Rediscovering

the

New

World

Rediscovering the New World

* * * * * * * * * *

Inter-American Literature in a Comparative Context

Ψ

University
of
Iowa
Press

Iowa
City

Earl E. Fitz

University of Iowa Press,
Iowa City 52242
Copyright © 1991
by the University of Iowa
All rights reserved
Printed in the
United States of America
First edition, 1991

Design by Richard Hendel

Printed on acid-free paper

Library of Congress Cataloging-in-
Publication Data
Fitz, Earl E.
    Rediscovering the New World: inter-
American literature in a comparative
context/by Earl E. Fitz.—1st ed.
    p.   cm.
    Includes bibliographical references and index.
    ISBN 0-87745-311-X (alk. paper),
    ISBN 0-87745-330-6 (pbk.: alk. paper)
    1. America—Literatures—History and
criticism.   2. Latin American literature—
History and criticism.   3. Literature,
Comparative.   I. Title.
PN843.F58   1991   90-20995
809'.897—dc20   CIP

TO JULIANNE,

who knows and understands

Contents

* * * * * * * * * *

Acknowledgments

* * * * * * * * * * * *

I would like to thank my wife, Julianne, and our children, Ezra, Caitlin, Dylan, and Duncan, for allowing me to steal time from their lives (chiefly from several years' worth of Saturday and Sunday mornings) in order to write this book. Your extraordinary generosity made it happen, and I thank you for granting me time to work.

Thanks, too, go to my friends and colleagues Leon Lyday (who heads the Penn State Department of Spanish, Italian, and Portuguese) and Caroline Eckhardt (the head of Penn State's Comparative Literature Department), whose steady support made the entire project possible, and to Leonard Rubinstein and Greg Rabassa, whose faith in the concept of Inter-American literature never waned.

Special thanks are also in order for my copy editor, Gail Zlatnik, whose sharp eye was ever on the lookout for the stylistic infelicities that mar a text's readability.

A sincere thank-you is proffered also to Karen Connelly, whose good humor and professionalism invariably made short work of the manuscript's seemingly endless revisions.

Finally, a promise must here be kept. Some years ago, in 1979, I told the students of my (and Penn State's) first class in New World literature that one day I would write a book about this subject and that I would dedicate it to them. I applaud you now (as I did then) for having been daring enough in your college careers to try something new and different. Bravo.

Introduction

* * * * * * * * * *

My purpose in writing this book was to show that, given the unique set of historical circumstances that governed the European discovery, conquest, and settlement of the New World, one could approach English and French Canada, the United States, Spanish America, and Brazil as constituting a community of literary cultures related to each other by virtue of their origins, their sundry interrelationships, and their sociopolitical, artistic, and intellectual evolutions. Their very real differences notwithstanding, the nations of the New World share enough of a common history that they can legitimately be studied as a unit, as different manifestations of the Americanism or New Worldism that each represents.

My methodology in this undertaking has been to identify several key issues that seem endemic to literature in the New World, to select certain representative texts from each of the five largest New World cultures (English Canada, French Canada, the United States, Spanish America, and Brazil), and to read these texts against each other. Since I begin with the Pre-Columbian era (and follow that with a discussion of the New World epic), there is a certain chronological order to the essays, though, as the later ones show, this was not a strategic part of my organizational plan.

One of several daunting problems encountered in an undertaking such as this was precisely the issue of text selection, for not all the works that relate to any given topic could possibly be discussed. Given the multitude of issues and texts that are available for consideration, on what rationale does one pick certain ones over others? If five texts from, say, French Canadian and Brazilian literature speak to the same issue, how does the scholar make the proper selection, the one that will most thoroughly or accurately exemplify the issue under consideration?

I have sought as often as possible to compare canonical texts because I wished to show how each of the ten issues selected for study manifests itself within the most established and influential works of literature that the various New World cultures have to offer. At the same time, however, it was my intention to feature lesser-known works and works by women. Happily, these goals often coincided, as evidenced by the presence here of such outstanding writers as Margaret Laurence, Alice Munro, Gabrielle Roy, Anne Hébert, Gertrude Stein, Willa Cather, Sor Juana Inés de la Cruz, Luisa Valenzuela, Clarice Lispector, and Nélida Piñon. Women are revolutionizing New World literature (as they are literature worldwide) and, without slighting male authors, I tried to cite as many important female authors and titles as I knew. Unjustifiable omissions are certain to have occurred and I apologize for these in advance.

Additionally, there is the thorny problem of depth. Once the representative textual selections are made, how, in the space of some forty manuscript pages, can one say something useful, revealing, or at least thought-provoking about the works being examined? An especially vexing aspect of this dilemma relates to the basic methodology employed; particular themes were chosen not merely because they were germane to all the New World cultures, but because they were primary features of the most "essential," most admired texts these cultures have to offer. I felt—and I continue to feel—that the issue of original literary insight notwithstanding, there is something to be gained by showing how the canonical works of New World literature reflect themes or ideas that are themselves fundamental to our better understanding of the entire Inter-American experience. It is my hope that what one loses in depth of treatment in these cases is outweighed by what one gains in breadth of coverage and in the comparative reassessment of established ideas. Thus, while in one sense it may be old hat to read such classics as *Huckleberry Finn* and *Facundo* in the context of the theme of civilization versus barbarism (chapter 10), in another it may be illuminating to compare these works with each other and to less well known Inter-American masterpieces such as *Agaguk* (which, on a crucial point, vividly contrasts with *Huckleberry Finn*), *Rebellion in the Backlands,* and *The Scorched-Wood People.*

A word, too, should be said about the immense bibliographic problem that confronts the scholar of Inter-American literature. Since most of the texts selected for closer examination are widely acknowledged masterpieces of their respective cultures, each comes replete with an extensive bibliography. Multiplying this problem by at least five (and by more if we are considering the many Native American literatures available for study), I came to realize that it would be virtually impossible to cite anything like a thorough bibliography of each work in each chapter. Instead, seeking readability and fresh reactions, I have chosen to keep references to a bare minimum, citing only those that relate directly to my topics.

Recognizing the importance of bibliography, however (and its special significance for a rapidly growing new area of scholarship), I have nevertheless included a Selected Bibliography, a listing of books, parts of books, and essays that in one fashion or another deal with the issues of Inter-American letters. I hope these titles will be of some use to scholars already working in or coming to this exciting and fast-developing field.

In many ways it is easier to say what this book is not than to say what it is. It is not, for example, an exhaustive study of the texts cited. Nor does it pretend to offer in any sense a comprehensive literary history of the several New World cultures under consideration. Finally, it does not presume to anything even approximating a definitive statement concerning the principles or praxis of New World literature. It is, rather, an invitation to further study, if only to correct the errors undoubtedly being made here.

A collection of ten chapters dealing with issues germane to all the literatures of the Americas, *Rediscovering the New World* arose out of my belief that the concept of "American literature" is not the exclusive province of one nation, that it is a concept that would link together all the literatures of the New World. I do not argue, however, that, having cast American literature in this particular hemispheric context, one must study it only in this fashion, for there are other approaches yet to be considered. Neither, finally, do I wish to imply that New World literature must in any sense be studied in isolation or that it developed devoid of any connection with Europe, for to do so would be patently absurd. What I have tried to show is that a great many problems of theme, form, and period resonate throughout the literature of the Americas and that, since the late fifteenth century, these have reflected the ongoing struggles of New World nations and cultures to define who and what they are.

Keenly aware of the daunting obstacles ahead, I initially despaired, feeling that they could not be overcome, at least not by me. To accept such a state of affairs, however, was tantamount to seeing the demise of the entire project, that being a condition I could not abide. The only alternative, therefore, was to forge ahead and make every effort to avoid the pitfalls as often as possible. The reader of these essays has my sincere apologies for those all too frequent moments when I fail to do this as well as I should have.

Fully conscious, then, of both the theoretical and the practical problems inherent in the kind of vast comparative study I had in mind, I began in January 1986 with the following plan: I would select ten topics that seemed especially significant to literature as it has developed in the New World; I would mention as many texts as I knew of that address these issues but (in nearly all cases) I would select only one or two texts from each New World literary culture to compare and contrast with the others; and, finally, I would strive to be as concise as possible in my critical commentary, hoping (instead of offering a series of close readings) first to show the reader what I had seen and, second, to entice her or him to investigate further, to read in their entirety the texts commented on only briefly here.

It is thus as an introduction to a fascinating and fertile new field of literary inquiry that this book is written, for it was conceived and developed more in the exploratory spirit of the French Canadian voyageur than in the conquering spirit of the conquistador. I trust, therefore, that the reader will regard the material discussed here as my attempt to paddle through some of the literary waterways of the New World and to report on what I have seen and experienced.

As the entire field of Inter-American literary relations continues to evolve, as I am sure it will, it is my hope that *Rediscovering the New World* will inspire other, better studies. If so, its writing will have been justified.

Rediscovering

the

New

World

1 The Pre-Columbian

✳ ✳ ✳ ✳ ✳ ✳ ✳ ✳ ✳ ✳ Era

Oral in its mode of transmission, the literature of the Pre-Columbian era is difficult to assess. With so much of it lost forever, the literary scholar is forced to rely on works and fragments of works that have evolved through centuries of change. Additionally, there are the related problems of translation and performance, for, as Ursula K. Le Guin has written, "reading an oral piece translated from its original language to English, and from voice to print, is like reading a musical score: you have to know a lot before you can hear what's happening. On the page, oral literature seems stiff and 'primitive,' because it's less than half there; it's only the notation of a performance." [1]

Yet in spite of these obstacles, the student of Pre-Columbian literature is encouraged by two facts: first, the Pre-Columbian era possessed not only a literature but one that ranged from the elementary to the highly sophisticated; and second, this vital and diverse native literature is undergoing something of a renaissance in the twentieth century. In various forms and in various ways, the rediscovery of American literature's ancient roots has proven to be an event of immense cultural significance for several New World republics. This movement is especially active in those Latin American countries like Mexico, Brazil, Guatemala, and Peru that still enjoy strong Indian populations, but it is also an important phenomenon in countries like Canada and the United States, which are likewise rediscovering their Native American heritage.

Were it needed, a third reason for undertaking a study of Pre-Columbian literature would be that no truly comprehensive examination of Inter-American letters could be possible without attempting at least to describe the nature of literature as it existed and evolved in the Americas during the approximately twenty thousand years that elapsed before the Europeans first set foot on the New World shores. American literature did not begin, as is all too commonly thought, with the discovery writings of such explorers as Columbus, Jacques Cartier, Pedro Alvares de Cabral, and John Smith. It began far earlier, with the songs, stories, dances, and dramatic productions of such peoples as the Chippewa, Choctaw, Osage, Pawnee, Sioux, Iroquois, and Papago, the Zuñi, Nootka, Kwakiutl, Inuit (Eskimo), Aztec, Maya, and Inca. Even the names by which we know some of these peoples today, the Zuñi (Spanish) and the Iroquois (French), for example, suggest the almost always violent impact the Europeans had upon these vastly different Native American cultures.

As a result, it does not surprise us to recognize how integral the issues of influence and reception have been to the ongoing process of intercultural literary development. In a living and regenerative fashion, then, much twentieth-century American literature has returned to its vibrant Pre-Columbian roots. The literary scholar who would trace the evolution of Inter-American literature must therefore begin at the real beginning, with the arrival of the first people on the single huge land mass that, since the sixteenth century, we have known as America.

Anthropologists tell us that the first "Americans" were probably Ice Age people from Asia who, following animal herds across the Bering land bridge, crossed over into the New World between fifteen thousand and thirty thousand years ago. The descendants of these Asian Cro-Magnons would, in one of the great misnomers of history, become known as American "Indians." By approximately twelve thousand years ago these people had fanned out to the south and east so that they spread over all of the land mass eventually to be called North America. Still later, some ten thousand years ago, descendants of these people finally reached the southernmost tip of South America. The Americas have been thoroughly peopled, then, for approximately ten thousand years. As a consequence, there is a sense in which American culture—and therefore American literature—can be said to be at least ten thousand years old.

So if the world "discovered" by the Europeans was new to them, it was not to the indigenous peoples already living here. Indeed, they, the true "discoverers" of the New World, possessed by the year 1492 an ancient world, one "based on a distinct concept of the universe. Tula, Teotihuacan, Monte Alban, Uxmal, Chichen Itzá, México-Tenochtitlan were all great centers of learning, having shared the wisdom of thousands of generations of pre-Columbian man."[2]

When one considers the radically differing terrains that the Americas offer— vast deserts and jungles, mountain ranges and grassy plains, frigid polar regions and sweltering tropical zones—it is easy to understand how not only diverse cultures but diverse literatures would have developed. As one studies these cultures, however, it becomes apparent that the three most complex Pre-Columbian cultures—those of the Mayas, the Aztecs, and the Incas—also produced the most sophisticated literatures. Some have argued that the Zapotecs, another advanced tribal group, even had a system of writing and that the Aztecs and Mayas, with their paper "books" and elaborate glyphs, were beginning to experiment with phonemic writing. Based on the oldest known literary works that we have from these different Pre-Columbian civilizations, there can be little doubt that the literature of the Aztecs, the Mayas, and the Incas was of a singularly high level of achievement, much of it on a par with the best European literature of the day.

Oral in nature, the literature of the Pre-Columbian era was characterized by such essentially poetic devices as euphony, imagery, symbolism, long and short pausing, cadence, timing, volume, repetition, parallelism, assonance, consonance, contrast, alliteration, and onomatopoeia.[3] Although there seems to have been no shortage of prosaic or dramatic literature, poetry does appear to have been the form that consistently produced the most exceptional efforts. Reflecting its oral expression and its social orientation, poetry for the aboriginal Americans was virtually synonymous with song. Throughout the New World, Pre-Columbian Americans showed themselves to be remarkable poets, singers of songs whose best work was richly evocative, succinct, and revelatory of the spirit of both the singer and the sharer. In contrast to written literature, the songs and stories of the Pre-Columbian era were commonly meant to be performed aloud in a communal exchange of intracultural revitalization between the performer and the audience. Structurally, we see (or hear) in this literature a constant reliance on repetition and parallelism, features fully characteristic also of the best oral traditions of Western civilization, including the Greek. One need not seek a Pre-Columbian Homer, however, to justify the worth of Pre-Columbian literature, the quality of which can be easily demonstrated by recognizing its elaborate structurings, its subtle techniques, and its varied thematics.

Critics believe that the early Americans viewed words as sacred entities that enjoyed a divine existence predating such natural phenomena as the earth, sun, and moon. Indeed, words were thought to possess so much magical force that they alone could have brought the physical world into existence. Margot Astrov has written that this important facet of Pre-Columbian literature is a "succinct statement of the Indian's relation to the 'word' as the directing agency that stands powerfully behind every 'doing', as the reality above all tangible reality."[4]

With this latter thought recalling Plato's theory of forms, Astrov states that "it is the thought and the word that stand face to face with the conscience of the native, not the deed."[5]

Because the aboriginal singers accorded such reverence to words, the poetry that they produced was judged to have the power to bring about a desired effect. Words were seldom used as mere embellishment, and this resulted in the creation of a literature possessed of a strong and dynamic social dimension. Nowhere is this social aspect of Native American poetry more clearly expressed than in the songs of healing and the songs of germination, fertility, and growth, the two categories of American Indian songs that outnumber all the others.[6] In *Chippewa Music*, Frances Densmore offers two examples that clearly demonstrate this basic social dimension. The first song, very short in its written English translation, is as follows: "The end only I am afraid of." In this work, a young man expresses a vision he has had in which the trees surrounding him are singing that they fear nothing except the winds.[7] The young man, a warrior, identifies animistically with the trees (that is, with the natural world) and in so doing prepares himself spiritually for his possible death on the battlefield. Like the trees with which he identifies, he will fear the wind, but by chanting the words of his song he will concentrate on the trees and thereby control his fear.

The second song, reminiscent of haiku, also shows a close and vital connection between the singer and the natural world that surrounds him:

> Sometimes
> I go about pitying myself
> While I am carried by the wind
> Across the sky.[8]

Here, as Astrov notes (paraphrasing the explanation of Densmore's Native American interpreter), "The dreamer becomes the companion of the swirling winds beneath the sky—torn away from his tribesmen, and therefore suffering, but close to the place where the powers dwell."[9]

Relating directly to the sacred quality of the word, these songs of personal vision and dream were deeply private creations. Expressive of a singer's innermost thoughts and emotions, such moving compositions are worthy additions to Western literature's venerable tradition of lyric poetry. Some, such as those produced by the brilliant Texcocoan poet-king Nezahualcóyotl, are, as we shall see, complex philosophical meditations on the vagaries of life and the mystery of death. Recalling the English metaphysical poets as well as the Greek tragedians, the poetry of Nezahualcóyotl is slowly beginning to gain renown as the most outstanding single-author body of literature in the known Pre-Columbian world.

Arguably the most distinctive feature of Pre-Columbian literature, the overwhelming belief in the word as a sacred object produces a kind of magical literature that, as in the magical realism of later writers like Gabriel García Márquez, John Nichols, Robert Kroetsch, and Miguel Angel Asturias, links its user to the mysterious but life-giving forces of nature that surround us. As much Pre-Columbian literature shows, the singer and the audience expect not to control or manipulate reality but to enter into it, to join with it and thereby become one with the universe. Reflecting its philosophical orientation as well as constituting a basic Native American aesthetic principle,[10] the thematic emphasis of this poetry is on kinship, balance, and harmony rather than on conflict and aggression. Because poems and songs of this kind stress equanimity both within oneself and with one's world, they also show how for people of the Pre-Columbian era (and in contrast to Saussurean linguistic theory) the word and its referent were indivisibly fused together. Words, sacred in essence, function in a way that is important to the stability of one's internal and external world. Songs were often used to invoke the forces of nature and thereby bring about some wished-for result such as rain, victory in war, or the healing of a sick or injured person.

Because in the Pre-Columbian world language was widely judged to be sacred, we find little use of irony or ambiguity in its literature. The reverence with which the word was held, in addition to the crucial cultural bonding of past, present, and future that occurs during a performance, precludes it. The literature of the Pre-Columbian people shows, moreover, an overwhelming sense of the necessity to use language only to reveal truth, never to deceive or dissemble.[11] The word was to be used in trust and mutual understanding between the singer and the audience and between people and their world. This sense of unity between the word and its object highlights a fundamental difference between much of the literature of the late twentieth century and that of the Pre-Columbian era.

As Karl Kroeber has noted, a final distinguishing feature of Native American poetry is that it is essentially metonymic and especially synecdochic, rather than metaphoric like most of traditional Western poetry. Kroeber argues that the synecdochic nature of oral American Indian poetry reinforces its already intentionally strong social and cultural dimensions. If this is true, it would substantiate his contention that "all Native American poetry is radically different from Western European poetry."[12]

A thematic approach also reveals a great deal about the nature of Pre-Columbian literature. Critics have broken this body of work down into five major thematic categories, examples of which can be found in virtually all known American Indian cultures: songs of healing; songs of germination, fertility, and growth; songs of personal vision and expression; death songs; and creation songs.

The first two categories (healing songs and songs of germination, growth, and fertility) are the dominant categories, the ones that generate the most examples for our Inter-American comparative context. Since the songs of the Pre-Columbian people were so intimately bound up with the functioning of their societies and with their ability to sustain themselves on this earth, it requires no stretch of the imagination to see why songs from these categories would be so important and so numerous. In *Chippewa Music 1*, Densmore records the following healing song, which Astrov calls "the healing song par excellence":

> You will recover; you will walk again.
> It is I who say it; my power is great.[13]

Though the sacred word is actually held to be the curative agent, the mechanism by which the healing process is set in motion is the singer's chant, the compelling and melodic repetitions in which the images of peace, tranquillity, and balance are unceasingly invoked, as in the process of hypnosis. The singer's chant, rhythmically accompanied by percussion and wind instruments, slowly works to relax and mesmerize the hearer, psychologically transporting the injured or ill person into the realm of pure beauty and perfection that is the American Indian's concept of the universe. Through the shaman's chant, built around the technique of repeating the sacred words, the hearer is transported spiritually into the cosmic force that, in the beginning, gave rise to all living things on the earth.

Another outstanding example of a Native American song of healing is cited by C. Daryll Forde in his *Ethnography of the Yuma Indians*:

> Your heart is good.
> [The Spirit] Shining Darkness will be here.
> You think only of sad unpleasant things,
> You are to think of goodness.
> Lie down and sleep here.
> Shining Darkness will join us.

> You think of this goodness in your dream.
> Goodness will be given to you,
> I will speak for it, and it will come to pass.
> It will happen here,
> I will ask for your good,
> It will happen as I sit by you.[14]

Even allowing for the inevitable distortions of sound, rhythms, and even meanings that Dennis Tedlock discusses in "The Question of Translation and Literary Criticism,"[15] one can in reading this drum-accompanied song gain a sense of its hypnotic effect, its soothing sound and message, and its curative inspiration. Even in its silent written form, the first line invokes the crucial notion that since the hearer's "heart is good" she or he will be well received by the positive and life-giving forces of the universe, forces which are themselves invoked in the second line. The Spirit, verbally rendered by an oxymoronic image, the "Shining Darkness," is a positive force, one giving comfort and succor, not fear and pain. The singer calls upon the injured hearer not to think of "sad unpleasant things," that is, of pain or the fear of death, but to concentrate instead on "goodness," on the beneficent "Shining Darkness."

The singer's next three lines, "Lie down and sleep here. / Shining Darkness will join us. / You think of this goodness in your dream," generate a more ambiguous meaning, particularly with regard to the word "sleep." If we take it literally, as the physiological act of sleep, and not metaphorically, as death, the lines collectively reinforce the idea that the human body requires rest to refresh or cure itself. The hearer will be lulled to sleep by the comforting (and holy) words of the chant and by its steady rhythm patterns and will then be visited while dreaming by the Spirit, Shining Darkness, who will revive and regenerate the hearer by immersing her or him in the purity of life's creative force.

The purpose of this very practical poem is thus achieved: the hearer sleeps, becomes rested, and then, finally, cured. The song has achieved its goal; the word has healed. By uttering the words aloud, the shaman is attempting to bring their meaning to pass. The leitmotif of the song is "good" or "goodness," and its steady, chanted repetition (it is used five times) expands and enhances the healthy concept of goodness in the hearer's mind as a positive and curative force.

The second category of Pre-Columbian songs, those that concern themes of germination, growth, and fertility, is also a very large one. Throughout Pre-Columbian America these songs linked the poet/singer/shaman with the uni-

versal life-giving forces that envelop us all and, as many of our Indianist modern authors remind us, are still very much with us today, even in our intensely
technological and mechanical world. As we shall see, several of these songs of
germination, growth, and fertility center on the cultivation of corn, which is to
the New World as rice is to Asia or wheat to Europe, that is, a staple of life. Of
the many songs of this type, the Osage "Song of the Maize" is prototypical:

> Amid the earth, renewed in verdure,
> Amid rising smoke, my grandfather's footprints.
> I see, as from place to place I wander,
> The rising smoke I see as I wander.
>
> Amid all forms visible, the rising smoke
> I see, as I move from place to place.
>
> Amid all forms visible, the little hills in rows
> I see, as I move from place to place.
>
> Amid all forms visible, the spreading blades
> I see as I move from place to place.[16]

Of this surprisingly complex song/poem, Francis LaFlésche has suggested
that the voice that speaks, the poem's "I" or persona, is that of the spirits of
ancestors, people dead and gone but joyfully and mysteriously come back to the
realm of the living in a way that parallels the way springtime (the season for
planting corn) joyfully and mysteriously returns to the earth after winter.[17]
Strongly evoking a number of archetypes, this beautiful song, working again
with repetition, long and short pausings, parallelism, and a simple but effective
symbolism, reflects the singer's belief (shared by the audience) that the growing
of corn, like singing about it, is a sacred act. Full of delicate but striking imagery, the first three lines reflect three related issues: the cyclicality of the seasons
(and by extension, for the Pre-Columbian people, the proper relationship of
human beings to the natural world); a human sense of past, present, and future
(that is, a sense of one's ancestors, one's own time, and one's progeny); and a
sense of movement that is at once psychological and physical, imbued with a
reverence for the eternal mystery of life.

The speaker's "grandfather" (or ancestors) has returned like the spring,
when the life-giving earth has been "renewed in verdure," that is, become
green with life once again. The image of "rising smoke" refers perhaps to the

early morning fog that hangs heavy and low over freshly plowed and planted cornfields. The dark brown and black of the earth, the silver gray fog or "smoke," and the delicate green of the corn shoots all come to life here in the poem's subtle color imagery, an imagery that would have been anything but arcane and abstract for the Osage themselves.

The third category of Pre-Columbian poetry consists of the songs of individuals, especially the songs of personal vision. Also sacred, since they express one's innermost feelings, these songs are often highly individualized and very pragmatic, frequently composed to effect a specific end. Less immediately functional than the songs created in response to some pressing need, the songs of personal vision or dream are considerably more metaphysical and contemplative. Intensely sacred to the singer and constituting a form that was (and is) endemic to Native American culture, many of these compositions belie the notion that the literature of the aboriginal Americans is somehow too simple, too childlike to warrant serious scholarly attention. Writing of the literary and philosophical importance these songs of personal vision have, Astrov reveals an unexpected parallel between Pre-Columbian literature and romanticism: "The Plains Indian . . . tries to prepare himself for a vision by seeking the solitude of nature, . . . until he gradually loses the sense of his own personality and identifies himself with the forms of his environment." [18]

Two exemplary songs from this important category, both of which project a philosophical stance in the face of the possibility of death during war, are a Pawnee war song:

> Let us see, is this real,
> Let us see, is this real,
> This life I am living?
> Ye Gods, who dwell everywhere,
> Let us see, is this real,
> This life I am living? [19]

and a warrior song from the Hethúshka (Omaha) society:

> I shall vanish and be no more,
> But the land over which I now roam
> Shall remain
> And change not. [20]

The Pawnee war song, as Daniel Brinton notes, has a decidedly metaphysical orientation. According to Brinton, this song was sung by a warrior who, about to go into battle, was keenly aware that one might well not survive.[21] The basic question being asked here is, interestingly enough, not whether the warrior-singer will return alive from the impending battle but, rather, what is real, what is the nature of reality? This question, crucial in Western art and philosophy at least since the time of Plato and Aristotle, is laid out here in pristine form by an unknown Native American preparing for war. This song, like others of its type, has a very specific and practical intent: to relax the warrior by freeing him or her from what a warrior society might hold to be a corrosive and enfeebling enthusiasm for the material comforts of this life. By chanting the song repeatedly, the warrior-singer is induced to believe that this life is not so precious after all, that if in dying one goes to the place of the gods, then death in battle need not be so fearsome. No longer burdened by the fear of loss of life, the warrior may perform even better in combat, thereby increasing the chances of survival.

The other warrior song, that of the Hethúshka society, generates a similar sentiment, one perhaps more stoic than that of the speculative Pawnee song. Echoing the idea of human impermanence in contrast to the permanence of the natural world, expressed in Ecclesiastes ("One generation passeth away, and another generation cometh; but the earth abideth forever"), the warrior-singer is also engaged in the process of freeing her- or himself from the fear of dying in combat. The warrior song of the Hethúshka society, like the Pawnee war song, clearly evokes heroic responses in both the singer and the hearer. The parallelism and repetition so typical of Native American poetry and song are more apparent in the Pawnee song than in the Hethúshka song, but both speak with dignified eloquence to the theme of reality and being, to our human anxiety over losing that fragile and enigmatic thing we call life.

A well-known song by one of Pre-Columbian America's most brilliant authors, the poet-king of Texcoco, Nezahualcóyotl, also undertakes a metaphysical consideration of the mysteries of life and death and the nature of existence. This increasingly anthologized composition offers a glimpse into the restless mind of a man who, had he lived in a culture with a phonemic writing system, might well rank among the giants of early Western literature:

1.

The sweet-voiced quetzal there, ruling the earth,
has intoxicated my soul.

2.

I am like the quetzal bird, I am created in the one
and only God; I sing sweet songs among the flowers;
I chant songs and rejoice in my heart.

3.

The fuming dewdrops from the flowers in the fields
intoxicate my soul.

4.

I grieve to myself that ever this dwelling on earth
should end.

5.

I foresaw, being a Mexican, that our rule began to
be destroyed, I went forth weeping that it was to bow
down and to be destroyed.

6.

Let me not be angry that the grandeur of Mexico
is to be destroyed.

7.

The smoking stars gather against it; the one who
cares for flowers is about to be destroyed.

8.

He who cared for books wept, he wept for the
beginning of the destruction.[22]

In what must surely rank as one of the most uncanny coincidences of history
(or, possibly, as the coming to pass of what had been preordained by Aztec cos-
mology) Cortés's arrival in Mexico in 1519 coincided almost exactly, according
to the Aztec calendar, with the expected return of the powerful god Quetzalcóatl, who would destroy the evildoers and followers of his eternal archenemy,
the god Tezcatlipoca, who at that precise moment was being paid obeisance by

the Aztecs. According to history (and, if we prefer, according to the natural laws of Aztec religion), the fierce Aztec army, vastly outnumbering Cortés's tiny force and easily capable of annihilating the Spaniards on the beach, held back and did not attack the strangers who had come out of the east (as it was predicted Quetzalcóatl, in disguise, would do). The Aztecs chose instead to bide their time to determine if these newcomers really were Quetzalcóatl and his minions returning to take their rightful place in Aztec culture.

The result of Montezuma's fatal strategic decision—which from his perspective he could hardly not have made—is of course a matter of well-documented historical record. Within two years, but only after a savage war, the Spanish conquest of Mexico was complete. In this brief, bloody conflict, Nezahualcóyotl, king of the pacific and intellectually inclined Texcocoans (a people subjugated by the warlike Aztecs), saw his prophecy about the destruction of Mexico come true. Nezahualcóyotl, who so loved literature and learning that he established an academy of science, music, and poetry, a gathering place for the artists and intellectuals of his time, must be considered as one of the great minds of the Pre-Columbian era.

Stanzas 1 and 2 of Nezahualcóyotl's song stress the essential unity of human existence and nature. Nezahualcóyotl first expresses this holistic sentiment in the simile "I am like the quetzal bird, I am created in the one / and only God." Then, by invoking two key metaphors, songs and flowers (which, as Irene Nicholson observes, are characteristic of the poetry of Nahua, the primary language of the Aztec world and a language still alive in modern Mexico), the poet-king moves to a general consideration of knowledge, language, and human existence. As Nicholson observes, "Communication between earth and heaven took place through the medium of song and flowers. Songs and flowers were symbols for the power of true speech, which a man had to acquire. 'A firefly in the night' was how the Nahuas described song, that is, the small point of illumination in the darkness of earth." [23]

Working within the elaborate Nahua poetic tradition, Nezahualcóyotl clearly utilizes this symbolic system: "I sing sweet songs among the flowers; / I chant songs and rejoice in my heart." For the Nahuas, flowers were the visual counterpart to song. In Nezahualcóyotl's poetry, then, flowers are not merely natural objects blossoming in the spring but symbols of visible truth, just as songs, in parallel fashion, function as the symbols of spoken truth. [24] Songs were for the Nahuas living organisms that spoke the truth in the mysterious corporeal world of unreliable forms, an attitude which bears some resemblance to Aristotle's famous defense of imaginative literature in the *Poetics*. For like Aristotle's poet, Nezahualcóyotl is a song-maker, a creature of vision not inspired mimetically to represent things as they "really" are but ideally, as they might be in a more perfect realm.

Acting as an interpreter between the ideal realm of the gods and the imperfect world of men and women, Nezahualcóyotl merges poetry with philosophy. Stanza 3 of his song, "The fuming dewdrops from the flowers in the fields / intoxicate my soul," might be read as a statement about how the blood ("fuming dewdrops") of humanity ("flowers in the field") "intoxicates" and inspires the poet to seek the answers to the eternal questions: What is the purpose of our life on earth? Where, if anywhere, do we go after we die? How should we live our lives? How can life be reconciled with death?

In stanza 4, Nezahualcóyotl voices a universal human concern, that we are pained to think that our time on earth is limited. In expressing his anxiety, he seems not ancient and culturally alien to us but a gentle, sensitive companion. We understand him in a profound way, for he speaks to us of our common human condition. Eerily, stanza 4 makes a prediction about the downfall of the Aztec reign, a prediction that comes true with Cortés's razing of Tenochtitlán, the Aztec capital, the ruins of which are the foundations for modern Mexico City.

Stanza 6, "Let me not be angry that the grandeur of Mexico / is to be destroyed," expresses the stoic resignation that many commentators believe to be one of the chief distinguishing characteristics of Pre-Columbian poetry. The "smoking stars" referred to in stanza 7 are probably comets that were visible for about a year before Cortés's arrival,[25] while the destruction of "the one who cares for flowers" can be read as referring to the man or woman who, like Nezahualcóyotl himself, is about to be plucked (like a flower) and consumed in the inscrutable plan of a god.

The violence of the Spanish conquest of the New World, and in particular its virulent attempts to extirpate all aspects of what for it was a pagan culture, spelled virtually immediate doom for the delicate, contemplative poetry produced by this extraordinary poet-king in the years just preceding the conquest. As Luis Valdez and Stan Steiner state:

América Indígena was obsessed with death. Or was it life? Man was a flower. A mortal, subject to the fugacity of all living things. Nezahualcóyotl, Chief of Texcoco (1402–72), was a philosopher king and one of the greatest poets América has ever produced. His poem "Fugacidad Universal" pondered the question of temporal existence:

> Is it true we exist on this earth?
> Not forever on this earth: only a brief moment here
> even jade shatters
> even gold tears
> even the plumage of quetzal falls apart
> not forever on this earth: only a brief moment here.[26]

Before leaving Nezahualcóyotl, we should mention an additional kind of Nahua lyric, a form which may have been developed by Nezahualcóyotl and which, in its longer forms (as examined here), seems probably to have been "'chanted' in rhythm, so that it sounds to our ears very like an Old-Testament psalm":[27]

> The passing vanities of the world are like the green willow; it falls before the axe and is uprooted by the wind. It is scarred and saddened by age.
> Life's splendours are like flowers, whose colour and whose fate they share.
> The beauty of flowers lasts only as long as their unsullied blossoms gather and store the precious pearls of dawn and let them fall in liquid dewdrops.
> But when the Lord of All causes the sun to cast its rays upon them, their beauty and their glory fade.
> The bright, gay colours which were once their pride, wither and fade.
> The reign of flowers is short. In the morning they boast of their beauty and strength, but by evening they mourn for the destruction of their thrones and the misfortunes which lead to loss, poverty, death, and the grave.
> All things on earth have an end, and in the midst of the happiest life our breath fails. We falter, and fall to earth.
> All the earth is a grave. Nothing escapes.
>
> .　.　.　.　.　.　.　.
>
> That which was yesterday is not today. That which is today may not be tomorrow.[28]

Recalling the *carpe diem* theme of the metaphysical poets as well as the stoicism and awe of the Old Testament poets, this elegiac and ontologically meditative lyric attests to the exceptional poetic expressiveness of Nezahualcóyotl, unquestionably the greatest of the known Pre-Columbian poet-singers.

Other noteworthy songs of personal vision come from the culture of the Mayas (in what is now eastern Mexico and Guatemala) and the Incas (in the mountainous region encompassed by the modern nations of Peru, Bolivia, and Ecuador). From the Yucatán Peninsula, a center of high Mayan culture and civilization, we have "A Maya Prophecy":

> Eat, eat, while there is bread,
> Drink, drink, while there is water;
> A day comes when dust shall darken the air,
> When a blight shall wither the land,
> When a cloud shall arise,
> When a mountain shall be lifted up,
> When a strong man shall seize the city,
> When ruin shall fall upon all things,
> When the tender leaf shall be destroyed,
> When eyes shall be closed in death.[29]

This Mayan song, which also sounds the *carpe diem* theme, is thought to be from "The Books of Chilam Balam." Balam, a Mayan prophet who lived during the closing decades of the fifteenth century, predicted that strangers coming out of the east and bringing a new religion with them would invade and conquer the Mayan nation. Collectively, the several "books" (consisting of folded paper) of Chilam ("priest") Balam are considered to be the sacred books of the Mayan people, containing their history, religion, laws, and, as we shall see, accounts of how the world began.

Another song of personal vision, "Supplication to the Creator God," is this Incan hymn:

> Viracocha, Lord of the Universe!
> Whether male or female,
> at any rate commander of heat and
> reproduction,
> being one who,
> even with His spittle, can work sorcery.
> Where art thou?

> Would that thou wert not hidden
> from this son of Thine!
>
> .   .   .   .   .   .
>
> Oh! Harken to me,
> listen to me,
> let it not befall
> that I grow weary
> and die.[30]

Despite the stylistic problems involved in translation, the typically Andean tone and spirit come through. We sense the magical quality of reality ("His spittle, can work sorcery"), the yearning of the Incan singer, whose song was often accompanied by flute music, to know Viracocha, the omnipotent power of the universe, and to be known by him or her. There is also a sense of resignation that, even though the singer asks that she or he never "grow weary / and die," stems from seeing how generation after generation marches "in orderly procession" to their "destined place," that is, to death. The Incas had a great appreciation of music and may have been preeminent among Pre-Columbian peoples in this regard. Especially skilled at the use of percussion and wind instruments, the Incan *haravecs*, or professional bards, were responsible for maintaining the strong and vital oral literature of their people.[31]

The fourth category of songs from the preconquest period is that of the death songs. These songs are of two basic types: those which were to be sung in a moment of utter desolation (or in the face of imminent death) and those actually composed just before death comes and actually sung with one's dying breath.[32] These death songs and their variations are mentioned by different scholars as characterizing the literature and cultural psychology of very diverse Indian tribes. The writings of the French Jesuits, who were called the "Black Robes" by the Indians, often note the importance death songs had among the Iroquois, the Hurons, and the Ottawa. Writing about the Crow people, Robert Lowrie cites this example of a death song, one that typifies the kind sung in the face of death:

> Eternal are the heavens and the earth;
> Old people are poorly off.
> Do not be afraid.[33]

Astrov observes of this song that while it has only a few simple words it succeeds, in its original chanted form, in expressing a grimly realistic yet serene world-view, one that does not demonstrate a consoling belief in a life after death but that calls for a calm acceptance of the inevitable.[34] In addition to the song's stoicism, there is also strongly evident a sense that it is a pitiful thing to be old and that, by implication, it is better perhaps to die young.

A representative example of a song from the second type of death song, to be composed and sung with the singer's dying breath, comes from the Chippewa. Densmore describes it as the death song of a Chippewa warrior who had suffered a fatal wound in a battle with the Sioux:

> The odor of death,
> I discern the odor of death
> In front of my body.

Then, with his dying words of farewell to his comrades-in-arms, the Chippewa warrior sings:

> When you reach home sing this song for the women to
> dance by and tell them how I died.[35]

About this song, Astrov makes the following comment, one of special interest to a comparatist:

> "There is something of Greek grandeur and Greek simplicity about the dying of this wounded Indian, high up in the northern woods of America. His words of departure seem like a faint echo of those words engraved upon the tombstone of the warriors fallen at Thermophylae ages ago."[36]

Another, more vivid and poetical song of this fourth category is the Papago "Death Song":

> In the great night my heart will go out.
> Toward me the darkness comes rattling,
> In the great night my heart will go out.[37]

The imagery and symbolism of this concise haiku-like poem are striking. "The great night," that is, death, is the all-encompassing entity into which the singer's "heart," that is, his "spirit," will go. The closeness of death gives line 2 of this song a powerful sense of both immediacy and palpable movement, the compelling suggestion that as the body loses its struggle to live, it is the "darkness" of death that "comes" to it. The word "rattling" is thus onomatopoetic in that it refers, denotatively and contextually, to the body's death throes. The third line, a repetition of the first, closes the thought and function of this song and thereby intensifies its psychological impact.

The fifth and final category of Pre-Columbian literature is that of creation songs, poetical compositions designed (as they are for other, more "advanced" cultures such as the Christian, whose Bible is often read as a creation song) to explain how the world came into being and how men and women came to exist on it. Examples of this category of song can be found throughout the thousands of different cultures that were in various stages of development at the beginning of the European conquest in 1492.

The Zuñi creation myth is a prototype of the Pre-Columbian creation song:

"Before the beginning of the new-making, Awonawilona solely had being.
There was nothing else whatsoever throughout the great spaces of the ages
save everywhere black darkness in it, and everywhere void desolation." [38]

The opening lines of this song call to mind the events depicted in the biblical Book of Genesis, with Awonawilona paralleling the Christian God. One difference, however, is that in the Zuñi tradition the all-powerful force magically transforms itself into the sun, which is said to be the father of the Zuñi. With his appearance, there comes not only "the brightening of the spaces with light" but the creation of Mother Earth and Father Sky. From a natural union of Earth and Sky the things and creatures of the earth, including women and men, are born; mountains, trees, clouds (a link with life-giving rain), and even nations are formed out of the procreative intercourse of Mother Earth (from whose "bosom" people will draw their nourishment) and Father Sky.

Father Sky, not a passive figure here, offers humankind the magic of seed (corn), which amounts to the gift of life itself. In a beautiful image of balanced interaction between nature and human beings, the singer tells how Father Sky, working in organic and fertile consort with Mother Earth, "set the semblance of shining yellow corn grains" into the "dark of the early-world dawn" so that they "gleamed like sparks of fire" for the humans who would sustain themselves with them.[39]

For the Mayas the cultivation of corn and its attendant religious symbolism were the cornerstone of their culture. Reflective of these and other aspects of the Mayas' complex civilization is the *Popol Vuh*, a work that, among many other things, tells how human beings were first created not out of mud, as in the Bible, but out of corn.

The *Popol Vuh*, a remarkably complete encyclopedia of Mayan theogony, cosmogony, and astrology (the Mayas were outstanding astronomers and mathematicians), is an extraordinary document, one of immense importance for our appreciation of Maya Quiché literature and culture in the Pre-Columbian era. Hubert Bancroft has written that "of all the American peoples, the Quichés of Guatemala have left us the richest mythological legacy. Their description of the Creation, as given us in the *Popol Vuh*, . . . is in its rude strange eloquence and poetic originality, one of the rarest relics of aboriginal thought." [40] Even more emphatic about the *Popol Vuh*'s unique value is Sylvanus Morley, who writes that "the *Popol Vuh*, or Sacred Book of the ancient Maya-Quiché, . . . is . . . the most distinguished example of native American literature that has survived the passing centuries." [41]

Arguably the most brilliant literary achievement of the Pre-Columbian era, the *Popol Vuh* is a two-part narrative, intensely mythic and poetic in nature, concerning the creation of the world and the arrival of the Maya Quiché in it. Part 1, dealing with the origins of the natural world and the creation (through corn) of humankind, is philosophical in the same way the better-known creation accounts of the Eastern and Western worlds are. Part 2, which centers (sometimes humorously) around the deeds of two mythical figures, Hunahpú and Ixbalamqué, the founders of the Maya Quiché people, has an epic dimension. "In the *Popol Vuh*," observes Abraham Arias-Larreta, "we find the magic participation of the animals, as in the *Ramayana*; the alternation of daring adventures in quimerical regions and pleasant common episodes of everyday life, as in the *Odyssey* and, as in the *Iliad*, we contemplate the intervention of the Gods in the human struggle." [42]

The opening section of the *Popol Vuh* establishes the work's Genesis-like qualities:

> "This is the account of how all was in suspense, all calm, in silence; all motionless, still, and the expanse of the sky was empty. . . . Then came the word. Tepeu and Gucumatz came together in the darkness, in the night, and Tepeu and Gucumatz talked together. . . . They united their words and their thoughts." [43]

It is interesting to note that here too, in the refined and sophisticated *Popol Vuh*, words (united with their thoughts) play central roles in the sacred process of creation. As Arias-Larreta points out, "The 'Divine Word' implies immediate creation. It is a synonim [*sic*] of power and action. The Gods met in the divine council and after deliberation they reached a unanimous decision. Having pronounced the exact word for earth, the earth appeared."[44] Like other Native American creation songs, the Mayan *Popol Vuh* shows the word to be a sacred object, humanity to be closely entwined with nature, and human fate to be tied inevitably to the laws and forces of the universe.

Another gem from this extraordinary era is the anonymous Incan verse-drama *Ollantay*, first written down by a Spanish priest, Antonio Valdés, in 1780. *Ollantay*, a drama of love, treachery, and war, is set in the time of the great Incan Empire, believed to date back to at least 10,000 B.C.

This play, interesting enough in itself, has aroused a good deal of controversy as to the purity of its Incan origins. As Margot Astrov, Abraham Arias-Larreta, Miguel Angel Asturias, and many others have noted regarding the Mayan "books" of Chilam Balam, they contain a wealth of material that is almost certainly preconquest, that is, exclusively Mayan in origin and expression, but there is also some material that seems at least partially European. It is at the juncture of the conquest that the study of the literature of the Pre-Columbian era begins to become complicated by many questions of influence and reception. These important issues are only now being examined in a comparative context, and much more needs to be done in this area. For scholars with the necessary cultural and linguistic skills, the literary relationships of this decisive period represent an immensely fertile area in which to work.

Thus, regarding *Ollantay*, some critics, such as Ricardo Palma, Bartolomé Mitre, and Marcelino Menéndez y Pelayo, believe it was completely colonial in origin, while others, such as Jesús Lara, Horacio Urteaga, and Sebastián Barranca, argue for its Pre-Columbian roots. Still others, such as José Cid Pérez and Dolores Martí de Cid,[45] believe it to be a hybrid work, essentially Pre-Columbian in theme and character but influenced by Spanish theater in its structuring.

The play's most notable features include its swiftly changing scenes, its humor, its political message and didactic intent, its dramatic irony, and its diverse dramatic structures, such as recognition scenes, numerous reversals, and an anticlimax. Other singular features of *Ollantay*, which was originally performed in the Quechuan language, include "an absence of supernatural elements, . . . an unexpected denouement, original use of songs and choruses . . . [and] unity of action, not of time and place."[46]

Regarding *Ollantay*'s artistic merit, Arias-Larreta is perhaps correct when he writes that "the *Apu Ollantay*, on account of its vigorous characters, its magnificent theme, the quality of its poetry, the dynamic interplay of human passions, and its splendid structure, is the most extraordinary example of the aboriginal theater in America. In fame and literary value [it] can be compared only to the *Popol Vuh*, considered as the richest mythological legacy of the pre-Columbian cultures."[47]

Another famous work, one that is judged by nearly all scholars who study it to be almost certainly Pre-Columbian in both theme and structure, is the *Rabinal Achí*, a Maya Quiché dance tragedy. Translated by Georges Raynaud from Quiché into French, and from French to Spanish by Luis Cardoza y Aragón, the *Rabinal Achí* is a fascinating theatrical work. As Miguel León-Portilla writes, "Both the subject and the action show a Pre-Hispanic origin. This is confirmed by the long dialogues with their many polite native phrases, parallel expressions, and pre-Columbian metaphors and symbols. Beyond a doubt the *Rabinal Achí* is one of the most authentic examples of indigenous drama prior to the conquest."[48]

Seemingly ritualistic in structure, the plot of the *Rabinal Achí* focuses on the capture, conditional release, return, and eventual sacrifice of an enemy warrior, a Quiché man, by a warrior of another tribe, Rabinal Achí, the son of chief Hobtoh. The work is divided into four acts or scenes. The first and third take place in front of the city of Rabinal Achí while the second and fourth unfold within the city. According to Cid Pérez and Martí de Cid, music and dance not only play a prominent part in the drama but are organically integrated into its action.[49] At the conclusion, for example, the eagle and tiger dancers surround the Quiché man and, as they dance close to him, come to symbolize his ritual sacrifice. The conclusion of the drama, which recalls the death songs we have seen, gives a sense of its uniquely Pre-Columbian nature. As the doomed Quiché man says:

"Oh eagles! Oh jaguars! Come then to fulfill your mission, to fulfill your duty; may your teeth, may your claws, kill me in an instant, for I am reaching out to my mountains, my valleys."[50]

Many critics believe there were many plays like the *Rabinal Achí* among the Mayas and Nahuas, in addition to other types of theater, including farcical pieces. In the closing decades of the text-oriented twentieth century, we can only wonder at the heights of oral literary sophistication achieved by these remarkable Pre-Columbian people.

But while in a strictly historical sense the Pre-Columbian era must end in 1492 with Columbus and the first wave of European conquerors, the evolution of Pre-Columbian literature—its cultivation, recognition, and development—does not stop there. Indeed, it remains a living American tradition, one that is with us today in the works of several of our most prominent New World authors, such as Miguel Angel Asturias (Guatemala), José María Argüedas and José Santos Chocano (Peru), Octavio Paz (Mexico), José de Alencar, Mário de Andrade, and Raul Bopp (Brazil), Robert Kroetsch, W. P. Kinsella, Leonard Cohen, George Ryga, Isabella Valancy Crawford, Emily Pauline Johnson, Duncan Campbell Scott, and John Newlove (English Canada), Yves Thériault, Remi Savaro, and Guy DuFresne (French Canada), and N. Scott Momaday, Louise Erdrich, Gary Snyder, Ursula K. Le Guin, Linda Hogan, Paula Gunn Allen, and William Carlos Williams (United States).

It is interesting to note, as Paul Zolbrod observes in *Diné Bahané*, that although literary scholarship concerning Native American literature, both oral and written, has been developing for well over one hundred years, it has been virtually ignored by mainstream literary critics.[51] One reason for this omission is undoubtedly the frequently encountered bias against oral literature. A second likely reason has to do with the small number of literary scholars fluent in American Indian languages, though, with the work of John Bierhorst, Paula Gunn Allen, Dell Hymes, Dennis Tedlock, and others, there is reason to believe this situation is changing.

A final reason relates to our cultural appreciation of what has happened to the first Americans in the several hundred years following the initial arrival of the Europeans in the New World. Viewed generally as impediments to progress, as enemies deserving extermination, or as uncultured beasts of burden who should provide a cheap labor supply for a growing society, the Pre-Columbian peoples of the Americas, along with their literatures and cultures, have been systematically effaced. Only through the actions of a few rare, often idiosyncratic individuals were these Native American cultures spared or artifacts of their cultures saved for posterity. This antagonism toward our most fundamental American culture—in all its original diversity—has left us virtually bereft of a preconquest past to draw upon positively. The result, as Octavio Paz has said, is that the United States (for Paz in contrast to Mexico) is a country "whose sole tradition is the future:

> . . . a country . . . built on the void left by destroying Indian cultures. The attitude of North Americans to the Indian world is part of their attitude to nature; they don't see it as a reality to be fused with, but to be dominated."[52]

Since the time of the conquest, then, but especially in the twentieth century, writers throughout the Americas have attempted to retrieve and revitalize the long-lost and once-rejected American past. They have sought, in a sense, to rediscover the New World and, in so doing, have come not just to discover the aesthetic and intellectual worth of Native American literature itself but to see how it can enrich our own twentieth-century existence. In short, many American authors have consciously begun to search for our roots not in Europe, which has largely neutered any such connection, but in the songs, poems, myths, and legends of preconquest America.

2

* * * * * * * * * * * *

The
Narratives
of
Discovery
and
Conquest

The European discovery and conquest of the New World produced a wealth of narratives that, in surprising contrast to their intended aim—to report as accurately as possible what the explorers were encountering—often blurred the tenuous distinction between fiction and nonfiction. The basic question of what was "real" in the New World, and how this reality could best be represented in language, was therefore often at the root of these works. This feature of the earliest of these New World texts links them directly to such later-developing concepts as magical realism, New Worldism, and the American Dream. Epitomized in the figure of Christopher Columbus, the men and women of the European Renaissance, and in particular those of its Baroque phase, held a number of preconceived and often fantastical notions about what the New World would be like, if, indeed, it existed at all. These fabulous preconceptions would exert a powerful and sometimes distorting influence not only on what was reported but on how it was reported. As a consequence, many of the early discovery chronicles are as full of what their authors fancifully hoped and expected to find (dragons, mermaids, fountains of youth, men with the heads of dogs or with a single eye in their foreheads, for example) as they are of meticulous descriptions of what actually was found. In a sense, then, the first written documents of New World literature can be regarded as self-conscious texts in which the idea of the real finds itself subsumed in notions of the fantastic and in preemptive authorial expectations; a "new narrative" was thus being forged at the outset.

Fired by Marco Polo's account of his exotic travels in the Orient, explorers like Columbus, John Cabot (Giovanni Caboto), and Jacques Cartier sailed west in hopes of getting to the East, where, it was believed, immense riches would be found. Both Columbus and Cabot, who as a Genoese sailing under the English flag first explored the area around Newfoundland ("new-found land") in 1497, believed they could reach China and Japan in a few weeks' sailing time.

The uniqueness of the new world they discovered, which included the extraordinary human civilizations of the Incas, Aztecs, and Mayas as well as such incredible geographic features as the great mountain chain that rims the western coast of the Americas, defied the ability of the Europeans to comprehend it. Often the newcomers' languages simply did not possess words to name the people and things they encountered. Imbued with a virtually palpable sense of awe and wonder about what their authors were seeing and experiencing, the letters, chronicles, and reports of the early European explorers call into question many of our basic assumptions about the nature of reality and about the ability of language to record it accurately. As one critic sums up:

> Even if the purpose of these documents was to present reality as it then was, they were permeated by the sense of wonder felt by the Europeans as they faced for the first time a reality totally unlike anything they had experienced before. A new image of man and nature was formed in the early days of the discovery and conquest. This image was the product not only of an observation of reality but also of the dreams and fantasies, of the sense of the "marvelous," that the Europeans brought to the New World. . . . The Renaissance appetite for discovery and wonder permeated such accounts, changing fact into fiction. . . . Everything was magic then.[1]

The narratives of discovery and conquest may be subdivided into those that offer a plotlike structure and those that do not. A further possible division, and one to be examined here, has to do with the nature of the basic conflict or conflicts that animated so many of these works. One sees that those texts with a definite plot configuration most often involve a conflict either between the individual and nature or between one human, or one culture, and another. Of the first variety, Captain John Franklin's *Narrative of a Journey to the Shores of the Polar Sea* may be taken as the prototype. Another example from this same category is Samuel Hearne's *Journey from Prince of Wales' Fort in Hudson's Bay to the Northern Ocean*, a work which many critics judge to be a classic of its kind. Of the second category, works in which the basic conflict is between two individuals or cultures, no finer example can be cited than Bernal Díaz del Castillo's *Historia verdadera de la conquista de la Nueva España* (*True History of the Conquest of New Spain*). The Spanish conquistadors and their minions produced a number of narratives of this type, such as Gonzalo Fernández de Oviedo's *A General and Natural History of the Indies, Islands and Mainland of the Ocean Sea* (part 1, 1535; part 2, 1557), but none surpasses Díaz's account. As we will see, the narratives in which the essential conflict is between two people were a direct result of the terrible clash of cultures that resulted when the European conquest of the New World began, pitting against each other men like Cortés and the Aztec monarch, Montezuma, or Pizarro and the Incan leader, Atahualpa.

For a very brief time (a matter of only a few years, really), the European adventure in the New World was one of discovery rather than military and cultural conquest. We begin our textual comparisons at this epoch-making juncture—the moment when suddenly, from the vast and seemingly endless expanse of ocean, the European voyagers first laid eyes on the New World. Fortunately for us, most of these earliest of European explorers, including Columbus, Cabral, Smith, Bradford, and Cartier, took pains to see that their thoughts and observations during those extraordinary moments of human history were recorded for posterity. The case of John Cabot remains something of a mystery, because of the apparent lack of a discovery text done in his own hand or upon his direct order. There is also a mystery as to the date of his earliest voyage—1494 or, as is widely thought to be more likely, 1497—to the New World.[2]

But if there remains some uncertainty concerning Cabot's first landfall in the New World, there is no mystery surrounding Columbus's reaction. The moment of discovery was recorded in a ship's log entry dated Friday, October 12, 1492: "At two hours after midnight appeared the land, at a distance of 2 leagues."[3]

While in general this historic shipboard account of the first encounter between the Europeans and the Americans is straightforward, descriptive, and fairly objective, a more detailed report appearing a short time later already shows the hyperbole, wild fantasies, and gross exaggerations that would soon come to characterize many of the Renaissance discovery narratives. This later document, Columbus's official letter to the Spanish sovereigns concerning what he found on his first voyage, is, as Samuel Eliot Morison declares, "the first and rarest of all printed americana. It tells not only what the admiral himself thought, but the most important things that he wished the sovereigns to know. It boils down from the Journal enthusiastic descriptions of the scenery, the flora, the abundance of the natives. He insists that his discoveries lie in Asia, and that the capital of the 'Great Khan' was not far away."[4] Ironically, so convinced was Columbus that he was close to Cathay (China) and Xipango (Japan) that to the end of his days he refused to acknowledge that his discovery was of the Americas, specifically the islands of Cuba, Santo Domingo, and the Bahamas, and not of Asia.

Because his mind was ablaze with the myths and legends of the European Renaissance, Columbus must have felt a keen sense of disappointment at confronting the less than supernatural realities of the New World. Regarding the disparity between what the great navigator expected to find and what he actually found, Emir Rodríguez Monegal, like Morison, has suggested that Columbus tried to disguise, through the use of standard rhetorical figures and conceits, what he felt was his "failure." As Monegal sees it:

> In describing the new land to his patrons, he resorted to literary models. He looked for and saw prodigies Pliny had described in his wildly imaginative *Natural History*; he also remembered Marco Polo's wonders; he exhausted the rhetoric of the "marvelous" he knew from romances of chivalry and Renaissance epic poems. His senses had been trained by European poets; he heard nightingales in Cuba, breathed May air in the tropical November of the Caribbean, vouched for the existence of Amazons and mermaids, of men with tails. A whole stereotype of the fabulous New World was being created.[5]

When Columbus, warming to his subject, begins to describe the island he calls Juana, he begins to write in a singularly effusive fashion, one that will become even more pronounced in the later Brazilian discovery narratives with their strong sentiment of *ufanismo*, or boastfulness, about the virtues of their newly discovered land. Columbus moves from his glowing account of the fertility of these islands, which he praises as earthly paradises, to comments about a commodity that would entrance the European conquerors for years to come—gold.

He begins this part of his narrative in a restrained manner, saying that there are many good fresh-water rivers and streams, but then—ever so hopefully, one feels—he asserts that most of these bear gold. From this rather startling statement, his enthusiasm for finding gold expands to the point that he declares that the islands he is exploring contain not just gold and spices but great mines of gold as well as other precious metals. In truth, Columbus found but little gold, and then only in the form of a few trinkets that the natives showed him; there were no gold mines or rivers full of gold.

In describing the people, who were pacific and not warlike, Columbus, a typical European of his time, shows himself to be more impressed by the fact that the natives went around naked than by anything else. Calling them Indians because he believed he had come upon an island off the coast of India, Columbus readily accepts the idea that on a nearby island called Avan men are born with tails, in accord with a popular European legend concerning the strange creatures who were said to inhabit the New World. Though he reports, accurately enough, that he personally had found no human monstrosities, as many European "experts" said he would, he also notes that on another neighboring island there were people who ate human flesh (probably a reference to the Caribs). Columbus also fuels another popular Renaissance myth about the New World—that it was the domain of the fabled Amazons—when he mentions that there is an island called Matremomio on which no men can be found. Ever the promoter, he observes how the "Grand Khan" will surely be interested in trading with the Europeans (presumably Columbus here means the Spanish) who will naturally assume control of all the gold mines and who will convert the "Indians" not only to Christianity but to service as slave labor.

Columbus's letter, with all its exaggeration, fantasizing, miscalculation, and misnomers (India, Indio, Indian), was an instant success in Europe, where it eventually went through eight Spanish editions, a Latin version that made Columbus's report known throughout Europe, and an Italian version. Moreover, Columbus's letter, describing as it did a kind of heavenly paradise on earth, became the textual inspiration for many future utopias, including those of Thomas More (1516), Montaigne ("On Cannibals," c. 1580), and Voltaire (the satirical version in chapter 18 of *Candide*, 1759).[6]

One final important dimension of Columbus's imaginative report was that in painting so idyllic a picture of what he saw (or wanted to see), he was helping to create the "factual" foundation for Rousseau's later concept of the *bon sauvage*, or noble savage, who lived in an Eden-like state of perfect nature, a place that Columbus, after his fourth voyage to the New World (one which, ironically, resulted in bloodshed) believed must exist somewhere in the Americas. Yet if Columbus failed to give as accurate a discovery report as he might have, he succeeded mightily in focusing the Old World's attention on the New. As Monegal succinctly puts it, "America as a literary and poetic subject was invented by this hyperbolic Genoese."[7]

The second European discoverer to reach the New World, John Cabot, is also one of the least known. Arriving most likely in 1497, only five years after Columbus's landfall further to the south, Cabot gave England a claim to a share of whatever riches were to be had in the Americas, a claim which the English would not capitalize on until 1607 and the Jamestown expedition. So while England was the second European power to arrive in the New World, it was the last to colonize it, coming with settlers only belatedly, after the Spanish, the Portuguese, and the French had begun to build civilizations in the New World.[8] While we lack in Cabot's case the kind of firsthand reportage that we have for Columbus, we can nevertheless get from the documents that do remain a sense of Cabot's impressions of the first American shore he saw.

A later report referring to the more likely 1497 voyage indicates that Cabot, like Columbus, was prone to gross exaggeration and to believing that he too was close not only to the fabled Seven Cities but to Asia and Xipango (Japan). This narrative, also reflecting Cabot's willingness to believe in the fecundity and bountifulness of New World nature, continues:

> They say that the land is excellent and temperate, and they believe that Brazil wood and silk are native there. They assert that the sea is swarming with fish, which can be taken not only with the net, but in baskets. . . . But Messer Zoane has his mind set upon even greater things, because he proposes to keep along the coast from the place at which he touched, more and more towards the east, until he reaches an island called Cipango, situated in the equinoctial region, where he believes that all the spices of the world have their origin, as well as the Jewels.[9]

As his report shows, Cabot's training and imagination led him, like Columbus, to expect things about the New World that were in fact not true.

Another important discovery narrative, written by the Portuguese scribe Pero Vaz de Caminha, the official chronicler of the Portuguese explorer Pedro Alvares de Cabral, dates from 1500. The Portuguese, like the Spanish (but unlike the English), began to colonize their portion of the Americas almost as soon as they arrived. Although it has long been suggested that Portuguese mariners had known about the existence of a huge western landmass long before Cabral's officially documented visit in 1500, credit for the Lusitanians' arrival tends to be given to Cabral.

Also written in the form of a letter (dated May 1, 1500), Caminha's account of what he first saw in the New World stands in sharp contrast to that of Columbus. While the latter's report is highly rhetorical and hyperbolic, Caminha's letter is restrained, less rhetorical, and not nearly so exaggerated. His style, in comparison to that of Columbus, is more realistic and matter-of-fact and perhaps less entertaining to read. The two documents, written at almost the same time, dealing with a similar subject, and coming from the pens of men of similar intellectual background (the Europe of the late fifteenth century), lend themselves naturally to a close comparative reading.

In his initial discovery document Caminha shows himself, in contrast to Columbus, to be more interested in the nature and behavior of the people the Portuguese meet than with the question of whether they possess gold, which, as we recall, was an almost obsessive concern for Columbus. Caminha's account of this meeting of two hitherto separated worlds even has a comic reader-response element in it regarding the question of gold and silver:

> He (a native) pointed to land and then to the beads and the Captain's collar, as if to give gold for the beads. Or rather we took this to be his meaning because we wished it to be so, while he really meant to say that he would take the beads and the collar together for himself; this we did not wish to understand because we did not have it to give.[10]

The entire letter has a tone of self-conscious objectivity, a refreshing change from the intense sense of expectation that permeates Columbus's account. Consciously or not, Caminha checks his Eurocentrism enough so that he does not feel compelled to judge the people he is meeting.

A final point of contrast between these two letters of discovery has to do not with their styles or the nature of their descriptions but with their literary histories. Unlike Columbus's letter, which in various translated forms was immediately disseminated throughout Europe, Caminha's letter was not published until 1817, more than three hundred years after it was written. Hence, Caminha's account of what the New World and its inhabitants were like, an account that stands in such sharp contrast to Columbus's version of essentially the same event, had no chance to influence European ideas about the New World as Columbus's letter had done. Caminha's natives were perhaps less noble or exotic than Columbus's but they were more real, a fact that might have been ignored anyway by the Europeans of 1500, for whom the Renaissance and its appetite for "the exotic and fantastic decisively favored hyperbole."[11]

Sailing under the French flag, the fourth European explorer to reach the New World was Jacques Cartier, who, on Sunday, May 10, 1534, sighted land at Cape Bonavista (Bonne Viste). As with Columbus and Cabral, we have from

Cartier firsthand documentation of what he saw upon arriving in the Americas. Like the other discovery documents we have seen, Cartier's log begins immediately to relate vividly detailed descriptions of the new flora and fauna he encounters. The prevailing climatic conditions also enter strongly into Cartier's account, just as they do in those of Columbus and Cabral, the difference being that rocky shores, ice, snow, and cold characterize the northern realms explored by Cartier.

Unlike Columbus, Cartier does not see his part of the New World as an earthly paradise; indeed, meeting the abundance of "stones and horrible rugged rocks" (on the coast of what is present-day Labrador), he says, "I am rather inclined to believe that this is the land God gave to Cain." [12] Yet Cartier's text shows that he alters his initial opinion of this new land somewhat as he investigates it, noting, finally, that the harshness of the wind and cold abate and that the land can support trees and grasses.

Also like Columbus and Cabral, Cartier discovers people in the New World. Since they are clothed (in animal furs), he has no problem with their nudity, as Columbus and (to a lesser extent) Cabral did. Describing them as "wild and savage folk," [13] Cartier is wary of their intentions. Later, when his men unexpectedly find themselves outnumbered by some natives, Cartier fires two cannon shots over their heads, hoping to frighten them off. This salvo constitutes, sadly, what may be the first recorded act of armed aggression by the Old World against the New.

In addition to their differing reactions to the people they encountered, one of the most striking distinctions between Cartier's account and those of both Columbus and Cabral has to do with the question of whether gold existed in the New World. Although Cartier's first voyage log does not make mention of this issue, that of his second voyage (1535–36) does. Echoing Columbus's interest in having his "Indians" possess gold, Cartier reports that the people of the Indian village Hochelaga (later Montreal) "gave us to understand that, in this country . . . there are many towns and tribes composed of honest folk who possess great store of gold and copper." [14] Conjecturing enthusiastically (if not with precision) on where these places might be, and keenly aware of the already well established Spanish presence in the New World, Cartier notes that these mineral riches lie to the south, toward Florida.

On his first voyage, however, that of 1534, Cartier's trade with the Indians involved various kinds of animal pelts, not gold or silver. This is significant, for in time, as furs became a commercially lucrative fashion item in Europe, the fur trade in Canada would do for the English and later the French what the quest for gold did for the Portuguese and, especially, the Spanish in the rest of the Americas. The pursuit of furbearing animals, like the otter and beaver, led to an opening of the hinterlands in Canada much as the pursuit of gold and silver had done in various parts of South, Central, and North America. (Furs, however, it might be noted, were taken from four-legged animals, while gold and silver were taken from people, people whose cultures equaled and in some ways surpassed the cultures of their European conquerors.)

Another prime discovery document, John Smith's *A True Relation of Occurrences and Accidents in Virginia* (1608), puts considerable stress on this clash of Old World and New World cultures, a clash that, as Smith's narrative shows, was violent from the beginning. Unlike the other discovery texts we have seen, which stress the longitude and latitude of the moment of arrival and which attempt detailed descriptions of everything that was encountered, Smith minimizes the geophysical data and instead takes his reader right to the most salient fact of his landfall—an Indian attack. As Smith, himself a seasoned soldier and Elizabethan adventurer, writes:

> The first land we made [April 26, 1607] we fell with Cape Henry, the verie mouth of the Bay of Chissiapiacke, which at that present we little expected, having by a cruell storme bene put to the Northward:
>
> Anchoring in this Bay twentie or thirtie went a shore with the Captain, and in comming aboard [on land], they were assalted with certaine Indians.[15]

As we can see by this account, the Native Americans encountered by Smith in 1607 were not as pacific as those encountered by Columbus in 1492, by Cabot in 1497, by Cabral in 1500, or by Cartier in 1534. An open hostility, bred possibly by the understandable fear that they were being invaded by strange foreigners who had come to take their lands away, characterizes the encounters described in Smith's account. Though open violence is lacking in the other discovery chronicles, it rather soon became a lamentably normal fact of life for the remainder of the European conquest, especially that involving the Spanish conquistadors, who would eventually confront and subjugate the three great Pre-Columbian civilizations. By 1607, then, bad relations between the aboriginal peoples and the Europeans were commonplace; indeed, the bloody conquest of the Aztec Empire had been a matter of historical record since 1521, a fact of which Smith, as is evident in his concluding remarks, was fully aware.

Smith's party was initially driven by a strong sense of social organization and settlement, although, as A. G. Bradley notes, it was not long before "a gold mania had broken out"[16] in the colony, just as it had on a larger scale in the colonies of Spanish America and to a lesser extent in those of Portuguese and French America. Nevertheless, Smith placed great store in keeping his group organized around the relatively democratic principles instilled in him by early seventeenth-century English society; as a comparative reading of New World history shows, that fact would make the sociopolitical experience of English-speaking America very different from that of its New World neighbors.

Problems with the Indians, then (in addition to those of sickness and famine), plagued the 1607 English (who initially came less to explore and exploit than to set up a new civilization in the New World) more immediately than they did the Spanish, the Portuguese, and the French. Although Columbus clearly intended to conquer and convert the Indians he encountered, his record indicates no immediate armed conflict with them, a state of affairs that would tragically change in the years from 1492 to 1607. Indeed, one of the most exciting parts of Smith's narrative, and one that helped to generate the later-appearing captivity tales (which as a genre have been cultivated throughout the Americas), is his account of his capture by the Indians.

Although all these discovery narratives deal with the unstable relations between the Europeans and the Native Americans, Smith's discovery narrative—the last to be written—is the only one to paint such a sorry picture of intercultural violence and enmity. Between 1492 and 1607, the nature of the European discovery of the New World had already undergone a radical shift. After dwelling on what he learned of the Indians' ways and, most important, what he learned about the cultivation of staple food crops such as corn and squash, Smith ends his account of the troubled 1607 Jamestown experience by declaring that the English colonists had "subjected the Savages [to their] desired obedience."[17]

From the perspective of the Europeans, the peoples first encountered in the New World had to be subjugated; for the Spanish, Portuguese, and French, these aboriginal Americans were to be converted immediately to Christianity.[18] All too often, however, they were abused as subhuman creatures and exploited for their utility as cheap labor. From the perspective of the indigenous peoples, the Europeans with their powerful technological advantages (ships, guns, armor, and horses) and their religions constituted very real threats.

When we compare these fascinating discovery documents, however, we can see more easily the nature of the particular European traditions that were being planted, albeit forcibly, in American soil. If Columbus's 1492 letter to the Spanish king and queen was the most self-consciously exaggerated of these accounts, then Cartier's 1534 account was the least fantastical. The 1500 letter by Cabral's official scribe, Pero Vaz de Caminha, is, as we have seen, more objective and restrained than Columbus's report and in this respect more similar to

Cartier's log. Smith's account, falling somewhere between Columbus's and Cartier's, possesses a sense of drama that the other accounts lack, a drama that springs directly from the desperate struggle to survive being waged by people who were for the most part settlers, not hardened soldiers or adventurers. But for all their stylistic differences and in spite of their differing levels of reliable reportage, the European discovery documents of the New World all possess a sense of great excitement, of expectation, and of new possibilities. Inescapably, the colonization of the New World would impose a new identity on everyone involved. Whether this process would be positive or negative was a question immediately taken up in the postdiscovery years, the years of epic struggle and conquest.

The many narratives that record these later years of struggle, the narratives not of discovery but of conquest, are stirring documents, vivid testaments to the courage and tenacity of the human spirit. Though these numerous New World conquest documents deal with a variety of subjects and areas, they can be divided into two large groups: those in which the essential conflict is with the environment and those in which the essential conflict is with other people. Put another way, one might say that the two primary obstacles to the European conquest of the New World were the American landscape itself, in all its diversity and extremes, and the very different human civilizations that were encountered.

The first group includes the journals of Henry Kelsey (perhaps the first nonnative to see the Great Plains of North America), the accounts of Anthony Henday and Matthew Cocking, and the exploration narratives of Cartier, La Salle, La Vérendrye, David Thompson, Samuel Hearne, John Franklin, Cabeza de Vaca, Coronado, Balboa, and Gaspar de Carvajal (who gave the name Amazon to the great river of South America); of these, the accounts of Franklin, Hearne, and Carvajal are classics of their kind. Carvajal, like Columbus and Oviedo before him, had been thoroughly conditioned by his reading of Renaissance mythology and so found it easy to "see" the fabled Amazon warriors when his group was attacked by a band of natives—some of whom may well have been female—along the banks of the Amazon. On the other hand, Cabeza de Vaca's harrowing account, full of dramatic events and offering a firsthand narrative of shipwreck, death, violence, incredible hardship, cannibalism, and capture by hostile Indians, helped to disprove the popular notions that the New World landfalls had been on a large archipelago just off the coast of Asia and that the New World contained the Garden of Eden.

The second group includes many of the narratives from the French Canadian *Jesuit Relations* (the central drama of which derives from the "Jesuit's evangelical zeal and the beliefs of the primitive nomads, between feudal theology and Stone Age superstition"),[19] the letters and reports of Antônio Vieira, José de Anchieta, Marc Lescarbot, and Samuel de Champlain, the accounts of the Brazilian Bandeirantes, Bernal Díaz del Castillo's *A True History of the Conquest*, and the various chronicles that deal with Pizarro's conquest of the Incan Empire. Bernal Díaz's extraordinary story of the fall of the Aztec nation emerges as the prototype of this category, the narrative of one individual's struggle against another.

Whether dealing primarily with a conflict between humankind and nature or between two individuals or cultures, the early conquest narratives, written by literarily unpretentious men, often possess a structural unity and an intensity that make them read as if they were fiction. Their style is typically simple and direct, yet they frequently generate the dramatic structuring, plotlike narrative development, and revealing characterizations that we associate with well-written adventure stories. In addition to Castillo's *True History*, Franklin's *Narrative of a Journey to the Shores of the Polar Sea* epitomizes this kind of writing, as do Hearne's *Journey from Prince of Wales' Fort in Hudson's Bay to the Northern Ocean*, Champlain's several chronicles (especially *Des Sauvages*, 1603), and Cabeza de Vaca's thrilling account.

The accounts of Hearne and, in particular, Franklin, epitomize the humankind against nature variety of these conquest narratives. As David Galloway has suggested, the English and French voyagers to Canada, beginning with Cabot and Cartier, always encountered sterner and harsher climes than did the Spanish and Portuguese, who more often came upon warm, sun-drenched beaches. Galloway also notes that because of the short summer season and the everpresent dangers of ice and winter storms, the early English and French explorers worked with a sense of urgency about their mission that becomes very evident in their chronicles:

> Prominent in accounts of . . . voyages to Canada . . . are descriptions of struggles against the elements. The time available for the completion of a northern voyage is limited. . . . In the voyages to Virginia and the Indies there is no such sense of urgency, and whatever the dangers of sailing to the South, there is no danger of having to experience the frozen horrors which Cartier endured in the St. Lawrence winter of 1535–36.
>
> From its very beginnings, the "literature" of Canada was stamped by a struggle against the climate and against the land itself.[20]

From the outset, then, the natural environment played a decisive role in the dramatic tension so apparent in the early English and French Canadian conquest narratives. The land and the climate often became the chief adversaries of the early explorers, who, as we see in their typically straightforward first-person accounts, gradually came to envision themselves as locked in a survival struggle with the elements. Margaret Atwood has even argued that the concept of survival, or *survivance* (in French Canada), can be taken as the defining motif of Canadian literature, much as the motif of the frontier is identified with the United States and that of the island is associated with England.[21] But whether the struggle for survival meant the conquering of a land or a people, it never failed to produce conquest narratives that are action-oriented, full of compelling characters (often seen in life-threatening situations), and organized around events of great drama and tension.

While Franklin's narrative, the prototype of this kind of writing, slowly comes to focus less on the completion of the 1819–22 mission (which was to map the northernmost shore of North America) and more on simple survival, the fact that Franklin and his men did accomplish what they had been charged to do actually heightens the dramatic tension of the narrative by giving it an organic and satisfying conclusion. Yet, as in a well-structured novel, the narrative's conclusion is not as gripping as the interplay of fortune—the ebb and flow of the conflict—that precedes and shapes it. Pitting his endurance and will to survive against the unforgiving Arctic wilderness and, increasingly, against the limits of human endurance, Franklin tells a story that, especially in its final chapters, possesses the unity and progression that we associate with good fiction. Rising to a natural climax, the events of chapter 11 surge toward what seems an inescapable conclusion, one the reader feels to be classically tragic in its inevitability.

As Franklin's party, inadequately equipped and ill-advised, struggled through the weeks and months of its journey, it began to suffer serious and unexpected problems: conflicting advice, internal dissent, mutinous conduct, and, with dramatic finality, even murder and cannibalism. As ever-higher levels of mental and physical exhaustion were reached, as the relentless Arctic weather and terrain drained more out of the men, and as their supplies dwindled, Franklin's group began to disintegrate. Only good luck, Franklin's iron-willed leadership, and the courage of several of his subordinates saved the expedition from total disaster. Struggling against the relentless adversaries of cold, hunger, exhaustion, and dissent, Franklin and his band persevered, finally reaching help on July 14, 1822, after an arduous journey of some 5,550 miles.

Franklin opens his account with an apology to the reader for an alleged deficiency of the text: "I ought, perhaps, to crave the reader's indulgence towards the defective style of this work."[22] In the first ten chapters, he describes in careful, scientifically quantified, and catalogued detail all the flora and fauna he sees, as well as the daily weather conditions, geological formations, and geographic data. As he becomes involved with different Indian peoples, whom he struggles to understand, he gains firsthand knowledge about the fur trade, an enterprise that he gradually comes to view less with objectivity than with criticism, even hostility. Franklin's text also offers a detailed account of the party's mode of traveling through the deep snow, an activity that, at this point in the narrative, has not yet become the cruel torture that it would later be. Though the ice, snow, and cold are problems here, the men are still strong, well fed, and rested, and they cope relatively well, a state of affairs that would later change dramatically.

As exhaustion and problems with the terrain, the climate, the food supplies, and the equipment mount, Franklin begins to have trouble with his "Canadian voyagers," the French Canadians and Métis who serve the group as guides, packers, and hunters:

> Our Canadian voyagers, who had been for some days past murmuring at their meagre diet, and striving to get the whole of our little provision to consume at once, broke out into open discontent, and several of them threatened they would not proceed forward unless more food was given to them.[23]

This is the first mention of dissent between the English officers and the Canadian voyageurs, a dissent that would grow until it yielded tragic results. Franklin, revealing both his rigid naval training and his own stern character, records in his journal how he responded to the initial rebellion:

> I, therefore, felt the duty incumbent on me to address them in the strongest manner on the danger of insubordination, and to assure them of my determination to inflict the heaviest punishment on any that should persist in their refusal to go on, or in any other way attempt to retard the Expedition.[24]

The incipient human rebellion momentarily quelled, Franklin and his men continue to battle the ice, snow, and cold:

> December 24 and 25 [1820] . . . The snow was so deep that the dogs were obliged to stop every ten minutes to rest themselves; and the cold was so excessive, that both the men were badly frozen on both sides of the face and chin.[25]

One entry provides both a kind of comic relief and an example of Franklin's astute if dogged leadership qualities. In order to divert their attention from their deteriorating condition, the men are ordered to go sledding down a snowy riverbank. Franklin, joining in, observes later, "On one occasion, when I had been thrown from my seat and almost buried in the snow, a fat Indian woman drove her sled over me, and sprained my knee severely." [26]

As the narrative moves toward its climax the reader is increasingly drawn into it, not because of the chronological progression of its entries but by a growing realization that as the men grow weaker, their chances of surviving in the unrelenting Arctic wilderness grow slimmer. Burdened additionally with the danger of attack from hostile natives, as well as with increasing numbers of fatigue- and weather-related accidents, some of which are suspected to be the result of sabotage, Franklin pressed on, knowing that to stop would be to perish. His log of September 6, 1821, records this scene of misery:

Heavy rain commenced at midnight, and continued without intermission until five in the morning when it was succeeded by snow on the wind changing . . . to a violent gale. . . . We had nothing to eat. . . . The covering of our blankets was insufficient to prevent us from feeling the severity of the frost . . . and . . . the drifting of the snow into our tents . . . our tents were completely frozen, and the snow had drifted around them to a depth of three feet, and even inside there was a covering of several inches on our blankets. Our suffering from cold, in a . . . canvass tent in such weather, with the temperature at 20°, and without fire, will be easily imagined; it was, however less than that which we felt from hunger. [27]

Subsisting more and more on *tripe de roche*, a lichen covering many of the rocks and stones in the region, Franklin's party struggled on. But as supplies and strength drained away, the men began to lose hope. Out of a growing sense of despair, arguments, fights, and even thefts of the precious food allotment began to occur; the degree of this heinous deed is thrown into sharp relief by a courageous act of heroism by Dr. Richardson, who dives into the icy water of a river to save a drifting supply raft that the party desperately needed to survive.

With supplies virtually exhausted, the men now eating burnt leather, Franklin decides upon a daring gamble: he splits his group and, taking the strongest men with him, sets out in a race to Fort Enterprise, where he believes help can be found. Though he and his men are facing imminent death, Franklin records the events in a detached, matter-of-fact style that only heightens the drama. The narration suddenly focuses all attention on Franklin, now clearly seen as its hero, as he struggles toward the fort. As if following a fictionalized plot, how-ever, Franklin discovers Fort Enterprise to be abandoned.

Franklin's next entry (for October 4, 1821), underscoring the anticlimactic pathos of this unexpected turn of events, heightens the tension of the narrative by understating the seemingly fatal significance of what has happened:

> It would be impossible for me to describe our sensations after entering this miserable abode, and discovering how we had been neglected: the whole party shed tears, not so much for our own fate, as for that of our friends in the rear, whose lives depended entirely on our sending immediate relief from this place.[28]

In an ironic inversion of the conqueror-conquered relationship (one also seen in the accounts of John Smith and Cabeza de Vaca), Franklin realizes that if he and his men are to be saved, help must come from the Indians of the area. Too debilitated by hunger and exposure to the elements, Franklin's men sink into a state of exhaustion so profound that, in a moment of tragic irony, they are unable to rouse themselves to action even when they see a herd of deer come close enough to be shot for meat.

Then, in another dramatic and unexpected change of fortune, Dr. Richardson and another man suddenly appear in Franklin's camp bearing unsettling news: Mr. Hood (one of Franklin's subordinates) and Michel (a French Canadian voyageur) are dead. Expressing apprehension about what could have led to the deaths of Hood and Michel, Franklin's narrative here incorporates Dr. Richardson's account into the *Journey*'s text.

Structurally, Dr. Richardson's commentary is a kind of first-person flashback that supplies information about the deaths of Hood and Michel that neither Franklin nor his reader could have known. The result is that his report is a story within a story, one replete with its own rising and falling plot structure, its own conflicts, its own vivid characterizations, and its own dramatic resolution. The events discussed in Dr. Richardson's account of cannibalism, mutiny, and mur-der also connect organically with the basic conflict of Franklin's text, that of these men against nature.

What is also seen clearly in Richardson's testimony is that this latter conflict has generated a secondary conflict, that of one man against himself, since what we learn (or what we suspect) about Michel's actions shows him to have col-lapsed under physical peril and psychological stress, becoming unable to con-trol his actions. According to Richardson's account, Michel murdered Hood but then is himself later "executed" for this alleged crime by Richardson, who in the absence of Franklin has assumed command of the party. The explanation offered is that Michel seemed about to kill Richardson, and perhaps the others, in an attempt to cover up his possible cannibalism of other members of the party. There is grim irony in Richardson's narrative in that he had once referred to Michel as "the instrument" the Almighty "had chosen to preserve all our lives."[29] Gradually, however, Richardson had begun to doubt the good intentions of Michel and to suspect him of both murder and cannibalism.[30]

Richardson's narrative, even more than Franklin's, shows the extreme urgency of their plight: "With the decay of our strength, our minds decayed, and we were no longer able to bear the contemplation of the horrors that surrounded us."[31] His entry for October 19, 1821, shows Michel, seemingly agitated and unstable, refusing to help his mates move a log to the fire. Richardson, like an omniscient author, quotes Michel as saying, in what might be construed as a revealing statement, "It is no use hunting, there are no animals, you had better kill and eat me."[32] The next day's entry describes in an unemotional way how, after an argument between him and Michel, Hood is found dead, "a ball having apparently entered his forehead."[33] Richardson's narrative of this event has a startling conclusion:

> I was at first horror-struck with the idea, that in a fit of despondency he had hurried himself into the presence of his Almighty Judge, by an act of his own hand; but the conduct of Michel soon gave rise to other thoughts, and excited suspicions which were confirmed, when upon examining the body, I discovered that the shot had entered the back part of the head, and passed out at the forehead. . . . Although I dared not openly to evince any suspicion that I thought Michel guilty of the deed, yet he repeatedly protested that he was incapable of committing such an act.[34]

Now convinced of his guilt, Richardson grows increasingly wary of Michel, who, heavily armed, suddenly becomes openly belligerent. In a moment of high drama, Richardson decides that "there was no safety for us except in his [Michel's] death . . . and immediately upon Michel's coming up, I put an end to his life by shooting him through the head with a pistol."[35] After explaining that he shot Michel to prevent him from attacking the group, Richardson moves to a conclusion that is as clinically analytical as it is objectively descriptive. His account of what he thought Michel had done and of what he himself did draws the reader into the narrator-protagonist's interpretation of what happened. In Richardson's account, then, the reader's response to the tale told by the narrator, who is decisively involved in the action, is just as crucial as it would be if this story had been a fictional creation.

Franklin is reunited with Richardson and the remainder of the group as the narration, back under the control of Franklin himself, draws quickly to a conclusion. The final scene contains a major irony, one that contrasts the wretched condition of the "conquering" Europeans with the relatively comfortable condition of the "conquered" Americans, here an Indian chief, Akaitcho, and his men. Written from the perspective of the "advanced" European who is saved from certain death by the generosity of the "barbarous" Indians, Richardson's recounting shows yet another ironic reversal of roles:

> November 8 [1821] . . . The Indians set about every thing with an activity that amazed us. Indeed, contrasted with our emaciated figures and extreme debility, their frames appeared to us gigantic, and their strength supernatural. These kind creatures next turned their attention to our personal appearance, and prevailed upon us to shave and wash ourselves.[36]

Even the concluding line of Franklin's narrative, written some eight months later, has a novelistic feel of plot closure to it, a sense that the central conflict has been resolved and that a logical conclusion has resulted:

> And thus terminated our long, fatiguing, and disastrous travels in North America, having journeyed by water and by land (including our navigation of the Polar Sea,) five thousand five hundred and fifty miles
> End of the narrative.[37]

While all eleven chapters of Franklin's *Narrative of a Journey to the Shores of the Polar Sea* deal with the conflict between humankind and nature, the final chapter has a unity and a dramatic intensity that make it stand on its own as a distilled and refined example of this type of conquest narrative. But beyond the power of its basic conflict, the narrative of chapter 11 also shows the crucial presence of another conflict, our need to control ourselves under adverse circumstances, a conflict which greatly humanizes the other, more fundamental struggle and which renders the outcome both more poignant and more ironic. A model of its kind, Franklin's *Journey* deserves a larger readership.

A conquest narrative that has won a somewhat greater audience is Bernal Díaz del Castillo's *True History of the Conquest of New Spain*, a novel-like first-person account of the Spanish conquest of the Aztec Empire.[38] The *True History*, completed in 1568 but not published until 1632, is oral history at its best. Written in a fresh (if not polished or sophisticated) style, Bernal Díaz's riveting eyewitness account is that of the Spanish foot soldier, the tough and disciplined conquistador who waged an always bloody and often hand-to-hand war with the fierce Aztec warriors and who came to respect them as only a soldier could.

Even more than Franklin's narrative, the *True History* has throughout the feel of fiction, the events it recounts having the kind of causally related sequentiality that we expect in the carefully structured war novel.

Although both Franklin's *Journey* and Díaz's *True History* have several features in common—they are nonfiction narratives that possess many of the qualities of fiction, they concern themselves with the two basic kinds of struggle that occurred when the Old World began to conquer the New, they make use of self-conscious narrator-protagonists, and they are dramatic stories—they also differ in several key ways. Díaz's account is not that of the leader of the expedition, for example. It is more novel-like in the steadily increasing tension of its structuring, and its narrator-protagonist is more revealingly self-conscious. It also relies more on dialogue than Franklin's work does, and it develops more thoroughly the complex personalities of its two great antagonists, the Spanish leader Cortés and the Aztec monarch Montezuma. Calling attention to the true spirit of this text, Monegal says of Díaz's literary talents, "He had the true eye and ear of the novelist." [39]

Without doubt "one of the greatest historical narratives of the Renaissance," [40] Bernal Díaz's account of the capture of the Aztec capital, Tenochtitlán, and the destruction of the Aztec Empire is one of the most exciting pieces of writing to come out of the era of New World discovery and conquest. The monumental events depicted in the *True History* were later revivified by Archibald MacLeish in his poem *Conquistador* (1932), a fact which underscores the significance that Cortés's epic undertaking continues to have for the people of the Americas. As his own narrative clearly shows, Díaz was quite conscious of having taken part in a great event: the overthrow of a powerful empire by a handful of tenacious adventurers, men driven partly by a sense of divine mission (to spread Christianity) but also by a materialistic lust for gold.

Like John Franklin, Bernal Díaz begins his narrative cautiously, with an apology to the reader for the plainness of his style: "What I myself saw, and the fighting in which I took part, with God's help I will describe quite plainly, as an honest eyewitness, without twisting the facts in any way." [41] Bernal Díaz is concerned, as John Franklin did not need to be, that the facts of the conquest of New Spain be presented accurately and in an unadorned manner. He was aware of and angry about other less than reliable accounts, such as Francisco López de Gómara's *Conquest of Mexico* (1552) which, according to Díaz, gave a distorted picture. Díaz wrote his own *True History*, then, to set the record straight.

His narrative succeeds as well as it does chiefly because of the author's extraordinary memory, his sure sense of the dramatic, his simple but vibrant style, and, above all, the grandeur of the actual events. While the plot structure of Franklin's *Journey* is essentially linear until chapter 11, when unexpected events come into play, the plot structure of the *True History* is from the very beginning full of reverses and unexpected changes of fortune. The Spaniards make an amphibious landing on Aztec soil in 1519 and, though vastly outnumbered, drive inland to the Aztec capital, which they take. Then, in an unexpected reversal, they are driven out. Rallying, they counterattack the capital and place it under siege. Finally, after bloody hand-to-hand fighting, they capture the Aztec leader and force their enemies to surrender.

In addition to the subjugation of the Aztecs and the military struggle, which Bernal Díaz describes dramatically and in detail, he also takes pains to make his reader understand the crucial importance of something else in the conquest of New Spain—translation. The Spaniards accidentally came into the services of an Indian woman, Doña Marina, who knew all the Indian languages of the region and quickly learned Spanish, thereby enabling Cortés to communicate with the Indian tribes who were at war with the Aztecs. Recognizing the importance of Doña Marina's language skills to the conquistadors, Díaz devotes an entire chapter ("Doña Marina's Story") to her, concluding by saying, "I have made a point of telling this story, because without Doña Marina we could not have understood the language of New Spain and Mexico."[42] The astounding implication of this comment is that the Spanish conquest of Mexico rested on the availability of an Indian translator; on such seemingly trivial things do momentous events sometimes turn.

Not long after first landing in Mexico (close to present-day Veracruz), Cortés made a decision that surely ranks as one of his most daring and dramatic. In order to ensure that none of his men, should they lose heart and become desirous of returning to Spain, could go back, the Spanish commander ordered that all his ships be burned; Cortés and his force (some six hundred in number) could only advance. They would have to fight or die, for they were in Mexico to stay.

One of the best-known sections of Bernal Díaz's narrative, and one that like the conclusion of Franklin's narrative shows an ironic inversion of the terms "civilized" and "savage," is the chapter entitled "The Entrance into Mexico." Seeing the magnificent Aztec capital through the eyes of our presumably reliable European narrator, we readers get a vivid sense of what an extraordinary vista greeted the Spanish upon their arrival at Tenochtitlán (a magnificent city built, possibly for reasons of defense, in the middle of a lake):

We were astounded. These great towns and *cues* and buildings rising from the water, all made of stone, seemed like an enchanted vision from the tale of Amadis. Indeed, some of our soldiers asked whether it was not all a dream. . . . It was all so wonderful that I do not know how to describe this first glimpse of things never heard of, seen or dreamed of before.[43]

Amazed at the grandeur of the Aztec capital, Bernal Díaz and his comrades-in-arms march from the shore of the lake into the heart of the city along a causeway some eight yards wide, their route packed with Aztec citizens staring with what must have been equal amazement at the Spaniards. Fully conscious of this extraordinary situation, nothing less than the meeting of two worlds hitherto unknown to each other, Díaz observes: "With such wonderful sights to gaze on we did not know what to say, or if this was real that we saw before our eyes."[44]

But soldier that he was, Bernal Díaz was not unmindful of the dangers inherent in the Spaniards' precarious situation, for he knew that the Aztecs might well annihilate them at any moment. By sounding such an ominous note at this point, when the Spaniards seem to be victorious, Díaz subtly increases the plot tension of his narrative.

Once safely inside the city, Cortés, working under a sign of peace, finally meets Montezuma face to face. The high drama of the moment is not lost on Bernal Díaz, who, like a good novelist, contrasts the characters of Cortés and Montezuma, the two leaders involved in what will become the classic example of the bloody clash between the Old World and the New. Through his description of what Cortés did, and by means of the words he attributes to him, Díaz portrays the Spanish leader as being cunning and duplicitous as well as noble and heroic, and the troubled relationship between Cortés and Montezuma is a kind of parallel to the events so vividly depicted in chapter 11 of Franklin's book. Portrayed as carefully as Cortés, Montezuma emerges from the text with a complex identity that sticks in the reader's mind long after the confrontation scene is past. The Spanish commander regards Montezuma warily but with respect, recognizing that he is the supreme ruler of a highly sophisticated if (in his view) barbaric culture.

Later in this same chapter, Bernal Díaz continues, again self-consciously, to describe the Aztec practice of human sacrifice. Other than its importance as factual knowledge about the Aztec civilization, this account also serves metaphorically to intensify the drama of the situation; the reader is reminded of how vulnerable the Spaniards are, how close to being annihilated by the soldiers of a culture the "barbarity" of which is symbolized by its systematic practice of human sacrifice and cannibalism. As Bernal Díaz puts it:

> I have already described the manner of their sacrifices. They strike open the wretched Indian's chest with flint knives and hastily tear out the palpitating heart which, with the blood, they present to the idols in whose name they have performed the sacrifice. Then they cut off the arms, thighs, and head, eating the arms and thighs at their ceremonial banquets. The head they hang up on a beam, and the body of the sacrificed man is not eaten but given to the beasts of prey.[45]

The plot tension suddenly intensifies when the Spaniards, who have been permitted to move about freely within the city, unexpectedly come upon the sealed treasure room of the Aztecs. Secretly breaking in, Cortés and some of his most trusted men, including Díaz, discover a treasure trove of gold, silver, and gems so fabulous that it holds them in awe. Díaz reports that "the sight of all that wealth dumbfounded me."[46]

Anxious that Montezuma might discover that they knew where the Aztec gold was kept and yet driven by their greed to possess it, fully aware that to seize it would certainly plunge them into a state of open war with the Aztecs, Cortés and his men determine to take Montezuma prisoner. Fearful that they might be attacked under any circumstances—and aware that they could not withstand an attack—the Spanish conclude that their best chance for survival (and for keeping the gold) would be to capture the Aztec monarch and hold him hostage.

But before Cortés can carry out this daring plan, another unexpected event takes place: the Aztecs attack a portion of the Spanish force stationed at a nearby village. Increasing the plot tension even more, Bernal Díaz comments, "God knows the distress this news caused us. It was the first defeat we had suffered in New Spain, and misfortunes, as the reader will see, were now descending upon us."[47]

Moving quickly now to capture Montezuma, Cortés is suddenly forced to quit the capital in order to check an abortive coup raised against him by a jealous fellow officer. This wholly unanticipated event is followed by more startling news: while Cortés was putting down this rebellion, the Aztecs had attacked his men inside Tenochtitlán itself. The scenario the Spanish feared most had begun to unfold.

Driving his men hard, Cortés reenters the Aztec capital and confronts Montezuma, who now knows he cannot trust the Spanish leader. Before the two leaders can conclude their deliberations, however, the Aztecs attack again, this time in force. Bernal Díaz, invoking the image of a pair of great classical warriors, captures the drama of the conflict:

> We fought very well, but they were so strong and had so many bands which relieved one another by turns, that if we had had ten thousand Trojan Hectors and as many Rolands, even then we should not have been able to break through. . . . We were struck by the tenacity of their fighting, which was beyond description. Neither cannon, muskets, nor crossbows were of any avail, nor hand-to-hand combat, nor the slaughter of thirty or forty of them every time we charged. They still fought on bravely and with more vigour than before.[48]

Realizing the extreme peril of his situation, Cortés prevails upon Montezuma to speak to his people, entreating them to lay down their arms. The effect, as Bernal Díaz recreates it, was again quite unexpected: "Barely was this speech finished when a sudden shower of stones and darts descended. . . . Montezuma was hit by three stones, one on the head. . . . Then quite unexpectedly we were told that he was dead." [49] Having murdered their own leader, the Aztecs closed in on the outnumbered Spanish, who now were forced to fight their way out of Tenochtitlán, the city they had entered so imperiously only a few weeks before. Speaking in the first-person plural as one of the combatants, Bernal Díaz brilliantly evokes the wild atmosphere of the battle:

> We saw them beginning to surround us. . . . We charged them, all together.
>   It was a destructive battle, and a fearful sight to behold. We moved through the midst of them at the closest quarters, slashing and thrusting at them with our swords. And the dogs fought back furiously, dealing us wounds and death with their lances and their two-handed swords.[50]

The scene ends with Cortés finally succeeding, despite heavy losses, in leading his men to relative safety outside the city.

The conflict between the Spanish and the Aztecs was far from settled, however, because Cortés had already resolved to retake the city, a fateful decision that would now generate another, even bloodier campaign. Gaining reinforcements from several tribes of Indians who had been harshly oppressed by the Aztecs and now saw a chance to defeat them, Cortés counterattacked. On the narrow causeways leading into the city and in canoes on the lake itself, the terrible second battle for the Aztec capital seesawed back and forth.

There is a moment of cruel irony in the account when Bernal Díaz, set upon by several Aztec warriors, thanks Jesus Christ for giving him the "strength to deal them a few good thrusts"[51] of his sword. Cortés too is nearly captured and killed, but the bravery of some of his men, who rush to his aid, saves him. These two episodes show Díaz's considerable skill as a narrator in reproducing scenes both of vast panoramic struggle and of intense individual combat. His skillful use of perspective keeps the reader's interest whetted and the story moving along with no loss of intensity or cohesion.

Finally, in a brilliant tactical maneuver, Cortés changed his basic strategy, a move that turned the tide of the battle in his favor. Unable to react effectively, the Aztecs, for all their numbers, courage, and tenacity, are defeated. This is the turning point in the plot structure of Díaz's narrative; the Aztecs' fate is now sealed.

With the outcome of the battle determined when Cortés alters his plan, the narrative begins to wind down toward its ineluctable conclusion, one that would be as appropriate for a work of fiction as it is historically accurate. The Spanish, having gained control of the lake, finally succeed in capturing Guatemoc, the new Aztec leader, as he tries to escape from his besieged capital. With this comparatively undramatic event the conflict comes to a halt. The short but ferocious war between the Aztecs and the Spaniards ends. Bernal Díaz moves quickly to bring his narrative to a conclusion, too, but not before he offers the reader another self-conscious reflection on the fear he felt going into battle and the wounds he received. He also offers a final comment on Cortés's dubious ethical conduct, suggesting that the Spanish leader may not have divided the spoils of war fairly with his men, and he offers an explanation—they had been led to believe there was no more gold or other wealth left to seize in the area— of why the conquistadors did not settle the area around the Aztec capital. With this abrupt and enigmatic bit of commentary, the narrative ends.

Of the two kinds of narrative produced by the arrival of the Europeans in the New World, the discovery narratives and the narratives of conquest, the latter are unquestionably more dramatic. Although an air of excitement and anticipation permeates the discovery documents, the two classes of conquest narratives (the human creature against nature and one individual or culture in conflict with another) generate the greatest degree of drama. Epitomized, respectively, by John Franklin's *Narrative of a Journey to the Shores of the Polar Sea* and Bernal Díaz del Castillo's *True History of the Conquest of New Spain*, the numerous texts of these two categories have captured forever the epic struggle that characterized the European conquest of the Americas.

3

The New World Epic

* * * * * * * * * * * *

As a literary genre, the epic was particularly well suited to the portrayal of the conquest and colonization of the New World. Both the bloody and violent clash of cultures that the conquest occasioned and the subsequent rise of the American nations lent themselves to retelling via the epic form. But just as the struggle for control of the Americas involved different types and degrees of conflict, so too did the numerous American epics come to differ in subject matter, mode of treatment, and style. Another key difference stems from the degree of self-consciousness with which these epic poems were written. *The Columbiad* (1807), for example, from the United States, is a very self-conscious epic, one that openly compares itself with some of the better-known epics of the past. The Iroquois narrative, *The Dekanawida*, on the other hand, is not at all self-conscious, though in its own way it does achieve most of the formal and thematic characteristics that we associate with the venerable form of the epic.

In the standard literary histories of English and French Canada the national epic is hardly mentioned, a fact that seems linked to the question of Canadian identity. Although this question can be said to lie restively at the heart of the entire American experience, several of the other American republics, most notably the United States, Brazil, and Chile, have produced national epics that follow the traditional form and overtly proclaim the uniqueness of their cultural and political identity.[1]

Given the historical facts of the New World experience, then, with its conquests and its long struggles toward political and cultural autonomy, it is not surprising that American epics would have been written. What is surprising is how different these New World epics are from each other and, often, from orthodox concepts of this ancient genre.

A few exceptions notwithstanding, one can say that the majority of the New World epics tend toward the genre of the literary or "art" epic rather than toward the "folk" epic.[2] As we will see, the hero of the American epic, though often symbolized in a single man or woman, is more likely to be collective in significance. This collectivized or socialized hero (like Aeneas) is able to help establish a new society, a new nation, and a new cultural and political identity. The representative epics we will compare here are the following: *The Dekanawida*; E. J. Pratt's *Towards the Last Spike* (1952); Louis Fréchette's *La légende d'un peuple* (1887); Joel Barlow's *The Columbiad* (1807); Alonso de Ercilla y Zúñiga's *The Araucaniad* (1569, 1578, 1589); and José Basílio da Gama's *The Uruguay* (1769).

In attempting to define the nature of the epic poem, C. M. Bowra has written:

> An epic poem is by common consent a narrative of some length and deals with events which have a certain grandeur and importance and come from a life of action, especially violent action such as war. It gives special pleasure because its events and persons enhance our belief in the worth of human achievement and in the dignity and nobility of man.[3]

Bowra's spacious definition is particularly useful as we begin to compare and contrast these several New World epics, poems which, though showing a diversity of forms, themes, and characters, also have a great deal in common, especially in regard to the nature of the hero and his or her relationship to the establishment of a nation. In addition, these poems also reflect, though in differing ways, other essential characteristics of the epic form with regard to setting, the nature of the action, the role of supernatural forces, the style, and the relationship between the epic poet and the song. The New World epics all offer a glimpse into the lengthy and complex process through which a culture gains (or, in the case of the Iroquois and their *Dekanawida*, retains) a sense of unity and identity.

Within this dimension of cultural amalgamation, the role of the hero in these epic poems is paramount. In the Native American *Dekanawida*, for example, the primary hero, Dekanawida, is born mysteriously, an occurrence typical of many epics:

> North of the beautiful lake (Ontario) in the land of the Crooked Tongues, was a long winding bay and at a certain spot was the Huron town, Ka-ha-nah-yenh. . . . In the village lived a good woman who had a virgin daughter. Now strangely this virgin conceived and her mother knew she was about to bear a child. The daughter about this time went into a long sleep and dreamed that her child should be a son whom she should name Dekanawida.[4]

Becoming manifest to his mother in a dream vision, an event typical of Pre-Columbian poetry and song, Dekanawida will have a dual role as an epic hero: he will become a great leader of his people, and he will unite warring tribes into a single great nation. Though initially misunderstood by his people, Dekanawida gradually assumes his two roles and succeeds in combat against his chief enemy, a supernaturally possessed man, and in the formation of what would later become known as the Iroquois Confederation.[5]

A very different kind of epic hero is found in Alonso de Ercilla y Zúñiga's *The Araucaniad*, the national epic of Chile and one of the outstanding (if little-known) epics of the Renaissance period.[6] For some critics the greatest epic in the Spanish language, *The Araucaniad* is unusual for several reasons: it is apparently the first epic poem in which the poet appears as a main character in the action he describes; it is the first to deal with events still in progress at the time of writing; it is the first to deal with the foundation of a modern nation; it is the first literary or art epic of the Americas; and it is the first epic in which the author, caught in a conflict between the ideals of historical truth and those of art, laments the poverty of his Indian theme and the monotony of the warrior theme and chooses to reveal self-consciously the intimate process of the poem's creation.[7]

Although *The Araucaniad* lacks a clearly defined epic hero in the sense of Aeneas in the *Aeneid*, Ercilla's epic transforms the defeated Araucanian Indians into epic heroes. For Ercilla, who actually participated in the battles he describes so vividly, and who worked on his epic whenever and wherever he could (on paper, animal hides, and, on at least one occasion, on tree bark), there was no single hero to his poem but a number of them. In the tradition of the Spanish hidalgos, Ercilla consciously chose to exalt the bravery not only of his comrades but also of his Indian foes, especially the great chief Caupolicán. Indeed, one senses a stronger and more animated defense of the Araucanians, who were defending their homeland from conquering invaders, than of the Spanish, some of whom (the Spanish commander García Hurtado de Mendoza, for example) are actually damned with faint praise. Equipped with a fine classical education, Ercilla saw in certain of the Araucanian chiefs warriors whose natural epic grandeur could best be shown by direct and indirect comparisons with better-known epic heroes. As Emir Rodríguez Monegal observes, "In transforming the defeated Araucans into epic heroes, he was also following a model that harked back to Homer: Ercilla praised Caupolicán and Colocolo in the way that the Greek poet praised Hector and Priam." [8] Caupolicán, the indomitable Indian leader who though a great warrior also embodies the best sociopolitical qualities of the Araucanian people, emerges as the primary character of *The Araucaniad*'s 21,072 lines.

In comparison to Dekanawida, Caupolicán shows himself to be the more formidable warrior, the leader of a people fighting not to achieve a union with other tribes but to survive, to resist foreign invasion and domination. Ercilla's greatest talent as an epic poet lies in his ability to depict battle scenes, which generate the most memorable parts of his poem. In this regard, Ercilla may surpass even Homer and the *Iliad*.[9] In both *The Dekanawida* and *The Araucaniad* the hero, whether mythic (as with Dekanawida) or historically verifiable (as with Caupolicán), is of singular importance to his respective people and their collective sense of national identity and unity.

The hero of a third New World epic, José Basílio da Gama's *The Uruguay*, is also especially prominent in his social and historical role.[10] Formally speaking, *The Uruguay* is the least epical of the poems under consideration here. Yet although it departs rather freely from the form of the traditional epic, it is nevertheless widely regarded as the best epic of its period in Brazilian literary history.[11] Unlike *The Araucaniad*, for example, *The Uruguay* does not have a single sharply delineated character around whom the narrative revolves and who dominates the action. Yet, this fact notwithstanding, the Portuguese commander, Gomes Freire de Andrade, is often read as the hero of the poem; it was his task to defeat the combined forces of the Jesuits and the Indians, to "free" the Indians from their "enslavement," and to drive the Jesuits out of Uruguay. Read this way, however, the poem generates a minimum of interest because Andrade, presented as a seemingly decent but ordinary man, simply does not achieve anything like heroic proportions. His struggle with the Jesuits and their Indian allies, moreover, was much more one-sided than Ercilla's bloody and protracted struggle with the fierce Araucanians.

The true hero of *The Uruguay*, the character who like Caupolicán gets vivid and sympathetic treatment from the author, is the Indian chief Cacambo.[12] With Cacambo representing the New World and Andrade the Old, the poem

can be interpreted as a distilled version of the struggle between two very different civilizations, for, as Andrade, expressing his sense of European hegemony,
says to his Guarani counterpart, "Cacique, . . . the Kings are in Europe."[13]
Clearly establishing the parameters of the now unavoidable clash between the
Old World and the New, Cacambo darkly responds:

> Ye sons of Europe, would that ne'er the wind
> And wave had borne you hither! Not in vain
> Nature between ourselves and you hath spread
> The water-wilderness, this vasty deep.[14]

The subsequent death of Cacambo (he is poisoned by one of the Jesuits)
symbolizes the demise of the New World and its native inhabitants. Whereas
Dekanawida and his ally Hiawatha emerge victorious from their trials and succeed in unifying disparate tribes into a powerful confederation, Cacambo, like
Caupolicán, dies, his nation defeated.

In a sense, the defeat of the latter two heroes also represents the victory of
technology over nature. This is true of Caupolicán and the evenly matched
struggle the Araucanians waged against the Spaniards in Chile, but it is more
vividly expressed in the uneven battle between Andrade's well-armed troops
and the Guarani. The violent victory of murderous European technology over
the Indians is symbolized by the battle scenes of canto 2, in which the firearms
of the Portuguese wreak havoc on the bow-and-arrow-wielding native warriors.

A different kind of epic hero is found in Joel Barlow's The Columbiad,[15] a
poem that grew out of an earlier attempt by Barlow to write a historical narrative poem called "America" for the New World and, in particular, the United
States. This earlier work, published as The Vision of Columbus (1783, 1787), a
fresher narrative than the later one would be, relies on the framework of a futuristic vision rather than the traditional epic-narrative form for which Barlow
finally opted in The Columbiad. In writing his epical accounts of the founding
and settling of the New World, Barlow was unquestionably influenced not only
by Voltaire's Essay on Epic Poetry, which would have lent credibility to his own
belief that a modern epic need not adhere strictly to neoclassical rules, but by
Garcilaso de la Vega's Royal Commentaries of Peru, Juan Francisco Marmontel's
Incas, and Ercilla's Araucaniad, the latter not yet available in English but discussed by Voltaire in his essay.[16] In The Columbiad, as in the earlier Vision of
Columbus, the Incan monarch Manco Capac is praised as a great New World
leader, surpassing many others from the ancient and modern worlds. In dis-

cussing at length the cultural history not only of Latin America but of French and English Canada as well, Barlow must be considered one of the earliest scholars of Inter-American literature, one of the first writers to draw the literature of the Americas together in a comparative fashion.

The hero of Barlow's poem is, nevertheless, problematic. Though several historical figures, including Manco Capac, Columbus, and George Washington, are extensively lauded, the real hero of *The Columbiad* gradually shows himself to be not so much a single human being but an idea: the greatness to be achieved ultimately by the New World, which Barlow tends to identify with the United States. Columbus, the "discoverer" of the New World, becomes for Barlow the eyes through which the New World might better see itself, but it is the concept of "America," epitomized in the philosophical and political ideals of the United States, that gradually emerges as the real hero of *The Columbiad*.[17] Another epical poet from the United States, Walt Whitman, would in *Leaves of Grass* attempt something similar a century later, but it was Barlow, with his unique Inter-American approach, who first attempted this particular kind of national epic.

The question of whether a true national epic exists in Canadian literature remains moot, but many commentators, including Northrop Frye, have considered *Towards the Last Spike* by E. J. Pratt to represent the genre of the national epic in the spirit if not the letter of the form.[18] Its theme, the union of Canada through the construction of the trans-Canadian railroad, is legitimately epic in national significance. As Frye notes, "While the choice of theme may have been easy, the theme itself is fantastically difficult. The poem is in the epic tradition, without any of the advantages of epic to sustain it."[19] If *The Columbiad* has for its epic hero the political possibilities inherent in the founding of a New World free of European kings and class restrictions, Pratt returns his epic hero to the vicissitudes of the human realm. The key difference is that Pratt makes his hero a highly collectivized character, the personification of a unifying social consciousness. As he writes:

> The east-west cousinship, a nation's rise,
>
> . . . .
>
> A nation, like the world, could not stand still.
>
> . . . .
>
> Thousands of men and mules and horses slipped
> Into their togs and harness night and day.
>
> . . . .

> As individuals
> The men lost their identity; as groups,
> As gangs, they massed, divided, subdivided,
> . . . like numerals only . . .[20]

Like *The Columbiad, Towards the Last Spike* focuses on specific historical figures, in particular Canadian Prime Minister Sir John A. Macdonald, who is the
political leader of the hotly debated transcontinental railroad project, and an
engineer from the United States, William Cornelius Van Horne. Although it
seems ironic that someone who is not Canadian effects the completion of the
great Canadian railroad project, it is also entirely fitting from an Inter-American
perspective that such an event occur. That Van Horne, an American (here I use
the word in its narrowest political sense), plays a major role in Pratt's Canadian
national epic ("The Yankee who had come straight over, linked / His name and
life to the Canadian nation")[21] merely parallels Barlow's extensive use of material and figures like Manco Capac from the Incan Empire and from Ercilla's
Araucaniad.

But the true hero of Pratt's poem is consciously collective and social in nature, much more so than in *The Uruguay, The Araucaniad,* or even *The Dekanawida,* where it is the social importance of the hero, his significance as a political
leader, that is most crucial. As the roles of Macdonald and Van Horne gradually
recede in the poem, the nationalistic need for the completion of the railroad
increases precisely because it symbolizes the kind of national unification that
can only come from the combined efforts of many people. Both Macdonald and
Van Horne can in fact be read as the agents by which the national will is acted
out. Thus, as Frye puts it, "the real hero of the poem is a society's will to take
intelligible form; the real quest is for physical and spiritual communication
within that society."[22]

Another epical Canadian poem, Louis Fréchette's *La légende d'un peuple,* also
features a distinctly social hero, one who, in this case, is collectivized into the
people of French Canada themselves.[23] Patterned after Hugo's *La légende des
siècles,* Fréchette's work, more than three thousand lines in length, attempts
nothing less than a grand telling of the entire history of French Canada. As if
invoking the Muses, Fréchette opens with a short dedication to France. He
then begins to speak to the North American continent, a place that he says is
destined to renew the energy and vitality of Europe. Setting up a kind of symbiotic relationship in which (recalling Lescarbot) the New World exists primarily for the benefit of the Old, Fréchette sings the praises of New France and

of such heroes as Robert de La Salle, the French explorer whose bold plan to colonize all of the land drained by the Mississippi River fell on deaf ears in the court of Louis XIV. By focusing on such characters as La Salle, *La légende d'un peuple*, uneven in epic stature though it may be,[24] remains the epic of a modern people, with the people's sense of cultural identity emerging as the authentic hero of the poem. Fréchette's usage of a highly nationalized epic hero generates a tone of ardent patriotism different from the nationalism one senses in, for example, Pratt's *Towards the Last Spike*.

Fréchette also pays considerable attention to descriptions of the land itself, often through Hugoesque epic similes and metaphors. This close attention to nature is a distinctive feature of his poem and one that goes beyond what Ercilla does in *The Araucaniad* and what da Gama does in *The Uruguay*. Less epic attention is paid to the land in Barlow's *Columbiad*, which does, nevertheless, catalog numerous New World rivers, regions, and mountain ranges. Similarly, there is also almost no overt praise of the land in *The Dekanawida*, but this is possibly explained by the fact that the Iroquois epic, which is not the product of a single author but a performance-oriented folk epic, lives through and for people who consider themselves part of the natural world around them.

A second key characteristic of the epic genre has to do with the scale of its action. On this score, too, the New World epics are not merely interesting but full of surprising similarities and parallels. Among these works only Barlow's *Columbiad* attains what might be called a truly celestial setting, however. Barlow was well schooled in the classical epics and patterned his own epic (which, as he notes in his preface, he felt would be superior to the earlier works) on them. Especially important to him was the device of divine revelation or vision because he needed a mechanism whereby the past, present, and future of the New World could be made manifest. As a consequence, of all the American epics only Barlow's approaches the cosmic scope that we associate with an epic like *Paradise Lost*. All of the other New World epics take place in geographically more finite and specific settings: *The Dekanawida* in and around the Lake Ontario region; *The Araucaniad* in the mountainous regions of southern Chile; *The Uruguay* in the lands incorporated into the modern state of Uruguay; *Towards the Last Spike*, the area of the union of eastern and western Canada; and *La légende d'un peuple*, the modern-day province of Québec.

Yet though the setting is truly vast for only *The Columbiad*, *Towards the Last Spike* generates a strong sense of immensity in regard to both the place and the obstacles—human and natural—that are involved. Pratt's poem possesses a unique brand of epic grandeur, on a smaller scale than what we find in the

Aeneid or *Paradise Lost* but effective nevertheless. Apropos of this, *The De-kanawida*, *The Uruguay*, *The Araucaniad*, and *La légende d'un peuple* all deal in differing degrees with the establishment of modern nations or cultures: the Iroquois League, Chile, Uruguay, and French Canada. If these are not great civilizations in the sense that Aeneas's Rome was, they are nevertheless real political entities, whose founding consciously became the subject matter of their epic narratives.

Four of these works—*The Araucaniad*, *The Uruguay*, *Towards the Last Spike*, and *La légende d'un peuple*—sing of the singular features of the American landscape. In Pratt's poem, for example, the treacherous North Shore area of Lake Superior, the area of the Laurentian Shield (which contains some of the oldest rocks on our planet), is brought metaphorically to life as the "Laurentian lizard." Of the towering Canadian Rockies, which many thought impenetrable for a railroad line, Pratt wrote:

> The big one was the mountains—seas indeed!
> With crests whiter than foam: they poured like seas,
> Fluting the green banks of the pines and spruces.[25]

And in a scene that invokes the bitter cold of the Canadian winter, the engineer Van Horne, contemplating the immensity of the task he has undertaken, has to use a jackknife to scrape the frost off a window of his room so he can see out:

> He saw the illusion at its worst—the frost,
> The steel precision of the studded heavens,
> Relentless mirror of a covered earth.
> His breath froze on the scrape: he cut again
> And glanced at the direction west-by-south.[26]

If Pratt and Fréchette tend to focus their Americanism on the geographic features of the landscape, writers like Basílio da Gama and Ercilla tend to devote their best efforts to descriptions of the land's indigenous people, concentrating upon and even idealizing the Indians of their poems. (This is not to say that either writer neglects the native geography, flora, and fauna; indeed *The Uruguay* includes such vibrant images of its American setting that one often feels it to be more lyrical than epic in its most basic appeal.) The Indian hero of *The Uruguay*, Cacambo, and his beautiful wife, Lindóia (who, upon learning of her husband's murder by a Jesuit, commits suicide), are an exemplary couple. So important has the figure of Cacambo been to Brazilian cultural history that during the nineteenth century, when Brazil had achieved independence from Portugal and its leaders were seeking a suitable national figure, they found in Cacambo precisely the qualities they needed.[27]

A similarly idealized *bon sauvage* is Ercilla's Araucanian chief, Caupolicán, whose dramatic rise to the highest level of tribal authority is vividly portrayed early in the poem:

> New-born light suffused that valley,
> As Caupolicán came striding.
>   With disdain and haughty bearing,
> Seizing hard and knotty tree-trunk
> As if 'twere a dainty yardstick,
> On his sturdy back he laid it.
>
> .   .   .   .   .   .
>
> With one voice the crowd attended,
> Rendering sentence, loud declaring:
> "On such shoulders we deposit
> Onus of our chieftain's office." [28]

So while nearly all these American epics tend to deal with the unique features of their New World settings, works like *La légende d'un peuple*, *Towards the Last Spike*, and, to a lesser degree, *The Columbiad* focus more on the physical environment, while others, like *The Uruguay*, *The Araucaniad*, and *The Dekanawida*, pay more attention to the plight of the human beings who inhabit the New World.

Traditionally, the action or conflict of an epic involves deeds of great valor requiring exceptional and even supernatural courage and prowess. Armed conflict is at the heart of all New World epics except for *La légende d'un peuple*, where the struggle involves a culture that is fighting for survival, and *Towards the Last Spike*, where the main struggle is between the people, or collective hero, and the social, political, and physical environment.

Of the epics that feature martial combat as a key dimension of their epicality, Ercilla's *Araucaniad* and da Gama's *Uruguay* stand out. And of these two works, *The Araucaniad*, "an authentic history concerning the things of war," [29] is unquestionably the one in which scenes of warfare dominate. Ercilla's genius as an epic poet, in fact, rests on his singular ability to create powerful and vivid battle scenes. Yet while such scenes are both lengthy and numerous in *The Araucaniad*, they are never repetitious or boring. Realistic and intense as only a firsthand account could be, Ercilla's consciously poeticized battlefield scenes make the reader feel as though she or he were actually in the midst of the fighting. Rivaled as a war epic only by the *Iliad*, *The Araucaniad* derives not only its conceptual genesis but its epical essence from the action it recounts, an action that, as in da Gama's *The Uruguay*, pits the forces of the technologically superior Old World against those of the courageous but doomed New World.

The central irony in *The Araucaniad* is that the author of the poem, himself one of the ultimately victorious Spanish soldiers, is clearly more sympathetic to the Araucanians than to the Spanish, even though he considers the latter's cause to be just and proper. As a soldier, Ercilla saw not only the deadly violence of war but the bravery of its contestants, Indian and Spanish alike. As he writes:

> Men flung taunts at one another;
> Sputtered seething wrath and uproar;
> Flowing blood o'erswelled the river,
> Spanish gore and Indian mingled;
>
> .   .   .   .   .   .
>
> Twice Hernán de Alvarado
> Struck lithe Talco to the greensward,
> But on one flank left unguarded,
> He was wounded by Guacoldo;
> And the Spaniard quite dumbfounded,
> Soon awoke from stunning thunder.
> As he lunged against the savage,
> In his breast his sword was buried.[30]

Da Gama also depicts scenes of violent warfare in *The Uruguay*:

> "Yield or die the death!"
> Exclaims the Governor; but the proud Tapé
> Bends his bow spurning parley and his shaft
> Speeds forth preparing for the enemy's death.[31]

Scenes of warfare also play a significant role in *The Columbiad*'s epical development. For Barlow, however, the central conflict is more political and philosophical than it is military, although he does chronicle several of the battles of the American Revolution. Scenes of overt violence such as we have in *The Araucaniad* and in *The Uruguay* are both fewer and less sanguinary than in the other epics. Barlow does, however, wax violent in a few scenes, the most effective of which involves the brutal murder of an innocent woman (Lucinda) by the Mohawks, who are cast as the paid assassins of the British:

> With calculating pause and demon grin,
> They seize her hands and thro her face divine
> Drive the descending ax; the shriek she sent
> Attain'd her lover's ear; he thither bent
> With all the speed his wearied limbs could yield,
> Whirl'd his keen blade and stretcht upon the field
> The yelling fiends; who there disputing stood
> Her gory scalp, their horrid prize of blood.[32]

The primary difference between Barlow's depiction of such bloody action as this and the way violence appears in *The Araucaniad* and *The Uruguay* is that, as he indicated in his prefatory statement to the poem, Barlow wrote *The Columbiad* in order to contrast the horror of war with the material, political, and moral advantages that international peace and cooperation offer. Barlow's historical epic is, then, about the potentially harmonious future of the New World; it is, like *The Dekanawida*, an epic of peace and hope, of what a better, more pacific world might be like.

Basílio da Gama's epic, which in its action is closer to *The Araucaniad* than to *The Columbiad*, is interesting because it features a dual conflict.[33] Read on one level, it is a virulently anti-Jesuit polemic whose vitriol is even more apparent in the inflammatory notes da Gama originally provided for his text. But read on another level, as Antônio Cândido and others have shown,[34] the more fundamental conflict in *The Uruguay* is the essential one in Inter-American literature, still unresolved in many ways, between the Old World and the New, between Europe and the Americas. Interpreted in this sense, *The Uruguay* can be seen to have some similarities to Barlow's effort.

But while this may be true in a general way, the cantos of *The Uruguay* focus primarily on the struggle between the combined forces of the Spanish and Portuguese and the Jesuits and their Tupí-Guarani allies. However, this war has less of an epic scale, lasts for a shorter time, and is more one-sided than the Spaniards' nearly even campaign against the Araucanians. Yet though the scale of the conflict in *The Uruguay* does not equal that of *The Araucaniad*, it does impart to the Brazilian poem a unity, cohesion, and focus that are lacking in the longer and often digressive Spanish American work.

Surprisingly similar in its structural compactness and unity of effect is the Iroquois epic, *The Dekanawida*. Here, too, we find a basic conflict that involves a hero, his struggles, and the formation of a people's sociopolitical identity. As the epic's anonymous singer presents it, a violent conflict has plagued the several tribes of the region for many years and is now widely perceived to be a scourge upon everyone involved: "Men were ragged with sacrifice and the women scarred with the flints. . . . Feuds with outer nations, feuds with brother nations, feuds of sister towns and feuds of families and of clans made every warrior a stealthy man who liked to kill." [35] Bloodshed had become a way of life for the disparate tribes of the Lake Ontario region: "Everywhere there was peril and everywhere mourning . . . everywhere there was misery." [36] Thus, as in Barlow's poem, in *The Dekanawida* a state of war is used to show how much better for everyone a state of peace would be.

Using the parallelism and repetition that are characteristic of Pre-Columbian literature, *The Dekanawida* differs from *The Araucaniad* and *The Uruguay* because it does not dwell in detail on the actual fighting itself; no individual battles or warriors are described or exalted. Overall, the poem is much less violent in its ethos than either the Chilean work or the Brazilian. The conflict, as with *The Columbiad*, involves a choice between political anarchy or political cooperation, that is, between war or peace. When at the conclusion of *The Dekanawida* the hero tells his appointed chiefs how and why they are to rule the people of the Five Nations of the Iroquois Confederation, he establishes a plan for the future that, though more collectivist in nature, compares favorably to Barlow's vision of America's future. As Dekanawida explains it:

> You must be patient and henceforth work in unity. Never consider your own interests but work to benefit the people and for the generations not yet born. You have pledged yourselves to govern yourselves by the laws of the Great Peace. All your authority shall come from it.[37]

In contrast to the basic conflict of these four New World epics, *La légende d'un peuple* and *Towards the Last Spike* are built around actions that involve armed struggle of a different sort. The basic conflict of Fréchette's historical poem, which is divided into different "eras," involves the decline of New France from a position of dominance (First Era) to one of struggle for mere *survivance*. The poem's action, which covers roughly the three centuries of Québec's existence, depicts the struggle between France and England for control of Canada, a contest which would end tragically in 1759 with a disaster for France and French Canada on the Plains of Abraham. Fréchette's poem, which extols both the endurance and élan vital of the French Canadian people and the physical beauties of their country, is the intensely patriotic song of an isolated and oppressed culture. The military struggle between France and Canada, which, understood in the larger context of cultural survival, constitutes a major part of the poem's epic appeal, is taken up by Fréchette chiefly in the episodes devoted to the Seven Years' War and to England's rule over Canada following the defeat of the French forces (Second and Third Eras). In contrast to that of *The Araucaniad*, however, the action of *La légende d'un peuple* is less bloody and militaristic and less dominant a feature of the poem.

Even less military in nature is the basic conflict of Pratt's historical narrative, *Towards the Last Spike*. There are really two essential actions in this work. One centers on the complex and protracted maneuverings between various politicians, such as Sir John Macdonald, the railroad's most powerful advocate, Edward Blake, the opposition leader, and Alexander Mackenzie, who became prime minister in 1873. The other action in *Towards the Last Spike*, and the one that most captivates the reader, is the long, dramatically portrayed struggle of humankind against nature, the same conflict that is played out in many of the New World discovery and conquest narratives. In Pratt's poem, humankind is better prepared for the struggle, which nevertheless remains a daunting undertaking. Summing up toward the close of the poem, Pratt writes, utilizing an image of birth and equating the building of the railroad to the work of nature:

> The Road itself was like a stream that men
> Had coaxed and teased or bullied out of Nature.
>
> .　.　.　.　.　.　.　.　.　.
>
> And where it could not climb, it cut and curved,
> Till from the Rockies to the Coastal Range
> It had accomplished what the Rivers had,
> Making a hundred clean Caesarian cuts,
> And bringing to delivery in their time
> Their smoky, lusty-screaming locomotives.[38]

An effective feature of the Pratt poem is that it merges these two lines of action, the human and the natural, into the same historical moment; that is, the two lines of seemingly antithetical action are intertwined so that an organically unified whole is attained. *Towards the Last Spike* surpasses even the tightly organized *Uruguay* in this respect.

A fourth feature of these New World epics, their reliance on supernatural forces, also shows both their conscious adherence to the epic tradition in Western literature and their determination to bring into play features that are unique to the New World landscape and cultural experience. Of the six poems under consideration, it is Barlow's *Columbiad* alone that employs supernatural intervention in the traditional epic fashion. The other poems do make use of extrahuman events and personages, but they tend to be less orthodox than the work of the classically trained Barlow.

A surprise in this respect, however, comes once again from the Native

American epic *The Dekanawida*, which features a magical and supernaturally malevolent antagonist, Adodarhoh, whose violent and even cannibalistic habits pose a chilling threat to the hero of the poem. As the eponymous singer presents him:

> South of the Onondaga lived an evil-minded man. His lodge was in a swale and his nest was made of bulrushes. His body was distorted by seven crooks and his long tangled locks were adorned by writhing living serpents. Moreover, this monster was a devourer of raw meat, even of human flesh. He was also a master of wizardry and by his magic he destroyed men but he could not be destroyed. Adodarhoh was the name of the evil man.[39]

By using what they learn in dream revelations and by magic, the heroes (for there are actually two, Dekanawida and Hiawatha) gradually overcome their enemy. However, they do not kill him; rather, by use of song (the healing force of the sacred word) they "cure" him by removing the evil that has twisted his body and unbalanced his mind. The warriors of Dekanawida are also able magically to invoke the positive forces of nature to help them, as when the ducks on a lake, rising up in a single body, lift up the water as they fly so that the hero can cut across the lake. These same men, the forces of good, that is, of peace, are also able to transform themselves into different animals. We can see clearly in *The Dekanawida* the merging of realism and magic into "magical realism," the twentieth-century style of writers as diverse as Gabriel García Márquez, John Nichols, and Robert Kroetsch, all of whom are cognizant of the powerful Native American heritage of Inter-American literature.

The Araucaniad also makes use of supernatural forces, as we see in the episode involving the Araucanian seer, Fitón (a *machi* or healer), of whom it is said:

> . . . so great his power and knowledge
> Is concerning beasts and pebbles,
> Plants and trees, that through his science
> He unriddles natural courses,
> And in Fright's dark, hideous kingdom
> He compels the close-lipped demons
> By atrocious conjurations
> To unveil the past and future.[40]

Like other epic poets (the parallel with Virgil is especially strong), Ercilla has a malevolent divine being[41] suddenly intervene in the action by means of a storm designed to becloud a warrior's vision and render him unable to act:

> Eponamon then swept on them,
> In the form of a hideous dragon,
> Whipped his fiery tail with lashings,
> Roughly spoke with rumbling accent.[42]

As if to balance the wrathful deity he has just introduced into the human world, Ercilla then employs a pacific goddess, to whom he also gives the task of influencing the action that follows:

> Ceased the tempest; . . .
> When in graceful flight, a goddess,
> Wrapped in gauzy veils of beauty,
> On a fleecy cloud swooped earthward, . . .
> Comfort shone, and fright was exiled
> Through her holy face of mercy.[43]

Deeply indebted to Homer, Virgil, Tasso, and Ariosto, Ercilla did not hesitate to employ supernatural beings liberally in his poem.

A more realistic epic poet (one following in the tradition of Luís de Camões's *Os Lusíadas*), José Basílio da Gama takes a rather different approach to the use of extrahuman elements in his poem. Da Gama is much more judicious than Ercilla in employing such creatures. Indeed, gods and other mythological machinery are exiled from *The Uruguay*, and the supernatural element is reduced to a mere two items: a prophetic vision granted the tragic Lindóia by the tribal witch, Tanajura, and a brief personification of the Uruguay River (canto 3),[44] the latter event showing how nature (the river) comes to the aid of the Indian hero, Cacambo. Da Gama's personification, however, is subtle and restrained:

> And where the current quietest rolls its course
> Spreading in reaches o'er the ruddy sands,
> In turbid thought, he dives and with the wave
> Breast-high already, hands and eyes he lifts
> To Heaven by him unseen, and to the waves
> Commits his body. Saw the new emprise
> For in his silty grot the patrial Stream
> And with propitious gesture tilts his urn
> To will its liquid crystal kindly smooth.
>> The Fortune-favoured Indian unperceived
> Upclimbs the farther stream-bank.[45]

Da Gama develops Lindóia's vision, in which she sees the Lisbon earth-quake, the rebuilding of the city, the avenging of her husband's murder, and the treachery of the Jesuits. The entire episode, culminating in Lindóia's suicide,[46] is in many ways reminiscent of the Fitón story in *The Araucaniad*. Yet da Gama consistently underplays the role of the supernatural, a feature of his poem that makes it significantly different from the other New World epics, all of which involve extrahuman forces to one degree or another.

The Columbiad, in sharp contrast to *The Uruguay*, makes extensive use of supernatural elements. Indeed, the entire poem is based on a vision afforded Columbus by Hesper, the guardian angel of the "Western Continent," that is, the New World. Barlow sets the scene for the triumphant coming of Hesper by showing the reader the desperate condition of the now vilified and maligned Columbus, who is unjustly locked away in a Spanish dungeon. After emo-tionally describing Columbus's pathetic plight, the poet creates this dramatic scene, one in which the wronged hero, Columbus, is finally treated justly:

> . . . a thundering sound
> Roll'd thro the shuddering walls and shook the ground;
> O'er all the dungeon, where black arches bend,
> The roofs unfold and streams of light descend;
> The growing splendor fills the astonisht room,
> And gales etherial breathe a glad perfume.
> Robed in the radiance, moves a form serene,
> Of human structure but of heavenly mien;
> Near to the prisoner's couch he takes his stand
> And waves, in sign of peace, his holy hand.
>
> .   .   .   .
>
> Thou seest in me the guardian Power who keeps
> The new found world that skirts Atlantic deeps;
> Hesper my name, my seat the brightest throne
> In night's whole heaven, my sire the living sun.[47]

Hesper magically frees Columbus from his cell and takes him, through the poem's ten books, on a tour of the New World, beginning with a review of Pre-Columbian history (which focuses, in books 2 and 3, on the brilliant reign of the Incan monarch Manco Capac) and ending with a vision of the New World's future greatness. Of all the New World epics, only *The Columbiad* gives the supernatural element a decisive role, one integrated not only into the action of the poem but into its very structuring as well. One might say, indeed, that the supernatural element constitutes *The Columbiad*'s basic structural presence.

The two Canadian epics, Pratt's *Towards the Last Spike* and Fréchette's *La légende d'un peuple*, utilize the supernatural less than any of the other American epics with the possible exception of da Gama's *Uruguay*. Like *The Uruguay*, *Towards the Last Spike* tends toward the historically verisimilar rather than toward the supernatural. But Pratt too, again like da Gama, personifies the American landscape when the development of his theme requires that he do so.[48] In *Towards the Last Spike*, this personification of nature takes the form of a huge prehistoric lizard aroused from its eternal slumber by the sound of the dynamite being used to blast through the ancient rock of the Laurentian Shield. The shield is metaphorically rendered into a female supernatural creature that struggles, unsuccessfully, against the railroad that is being cut through her.[49] The lizard's extrahuman presence makes for a formidable foe:

> On the North Shore a reptile lay asleep—
> A hybrid that the myths might have conceived,
> But not delivered, as progenitor
> Of crawling, gliding things upon the earth.
>
> .   .   .   .
>
>   In continental reach
> The neck went past the Great Bear Lake until
> Its head was hidden in the Arctic Seas.
> This folded reptile was asleep or dead:
> So motionless, she seemed stone dead—just seemed:
>
> .   .   .   .
>
>   Was this the thing Van Horne set out
> To conquer?[50]

Stylistically, the six New World epics vary widely, from the demotic to the formal and from rhyming couplets to blank verse, yet none of them achieves quite the sustained elevation, rhythmic fluidity, and grand simplicity of language that we commonly associate with epics like the *Odyssey*, the *Iliad*, and the *Aeneid*. Of the six, only Barlow's *Columbiad* comes close in this regard. Although its language seems awkward at times, and although it too often strains for effect, *The Columbiad* hews closer, stylistically, to these better-known models of the art epic genre. In book 5, for example, Barlow labors to attain an epic aura for his hero, General George Washington:

> Swift on a fiery steed the stripling rose,
> Form'd the light files to pierce the line of foes;
> Then waved his gleamy sword that flasht the day

> And thro the Gallic legions hew'd his way:
> His troops press forward like a loose-broke flood,
> Sweep ranks away and smear their paths in blood;[51]

The Brazilian epic, *The Uruguay*, a poem that is often as lyrical as it is epical, achieves in the original Portuguese a level of freshness and clarity that gives it a stylistic distinction unique among the New World epics. By omitting allusions to classical mythology, which the classically trained Ercilla had employed, and by using imagery that though Baroque in its conception remains remarkably unobscure, da Gama succeeded in creating a new kind of epic, a modern one that proves how flexible and adaptive the epic genre is.

Fréchette's poem, which has never been translated from the original French, has a Hugo-like grandiloquence that oddly seems to undercut the poem's modest aspirations to epic status.[52] Written almost entirely in Alexandrine couplets (in contrast to da Gama's ten-syllable blank verse), *La légende d'un peuple*, though sonorous, is, as David Hayne suggests, sometimes wanting in unity, action of epical proportion, and focus.[53]

The translation problems provoked by the style of these epics reach their zenith in *The Dekanawida*, a "living American epic"[54] that Seth Newhouse, an Onondaga Indian fluent in English, has set down on paper. The Newhouse version, said to be that most favored by the Iroquois,[55] takes the form of an artfully constructed narrative, one energized by vivid poetic images and metaphors and held together by the parallelism and repetition typical of indigenous literature. The language throughout is simple but elegant and, in its own way, does seem consistent with the grand simplicity of epic style, if not necessarily with the sustained elevation of its diction.

Pratt's epic presents a similar state of affairs. Here, too, the language is unpretentious, but it does create a tone of grandeur, a consistently attained level of epicality that carries the reader out of the realm of the ordinary. Describing the culminating scene when the last spike is driven home, Pratt, who like da Gama eschews classical mythology, writes with a deft and distinctly modern touch of ironic humor:

> The job was done. . . .
> At last the spike and Donald with the hammer!
>
> . . . .
>
> What made him fumble the first stroke? . . .
>
> . . . .
>
> Now here he was caught by the camera,

Back bent, head bowed, and staring at a sledge,
Outwitted by an idiotic nail.
Though from the crowd no laughter, yet the spike
With its slewed neck was grinning up at Smith.
Wrenched out, it was replaced. This time . . .
The Scot, invoking his ancestral clan,
Using the hammer like a battle-axe,
His eyes bloodshot with memories of Flodden,
Descended on it, rammed it to its home.[56]

Tempering the grandeur of the achievement described here with a touch of frailty and error, Pratt humanizes his poem in a way that sets it apart from the other New World epics we have examined.

Finally, we turn to Ercilla's *Araucaniad*, a poem that has been called "the first literary masterpiece of the New World."[57] Although the reader who does not know Spanish will find it difficult to assess the epic style of *The Araucaniad*, one thing is clear even in translation: unlike da Gama, but like Barlow, Ercilla consciously places his work within the epic tradition established by Virgil. Ercilla also shows the influence of Lucan (who was praised by Barlow in his introduction), Boiardo, Tasso, and, especially, Ariosto. While da Gama generally avoids classical allusions in *The Uruguay*, Ercilla, working with the traditional hendecasyllabic meter in eight-line stanzas showing a regular rhyme scheme (*abababcc*), hardly ever departs from the classical tradition. In canto 32 (there are thirty-seven in all), for example, commenting on the "loyal faith" of the Indian women, Ercilla compares them to Queen Dido. Showing his classical education (as well as his critical temper), Ercilla then takes Virgil to task for what he considers to be improper treatment of Dido.

The sixth and final point of comparison between the New World epic poems is that of the extent to which their authors objectively recount the deeds of their heroes. The chief exception in this regard is, surprisingly, Ercilla's *Araucaniad*, the most classically orthodox of all these works. Because the poet himself is a participant in the events he narrates, *The Araucaniad* is highly subjective, as well as the first known epic by an author who writes about his own exploits. Beyond this, however, Ercilla gradually develops within the poem a metacritical self-consciousness not only about what he is writing but about how and why he does it as well. Speaking directly to the reader and reflecting on the nature of his theme and on his insistence that his story be presented in full and in detail, Ercilla writes, for example, in canto 15:

> How can I, so crude and loveless,
> Lorn of wit's resplendent ermine,
> Have the hardihood to venture
> 'Neath the chiseled edge of poesy?
>
> .　　.　　.　　.　　.　　.
>
> I exhort your thoughts' indulgence;
> If my script be long and labored,
> Know that truthfulness exacts it.[58]

A fascinating sidelight of this intense involvement by Ercilla himself in his own poem is his commentary on the difficulty he gets into with his commanding officer. The penultimate canto (36) relates digressively how Ercilla, having returned to camp from leading what modern soldiers would call a reconnaissance patrol in hostile territory, is unexpectedly rebuked by his superior and sent back to Spain. Ercilla is singularly vague about the details of the event, but the text shows clearly that he felt he had been unjustly punished. As he tells it:

> Unexpected altercations
> Stopped the fête; . . .
> Gossip has exaggerated
> Into a crime a simple gesture.
> Hilt of sword I merely fingered,
> Ne'er unsheathed without good reason.
> 　　This event of little moment
> Banished me henceforth from Chile.[59]

After describing his arduous trip home, Ercilla, with characteristic self-consciousness (and not without a touch of irony), returns at the conclusion of canto 36 to a critical consideration of his own poem:

> Why should I persist in boring
> Wearied ears and languid senses
> With tales of unknown Indians,
> Wars in far, obscure meridians?
> Why should I heed strident rumblings,
> Stumble on with conquering legions,
> Following the clash of weapons,
> Burned with Mars' consuming passion?[60]

Far from reporting the deeds of his heroes with epic objectivity, Ercilla enters his own text both as a character and as a critically self-conscious commentator.

The result of this unique approach to epic writing is an intensity and a complex interplay of reader, main character, and author that cannot be found in any other epic poem. Though *The Araucaniad* violates the so-called rule of epic objectivity, it does so necessarily, for the author was writing his poem in lulls between the very battles in which he was participating.

In comparison to *The Araucaniad*, the other New World epics are more conventional with regard to the objectivity of the poets and the events they narrate. Typical of this approach are Barlow's *Columbiad* and Pratt's *Towards the Last Spike*, works which reflect a clear distance between the poet and the action of the story. The same is true of da Gama's *Uruguay*, except that here one senses (in da Gama's personal antipathy toward the Jesuits) that the poet has moved into an open advocacy of the exposure of the Jesuit order's alleged mischief. Yet even so, the degree of da Gama's authorial involvement is nowhere as systematic as Ercilla's. A similar comparison might be made between *The Dekanawida* and Fréchette's fervently patriotic *La légende d'un peuple*. In the Iroquois epic, there is a sense that the Iroquois people themselves participate in the action of the poem, that in a way they are the present-day embodiments of Dekanawida and Hiawatha. Yet for all its collectivist spirit, *The Dekanawida* cannot be said to possess the same kind or degree of authorial involvement that we see in *The Araucaniad*.

It is quite natural that the epic should have been cultivated in the Americas. The entire process of the New World's discovery, conquest, and colonization by the Old World involved a complex struggle of epic proportions. Moreover, writers like Ercilla and da Gama had before them wonderful examples of how expressive and adaptive the epic poem could be. These and other New World epicists felt the need to enter into the epic tradition but to do so by writing new epics, works that, though deriving from the European models, would adapt themselves formally, thematically, and stylistically to both the extraordinary realities and the vast potentialities of the New World experience. The epic, practiced since before the time of Aristotle and prized by the Renaissance critics, was the obvious choice for those poets who wished to give heroic proportions to the immense achievement that was the conquest and colonization of the New World. These New World epics mark important steps in the ongoing quest for New World identity and expression.

4

The Theme of Miscegenation

* * * * * * * * * * * *

The theme of miscegenation is endemic to the literature of the New World. Given the violent clash of cultures involved in the conquest, it could hardly have been otherwise. Primarily through rape and concubinage, though also on occasion through genuine love and affection, a new group of people—the mestizos—was born in the Americas, a group that dates from the earliest days of the conquest. Doña Marina, for example, was not only Cortés's interpreter but his mistress as well. Their sexual liaison—of the conquered with the conqueror—led to Doña Marina's being contemptuously referred to as La Chingada, a derisive term implying that she was violated sexually, politically, and psychologically by a more powerful person. As Octavio Paz describes this phenomenon in *The Labyrinth of Solitude*, the word lives in today's Mexico to categorize a variety of relationships, including international politics.[1]

But modern Mexico is not the only American nation where there still exists an active social consciousness of the abuses that took place when the militarily superior Old World overcame the New. The continuing problems of the Métis in Canada, of the "half-breeds" in the United States, and of the mulattoes, cafusos, and mamelucos in Brazil and Spanish America give ample evidence that questions not just of race relations but of racial heritage are acutely (and all too often painfully) alive in the Americas.

Historically and sociologically, there are five basic issues involved in the question of miscegenation in the New World. First, there is the issue already mentioned, that of the abusive relationship between the conqueror and the conquered, and, specifically, the idea that the conqueror has the right to do with the conquered as he or she wishes. Second, there are the differing attitudes about race relations that the Europeans themselves brought to the New World. The historian E. Bradford Burns has written that the Portuguese, for example, with their long history of overseas trade and commerce, were psychologically flexible about miscegenous unions, and that this attitude made their colonial experience unique.[2] This same position is also taken by Samuel Putnam, who in *Marvelous Journey* compares the literary history of Brazil with that of the United States and finds that one of the key differences between these two cultures has to do with sexual relations between men and women of different "races."[3]

Third, there is the question of whether we want to use the term "miscegenation" to refer only to interracial sexual acts or also to the progeny produced by such sexual activity. In Latin America, especially in Mexico, Cuba, Peru, and Brazil, the latter meaning is more applicable; it suggests the creation of a new "race" of people, that called by the Mexican intellectual José Vasconcelos the *raza cósmica* or cosmic race. The question of the Métis in Canada is also of this type. The United States and English Canada, with their English heritage, seem comparatively less comfortable with the entire issue of miscegenation than do the people of the Caribbean, Spanish America, or Brazil. As we see in the works of writers like James Fenimore Cooper, William Faulkner, and James Baldwin, the United States has had a difficult time dealing with either the concept of interracial sex or with the offspring produced by it.

A fourth basic issue is that of the interbreeding of American Indians, European settlers, and Africans brought over as slaves. This question is, of course, not just biological but psychological and political. Slavery, we recall, was prophetically identified by Joel Barlow in *The Columbiad* as the great evil that could destroy the Americas. Slavery, in all its moral, political, and cultural dimensions, was also a central concern of Bartolomé de Las Casas, who lived to see the enslavement not only of the Indians but of the Africans as well.[4] A little-recognized corollary of the slavery issue, and one that is crucially related to the theme of miscegenation, is the question of female/male relationships, a special kind of sexual politics in that sex roles and issues of gender identity are as profoundly involved as are the questions of sociopolitical power, social mores, and "race."

Finally, there is the fact that of the four European nations that undertook the settlement of the New World, only the English came with families; the early French, Spanish, and Portuguese men generally came alone. This does not mean, of course, that miscegenous relationships did not occur between the English and the Indians or, later, the Africans but that male English settlers could look to their wives for sexual activity rather than to the Indian and African women, as the early French, Spanish, and Portuguese men did. For a number of historical, political and sociological reasons, then, miscegenous relationships began to develop very early in the American experience and, though with surprising differences and results, have continued unabated up to the present time. As we shall see, even now we can justifiably speak of miscegenation, in its varying forms and expressions, as one of the fundamental themes of Inter-American literature.

The theme of miscegenation in the Americas can be subdivided into two main categories: the presentation of interracial sex itself, focusing on the private stories of individual men and women (and on the political aspects of interracial sex), and the presentation of material that focuses more on the future of children produced by miscegenous sex. Works of the former category, including James Baldwin's *Another Country* (1962) and *Tell Me How Long the Train's Been Gone* (1965), Malcolm X's *Autobiography* (1965), Eldridge Cleaver's *Soul on Ice* (1968), Antônio Callado's *Quarup* (1967), Darcy Ribeiro's *Maíra* (1983), Georges Bugnet's *Nipsya* (1924), Dany Laferrière's *Comment faire l'amour avec un nègre sans se fatiguer* (1985), and Alix Renaud's *A corps joie* (1985), tend to concentrate on the sundry sociosexual problems inherent in developing a private or personal sense of identity. Works of the latter category, such as Jorge Amado's *Tent of Miracles*, Rudy Wiebe's *The Scorched-Wood People*, Vasconcelos's *La raza cósmica*, William Faulkner's *The Bear* and *Absalom, Absalom!*, José de Alencar's *O Guarani* and *Iracema*, the poetry of Pierre Falcon, the dramas of George Ryga, and Juan Zorrilla de San Martín's *Tabaré* (1886), focus much more attention on issues of public, cultural, and even national identity. The list of New World literary texts that deal in whole or in part with the theme of miscegenation is a long and growing one and includes some of the masterworks of American letters.[5] Many of these texts, like Amado's *Tent of Miracles*, Margaret Laurence's *The Diviners*, Faulkner's *Absalom, Absalom!*, San Martín's *Tabaré*, and Bugnet's *Nipsya*, could be placed in both categories. The distinction between them derives not from the content of these works, all of which merge questions of human sexuality with issues of social and political significance, but from the way this sexual and political material is handled, its primary focus and thematic orientation.

James Baldwin's *Another Country* is the New World prototype of the sexually oriented interracial novel. Dealing with a tangled matrix of human sociosexual relationships that evolve from a casual sexual encounter between a black man and a white woman in New York City, *Another Country* develops into a powerful commentary on the politics of interracial sex, of female/male relationships, of political identity, and of race relations. By focusing on the broadly cultural dimensions of two different but intimately related love affairs, Baldwin shows how the abuse of power and the perverting force of master/slave relationships, whether they be of a sexual, racial, or political nature, eventually debase and destroy everyone involved. Thus Baldwin's novel transcends the level of a lurid interracial sex story and becomes a plea for more humane, less exploitive conduct in our personal and public lives.

Yet the novel's undeniable power really stems from Baldwin's effective union of the theme of miscegenation, which stands at the core of the story, with the allied theme of sociosexual inequality. The unequal social status of women and men is merged thematically with the more attention-getting motif of interracial sex. Baldwin thus deftly connects the question of race relations in the United States to that of how women and men feel about themselves and how they deal with each other. The story of Rufus, an urban black man, and Leona, a poor white Southerner he meets by chance on a New York street, is lacerated by currents of both love and hate. This violent emotional contradiction is a central fact of their tempestuous relationship and one that, through Baldwin's artful telling of their story, reflects the larger social and historical forces that have produced them both, the forces that have made them so different and, tragically, that destroy them.

Using the sexual union of Leona and Rufus to encapsulate the divisive racial situation in the United States during the late 1950s, as well as to suggest subtly the unequal status of women and men, Baldwin develops a story that is at once intimately private and broadly public:

> Rufus opened his eyes and watched her face, which was transfigured with agony. . . . Tears hung in the corner of her eyes. . . . He wanted her to remember him the longest day she lived. And, shortly, nothing could have stopped him, not the white God himself nor a lynch mob arriving on wings. Under his breath he cursed the milk-white bitch and groaned and rode his weapon between her thighs. She began to cry. "I told you," he moaned, "I'd give you something to cry about," and, at once, he felt himself strangling, about to explode or die. A moan and a curse tore through him while he beat her with all the strength he had and felt the venom shoot out of him, enough for a hundred black-white babies.[6]

This early scene, conveyed from the perspective of Rufus, plays an important part in Baldwin's development of the theme of miscegenation in the novel. By describing Rufus's ejaculate as "venom," Baldwin suggests that Rufus's entire being is poison, that Rufus is a venomous and therefore lethal creature. The references to the "lynch mob," the description of Leona as a "milk-white bitch," and the curses that Rufus utters all reinforce the reader's awareness of the violence and hatred that are destroying Rufus, who had earlier felt an unexpected tenderness for Leona. Leona herself, who is cast as a willing if pathetic participant in this sexual encounter, is a victim like Rufus. Having already told Rufus why she left her home and that she did not fear or loathe blacks, that, for her, "people's just people," Leona now kisses a very surprised Rufus, her lips "curved slightly in a shy, triumphant smile."[7] When Rufus rather coyly asks Leona what her husband will think when she returns home with a little black baby, she replies in a way that underscores the physical violence that husbands are permitted to direct against their wives: "'I ain't going to be having no more babies,' she said, 'you ain't got to worry about that. . . . He beat that out of me, too.'"[8]

Although on one level Rufus and Leona seem a highly unlikely couple, on another level, that of victims, they have a great deal in common. Leona, victimized by poverty, lack of opportunity, and a husband who beats her, has left home in search of a better life. Rufus, victimized by all the social, psychological, and economic wounds of racism, stays at home but is devoured by his own anger, an anger that, as we have seen, surfaces violently when he and Leona first have sex together.

Things go from bad to worse for the couple, however, and Leona, invalided by a mental breakdown, is taken back to Georgia by her brother, never to return. Rufus, now suffering from guilt and the pain of separation and increasingly tormented by the conflicting demands of love and a by now highly politicized racial consciousness, commits suicide by leaping off the George Washington Bridge.

Though the story of Rufus and Leona concludes at this point, its tragic legacy is paralleled in another interracial love affair, that of Vivaldo, Rufus's white friend, and Ida, Rufus's keenly intelligent and racially militant sister. In a certain sense, *Another Country* is less about miscegenation per se than it is about love or the impossibility of love, heterosexual or homosexual, in a world dominated by hatred, intolerance, and violence. This becomes more apparent as the story of Ida and Vivaldo unfolds. The problems faced by this couple are in many ways more poignantly presented than are the intractable problems encountered by Leona and Rufus, whose relationship, the reader feels, was doomed from the start. Vivaldo and Ida, in contrast, can perhaps learn from the tragedy that befell Rufus and Leona, a possibility which intensifies the drama of their affair because they seem to have at least a chance at happiness. Artfully merging the problems of race relations and sexism, Baldwin's focus shifts increasingly to showing the difficulty of love in a world dominated by racists and sexists.

From this concern for the possibility of human love Baldwin moves the reader toward a consideration of Ida and Vivaldo not just as interracial lovers but as interracial parents. As Vivaldo and Eric (who eventually becomes Vivaldo's lover) are discussing the need for love in human existence, Vivaldo declares:

> "Ida and I could have great kids," said Vivaldo.
>
> "Do you think you will?"
>
> "I don't know. I'd love to—but"—he fell back on the bed, staring at the ceiling—"I don't know."
>
> He allowed himself, for a moment, the luxury of dreaming of Ida's children, though he knew that these children would never be born and that this moment was all he would ever have of them. Nevertheless, he dreamed of a baby boy who had Ida's mouth and eyes and forehead, his hair, only curlier, his build, *their* color. What would that color be?[9]

This is as close as Baldwin gets in *Another Country* to linking the sexual, political, and racial dimensions of miscegenation with the even more significant issue of miscegenous children. It is interesting that Vivaldo stresses the theoretical independence of these children of mixed racial lines by speaking of *their* color, not the color of their parents. Moreover, his question—"What would that color be?"—is both biological and sociopolitical, a question about the presence of some degree of melanin in the skin, but also a more fundamental question about human rights and individual identity. (In raising this crucial but often overlooked point, Baldwin, as we shall see, anticipates the remarkable message provided by Brazil's Amado in *Tent of Miracles*, a work dealing with the same subjects as *Another Country* but in a very different way.)

While a great deal of Inter-American literature deals with miscegenation by emphasizing the sexual and political dimensions of interracial couplings, an even greater number of works emphasize the creation of a new race of people. In these writings children, rather than the miscegenous sex act itself, become the focal point of the story. This preoccupation with progeny rather than sex (which is limited in significance even when, as in *Another Country*, it has a powerful political dimension) can be found throughout the literature of the Americas. Sometimes, as in Laurence's *The Diviners*, Nélida Piñon's *The Republic of Dreams*, Amado's *Tent of Miracles*, Alencar's *Iracema*, or Vasconcelos's

La raza cósmica, it is presented very positively, while other times, as in Faulkner's *The Bear* or *Absalom, Absalom!*, it is cast in a negative light. But in all these works the emphasis is on the new human beings who are created from a sexual mixing of "races," the people known as mulattoes, half-breeds, or Bois-Brûlés, the French Canadian Métis.

One of the most forceful works of this type, and a work that amounts to a thesis novel on the subject, is Jorge Amado's *Tent of Miracles* (1969), which not only celebrates miscegenation but openly advocates it as the solution to the worldwide problem of racism. Moving back and forth in time between 1969 and the years of its protagonist's lifetime (which ends in 1943), *Tent of Miracles* tells the tale of Pedro Archanjo, an Afro-Brazilian folk hero who champions not just miscegenation and the elimination of political oppression and racism but the brotherhood of man.[10] As the comically self-conscious narrator, Fausto Pena, describes Archanjo, "He was a standard-bearer in the struggle against racism, prejudice, misery, and unhappiness."[11]

The situation presented in *Tent of Miracles* is almost diametrically opposite to that presented by Baldwin in *Another Country*. In the Brazilian novel, miscegenation is not merely accepted but espoused, even lauded, as the logical result of the victory of love and freedom over hate and repression. In what one feels is an intentionally symbolic scene, Archanjo, who is proudly mulatto, is smitten by Kirsi, who is white. Powerfully attracted to each other, the two of them enter into a sexual affair, the point of which (according to Archanjo) is to produce a mulatto child. Speaking "words of love," Archanjo declares to Kirsi: "'Gringa, . . . let's make a mulatto together, you and I.' . . . Their words crossed in the air, and all of them were words of love."[12]

Although Amado could be taken to task here (and elsewhere) for sexism and sexual stereotyping, the points he makes about miscegenation in this scene are two: first, its purpose is to produce a mulatto child, and, second, the miscegenous sex act can be based on mutual love and admiration; it does not have to derive from hatred or rape, an approach taken by such 1960s writers as LeRoi Jones (Imamu Amiri Baraka), Malcolm X, and Eldridge Cleaver. The child produced by Archanjo and Kirsi symbolizes the mixing of races that Brazil (too often more in theory than in fact) prides itself on, a racial mixing that (as we shall see) echoes Alencar's *Iracema* and contrasts sharply with what happens between Cora and Uncas in Cooper's *Last of the Mohicans*. Structurally, the basic conflict in *Tent of Miracles* is polarized between Pedro Archanjo, the champion of peace, miscegenation, love, and human freedom, and Dr. Nilo Argolo, the advocate of violence, political repression, racism, and apartheid.

Argolo's oppressive position is comically and ironically undercut and the conflict dissolved when, late in the novel, he is discovered to be himself a mulatto.

Through comparative references in *Tent of Miracles* to the turbulent racial
situation in the United States during the late 1960s, Amado shows how different the Brazilian racial scene—itself far from perfect—was. Archanjo declares
at one point that North American racism is "unacceptable to a Brazilian." He
asks, Is it not true that "the race problem and its solution were completely
different, in fact quite opposite, in Brazil and the United States? That the
tendency here, in spite of all the obstacles, was the mingling and mixing of
races?"[13]

The racially mixed society that Archanjo advocates is a far cry from the
bitterly divided world described by Baldwin in *Another Country*, by Malcolm X
in his *Autobiography*, by Cleaver in *Soul on Ice*, and by V. S. Naipaul in *Guerrillas*,
in all of which questions of interracial sex are interwoven with issues of violence, sociopolitical identity, and sexism. Though based on the Brazilian experience, Archanjo's social vision is universalist and liberating. He envisions a
society in which racial differences are accepted for what they are and both
interracial marriages and the children they produce are not only accepted but
prized. Archanjo expresses this noble sentiment: "I want one thing only: to live,
to understand what life is, to love my neighbors and all men."[14]

The entire thrust of *Tent of Miracles* is therefore utopian, a passionate if idealized argument for the creation of a more tolerant and integrated society, one
that could free itself from the ravages of racism and political oppression by
means of miscegenation based on love and respect. The unique stance of *Tent of
Miracles* offers a powerful contrast to the destructive ways miscegenation is presented in many other American cultures.

Margaret Laurence's *The Diviners* (1974) presents a Canadian perspective on
the issue of miscegenation. It stands thematically and philosophically between
Baldwin's *Another Country* and Amado's *Tent of Miracles*, incorporating the
theme of social ostracization as it applies to the Métis, a people of French and
Indian ancestry, with the allied problem of female and male identity (social as
well as individual). The latter, in Laurence's world, is made more complex
because of the racially mixed but nonharmonic heritages of her characters.
Laurence also weaves into her story the nature of the problematic relationship
that can exist between an artist and her or his society. This conflict is made
more complex in *The Diviners* because the protagonist, Morag, is not only a
social pariah (the unconventional child of an unconventional garbage collector)
and an aspiring artist (a writer) but a woman as well.

The perspective of *The Diviners* on miscegenation is thus significantly different from that of both *Another Country* and *Tent of Miracles*. In the latter two works, the primary perspective was male, even though, especially in Baldwin's work, considerable emphasis was placed on a female perspective, first Leona's and then Ida's. In *The Diviners*, as in Laurence's four other regionalistic "Manawaka" novels, the theme of miscegenation appears not explicitly but implicitly, through the alienated Tonnerre family, a Métis clan looked down on by the non-Métis society of Manawaka, a fictional town reminiscent of Yoknapatawpha or Macondo.[15] *The Diviners* differs from works like *Another Country*, *Quarup*, and *Maíra*, however, because a child is born, from a complex and tempestuous love affair between Morag and Jules Tonnerre, whose psychological torment parallels that of Rufus. The child, a girl, struggles to find her personal identity, which, as she comes to discover, is ineluctably tied to her mixed ancestry.

The conclusion of *The Diviners* is guardedly optimistic and recalls the way the reader last sees Ida and Vivaldo in *Another Country*. The girl has become not only conscious of her mixed heritage but proud of it as well. When the novel ends, she is preparing to leave her home and begin a new life, one that promises to be difficult but appears to offer the possibility of satisfaction. The crucial factor here, as in the case of Tadeu (a mulatto) and his fiancée, Lu (a white woman) in Amado's *Tent of Miracles*, is that miscegenous sex results in the birth of a child who symbolizes a more racially tolerant future. Moreover, the interracial sex in *The Diviners* is based on love, not (as with Baldwin, Cleaver, Jones, and Naipaul) on rape, violence, and debasement.

In all three novels, however, the political and historical ramifications of miscegenation play an important role. The difference is that in *Another Country*, for example, interracial sex remains an end in itself, a political and psychological factor of such divisiveness that it makes the growth of love impossible and thereby all but guarantees disaster for everyone involved. In *Tent of Miracles*, Amado, too, amply demonstrates the social and political volatility of interracial sex, but he also succeeds in showing how men and women of different races can free themselves socially, sexually, politically, and psychologically and deal with each other not as masters and slaves but as gentle, caring, and socially conscious equals. The message in *Tent of Miracles* is similar to that of *The Diviners*, a sophisticated piece of extended narrative that achieves a compelling sense of psychological reality by merging the past with the present and the present with the future, showing how a better world might eventually be. Amado does this as well, but Laurence's interweaving of a painful and violent past with an unstable and exploitive present, and her portrayal of the pressure this brings to bear on the love affair of Jules Tonnerre and Morag, achieves a level of pathos and unity lacking in the more loosely structured and digressive Brazilian novel.

Seen from this perspective, it is clear that both Morag and Jules suffer from the same kind of racial and political injustice that poisoned Rufus and Leona in *Another Country*. The difference between the two novels on this point is one of degree, not of kind. The intense tangle of love and hate that characterizes the feelings Jules and Morag have for each other reaches a climax in the scene where Morag, painfully conscious that she is an outsider not only to Métis culture but to the larger white society that disparages the Métis, tells Jules what she saw when she went to view the charred remains of the house and children of Piquette, Jules's sister:

> "The air smelled of—of burnt wood. . . . I thought Bois-Brûlés."
>
> "Shut up!" Jules cries out in some kind of pain which cannot be touched by her.
>
> Silence.
>
> "Go on," he says finally.
>
> Why does he have to inflict this upon himself? Why can't he let it go? Perhaps he has to know before he can let it go at all. . . . Then slowly he raises his head and looks at her.
>
> "By Jesus, I hate you," he says in a low voice like distant thunder. "I hate all of you. Every goddamn one." [16]

The terrible pain, anger, and resentment that Jules and Morag are trying to come to grips with in *The Diviners* are similar to those of the anguished and violently self-destructive relationship that exists in *Another Country* between Rufus and Leona. For Baldwin's two characters, however, in contrast to Laurence's, there is virtually no chance for happiness, much less love. Historical in their malignant potency, compounded by the myriad problems of political oppression and sexism, the evils of racism are simply too great for Leona and Rufus to overcome. In *The Diviners*, moreover, it is the man, Jules Tonnerre, who first rises above the murderous pain that is destroying him and reaches out, physically and psychologically, to the love Morag extends to him. Rufus, in contrast, is too far gone when he meets Leona to be saved. Though both couples must battle the various prejudices against miscegenous affairs that characterize their respective societies, Rufus and Leona (and, later, Ida and Vivaldo) stand much less chance of attaining a state of love and respect for each other than do Morag and Jules, who ultimately do achieve an intimate though still troubled happiness with each other.

Within *The Diviners*, however, the story of Morag's growth into a strong, free woman (a novelist) is bound up in the nature of her unusual affair with Jules. She is never dependent on him, sexually, economically, socially, or psychologically, and he, in a reflection of his painful awareness of his own status as an outcast, never attempts to possess Morag or determine her fate. Since both are pariahs—Jules because he is a Métis and Morag because she is a free-thinking woman and artist—they deal respectfully and honestly with each other, taking pains never to commit the duplicities, deceits, and manipulations that debase other, more "respectable" love affairs. Jules and Morag not only never marry, but they spend most of their lives apart, leading separate lives but keeping in touch, sometimes by accident and sometimes by design. Their affair implies that only if both parties are completely free and equal, dealing openly with each other, can a loving and caring relationship ever hope to take root. Marriage vows do not create love; honesty, respect, and concern for the other person do, and these are the qualities that Jules and Morag, misfits in orthodox society, struggle to practice in regard to each other.

When a daughter is born to Morag, Jules is absent. Indeed, he learns of the event only when Morag, after some deliberation, writes to him to tell him, not knowing if he will ever get her letter. After a month, Jules replies, thanking her for letting him know about the birth. Morag, who has assumed responsibility for rearing the child, does not beg Jules to return, nor does Jules promise to do so. The child, named Pique by Morag in honor of Jules's deceased sister, Piquette, becomes like Jules a folksinger who specializes in the songs and stories of Métis culture. Eventually, after Jules's death, she writes a song that is a moving tribute to her tormented father and to her own mixed heritage. Acutely aware of her dual background, Pique had for some time been engaged in a personal struggle to find her own identity. Though aware of Pique's efforts and of the role Jules played in her struggle, Morag, herself in quest of an identity, becomes painfully conscious of not being able to provide her daughter with the answers she seeks:

> "You look different, Pique. It's your hair. Why braids?" . . .
>
> "Cooler. Keeps it away from my face in this weather. Also, I'm part Indian—it's suitable, isn't it?"
>
> "I don't think I'm hearing you very accurately. What're you trying to say?"
>
> "I don't know," Pique said. "I don't want to be split. I want to be together. But I'm not. I don't know where I belong."
>
> "Does it have to be either/or?"

Pique's eyes became angry.

"I don't guess you would know how it feels. Yes, maybe it does have to be either/or. But I was brought up by you. I never got much of the other side."

Once again, the reproach. Not to Jules; to Morag. When Pique wielded that particular knife, it always found its mark, as she very well knew.[17]

Pique, like Piquette before her, suffers discrimination and sexual harassment in school because she is known by her schoolmates to be a "half-breed." Unlike Piquette, however, who sank into alcoholism and suicidal self-debasement, Pique seems strong, resilient, and able to move toward a better life for herself. She is, in this sense, a symbol of a better future not only for people of diverse racial heritage but, as we see in her relations with non-Métis people, for all Canadians and by extension for all people. Like Tadeu in Amado's *Tent of Miracles*, Pique proves that a miscegenous sexual liaison can produce a strong, free, and beautiful human being, one consciously proud of having a racially mixed heritage. Symbolically, then, the survival of the Métis people is implied through the survival of Pique, who tells her mother toward the close of the story that she is leaving home to travel to a Métis settlement in Manitoba, where she hopes to realize more fully who she is. The novel thus ends on a hopeful note.

Another Canadian work that confronts the theme of miscegenation is Georges Bugnet's *Nipsya*, the story of a young Métis woman who is forced to choose between her Indian heritage and her "white" heritage. Three suitors come forth to complicate Nipsya's decision: the first is her cousin Vital, a strongly religious Métis; the second is Mahigan, a pureblood Indian; the third is Monsieur Alec, the factor for the Hudson's Bay Company. Refined, cultivated, and above all white, Alec is the opposite of Mahigan, whose Indian ways exert a powerful hold on Nipsya. Vital, like Nipsya of mixed racial ancestry, represents not a compromise choice for her but, as Bugnet presents it, the best possible choice, the only suitor who can offer her true happiness and love, both of which are cast in a distinctly religious and noncarnal context. The narrative voice here suggests that the Métis are already "tainted" because of the "illicit" nature of their engendering and that only by living a saintly existence can they ever hope to remove this "blemish" from their race and gain respectability.

Bugnet's text expresses neither the direct praise for people of mixed racial backgrounds of Amado's *Tent of Miracles* nor the vast reservoir of racial hatred and political inequities that fill the pages of *Another Country*, Malcolm X's *Autobiography*, or *Soul on Ice*. *Nipsya*, however, recalls *The Diviners* because it implies that people like Nipsya and Vital continue to suffer from various kinds of social and political discrimination. Although Mahigan looks upon Nipsya as an inferior being upon whom he can force his sexual advances, it is the world of the white people that ultimately is the most disparaging to her. Even Alma, Vital's sister, discriminates racially between what she regards as "lowly" Indians and, from her perspective, superior Métis.

Bugnet's most telling scene in this regard, however, is reserved not for Alec, who actually defends the Métis, but for the white woman, Flora, who becomes his wife, much to the disappointment of Nipsya, who mistakenly had fancied herself in love with Alec. The sharp contrast that Bugnet establishes between the white skin, blond hair, and elegant apparel of Alec's racist wife and the dark-haired, dark-skinned, buckskin-clad Nipsya marks a crucial step in Nipsya's psychological development and therefore in the novel's plot structure. Feeling rejected and racially inferior, Nipsya attempts suicide. She is rescued by Vital, and she begins to see in her Métis counterpart her best chance for the love and contentment she seeks. Nipsya and Vital begin to work together to control their physical attraction to each other and to place their vows of sacred love above their desires for physical love.

Vital, however, is suddenly called away to fight in Riel's 1885 rebellion, a conflict which represents for Canadians what the Canudos revolt (1896–1897) represents for the people of Brazil. (Throughout *Nipsya*, the name of Louis Riel turns up frequently, as it does in virtually every work of Canadian literature that involves the issues of the Métis and miscegenation.) Vital's sudden departure is symbolically important to the novel's conclusion, which, reminiscent of both *The Diviners* and *Tent of Miracles*, suggests not merely that the Métis will survive but that they will flourish. This reading gains credibility when Vital returns home to begin a new life with Nipsya. Although Bugnet, his sexism showing, portrays Nipsya as the decidedly weaker part of the Nipsya/Vital union ("Won't you help me, Vital? I am only a girl, and so weak and proud!") [18] the final chapter employs an effective metaphor, that of the willow tree, to show how Vital and Nipsya will serve both God and Canada. Identifying the future of the Métis people with Nipsya, and symbolizing both in a plain yet enduring plant, Vital poetically observes, "Your soul is like that of the willows, Nipsya, like the soul of our race—perennial and ever-varying." [19] Then, concluding the novel on a guardedly optimistic note, Vital declares: "Nipsya, may our sons be like yourself and the willows—humble, useful, diverse—and may they, too, become the blood and the soul of the country, the obedient servants of the Great Wisdom!" [20]

Appearing first in Rousseau's concept of the *bon sauvage* and later in that of Chateaubriand, the theme of the indigenous "Americans" and their problematic relationship with their conquerors, as we see in *Nipsya, The Last of the*

Mohicans, *Quarup*, and many other works, is one that runs throughout the literature of the New World. But because the realities of the flesh-and-blood "Indians" often did not correspond to the French visions of what these supposedly
"primitive" beings must be like, several problems arose in regard to how they
were to be treated by the Europeans who came to the Americas.

Among these, however, the issue of miscegenation looms larger than most.
This is so perhaps because the mixing of races would have been a logical and
desirable development for anyone who wished to act upon what Rousseau and
other Europeans advocated about the Native Americans. What, after all, could
be more beneficial than to blend the blood of the New World "noble savages"
with the elite of Old World culture and civilization? The problem in all this, of
course, is that what was acceptable in theory was often not acceptable in fact;
while male Europeans could easily embrace in the abstract the notion of the
noble savage, they weren't always anxious to have their daughters marry one.
Approached from this perspective, it is clear how the closely related issues of
sexism and racism are bound up in the more general concept of miscegenation.

Although the theme of miscegenation is found, as we have seen, throughout
the literatures of the New World, I have chosen to focus my final comments on
the role it plays in works written by James Fenimore Cooper of the United
States, José Martiniano de Alencar of Brazil, Juan León de Mera of Ecuador,
and Juan Zorrilla de San Martín, of Uruguay. My contention is that of these
four authors, whose best-known works can be said to represent the social
norms of English North America and Portuguese and Spanish South America,
only Brazil's José de Alencar took a definitively affirmative stand in regard to
the issue of miscegenation. Even more than Margaret Laurence and Georges
Bugnet, Alencar saw in miscegenation the bright future of his country. He saw
it, moreover, not only as a question of interracial sex, as Baldwin and others do,
but, anticipating both Vasconcelos and Amado, as the creation of a new race of
people, one that would symbolize the merging of the Old World with the New.

In the literatures of both Brazil and the United States, the theme of In-
dianism links the style and motifs of neoclassicism with those of romanticism.[21]
Although writers of both countries had been concerned since their respective
colonial eras with how Indians would be depicted artistically, the poets and novelists of Brazil had by the mid nineteenth century transformed them into romantic stock figures or heroes. Only James Fenimore Cooper would attempt to
do something similar in the United States.

Much has been written about the parallels that exist between Cooper and
Alencar and the supposed influence, direct or indirect, of Cooper and Chateaubriand on Alencar. In *Como e porque sou romancista* (*How and Why I Am a*

Novelist, 1893), however, Alencar categorically denies that either Cooper or Chateaubriand ever influenced him. He says, in fact, that the efforts of the North American and the Frenchman were no more than copies of the "sublime original" (that is, "glorious Nature"), which Alencar claims to have known intuitively in his heart.[22] But the question that concerns us here is not the matter of influence, though, as in the case of Cooper and Richardson, this thorny problem is of considerable interest to a comparatist and deserves closer attention; rather, we are concerned with the ways Cooper and Alencar handled the potentially explosive theme of miscegenation in three of their better-known novels: *The Last of the Mohicans* (1826), *O Guarani* (1857), and *Iracema* (1865).

Everyone is familiar with *The Last of the Mohicans*, the stirring tale of chase, capture, and escape set in the era of the French and Indian War (1754–1763) in North America. Cooper's dauntless frontier scout, Hawkeye, and his faithful Mohican companions, Chingachgook and Uncas, inseparable comrades, stand in stark contrast to the evil Hurons and violent Iroquois, who are led by the wily and vengeful chief, Magua.

The novel's love interest and the theme of miscegenation develop in the following way. The English commanding officer has two daughters, Alice, who is fair-skinned, blond, and blue-eyed, and Cora, who is dark-complected, black-haired, and dark-eyed. The handsome and dashing (but feckless) Englishman, Major Heyward, falls in love with Alice, but the young women's father mistakenly believes that Heyward loves "dark" Cora rather than "light" Alice. The scene (chapter 16) in which this confusion is revealed is crucial for understanding the way the issue of racial mixing is handled in the novel, because it illustrates the strong strain of racism that characterizes the English settlers and, therefore, the roots of North American social structure. The "problem," as Cooper presents it, is this: Cora turns out to be the granddaughter of a white West Indian planter and a woman descended from black slaves, so when Colonel Munro learns that Heyward loves not Cora but Alice, he fears that the English Heyward has rejected the daughter he considers to be racially tainted in favor of the racially "pure" one.

As the novel's several breathless chase scenes begin to unfold, the attentive reader begins to notice Uncas, the epitome of the *bon sauvage*, taking greater interest in the welfare of Cora, who in turn seems to grow increasingly receptive to the young Mohican's always-restrained behavior and honorable intentions. Although the novel's primary love interest is clearly that between Alice and Major Heyward, the subtly developed relationship between Cora and Uncas leads us to suspect that Cooper wanted to titillate the reader with the possibility of a budding interracial love affair between the noble Indian warrior and the plucky white woman. There is simply too much carefully worded textual evidence in the novel to accept the arguments that such an interpretation represents an overreading of the novel or, as David Driver has suggested, that the Cora/Uncas relationship was of minor importance to Cooper.[23] Indeed, there is much evidence that Cooper was quite conscious of how the combined issues of race relations and Indian male/white female relations might play a significant role in his fiction. But Cooper, owing perhaps to his own doubts about the propriety of a racially mixed world, apparently could not bring himself to write such an ending to the tale. Undoubtedly aware that a miscegenous union between a white woman and an Indian man would have scandalized his reading public, Cooper solves his literary problem by having Uncas die, struck down by the malevolent Magua (who had abducted Cora) while attempting one final time to rescue her. She also dies, conveniently dispatched by one of Magua's braves.

But while Cooper does defuse his problem with the deaths of Uncas and Cora, he does not let the idea of a miscegenous relationship die. To the contrary, during the Indian burial scene which concludes the novel, the possibility that Cora and Uncas might be united in the afterlife is strongly if problematically implied. Thus, the conclusion of the novel not only returns the reader to the tantalizing relationship between Cora and Uncas but suggests that what they could not attain in life, a loving and admirable union sanctioned by their respective societies, they might attain in death. Yet even in this crucial final scene there is ambivalence on Cooper's part; Hawkeye, who seems here to speak for Cooper, rejects the possibility (or at least the rightness) of a union between Cora and Uncas, and the reader can only agree with Leslie Fiedler that "even beyond death, the ferocity of Cooper's dread of miscegenation will not yield." [24]

But while Cooper felt compelled to restrain, camouflage, and finally denounce the possibility of a love affair between an Indian warrior and a white woman, his Brazilian contemporary José de Alencar felt considerably less restricted. Samuel Putnam believes that the explanation rests in what he sees as a fundamental difference between the cultures of Brazil and the United States: from the beginning the Portuguese not only tolerated miscegenation but accepted it, while the Puritans with their "feeling of superiority to colored peoples" did not. Although both the Portuguese and the English warred with the Indians, Putnam says, the English segregated themselves from the Indians and tried to exterminate them, whereas the Portuguese "solved the problem by absorbing and assimilating [them]." [25]

It is not my intention here to argue the legitimacy of Putnam's sociological observation, for its correctness regarding Brazil and the United States (to say nothing of French or Spanish America) is surely a matter of degree and not of kind. Yet because both Cooper and Alencar were so consciously committed to chronicling and perhaps mythologizing the formation of their respective societies, one cannot disregard here the sociopolitical implications inherent in the treatment of the theme of miscegenation in their novels.

The earlier of Alencar's works, *O Guarani* (*The Guarani*), is concerned with the emotional (but, recalling *Nipsya*, not sexual) relationship between an Indian warrior, Peri, and Cecília, the white daughter of a Portuguese *fidalgo*.[26] Peri, who like Cooper's Mohicans talks like a French philosopher, is the quintessence of the brave, modest, and gallant "noble savage." After a series of chases, captures, and escapes (which together closely resemble the structure of Cooper's *Last of the Mohicans*), Cecília's father asks his friend and ally, Peri, to save Cecília from the Indian enemies who threaten their settlement with annihilation. In *O Guarani*, as in Cooper's novel (or, as some prefer, his "historical romance"), there are "good" Indians and "bad" Indians, although only Cooper's Indians embody the Puritan sense of evil that so permeated the intellectual formation of the United States. There is, for example, no close equivalent to Magua in Alencar's more idealized world. (Magua was presented by Cooper as having been corrupted by the evils of the colonists' world, principally alcohol; we recall Rousseau's important, debatable ideas that mythical humanity-before-society is naturally good and that it is the vices produced by society that corrupt.) But Peri, like Uncas, is pure. Both heroes come to demonstrate a virtually sacred devotion to the women they love, a devotion that (fortunately for the settlers) is extended to their families as well. At one point, Peri even confuses his vision of Cecília with a vision he has of the Virgin!

Although Peri and Uncas are similar characters, substantial differences exist between Cora and Cecília; the former is from the outset braver and more resourceful than the latter, whose early capriciousness gives way eventually to reveal a more determined woman than one would expect, given her stereotypical characterization early in the novel. (The ways Cooper and Alencar deal with their female characters have yet to be studied comparatively; such a perspective could yield new and valuable insights into the merits of Cooper and Alencar as social critics and historically aware narrativists. This approach could be especially rewarding in the case of Alencar, who in his later feminine portraits, like *Senhora*, 1875, is quite capable of creating independent and strong-willed female characters.)

But it is only in the conclusion of *O Guarani* that the theme of miscegenation really comes to center stage. Up to that point, the love between Peri and Cecília has been basically platonic, even filial in nature. Their love has not yet been acknowledged, much less consummated; this presented Alencar with a serious problem, just as the Cora/Uncas relationship had left Cooper with an awkward situation at the end of his story. Perhaps because he felt his society, in 1857, was close to accepting racially mixed marriages, Alencar resolved his thematic dilemma with a symbolic conclusion: Peri, threatened by rising floodwater, tears a palm tree out of the ground and, as the novel ends, he and Cecília float away together, presumably, one supposes, to engender a new race, the Brazilian people. This highly stylized scene echoes Cooper's conclusion to *The Last of the Mohicans*, where, as we have already seen, the possibility of a Cora/Uncas marriage in the afterlife is intimated if not advocated. In *O Guarani*, Cecília begins to suspect at the last moment that she has a woman's love for Peri, but she also feels strongly that she cannot openly admit to wanting to marry an Indian. Like all of Alencar's "civilized" (that is, white) female characters, Cecília feels duty-bound to respect the proprieties of her social class. So in spite of the love she now knows she feels for Peri, she is compelled to refer to him as her *irmão*, her brother. As if to sanction their love, she declares that should they die in the flood (which she feels they will), they will live on in heaven—as brother and sister. Since Alencar probably did not mean to add incest to the problems of Peri and Cecília, it seems a proper reading of this passage to view Cecília's words as pure artifice, as a way of easing her own socially conservative conscience as to what would happen between her and Peri—who makes it quite clear to Cecília that they will not die in the flood.

The key point in all of this is that the miscegenous implications of the integral and exciting relationship between Peri and Cecília are not explicitly presented. Alencar only intimates them, but he does so in a way that is considerably more positive than in *The Last of the Mohicans*, where Cooper first brings the issue up and then labors to disavow the possibility that Uncas and Cora should ever marry. To this end, Cooper even has his protagonist, Hawkeye—who throughout the work is portrayed as the embodiment of the "American moral ideal"[27]—cast serious doubts on the feasibility of Indian/white love affairs.

But if in *O Guarani* Alencar broached the issue of miscegenation, it was in *Iracema* that he left no doubt as to its implications for Brazilian society.[28] Written as a legend in the manner of a prose poem rather than a realistic narrative, *Iracema* (an anagram of "America") recounts the poignant tale of a beautiful Indian woman, Iracema, who falls in love with Martim, a Portuguese colonizer who represents the European struggle to adapt to life in the New World.

Iracema, a symbol of the beauty and fertility of the American landscape, is characterized as the "virgin of the honied [sic] lips whose hair was blacker than the wing of the grauna bird and longer than her palm tree figure." [29] A feminist critic might reasonably argue that Iracema's relationship with Martim (like that of Doña Marina with Cortés) could also be said to symbolize the European conquest (or rape) of the New World; such a reading is essential to understanding the work's political aspects, particularly those dealing with the issue of gender identity.

Seen strictly in terms of the theme of miscegenation, however, the fundamental difference between O Guarani and Iracema is that in the 1865 work the interracial love affair is played out to its logical and natural conclusion. The result, still symbolic but here more explicitly so, is the birth of a child, Moacir, whose name, in the language of Iracema, means "child of pain." Iracema's pain is of three kinds: the physical pain of childbirth (Iracema dies not long after giving birth to her child); the emotional pain of seeing Martim's ardor for her cooled by his longings for his homeland; and the psychic pain caused by the fighting between the Indians involved (the Tabajara, Iracema's people, and the Pitiguaras, allies of the Portuguese) and between the Indians and the Portuguese. If in O Guarani the possibility of interracial offspring is left to the reader's imagination, in Iracema it moves openly into the realm of a dramatically (some might say melodramatically) depicted mythos.

But while the development of the miscegenation theme is clearly apparent in O Guarani and Iracema, there is an additional factor, sexism, which also catches our eye. In both The Last of the Mohicans and O Guarani, it is an Indian man who becomes enamored of a white woman. In Iracema, however, published eight years after O Guarani appeared, it is an Indian female, a princess to be sure (she is the daughter of the chief of the Tabajara tribe), who gives herself unabashedly to a Portuguese soldier, who, it should be noted, is not as firm in his devotion to her as she is to him. One can only speculate about why Alencar chose to reverse the female/male roles in these two novels. Did he feel that for all the considerable Indianist literature his country had produced, and for all that racial mixing had already been a vital and recognized part of Brazil's heritage, his compatriots were not ready for a detailed discussion of both the female/male and the Indian/white themes until 1865? Could Brazilian society, long dominated by white males, find the theme of miscegenation socially acceptable only if the man involved were a white Portuguese nobleman and not an Indian? Or is it simply that Alencar is recasting the epic story of the Old World's conquest of the New? If one considers the female/male thesis as offering a possible new reading of *O Guarani* and *Iracema*, then these stories become socio-logically interesting for reasons beyond those involving the simple question of racial mixing. The issues of the sociopolitical status of women and men, as well as of the indigenous people and the Portuguese, also come into play, and in a profoundly interactive and even antipatriarchal fashion.

In considering these three novels, one can easily come to the conclusion that the female/male question is bound up not only in the way Cooper and Alencar portray their characters but in the way they develop the theme of miscegena-tion. Because, as Colonel Munro himself implies, Cora "suffers" from having "tainted blood," she is a suitable mate, if one accepts racist theories, for the nonwhite Uncas. Ironically, though, and to Cooper's credit (if indeed he planned it this way), in her courage and daring Cora was the only proper match for the brave Uncas. The pure-blooded but fainthearted Alice, on the other hand, was the proper love object of the well-intended but inept Major Heyward. In Alencar's work, however, it is first the redoubtable Peri (virtually a clone of Uncas) who devotes himself to the safekeeping of the Alice-like Cecília and then, in a different novel and a reversal of sex roles, the tough but adaptable Martim unites with the more Cora-like Iracema.

Cooper, long known as the American Scott, may or may not have exerted an influence on Alencar. Either way, however, as Driver has argued, certain struc-tural aspects of Alencar's work (his melodramatic chase-and-escape scenes, for example) do seem to recall much of Cooper's work as well as some of that of Ferdinand Denis ("Les Machakalis," for example), who may himself have been influenced by Cooper and whose work, *Le Bresil* (1837), was known to Alencar.[30]

If Scott, with his concept of the historical romance, and Rousseau, with his theories of nature and the natural man untainted by civilization, were important in Cooper's development as a writer, the impact of Chateaubriand on Alencar's work cannot be discounted either. Alencar, we know, especially admired *Atala*, a work which one recalls in reading *Iracema*, although Alencar insisted that while Chateaubriand provided him with a "model," he did not provide him with his "inspiration."[31]

Noting several parallels between Alencar's novels and Cooper's, Driver ob-serves (only half correctly, I think) that the miscegenation theme in *The Last of the Mohicans* is a "minor one" whereas, in the story of Peri and Cecília, Alencar makes it "the central theme."[32] Because the specter of miscegenation turned up in so many of Cooper's works, and because it is always shrouded in a mixture of fear and perverse fascination, one is led to believe that the theme of interracial sex was not merely of minor importance for Cooper. And while Cooper never brought it into the open, as Alencar did, it nevertheless remained a powerful though repressed issue for the more prejudiced North American writer. It is possible that if he had indeed read the earlier Cooper novel, Alencar might have seen how the theme of miscegenation could be handled in a Chateaubriand-like Indianist novel by a writer well aware of his country's traditions and of Rousseau's concept of the noble savage.

In summary, we can say that three features distinguish Alencar's treatment of miscegenation from that of Cooper. First and foremost, while Cooper abhorred racial mixing (and yet was clearly enthralled by the prospect) Alencar was disposed to accept and even champion it as a natural course of events. Second, and perhaps as a direct consequence of the first, Alencar came to develop the theme of miscegenation openly in his work, while Cooper, for reasons probably both psychological and cultural, cultivated the issue of miscegenation as what Fiedler calls "the secret theme" not only of *The Last of the Mohicans* but of the entire *Leatherstocking Saga* as well.[33] Third, Alencar's sympathetic handling of this sociological issue reflects a lyrical sensitivity that is lacking in Cooper's often awkward novels, which are as confused and stereotypical about sexual matters as they are obsessively rigid about the supposed need to maintain racial segregation in the United States and the world. But, as we shall now see, while Cooper's handling of this complex theme may have represented the orthodox view of his culture, it was by no means the only one being advanced.

Another novel to address—though in a more distinctly feminist fashion—the entwined issue of racism and sexism is Lydia Maria Child's *Hobomok* (1824),[34] the primary thesis of which (that interracial marriages between white women and nonwhite men could be a positive force in American culture, one working to subvert sexual and racial hypocrisies) may well have inspired Cooper to write *The Last of the Mohicans*.[35] The story of two "marginalized" men, an Episcopalian named Charles Brown and an Indian, Hobomok, and a freethinking Puritan woman, Mary Conant (who, marginalized because of her sex, loves them both), *Hobomok* can easily be read as an indictment of the same white male–dominated culture that Cooper so unquestioningly upholds. Upon learning (erroneously, it turns out) that the man she initially loves (Brown) has died, Conant comes to accept the love she feels for the noble Hobomok, whom she marries, observing the customs of his people. A child is born to this union and, as in Alencar's *Iracema*, it is with this child that a large portion of the novel's primary symbolic significance rests.

A plot complication arises, however, when, after a period of three years, Brown suddenly reappears. In an extraordinarily magnanimous act that highlights his inherent nobility, Hobomok effectively renounces his claim to Conant and, returning to the forest, frees her to marry Brown, which she does. The child, who is given the name Charles Hobomok Conant, is educated at Harvard and in England, while his mother and nonbiological father are reintegrated into the same cultural milieu that had earlier censured them for their beliefs, attitudes, and conduct. Thus, Mary Conant appears to emerge victorious on both of the novel's primary thematic fronts: she upholds the validity of an interracial love, and she overcomes the restrictions of her patriarchal Puritan society.

Yet in spite of the novel's felicitous merging of these two themes, the conclusion of *Hobomok* raises some troubling questions. What, for example, is the reader to make of the fact that the miscegenous union that originally liberates Conant from her repressive Puritan culture is later abandoned in favor of a more conventional one, when her white lover reappears? Why is the child completely subsumed in his mother's culture, seemingly in rejection of that of his natural father? Why does Hobomok disappear from the story when Brown returns to reclaim Conant? And, finally, how can the tough and determined Mary Conant so easily drop one lover (the man she chose to marry) in favor of another? Even though the text repeatedly mirrors one man in the other (thus allowing for the possibility that from Conant's perspective they represent a single ideal lover), the resolution of *Hobomok*'s basic plot conflict is fraught with problems. Nevertheless, as Carolyn Karcher notes:

> What reviewers found so "unnatural" and "revolting" was the sexual freedom Child had allowed a woman of their own class—freedom to choose her mate without regard to race or class, freedom to take the initiative in proposing marriage, freedom to divorce and remarry, retaining custody of her child to boot—freedom, in sum, to flout every law of patriarchy without suffering the consequences.[36]

Dealing deliberately, then, with the combined themes of sexism and racism, *Hobomok* merits comparison with *O Guarani* and *Iracema* on several key points: the symbolic importance of interracial marriage to their respective cultures; the rights and privileges of children born to these marriages; and the social, political, legal, and economic status of women in these societies. Offering a sharp and vivid alternative to Cooper's *Last of the Mohicans*, *Hobomok* ranks with Alencar's works as one of the most provocative New World novels of its time.

But if the positions taken by Child and Alencar in *Hobomok*, *O Guarani*, and *Iracema* stood in opposition to the prevailing mores of their respective cultures, much the same could be said of their relationship to Spanish America. Surprisingly, nowhere does the theme of miscegenation gain the early formalized centrality that it possesses in *O Guarani* and *Iracema*. Although many well-known works deal with issues related to miscegenation, few of these develop the theme as positively as Alencar does. Works like Esteban Echeverría's *La cautiva* (1837), Juan Zorrilla de San Martín's *Tabaré* (1886), Manuel de Jesús Galván's *Enriquillo* (1882), and Juan León de Mera's *Cumandá* (1879) all involve the issue of miscegenation, for example, but they incorporate it as an ancillary theme, the main one being an essentially historical or political treatment of the clashes between the Indians and the conquistadors. Two of these works, however, Mera's *Cumandá* and San Martín's *Tabaré*, go further than the others in taking up the issue of racial mixing and giving it a larger measure of thematic significance.

Showing again the influence of both Chateaubriand and Cooper,[37] the Ecuadorian Juan León de Mera liberally mixed in *Cumandá* European images of the noble savage with accurate descriptions and firsthand observations of native flora and fauna, especially that of the vast American selva or jungle. The plot of Mera's novel is based on a colonial legend in which a beautiful Indian woman, Cumandá, dies tragically before her love for Carlos, the son of a white settler-monk, can be consummated. Upon her death, the reader learns that she and Carlos were siblings, both fathered by the same man, José Domingo Orozco.

In contrast to Alencar, Mera (like Cooper) cannot permit himself openly to countenance love between Indians and whites. The character Orozco, however (in a revealing display of phallogocentrism's double standard), is casually permitted sexual activity with Indian women, the birth of Cumandá being the miscegenous outcome of one such affair. Yet whereas in *Iracema* the love affair between an Indian woman and a white male settler is based on authentic love and the hope for a unified, peaceful future, in *Cumandá* it is based on rape and concubinage. Further, it results in the creation of an outcast "half-breed" race similar to the Métis of Canada and not easily accepted by the society of either parent. So while a narrative like *Iracema* shows how the races can come together for the benefit of all concerned, novels like *Cumandá* (and *The Last of the Mohicans*, which in this regard has much in common with *Cumandá*) show the depth of the racial divisions that already existed in Spanish and English America and that would bitterly divide the Europeans and the indigenous peoples for generations to come. Mera could not accept the sexual and social implications of Rousseau's noble savage theory, which by postulating the natural goodness of humanity, had logically to accept as equally good the procreation of a mestizo race. Instead, as we see in Mera's text, the noble savage had to be baptized before she or he could even hope to be accepted, and even then acceptance came only within limits.[38] This hypocritical aspect of *Cumandá*'s handling of miscegenation has a close parallel in Bugnet's *Nipsya*.

A more refined work, yet one no less revealing of the racial problems that existed between the Spaniards and the Indians, is Juan Zorrilla de San Martín's *Tabaré*. Long considered to be Uruguay's national epic, *Tabaré* deals with the conflict between an aboriginal people, the Charrúas, and the Spanish. The tone of *Tabaré*, however, is often less epic than elegiac, an aspect of its composition that derives from the haunting evocation of the past that San Martín offers in his poem, an evocation that though lyrically rendered also shows clearly why the Charrúas faced certain extinction.

San Martín's hero, Tabaré, is like Cumandá a mestizo, but he is a more tragically rendered character, one whose biological parents cannot break through the walls of racial, sexual, and social prejudice that separate them and make them enemies. Additionally, because Tabaré's father was a Charrúa chieftain and his mother a Spanish captive of the Charrúas, his very lineage implies rape and domination, a theme that (as in *The Royal Commentaries* of Inca Garcilaso) reverberates throughout the work. Though reared as an Indian (a blue-eyed one), Tabaré has been baptized and lives by the Christian moral code. He falls in love with Blanca, the orphaned sister of the commander of the Spanish garrison, Don Gonzalo de Orgaz, and thus the specter of miscegenation is raised in yet another generation. Tabaré, who belongs neither to his Indian race nor to the white race, anguishes (like Pique) over not possessing a social or cultural identity, a problem that does not afflict Blanca. Mirroring the conflicts inherent in the war that surrounds him, Tabaré and his Charrúa heritage stand in sharp and painful conflict with his Christian heritage, and it is this fateful psychological and cultural schism that proves to be his downfall. During a battle, Blanca is abducted by rebellious Charrúas, but Tabaré intervenes to save her and return her to the safety of the Spanish outpost. On his way back with her, Tabaré is discovered by Don Gonzalo and a Spanish patrol, who kill him, thinking mistakenly that he was attacking Blanca. Tabaré's ironically tragic end symbolizes for San Martín the similarly tragic demise of the once-great Charrúa nation.

Tabaré is similar to *Iracema* and *O Guarani* in that the authors of both rely heavily on symbolism to convey their respective themes. But it is precisely in regard to the issue of theme that the works part company. For Alencar, the conclusion of *Iracema* represented the future of Brazil, a future that would be difficult but that held considerable promise for those who approach it with love and open-mindedness. For San Martín, on the other hand, the symbolic conclusion of *Tabaré*, like that of *The Last of the Mohicans*, points unhappily toward a future full of rancor, oppression, and strife, based not on unity, love, and cooperation, as Alencar had stressed, but on the extermination or domination of one race by another. In *Tabaré*, as in so much Spanish American and English American literature, the theme of miscegenation is secondary to the larger theme of epic conquest, to the struggle between the forces of the Old World and those of the New. Although interracial sex and miscegenous progeny are common elements in Spanish American literature, they are not presented as positively or as symbolically as they are in Brazilian works, particularly in Alencar's *O Guarani* and *Iracema* and in Amado's *Tent of Miracles*.

The theme of miscegenation is one of the key themes of Inter-American literature, bound up with the closely related problems of slavery, racism, and gender identity. As we have seen, works using the theme divide themselves naturally into two major categories: those that focus primarily on interracial sex, typified by Baldwin's *Another Country*, and those that, working to break down social, political, and racial taboos, emphasize the future of racially mixed children. The literature of the latter type, typified by Amado's *Tent of Miracles* and Laurence's *Diviners*, is as politically sensitive as that of the first group but tends to look beyond the social and psychological problems inherent in interracial sex and toward the creation of a new, more harmonious race of people. This orientation toward the future is consistent with the overall outlook of the American republics for whom the creation of a cultural, political, and racial identity is an ongoing issue.

Though no one would claim that the theme of miscegenation is unique to the New World, one can argue that miscegenation has always been a vital, if rarely pacific, part of the American experience. Indeed, the first American-born writer of real distinction was of mixed blood. Inca Garcilaso de La Vega, the son of a Spanish conquistador and an Incan princess (the niece of the last Inca),[39] is often credited with having founded Spanish American literature, a point of literary history made interesting because of Garcilaso's racially mixed heritage, both sides of which he praises in his masterpiece, *The Royal Commentaries* (1, 1609; 2, 1617). From El Inca in the sixteenth century to Alix Renaud's *A corps joie* in the twentieth century, the theme of miscegenation has been a constant force in Inter-American literature.

5

********** Refining the New World Novel

Henry James and

Machado de Assis

When one begins to consider the refinement of the novel form in the New World, one thinks almost immediately of the great American writer Henry James. No less an American, however, and a writer of similar sophistication and innovation, was James's egregiously overlooked contemporary, the Brazilian novelist and short-story writer Joachim Maria Machado de Assis. Although there is no evidence that they ever knew of each other's work, both men, one the well-bred scion of a cultured New York family, the other a lower-middle-class Rio de Janeiro mulatto, changed forever the ways in which the craft of fiction would be practiced in their respective countries.

While the story of Henry James and his contribution to the novel form is thoroughly documented, the equally significant contribution of Machado de Assis is with but few exceptions known only to those few people whose reading has taken them into the ken of Luso-Brazilian literature. The fact that Machado, as he is known in Brazil, has been permitted to languish virtually unacknowledged must surely constitute one of the major literary travesties of the modern age. The sad truth is that Machado has suffered from a near-fatal malady (one that, with the exception of the United States, has long afflicted New World writers), that of being born in the "wrong" country, one not ordinarily ranked among the literary elite of Western culture. If Machado had practiced his art in

France, Germany, Russia, England, Italy, Spain, or even Portugal, his name would now be as familiar to students of literature as are those of Flaubert, Goethe, Dostoevsky, Dickens, Pessoa, or Cervantes. Moreover, in discovering Machado de Assis, the comparatist quickly realizes that the Brazilian master, like the better-known authors cited above, belongs not merely to a particular national literature but to world literature. He is, simply put, one of the finest writers of the modern era, and a systematic analysis of his work in comparison to that of Henry James, his New World contemporary, bears this out. Indeed, Machado's numerous structural, stylistic, and semantic innovations were so ahead of their time that (with chapters 9, 55, 124, and 138 ironically and self-consciously "explaining" how and why this text differs from what the reader of this time was expecting) his *Epitaph of a Small Winner* can easily be considered not only Latin America's first "new novel" but that of the Americas and of the Western tradition as well.

Both writers were technically—and brilliantly—innovative, particularly with regard to the nature and function of point of view in narrative. And although James is decidedly the better known of the two in this regard, a thorough reading of both men's work indicates that on this very point, long held to constitute one of James's strongest suits, Machado de Assis was actually the earlier experimenter. As early as 1880 he recognized the possibilities inherent in the kind of fiction that could, by means of its style, structuring, and perspectives, establish new relationships between the characters, the author, and the reader. Machado's final five novels, two of which—*Epitaph of a Small Winner* (1880) and *Dom Casmurro* (1900)—may fairly be judged as world masterpieces, constitute five highly innovative narratological experiments, texts that brilliantly convey Machado's strikingly modern representation of the human experience.

This latter feature, Machado's profoundly ironic *Weltanschauung*, takes form in his narratives as a wryly expressed but keenly felt disenchantment over the discrepancy between humanity's potential for noble activity and its deplorably selfish performance. James, for all his marvelous ambiguity, his subtlety of statement, and his ability to express the ineffable, cannot consistently quite match the affective, tragicomic union of laughter and tears, of pathos and bathos, of idealism laced with baseness that for Machado (as for Cervantes) characterizes the human comedy.

Both James and Machado enjoyed long, active careers that enabled them to experiment with and react to different influences, undertake various technical experiments, and try their hand at other genres, such as poetry, theater, the essay, and criticism. Machado additionally did a great deal of translation work and can be credited with having introduced many new forms and techniques to Brazilian literature. But the outstanding feature of their careers was that both clearly show a steady growth in terms of their technical control, their ability to develop characterization, and the enlargement and elaboration of their basic themes and concerns. Few writers have ever matured as progressively and felicitously as did Machado de Assis and Henry James. Coming from backgrounds that were starkly different, both men early on recognized in themselves what would eventually grow into an unquenchable thirst for the creation and study of literature. Interestingly, while James rather casually gave up a career in law to become a writer, Machado sought a bureaucrat's post in the government, because he felt such a job would provide him with both a steady if modest income and enough free time to allow him to pursue his true passion—literature. But whereas James traveled to Europe to study French and to steep himself in European culture, Machado learned his French (and his European culture, one supposes) by working in Madame Gallot's corner bakery in Rio de Janeiro and by checking out books from the library.

Many critics have tried to explain the supposed pessimism of Machado's work by referring to the hardships of his early years, and while this approach seems open to considerable conjecture, it does serve to remind us that James's fiction has often been approached from a similar perspective, one that places an unjustified importance on biographical data regarding the author and his well-off family.

This has also occurred with studies of Machado and his work, though Machado himself resolutely insisted that the two issues be kept quite apart, that his work was not about him or his life. While no one would deny that James's educational background or his well-financed sojourns in the literary salons of Europe had an effect on what he wrote or that Machado's lack of formal education, his penury, and his physical ailments must have had an impact on his fiction, we should never lose sight of the key issue here: neither James nor Machado was an ordinary writer; they were, on the contrary, inspired, deeply committed artists who, drinking in the literary and cultural trends of their time, sensed in themselves the ability and the need to break new ground, to take the "pale little art of fiction," as James put it, to previously unexplored realms of refinement and subtlety. In order to gain the critical acumen and the national and international perspective necessary to do this, both James and Machado read widely and made important critical statements about several of the leading European masters of the time, including Flaubert, Balzac, Turgenev, Eliot, and Zola, among others. What James had to say about Zola and the naturalistic novel, for example, is similar to what Machado, writing at almost the same time, had to say about it, which supports a point to be made later in this chapter, that James and Machado were surprisingly close in their critical thinking.

Many of the same European writers, then, provided James and Machado with models and theories of fiction writing against which they could measure and develop their own work. But in looking at James's three final novels and at Machado's final five, we can see that both New World writers had actually gone beyond their Old World counterparts in artistic experimentation and refinement. In the case of Machado, the importance of Dante, Voltaire, Flaubert, Zola, Fielding, Sterne, Cervantes, Shakespeare, and Pascal cannot be overestimated, while in the case of James one cannot miss the influence of Hawthorne, Balzac, Eliot, Turgenev, Maupassant, and, of course, Flaubert. As a result of these influences, both James and Machado exhibit, even in their early work, a marked tendency to merge some quite diverse modes of expression. We find, for example, aspects of the romance mingled with aspects of the novel, an abiding interest in depicting the variety and complexity of emotional and intellectual phenomena, an enthusiasm for developing the themes and techniques of what would later become known as the psychological novel, and an open, even enthusiastic acceptance of both realistic description and lyricism in their narratives. Perhaps most important, however, is that both James and Machado endorsed the idea of the "well-crafted novel," the notion that novel writing was an art that could be refined a good deal more than it had been, something which both these writers would succeed mightily in doing.

Distinct periods of development are readily recognizable in the careers of both writers. James's so-called early phase, from about 1875 and the publication of his first major novel, *Roderick Hudson*, to 1881 and the appearance of *The Portrait of a Lady*, was characterized by a painstaking dissection of American "innocence" as it manifested itself in contrast to the "experience," or "worldliness," of the Europeans. The other novels from this period, *The American* (1877), *Daisy Miller* (1878), and *The Europeans* (1879), continue this trend while also showing James's penchant for crafting novels of manners and customs and his ability to depict prototypically distinctive social types, Europeans as well as Americans.

James's middle period, which is often said to run from about 1882 to 1900, includes three long social novels: *The Bostonians* (1886), a satirical treatment of the women's suffrage movement in Boston; *The Princess Casamassima* (1886), a journey into the seamy world of London's anarchist movement; and *The Tragic Muse* (1890), a study of the conflict between the value systems of the world of artistic endeavor and those of a materialistic society. This, as we know, came to be one of James's major themes, one paralleled (though not as openly) in Machado's work, which tended to be more universal than international in focus.

During this same period, James also wrote literary criticism and began to refine his concept of the role a "central consciousness" would play in his fiction. This latter idea involved the development of a technique by means of which James felt better able to depict the subtle interplay of social and psychological perspectives, of stimulus and response, which would later become the hallmarks of his best work. And, again like Machado, James began to experiment with the use of poetic symbols, to expand the role of metaphor in his otherwise realistic narratives, and to sharpen his sense of how dialogue could be utilized in a novel to convey the flux and tentativeness of human thought that, increasingly, he desired to centralize in his fiction.

The 1890s were the famous and frustrating dramatic years for James, when, to his great disappointment, he discovered that his interest in psychological drama could not easily be framed in the rigid and restrictive forms of the classical French theater, the dramatic form which held the greatest attraction for him. The result of this unhappy though certainly not wasted experience was, in 1899 (and *The Awkward Age*), to drive James back to narrative, yet a narrative that from 1899 on would be characterized by a pictorial, or scenic, style clearly reflective of James's interest in the drama as a vehicle of literary expression.

James's mature period encompasses the three long novels usually cited as his masterworks: *The Wings of the Dove* (1902), *The Ambassadors* (1903), and *The Golden Bowl* (1904). Comprising a tripartite statement about manners and morals and New World/Old World relations (the latter being another fundamental theme for James), these three works offer a contrast in their respective modes of expression. In the story of Milly Theale, we experience an essentially tragic mode; in that of Lambert Strether, we sense a comic or ironic mode; and in the story of Maggie Verver, we encounter a generous and philosophically conciliatory mode that comes to pervade all aspects of the tale.[1]

Paralleling closely in time, experience, and influence the career of Henry James yet developing wholly apart from it, Machado's growth as a craftsman of the novel form shows an equally sustained pattern of development. Machado's career can also be divided into clearly defined periods, though most critics recognize only two major divisions, the pre-1880 Machado and the post-1880 Machado. It is often said that Machado de Assis was a romantic who, committing a kind of theoretical apostasy, became a realist (though one more in the vein of Maupassant or Joyce than, say, Dickens), and, indeed, a careful reading of his later novels and stories seems to bear this out. However, as in the case of the maturing Henry James, one can argue just as cogently that the seeds of the post-1880 Machado had always been present, even in the first novel, *Resurrection* (1872). To take this plausible position, however, still leaves the critic obliged to explain the striking shift in style, tone, and technique that characterizes Machado's last five novels: *Epitaph of a Small Winner*; *Philosopher or Dog?* (1891); *Dom Casmurro*; *Esau and Jacob* (1904); and *Counselor Ayres's Memorial* (1908). One of these latter works, *Dom Casmurro*, has been lauded as being perhaps the finest novel ever written in North or South America.[2] Machado's earlier novels, *Resurrection*, *The Hand and the Glove* (1874), *Helena* (1876), and *Iaya Garcia* (1878), all exhibit a growing confidence in the author's technical control, an authorial frustration at the restraints imposed by romantic modes of characterization, and an increasing interest in developing new forms, structures, and techniques. *Resurrection*, for example (told, like *The Wings of the Dove*, in an essentially tragic mode), is a sobering tale about human failure; specifically, it is about the triumph of jealousy over love and the concomitant hardening of a human heart, all of which became as much a defining theme for Machado de Assis as did the New World/Old World contrast for Henry James. The next novel, *The Hand and the Glove*, is a romantic comedy reminiscent at times of *The Ambassadors*. It affirms another preoccupation of the author (one that recalls Maggie Verver's magnanimity in *The Golden Bowl*), namely, that only a conscious collaboration of love and will power can overcome egoism and the all-engulfing indifference of the universe. *Helena* and *Iaya Garcia* are sharply worded commentaries on social types and customs and, for that reason, very much in the Jamesian vein, especially similar to the novels from his middle period.

Although it is primarily the novel form that has permitted Machado to gain even the small degree of international recognition he enjoys, he like James worked in other literary genres as well, most notably the short story, a genre in which Machado must be regarded as a modern master. His first published work, the poem "Ela" ("She," 1852), reflects the prevailing romantic aesthetic of the time and shows a not insignificant talent for verse which shines through clearly in later poems. "A Mosca Azul" ("The Blue Fly"), sharply ironic in tone, was written in the parnassian mode, which Machado was instrumental in establishing in Brazil.

Also like James, Machado wrote extensively for the theater. Machado's experience, however, was considerably happier than James's because with one exception (the 1862 drama, *Gabriela*), he restricted himself to the creation of repartee-filled drawing-room comedies about upper-middle-class society. He did not attempt, as James had, to do on the stage the kind of psychological analysis that is better done in the more flexible and spacious novel form. Like James, Machado's later narratives were almost certainly influenced by his earlier efforts in theatrical writing. While James more or less devoted the entire decade of the 1890s to his fling with the theater, Machado largely abandoned drama after 1869, the year of his marriage, choosing instead to cultivate the novel and short-story genres.

If we can say in summary that James's career was marked by a progressively more integrated view of cultural intercourse and human consciousness, the expression of which depended on a proper rendering of the psychology and background of the characters involved, we would have to characterize Machado's career as being an equally progressive though psychologically more profound attempt to examine the issues of human motivation and identity. Additionally (and in a way that universalizes his work), Machado goes further by making a particular human psyche a microcosm of the human race, an effect he achieves metafictionally by systematically drawing the reader into the mind of his protagonist. This technique establishes a sense of kinship between the reader and the protagonist (who is often the self-conscious narrator), allowing Machado to develop unobtrusively the patterns of moral and philosophical contrast that gradually entwine the reader's views and those of the protagonist. The primary difference here between James and Machado is one not of subject matter but of the nature of the treatment, the depth of the psychological plunge, and the degree of its universality.

To achieve his goal, Machado, like James, consciously shifted the focus of his work away from a concern with the external world, an orientation which in both Brazil and the United States had long dominated the writing of fiction, and moved it toward a finely detailed, poetic depiction of the inner world of psychological motivation and subjective contemplation. Both writers seem to have moved decisively toward a presentation of the psychological realm at almost the same moment, Machado in 1880 and James in 1881.

To appreciate fully the arresting changes in style and technique that were required to make such a major thematic shift successful, we can look at the two works which first accomplished this very similar function for their respective authors, *Epitaph of a Small Winner* (1880, serialized version; 1881, book version) and *The Portrait of a Lady* (1881). The year 1881 can be said to be a watershed in the development of literature in Brazil and the United States, after which the art of novel writing in these two countries would be forever changed.

By 1881 both Machado and James were attempting to establish a sense of sub-stance in their novels not by concentrating on a Flaubert-like detailing of the three-dimensional world but by tracing the growth of a particular human con-sciousness: in one novel, that of a wealthy and sardonically nihilistic Brazilian gentleman, Braz Cubas, and, in the other, that of a strong-willed but vulnerable young American woman, Isabel Archer.

In both novels, "reality" is portrayed not as external to us but as something private and psychological, the sense of awareness or consciousness, moral choice, and will power that each of us possesses. Hence, in each work it is by means of a unique characterization that we enter into the minds of Isabel Archer and Braz Cubas; for Archer, this ingress occurs relatively late in the novel, while for Cubas it is there from the opening page. Cubas, however (and in this he shows himself to be a more sophisticated creation than Archer), is the wryly self-conscious but fallible narrator of his own story, and, as a result, in ways seemingly unknown to him he repeatedly reveals more about himself than he wants the reader—to whom he directly and often disparagingly speaks—to know. As Cubas breezily avers in his preface, "To the Reader": "The book must suffice in itself: if it please you, excellent reader, I shall be rewarded for my labor; if it please you not, I shall reward you with a snap of my fingers, and good riddance to you." [3]

We cannot fail to note, however, that both James and Machado were skillful at utilizing social situations, with their cultural, psychological, and material ac-couterments, as vehicles for depicting the evolving emotional states of their characters. To do this, they rely heavily on many of the traditional techniques of poetry and realistic or mimetic narrative while plunging headlong into the new kind of fiction writing we now call psychological realism. In James's novel, we enter into Isabel's perspective only in the latter part of the story, and even then we have the feeling that we have entered into only the upper levels of Isabel's conscious, ratiocinative mind; we haven't peered deeply into the complexities of her being. While we can certainly admire James for realizing the benefits to be gained by shifting his novel's dominant point of view to that of Isabel herself (a radical departure from the established modes of storytelling in the United States up to 1881), we are amazed at how deftly Machado leads the reader into the vicissitudes of Braz Cubas' egocentric view of life, a view as chilling as it is calculating. The result of Machado's effort is that the reader comes to know more about Braz than, seemingly, he would want us to have known, and this, generating a definite response from the reader, establishes itself as the source of the novel's power. Machado's metafictional techniques, which are replayed in virtually all his post-1880 narratives, are highlights of this 1880 narrative in which a fully self-conscious and wholly dramatized (but unreliable) narrator tells a story about the writing of a book, in which he himself is the dominant figure, and about its alleged significance. The textual interplay of author, narrator, and reader in *Epitaph of a Small Winner* thus becomes what the novel is really about.

Machado does not stop here, however. Aside from his experiment with an unreliable narrator, the real author of Braz's book (Machado himself) builds his own "house of fiction" on a foundation more fundamentally ironic than even the surprising turn of events in *The Portrait of a Lady* (Isabel, hopeful but unaware, abandons her "unsophisticated" American house, only later to embrace, now aware but disillusioned, a "sophisticated" European house). The ironies in the James novel are essentially ironies of language and isolated event, as they also are in *The American, The Europeans,* and *The Bostonians*; they do not reflect an essentially ironic world view, as is the case in Machado's novels. Isabel Archer, in *The Portrait of a Lady,* does not get what she wants, though during the first two-thirds of the novel we see her thinking that she does or that she will. The central irony of her story is that she ends up with exactly what she sought all along to avoid, a fettered and unfulfilled existence. Because of her unhappy marriage to Osmond, a marriage she had thought would set her free, she becomes more of a prisoner in her fancy European mansion than she had ever been in her less elegant American house, which in turn symbolizes the American life she had initially condemned as too confining.

As in Machado's *Resurrection,* there is more than a hint of tragedy here, for Isabel is a thoroughly likable and admirable young woman. She tries very hard to see things as they "really are" but falls prey to her own harmartia, an error of judgment that places her, ironically, in Osmond's gilded cage rather than in Lord Warburton's more human, more honest way of life. But, in the novel's famous fireside scene (chapter 42), when Isabel finally comes to realize the full implications of her action, James mutes the tragedy by allowing us to observe Isabel in the process of resolving to endure, to do the best she can with what she knows is a hopeless situation.

The irony of Braz Cubas' story is more tragic than that of Isabel Archer. And though it is present throughout the novel, nowhere is Machado's deeply (some say bitterly) ironic view of life more succinctly expressed than in the final scene, in which Braz, speaking to us from the hereafter (as he has been doing from the first page), declares, "Upon arriving on this other side of the mystery, I found that I had a small surplus, which provides the final negative of this chapter of negatives: I had no progeny, I transmitted to no one the legacy of our misery."[4] Coming from our affable, urbane guide through his own posthumous memoirs, these final words and the terrible judgment they deliver about the nature of human existence stun us. We are struck by the momentous shift in tone here, the abrupt movement from the witty, sarcastic banter we have come to expect from Braz to the savage indictment of human life that concludes the story.

But when we put Braz's final words in the context of what he has often said or implied about people and why they do the things they do—those desultory aporias in which he seems to make a slip, to reveal some of the reservoir of rancor, coldness, and selfishness that distorts his vision and makes him unreliable as a narrator—we are not so surprised at the ferocity of this stunningly nihilistic pronouncement. When we reflect on what we have read, it becomes plain that the same Braz Cubas who could say (suggesting that it flattered him to do so), "One endures with patience the pain in the other fellow's stomach,"[5] was all along the same Braz who finally declares, "I had no progeny. I transmitted to no one the legacy of our misery." In fact, the final scene—which is the key scene in terms of the novel's real theme, that unchecked self-centeredness or "egoism" (as Machado often put it) is ultimately self-destructive—can be interpreted as an exceptional example of dramatic irony: while Braz Cubas does not share the real author's views about the value of human life, the reader does.

Only at the very end of Braz's narrative, then, does his misanthropy burst the bonds of decorum that, except for occasional slips, have held it in check, blunted it, and even transmuted it into an instrument of pungent humor, obliquely warning the reader not to adopt Braz's alluring point of view. From the opening page of the narrative, Braz labors to draw the reader close to him and to gain her or his confidence, and the reader, willing to play a participatory role in the game of fiction (as Machado insisted that she or he do), responds just as Braz desires. The surprising result is that because we are shocked and dismayed at Braz's final comment, our reaction is to reject Braz's callousness and self-centeredness and turn instead to Machado de Assis, the author whose beneficent presence seems to leap out of the text to offer us hope for a more humane approach to life. Hence we move away from the cynical, selfish Braz Cubas and toward the gentle, loving Machado, the real author, whose thoroughly effaced role in the novel is restricted to this final scene. Ever the master craftsman, Machado brings all this about in a moment of rare and dramatic irony in which, suddenly and with no advance warning, we sense that the perceptive reader and the real author share a knowledge (that egoism is destructive) which the main character, Braz Cubas, does not possess. The message of this novel, its theme, is thus brought home to us in a wholly unexpected and ironic fashion.

Yet while it is clear that as early as 1881 both Machado and James were striving to move their novels away from a fictional world dominated by action toward one composed of shifting levels of awareness and mental flux, we should not overlook the greatest single difference between their respective treatments of the inner realm. James, working on a level of carefully articulated consciousness, wrote in *The Portrait of a Lady* a novel of social manners and "sensibility" in which the rendering of Isabel's movement toward comprehension of her situation is clearly connected to a certain facet of the outside world, to a particular social milieu. Though the primary technical uniqueness of *The Portrait of a Lady* lies in its shift of perspective from omniscience to that of Isabel's mind, this process is still linked to a particular external reality, the totality of Isabel's psychological and sociopolitical vision of herself as Mrs. Gilbert Osmond.

In *Epitaph of a Small Winner*, however, the psychological plunge is more comprehensive, more exclusively personal, and more exhaustive in its ontological implications for the reader, whose response to the work—especially to its conclusion—is adroitly engineered by both the real author and his narrator. Machado's novel, true to his aesthetic credo that plot should derive from a conflict of motivation or emotion within a single mind, puts a more sharply focused emphasis on extensive interior characterization than does James's work. Although Braz Cubas talks a great deal about other people and things, implicitly contrasting himself to them, the novel actually chronicles the growth of his own fatal flaw, the problems inherent in the numbing egotistical way he sees himself. His becomes a kind of death in life, and the silent, unrecognized, or simply unacknowledged drama that centers on the struggle between the forces of love versus egoism in the soul of Braz Cubas seems more compelling, more timeless, and more poignant than does Isabel's slow realization of the errors of judgment she has made. We feel sorry for Isabel Archer, but the impact of Braz Cubas' story is tragically cathartic. Hence, in terms of their respective experiments with psychological realism, it must be concluded that the Brazilian's efforts were deeper, more psychologically complex, and less moored to a social environment than was the American's effort. Given the disparity between the basic orientation and the relative profundity of their treatments, Machado de Assis, not Henry James, should be given credit for having written the first modern psychological novel.

Linked to the concern shared by both writers over the depiction of the inner world is the crucial issue of technique, which sets the work of both men apart from all that was written before them. Because both writers were consciously concerned with the purely technical aspects of fiction writing, the affinities between them in this regard are numerous and strong. But there is one issue, the question of point of view, that illustrates better than any of the others how the technical innovations wrought by James and Machado provide the key to our appreciating fully the excellence and originality of their work.

More than anything else, it is their experiments with perspective that distinguish the fiction written by James and Machado. The later novels of both men, especially James, show increased psychological depth, refined methods of characterization, and an increasingly complex style. But it remains the way in which the reader is presented with the story (and lured into it), the point of view from which it is told, that really permits James and Machado to carry out their forays into the recesses of the human mind.

When speaking of the depiction of human consciousness or awareness, we are necessarily speaking of characterization as well as of the nature and function of point of view in a novel. And in terms of his delineation of character, Machado de Assis has few equals in the Americas or elsewhere. Through the controlled manipulation of the relationship between the reader (implied and real), the author (implied and real), and the narrator, who in several of the last five novels is in different ways both self-conscious and unreliable, Machado dives deep into the souls of his characters and, simultaneously, into the soul of the human creature. The depth of this plunge is surely what led Samuel Putnam to suggest that Machado shows in his work more *sabedoria*,[6] or profound life-wisdom, than Henry James, even though both writers were concerned with the same issues. In contrast to Machado who in works like *Epitaph of a Small Winner*, *Dom Casmurro*, and "Midnight Mass" dealt with language and event in terms of personal ontologies, James was primarily interested in the various ways a literary artist might represent the tenuous, ephemeral effects that an event or word in the external world could produce in the psychic life of his characters.

But though both Machado and James worked with a flow of ordered, conscious, intellectual activity and emotional flux, it is Machado, with his special talent for making the private psychological conflict of a particular character serve to symbolize the same dilemma in a universal context, who is more satisfying in his development of characters.

The protagonists of *The Ambassadors* and *Dom Casmurro*, the latter a novel that in its treatment of the role time plays in the human experience presages the

Proust of *A la recherche du temps perdu*,[7] bear this out. Lambert Strether and Bento Santiago are both wealthy and cultured gentlemen whose stories are laid out on a fully rational, highly articulate plane, yet it is Santiago who, in the course of telling his story from the vantage point afforded him as he approaches the end of his life, shows us best how he has evolved from being a rather callow, diffident lad into the curmudgeon nicknamed Dom Casmurro. Santiago and Strether are alike in that both undergo radical changes in their understanding of life, yet the great difference between the two novels resides in the point of view utilized to convey the story to the reader. Moreover, this same difference, which shows Machado and James at their experimentally most brilliant, mirrors the kind of emphasis that the psychological novel tends to place on the processes involved in interior characterization.

In his novel Machado relies entirely on the viewpoint of a single character, Dom Casmurro, a bitter old man who, we slowly come to discover, has hidden even from his own rational mind a powerful motive for altering the facts of the story he tells us, a story which in its ethical and moral implications is a towering human tragedy resting ironically upon an authorial and readerly (and not protagonal) condemnation of jealousy, cruelty, and selfishness. The point of view employed here is overwhelmingly—and manipulatively—first-person, that of the character who figures most centrally in the overall plot, whose veracity and forthrightness most influence the way the reader reacts to the story.

As a consequence, the crucial element in appreciating the technical uniqueness of *Dom Casmurro*, and one that directly involves the reader's ability to enter into the story, to participate actively and knowingly in Casmurro's tale from the outset, is the reader's ability—when the narrator asks the reader to make the judgment on the narrator's innocence or guilt—to discern the underlying duplicity of his being and his discourse. To complicate this situation even more, Machado develops a meticulously structured and interwoven ambiguity regarding what actually happened between Casmurro's wife, Capitú, and Escobar, Casmurro's erstwhile best friend. The narrator, an attorney who knew well how to arrange evidence to sway a jury (or a reader), amasses a great deal of evidence in the progression of the text. Though it is purely circumstantial, this evidence seems to suggest strongly that Casmurro's wife and best friend did have an affair that resulted in the birth of a child. In the novel's final chapter, Casmurro demands that the reader agree with his presentation of the "facts" of the story and that he be absolved of any part he might have had in causing its tragic outcome—a denial of even filial love, in all-consuming jealousy and a bitterness that results in rejection and death.

As Helen Caldwell and Paul Dixon have shown,[8] the deliberate ambiguity that cloaks the pivotal question of guilt or innocence on the narrator's part rests at the heart of the work and thus becomes an aspect of Machado's artistry that cannot be separated from his innovative implementation of a fallible first-person narrator (a technical device that had held his attention ever since its appearance in *Epitaph of a Small Winner* twenty years earlier). In *Dom Casmurro* we have an exemplary wedding of form and content, a modernistically organic unity in which the essential ambiguities of the story are paralleled and embodied in the larger, more philosophical issue of the nature of truth in the process of artistic representation.

With the appearance of *Dom Casmurro* in 1900, however, we begin to note one of the most striking distinctions between the mature work of these two authors, one that calls attention to James's sophisticated and elaborate usage of the third-person limited point of view, a technical breakthrough which, according to many critics, constitutes his major stylistic contribution to the development of extended prose fiction in the United States. Yet if in this use of a third-person limited point of view we can see traces of Flaubert's influence on James, we must not neglect to appreciate the extent to which Machado took to heart and refined what he saw Sterne do with the self-conscious first-person point of view and narrative structuring in *The Life and Opinions of Tristram Shandy* (1759–1767). In *The Ambassadors*, a work that James himself especially liked, the perspective from which the story is told changes in accordance with the shift in focus from one character to another. In each case, however, the third-person limited point of view still expresses the inner drama of the character in question as well as her or his relationship to the larger story, to the comings and goings of the outside world. We have in this novel the culmination of James's longstanding enthusiasm for a scenic or pictorial structuring of fiction, for a cultivation of the dramatic methods of objectivity and dialogue, and for the employment of a central consciousness, a character through whose observing, interpreting mind the story unfolds.

The role of Strether as the central consciousness of *The Ambassadors* suggests an interesting comparison with the similar function of Bento Santiago in *Dom Casmurro*. I refer here to their relationship with the reader (both real and implied), which demonstrates the basic unreliability of each of these characters and which prevents us from accepting what they tell us as the complete "truth," a poststructuralist problem often at the heart of Machado's narratives. Because Strether is the one character whose viewpoint holds the entire work together, we note that he is often mistaken in his conclusions about what goes on around him and about what truly motivates the other characters. But in a way that high-lights James's masterful control of the novel's point of view, we as readers must wait until each separate situation is resolved in order to find out when, where, and how Strether is wrong. This technique has a parallel in Santiago's position in *Dom Casmurro*, where the self-conscious narrator/protagonist may also be guilty of error. In both novels, then, we have a viewpoint character who misin-terprets events—Lambert Strether because he is often ingenuous, but Bento Santiago because he is (or may be) self-servingly devious. The use of this type of viewpoint character requires that the reader make judgments about the char-acters and their actions without knowing for certain whether such interpreta-tions are "correct" or whether they are intended by the real author. This strat-egy, brilliantly deployed in these two singular New World novels, is developed by both James and Machado into a structural ambiguity which is decisively re-lated to both the question of Casmurro's guilt or innocence in *Dom Casmurro* and the meaning of Strether's new understanding of himself at the close of *The Ambassadors*.

Closely connected to the key issue of point of view in the later work of these two writers is the even more revealing function of irony. Irony, the art of saying one thing but meaning or implying something else, is present in Machado's novels, for example, from the very beginning. In *Resurrection* and *Helena*, his first and third novels, Machado works with dramatic irony, a technique he had perhaps learned from his early work in the theater and which he had thoroughly mastered by the time of the 1881 publication in book form of *Epitaph of a Small Winner*, the novel which, as we have seen, turns on the reader's ability to react to the ironic shift in perspective effected by the narrator/protagonist's final words. But even in *Helena*, Machado's interest in dramatic irony as a way of enhancing the reader's participation in the story is obvious. Yet Machado's great talent in developing dramatic irony as a basic structural feature is that he never tells us outright what we wish to know; he invariably shows or suggests something to us (which the character in question does not know) by utilizing the traditional tools of the poet—allusion, symbol, and metaphor—to advance the plot of an essentially mimetic narrative.[9]

It is difficult, at first glance, to grasp the full extent to which Machado devel-ops irony in his work, even in a masterpiece of ironic structuring like *The Psy-chiatrist* or *Dom Casmurro*. This is so because in the closing decades of the twentieth century we tend, in our canonical way, to think of any extensive use of irony as somehow the special province of modern European literature, not that of a little-known late nineteenth-century Brazilian writer. In all his ironic narratives Machado mined the uncertain terrain that lies, forever intangible, between the sundry realities of human existence and the words we use to re-present them. Taking this perspective on the question of style may help explain why, in James's refined but volatile world, the irony seems more often to exist beyond his characters, bound up in the labyrinthine ways they use language to relate to the world of social intercourse, whereas for Machado it is more an ontological problem, a matter of a philosophically skeptical and yet resigned view of life. Given Machado's wrier outlook, the irony of his novels originates in the soul of his characters, each of whom embodies some conflictive and contrastive world view, such characterizations being ever more successfully brought about after 1880, primarily by means of the author's use of different kinds of self-conscious and unreliable narrators.

Yet even in the early novels, Machado had begun to recognize in irony the technical device that would enable him to go deeper in his explorations of the human psyche at the same time he created a new kind of narrative hero, one who plays a key role in the action but whose understanding of it was, for differing reasons, often in error. As Machado saw it, only an ironic interpretation of life—and life was always Machado's real subject—could accurately account for the ambiguousness of words, the terrible finality of deeds, the constant struggle between good and evil (or, for Machado, between love of others and self-love), and the ever-present threat of self-deception that plague human activity.

For Machado, literary irony was not merely a technical achievement existing "out there" in the narrative world of action and event, as it regularly was for Henry James, but a Doppelgänger-like reflection of an immutable characteristic of human existence, one constantly at work, often unconsciously, deep within us and affecting all we do, all we think we do, and even the way we interpret (and thereby create) life around us. Machado's notion of irony, then, was philosophical in nature, but as a stylistic device—as a function of language and its power over us—he gave it an ever-greater role in the creation of his best characters and plot structures. A master of realistically detailed portraiture, of the art of controlled ambiguity and understatement, and yet a writer who like James relied heavily on symbolism, allusion, and metaphor, Machado developed an ironic style that reflected his understanding of the arbitrary and differential relationship between language, literature, and human existence.

The reader is impressed by the extent to which both Machado and James recognize the possibilities inherent in making irony play a fundamental role in their novels. Even in their early efforts both writers attempted to integrate irony, especially verbal irony and irony of event, into the main story. But, as we see in

The American and *Resurrection*, for example, these relatively unsophisticated attempts fail in general to develop into the thematically and structurally crucial issues and patterns of development they would become in such later works as *Philosopher or Dog?*, *Esau and Jacob*, *Counselor Ayres's Memorial*, *The Wings of the Dove*, and *The Golden Bowl*, in addition to *Dom Casmurro* and *The Ambassadors*.

In this latter novel, for example, the recall of Strether at the end of book 6 reverses the entire movement of the story and thereby establishes its most fundamental irony, that the person initially charged with bringing home the wayward Chad must now himself be brought home. Strether, whose assignment it was to extricate Chad from the wiles of a worldly French woman, is himself transformed by the delights of European society, converted to an opposite view of life and of himself. Realizing this at the same time that the reader does, Strether comes to believe that Chad, who like Braz Cubas is an egoist, should remain in Paris with his lover, Madame de Vionnet, that he should not abandon her, and that he should not return home to Wollett, Massachusetts, as his moralistic mother, Strether's fiancée, demands. His unexpected reaction heightening the delicious irony involved here, Chad (showing his shallowness) now feels he is ready to go back home, to quit Europe and return to the United States. As Leon Edel has noted, this particular reversal of roles is significant; as the reader, who accompanies Strether in his expanding awareness and comprehension, discovers, Chad has been superficially changed whereas Strether's consciousness has been permanently altered.[10] Strether's realization that he has let life slip through his fingers is powerfully expressed in book 5:

> Live all you can; it's a mistake not to. It doesn't so much matter what you do in particular, so long as you have your life. . . . I see it now. I haven't done so enough before—and now I'm old; too old at any rate for what I see. . . . It's too late.[11]

As we see in this famous passage, though irony is strongly present in James's best psychological portraits, it remains predominantly linked to external events, a fact amply demonstrated by the ironic reversal of roles undergone by Strether and Chad in *The Ambassadors*.

Machado, on the other hand, began as early as 1881 to conceive of irony not in a cosmetic or ancillary capacity but as his work's basic philosophical ground, the organizing principle around which all other narrative functions, including plot, characterization, and imagery, would be grouped. He first demonstrated this orientation in *The Psychiatrist*, an intensely satirical novella in which the old problem of sanity versus insanity is given a thoroughly ironic treatment. This venerable theme is not presented in a traditional way, as in the manner of *Don Quixote* (which did significantly influence other Machado works, especially *Philosopher or Dog?*). Rather, the irony in *The Psychiatrist* arises organically out of the author's most deeply held convictions about the nature of human existence, about how our sense of sanity and insanity is little more than an extension of the private and often idiosyncratic ways we interpret ourselves and our world. Or, to put it another way, the most ironic aspect of this short narrative stems from Machado's pummeling of our excessive belief in the ability of scientific analysis to explain human behavior and our vainglorious and hypocritical methods of self-appraisal. While the events so mimetically depicted in the story appear in their social context to mean one thing, when read symbolically they actually suggest something quite different, something more philosophical and universal in nature.

Though they form a cohesive, tightly woven story line, these same events give rise to only part of the tale's ironic appeal. The rest derives from Machado's effaced but still strongly sensed presence in the novel. It is the style of *The Psychiatrist*, not its ironic world-view, that emerges as the book's real brilliance. This powerful marriage of style and theme, which in its satirical aspect reminds us of James's *The Bostonians*, is refined even more in Machado's last four novels, *Philosopher or Dog?*, *Dom Casmurro*, *Esau and Jacob*, and *Counselor Ayres's Memorial* (though the latter work, through its poignant affirmation of the curative powers of love and fidelity, reminds us most of James's final work, *The Golden Bowl*). On this point—the integration of form and content—the similarities between James and Machado in their mature periods are again numerous and striking. But perhaps more than any other single facet of their art, it is the manner in which James's and Machado's expanded scope of irony functions that suggests just how far ahead of their time these two American authors were.

While in general it is readily apparent that both James and Machado liberally mixed the traditional stylistic techniques of narrative realism with those of poetry, utilizing symbolism, imagery, and allusion rather than rote realistic description to advance their stories, we must note how each achieves this end. In truth, James and Machado go about it very differently, in ways that directly reflect their respective views about how language relates to reality and to the syntax of their sentences. Like Flaubert, both the Brazilian and the North American were aware of the tenuous, symbolic nexus between words and reality, and both recognized that the weakness of this connection was exacerbated if one wished to delve into the psychological world of half-formed thoughts and inchoate feelings. This acute sensitivity to language, reality, and language's communicative function is illustrated consistently in the style of each writer. In his later stage of development, James became virtually obsessed with achieving an exact representation of human consciousness, and his style became intricately patterned in an attempt to effect this end.

The result of his concern is that the sentences of James's post-1902 novels become long, complex, and full of carefully weighted clauses and qualifiers. James's mature style, in contrast to that of Machado (who leads his reader to determine the pertinent decisions as to the text's theme, meaning, and significance), holds the reader in a state of suspended animation; it is his ornate style that makes the reader defer an interpretation of the events taken up in the text until the author's long compound-complex sentences finally congeal and come to life as an intricate web of suggestion and insinuation. In such works as *The Wings of the Dove*, *The Ambassadors*, and *The Golden Bowl*, his sentences, when read aloud, give ample evidence of the rhythm and euphony that we normally associate with poetry, which strongly supports the argument that James's best writing, like that of Machado, was substantially poetic in essence. The suspension of judgment on the part of the reader, who is swept along by an artfully modulated prose, comes, finally, to characterize James's personal attitude toward human existence, our consciousness of it, and the ability of our language to reproduce it.

As noted earlier, a shift in the focus of attention from one character to another, a process accompanied by an appropriate shift in the perspective established, is achieved by James in the use of a new third-person limited point of view. That he was able to achieve this constituted a major technical breakthrough for James and provided him with the freedom and flexibility he needed to create the kind of delicate, subtle psychological realism that, for him, represented the highest levels of the writer's art. In book 7, chapter 1, of *The Amabassadors*, for example, we see Strether develop about as far as he will go in terms of his efforts to understand the now restive and confused state of his own mind. We as readers believe that Strether's awareness of his situation, his consciousness of who he is and of what is happening around him, has here been stretched to its limit. Thanks to his new concern over style, James succeeds in balancing both temporally and spatially some diverse and even antithetical elements. He uses sentences that seem to become living parts of Strether's mind, which is presented to the reader as being in the process of psychic expansion. The climax of *The Ambassadors*, the scene in book 11, chapter 3, in which Strether, strolling about the French countryside and imagining it to be like a picture, suddenly seems actually to walk into and become part of the very picture he is describing to us, rests squarely on this same stylistic feature, on James's extraordinary ability to draw the character and the reader together in a single moment of psychological and emotional insight, a privileged moment of intense self-revelation.

Syntactically, the sentences that generate this "picture" are distinctive as well, for as he matured as a writer James increasingly rejected the use of simple, compound, and even complex sentences in favor of long compound-complex sentences. The progressiveness of this syntactical evolution becomes quite evident as one compares the work of James's three periods. Specifically, this pattern can be traced through *The American*, *The Portrait of a Lady*, and *The Golden Bowl*. In this final work, as in *The Ambassadors*, James's sentences are graceful yet elaborate, characterized by compound-complex constructions, numerous subordinate clauses, and qualifying phrases, by seemingly endless interpolations, and a steady use of two and even three modifiers for each noun and verb. In sum, Henry James's fictive world was marked by intellectual conversation, innuendo, irony, verbal interplay, and a flow of highly charged and deeply complex elliptical phrasings. Writing of the emotionally and intellectually tangled inner lives of refined and educated people, of what has been called the subjective accompaniment of a story rather than the story itself, James felt it necessary to develop a style of writing that would permit him to recreate as authentically as possible the half-tones, misdirections, and unspoken suggestions of human discourse.

But if James believed that in order to write about the nuances of human awareness he would have to create a style that could convey the extra-linguistic intricacies in which he was interested, we must note that Machado de Assis held a very different view about how this same goal might be achieved. Like James, Machado was committed to creating literary studies, or portraits, of the conflicting desires (including those of a sexual nature) and the obscure, unpredictable impulses of the human mind. Unlike James, however, Machado came more and more to believe that the complexities of this world could be more tellingly expressed by means of a style that became olympian in its serenity, syntactically clear, and classically direct in its expressiveness, even while generating a poststructural sense of instability, ambiguity, and unreliability in regard to its truth-telling ability. As is evident from much of his critical writing, Machado, too, was very much aware of the symbolic and arbitrary relationship that exists between language and reality. But he chose to rely upon relatively short, simple, compound, or, on occasion, complex sentences to give form to his own representation of reality, which, in a pre-Borgesian vein, he clearly understood as a verbal artifice, that is, as a self-contained and self-referential structure of art, the sociopolitical implications of which would be determined in the mind of the reader. So while James and Machado concentrated on essentially the same subject matter, their styles, or modes of expression, differed greatly. To appreciate more precisely why they differed is tantamount to realizing why Machado de Assis, even more than Henry James, made irony the dominant aspect of his last five great works.

But aside from the relative simplicity of Machado's style, and setting aside for the moment the differing treatment of irony demonstrated by these two writers, we must note the other eminent characteristic of Machado's style, its whimsicality, its breeziness, its supreme chattiness. Humor, in fact, can be said to be the one element present in virtually all of Machado's mature work. Moreover, the comic aspect of Machado's work can be seen in a wide range of forms—puns, satire, sarcasm, irony (of several stripes), parody, structural shenanigans, self-deprecating parody, and even burlesque. Henry James, on the other hand, is with one major exception more selectively funny; in his own favorite work, as Robert Spiller points out, a truly comic spirit controls the action from start to finish.[12] But while in *Dom Casmurro* an archness and an amiability permeate the telling of the story, these qualities are there to mask the tragedy implicit in Casmurro's version of his life story. More than in any of his other novels, with the possible exception of *Epitaph of a Small Winner*, Machado here makes full use of his considerable comic vision, even in chapter 54, "The Panegyric of Saint Monica," which is devoted to self-parody and in which Machado allows Casmurro to ridicule a poem which may have been written by Machado himself.[13] Other humorous elements brought into play in *Dom Casmurro* include chapter headings such as "Let's Proceed to the Chapter," "Let Us Enter the Chapter," "Shake Your Head, Reader," "Anterior to the Anterior," and "Well, and the Rest?," ludicrous characters, such as the Polonius-like José Dias, and numerous protestations to the reader about what she or he should think of the book Dom Casmurro is writing.

Overall, it can be said that while James's tone is periodically comic, though pervaded (as in the case of Machado) by an unmistakable but elusive sense of sadness or failure, Machado's tone is steadily comic, though often in an ironic fashion. Indeed, Machado actually uses humor to intensify the darker impact that he hoped his stories would have on his readers, the same alert and patient readers for whom James, like Machado, wrote his finest work, and who like James himself had to be among those people upon whom nothing is lost. And for Machado the attention-grabbing contrast between a light, humorous style and a somber, thought-provoking theme—the wasting of one's own life and the ruination of other lives through jealousy and selfishness—is nowhere better illustrated than in his trilogy, *Epitaph of a Small Winner, Philosopher or Dog?*, and *Dom Casmurro*, the acknowledged masterpieces of his late period.

Our final point of comparison between these two authors concerns their critical writings. Both James and Machado wrote extensively about fiction at the same time that they were creating it, and, in both cases, what they theorized about narrative came inevitably to appear in what they wrote. While their respective refinements of point of view offer a case in point, there are numerous other examples as well, including the questions of subject matter preferred, modes of characterization, and style. But aside from their affinity for putting into practice the theories they postulated about the craft of fiction, both James and Machado took a keen interest in the critical trends of their day and wrote what still rank as some of the most penetrating literary studies of the time, commenting incisively on the fiction of such diverse writers as Turgenev, Flaubert, Balzac, and Zola. So while James and Machado were deeply committed to new ways of crafting fiction, they were also thoroughly familiar with the debates on critical theory then raging in Europe and the Americas.

James, like Machado, was the first major author of his country to write both first-rate fiction and criticism. James, again like Machado, rejected the then-prevalent notion that authors were somehow obliged to put a clearly defined moral in their stories, to let the reader know exactly where the author stood in relation to the events depicted in the story. In refusing to play this role, James argued that only two relevant critical questions could be asked about a work of fiction: what is the author trying to do, and how well does she or he succeed in doing it (how skillful is the author)? Eschewing the need or even the desirability of a moral in his work, James asserted the primacy of a greater need, that of portraying the shifting states of human consciousness, which he defined in terms of both form and content, the ability to infer or intuit the unseen and unheard from the "seen" and "heard," to trace patterns of implication and influence.

In doing for American fiction what Emily Dickinson had done for American poetry,[14] that is, in shifting the ground for the novel away from the outer world and toward a contemplation of the inner world, James saw the need for the formulation of a new critical approach, one that would allow him to discuss the merits of the technique he would employ and the defects of the one he would replace. Thus in 1884 he wrote his famous essay "The Art of Fiction" as a response to comments made by the British critic Walter Besant, an advocate of popular and "realistic" standards for fiction. James, who had long decried the paucity of good American literary criticism in his day, asserted that the novel was the "most magnificent" literary art form (and that the single most important requirement of the novel is that the story be "interesting"), but also that the novelist should be perceptive, intelligent, and true to her or his personal vision of art.[15] James thereby made a sharply defined distinction between a realism of fact (content) and a realism of method (form), an approach to fiction writing that permitted him to write about what he felt was most compelling, the question of human consciousness and sensibility, and to do so in such a way as to intertwine indivisibly the form of his work with its content.

As evidenced in several of his critical essays, Machado de Assis likewise made a clearly defined distinction between realism as a way of apprehending life and realism as a mode of expression.[16] As Machado understood it, there was a great difference between "reality," which in its unfathomable power and mystery fascinated him, and "realism," which as a restrictive, superficial, and formulaic method he deplored as being too limited in its aesthetic possibilities (Borges would later make a similar point in two important essays, "The Postulation of Reality" and "Narrative Art and Magic"). This rather avant-garde theoretical orientation is clearly evident in each of Machado's novels, even those written during the allegedly romantic pre-1880 period. The originality and iconoclasm of Machado's creative mind would not allow his personal vision of life and art to be hampered by what he eventually came to feel was an outdated and unwarranted mode of expression, realism. Like James, Machado inveighed mightily against the conventional critical wisdom of the day and hoped to discover open-minded readers who would be receptive to the revolutionary things he was trying to do in his fiction. Unfortunately, though Machado was immensely successful in achieving the former, he was not so fortunate in terms of the latter; the absence of a sophisticated reading public and especially the dearth of perceptive, imaginative critics in the Brazil of the 1880s and 1890s explain in part why Machado was not fully appreciated until the final years of the century, when he began to receive the critical and popular acclaim he had deserved for so long.

As he often reiterated in his newspaper columns, for Machado de Assis, art, in literature, was everything; like Flaubert, Machado revered *le mot juste* and, like Henry James, he was a writer for whom technique was paramount in importance. While James regularly made forays into social and verbal intercourse in attempts to portray the ebb and flow of a carefully articulated human consciousness, Machado, bent on exploring deeper levels of the inner world, concentrated on creating psychological studies of human motivation, of the interplay of conscious and subconscious drives (including, like Freud, sexual ones) that compel us to act in ways that, seen by others after the fact, are both noble and base. As an artist Machado was captivated by what he considered the most striking characteristic of the human creature, our seemingly infinite capacity for contradictory and incompatible behavior and our rational capacity for self-deception. Driven by such problems of motivation and desire, Machado's fiction is possessed of a distinctly moral tone, even when draped in irony and self-conscious criticism. This moral tone is never preachy or tendentious, however; indeed, it is so thoroughly hidden behind the sardonic humor of his texts that one must consider it carefully before its function can be charted. Machado's cynicism is really that of the failed idealist, the man who loves life and human beings but who, in his stoic, honest view of life, cannot accept our tragic insistence on acting in ways that are an insult to our noble potential.

In an early statement of his critical theory in the preface to his first novel, *Resurrection*, Machado declares his intention not to write a novel of manners, a form he took to be both frivolous and spurious, but to sketch out a situation and allow the characters involved to develop in contrast to each other. And in the preface to Machado's second novel, published in 1873, we have an even more succinctly stated interest in exposing the inner drama of conflicting desires that motivates his characters, even early ones like Guiomar, the protagonist in *The Hand and the Glove*: "My portrayal of these characters—and, especially, of Guiomar—has been my main objective, if not my only one. The action serves as no more than a canvas upon which I could paint the figures in broad strokes." [17]

Then, in his 1878 critique of Eça de Queirós' *Cousin Basilio* (1878) and the school of French naturalism, Machado outlined his position on literary theory and criticism. As Machado envisioned it, the plot of a well-written novel must arise not out of forces exterior to the nature of the protagonist but from a conflict of ideas deep within, from the unceasing interplay between the will to do good and the compulsion to do evil. The plot of any novel that purports to tell the truth about the human experience must therefore derive from the complex nature of the characters involved. Not surprisingly, then, his chief objection to Zola and his imitators, who, along with their naturalistic doctrine of positivism, were immensely popular in Brazil during Machado's lifetime, was that naturalism was superficial and simplistic. It was odious not because it was occasionally lurid but because, as Machado and James both saw it, it was boring.

In *Machado de Assis* Caldwell argues that while Machado's fundamental concern about human existence may have been tragic in nature, Machado in the main chose comedy as his primary mode of expression. As noted earlier, Machado felt that he could actually enhance the serious thematic concerns of his work by utilizing a style that emphasized the way comedy and tragedy go hand in hand in the human experience. This delivery of an often tragic theme by means of an offhand, seemingly flippant style is most evident in the post-1880 stories and in *Epitaph of a Small Winner, Philosopher or Dog?*, and *Dom Casmurro*, in which the ironic union of form (comedy) and content (tragedy) is seen most convincingly to be wholly organic in nature.

These works are as far from the naturalistic novel and its tenets as the late James novels are.[18] Indeed, when we read James's insightful 1880 review of Zola's *Nana*, we discover that his primary reservation about this novel closely paralleled Machado's objection to naturalistic fiction. Interestingly, neither writer was bothered as much by the alleged prurience of naturalistic fiction like *Nana* as by the lack of the kind of inner motivation that James and especially Machado demanded in their main characters. For James and Machado, the "what" of life, lurid or not, was never as important as the "why," but the "why" had to be rooted within a character's own tangled personality. James, echoing Machado's objections to even the best of French naturalism, summarizes this objection: "It is not his choice of subject that has shocked us; it is the melancholy dryness of his execution, which gives us all the bad taste of a disagreeable dish and none of the nourishment."[19] Machado, in a remarkably similar vein, castigated the Portuguese naturalist Eça de Queirós for his clumsy handling of the character Luisa in his novel *Cousin Basilio* (which, Machado had earlier alleged, was plagiarized from Zola's *La faute de l'abbé Mouret*). Anticipating James and taking Eça and the entire naturalistic novel to task, Machado wrote:

> The beginning of her fall was such that no moral reason, no passion, sublime or base, no love, no spite and no perversion can explain it. . . . She simply wallows. . . . And what does the reader of the book feel about these two creatures, without will or feelings? Absolutely nothing.[20]

As is evident, both James and Machado were profoundly concerned with the process of characterization and how these characterizations would fit into the overall structure of the narratives in which they appear. And yet when in "The Art of Fiction" James asks, "What is character but the determination of incident? What is incident but the illustration of character?"[21] he is underscoring a fundamental critical distinction between James and Machado: while James was more interested in cultural situations and in the actions and reactions, often psychological, of his characters to these, Machado focused more intensely on the forces, conscious and unconscious, that control our inner being and cause us to do the things we do. James's characters are ultimately determined, therefore, in a social and/or psychosocial context, while the real drama of Machado's characters (who nevertheless do not lack a strong sociopolitical dimension) stems primarily from the intensely private, jealously guarded insularity of their own self-centered and contradictory natures.

It should be noted, finally, that the impact of Machado's critical writings on the craft of fiction writing in general and on the novel form in particular was, in Brazil, significantly less than was the case with Henry James in the United States. For Machado, there was no one of the stature of Ezra Pound to declare, as Pound did for James (in reference to the critical prefaces that James himself wrote late in life for a collected edition of his work), that the American stood alone in having written the one great treatise on the novel form that had, up to his time, been done in English. In *Ideas and the Novel* Mary McCarthy reinforces this influential critical evaluation of James, arguing that because of his style and choice of subject matter, James changed the novel's course of development as a literary genre.[22]

In Machado's case, however, the sociological and political novel dominated the literary scene in Brazil during the years following his death in 1908. With the exception of a few writers, like Oswald de Andrade (whose *Seraphim Grosse Pointe*, 1933, owes a considerable debt to Machado), it is only now, late in the twentieth century, that we are beginning to appreciate the technical breakthroughs achieved by this great Brazilian master, whose influence remains a potent force, both at home and abroad.[23] Taking note of Machado's metafictional texts, his trenchant wit, his biting irony, and his droll, laconic style, many readers, including the novelist John Barth, find Machado a surprisingly "modernist" and even "postmodernist" novelist and theoretician.[24] His work is a tailormade subject for the inquisitive student of comparative literature, and much more needs to be done on all aspects of it, including the challenging but rewarding problem of literary influences.

6

* * * * * * * * * *

The
Five
(Six?)
Faces
of
American
Modernism

As a literary period or movement, modernism stubbornly resists narrow definition. Chronologically, it encompasses roughly the years between 1890 and 1930, with the peak years coming just prior to World War I and in the early 1920s, especially from 1922 to 1924. While in literature modernism shows itself to be a type of writing that stresses formal experimentation, "shocking" new uses of language and imagery, and thematic concern over what was felt to be the despair, alienation, and disillusionment of a newly mechanized (and perhaps dehumanized) world, in painting and music it features the splintering effect of cubism and the nonharmonic scores of atonalism. Characterized by its preoccupation with consciousness, identity, and perception, the literature of modernism is less concerned with action and event in the external world than with the way a mind reflects on itself and on the universe surrounding it. Yet even though the basic perspective of such modernist classics as *Six Characters in Search of an Author* (1921), *Ulysses* (1922), *The Waste Land* (1922), and *The Magic Mountain* (1924) is private and even arcane, these works nevertheless possess a definite sociopolitical significance, a feature of modernism that becomes quite evident when one compares the diverse ways this enormously important movement evolved in the Americas.

American modernism is of two distinct varieties: in one, principally that of Spanish America and Brazil, there were the formally defined (though aesthetically distinct) movements bearing the generic title of "modernismo," while in the other, as we see in Canada and the United States, there were many "modernist" writers and texts but no official movement of the same designation. Modernismo, then, existed as a definite and well-documented literary movement in both Spanish America and Brazil, though, as we shall see, the term refers to something very different in each case.

In Spanish America, moreover, there were really two modernisms, the better-known one centering around the work of the Nicaraguan poet Rubén Darío and running from approximately 1888 (and the publication of Darío's *Azul*) to around 1916. The other Spanish American modernism, sometimes loosely termed "vanguardismo," or vanguardism, runs from about 1916 to the early 1930s and includes the early work of some of twentieth-century Spanish America's most important writers, such as Vicente Huidobro, Pablo Neruda, Jorge Luis Borges, Alejo Carpentier, César Vallejo, and Miguel Angel Asturias. Two other important poets, Leopoldo Lugones and Julio Herrera y Reissig, may be considered transition figures whose best works (Lugones' *Lunario sentimental*, 1909, and Herrera y Reissig's "La torre de las esfinges," 1909) are decisive precursors of the later vanguardist poetry.

Brazilian modernism, which must be clearly distinguished from its Spanish American counterparts, dates from 1922 to around World War II and shows a very definite chronological and aesthetic evolution, one that from the outset was not only theoretically oriented but socially conscious and formally innovative as well. Indeed, one of the unique features of Brazilian modernism is that it strove consciously to develop nationalistic themes and types while at the same time utilizing imported formal influences, such as cubism in painting, nationalism (and atonalism) in music, free verse in poetry, and stream-of-consciousness subject matter in narrative. Artists like Mário de Andrade, Oswald de Andrade, Heitor Villa-Lobos, and Anita Malfatti were attempting to forge their own brand of modernism, one that was technically avant-garde in an international sense but nevertheless intensely nationalistic in terms of its themes, characters, and motifs.

In contrast to what are really the three established modernismos of Spanish America and Brazil, there is the second type of American modernism, in which there exists a group or generation of innovative writers reflecting an amorphous, iconoclastic set of artistic attitudes and styles but no clear-cut literary movement. This is the situation of modernism as it existed in English and French Canada (where further distinctions must be made) and in the United States.

In sum, then, there were really six modernist or modernistically inclined movements in the Americas: one each (with different levels of development) for English and French Canada, the United States, and Brazil and two for Spanish America. Though these movements are not closely related, they do, as we shall now see, possess a number of features in common.

Like Spanish American modernism, the modernism of English Canada has two subdivisions, one an early or pioneering modernism and the other a later, more sophisticated variety. The early English Canadian modernists like Arthur Stringer, Raymond Knister, W. W. E. Ross, and Dorothy Livesay evinced a strong sense of nationalism in what was often formally experimental work. Their modernistic Canadianism thus parallels quite closely what was happening in Brazil. The later English Canadian modernists, closely associated with the so-called Montreal Group, include such luminaries of modern Canadian literature as A. J. M. Smith, Leo Kennedy, A. M. Klein, and F. R. Scott. If the early English Canadian modernists can be characterized by a general preference for Canadian themes and types, the writers of the Montreal Group are much more cosmopolitan and urbane, in both their outlook and their thematics. Both groups, however, recognized the need to revivify English Canadian letters, a task they hoped to accomplish by combining certain foreign influences, especially imagism, free verse, and cubism, with native material. The result, in English Canada and Brazil, was the creation of a new kind of writing that authenticated the literatures of Brazil and English Canada not as secondary, derivative national literatures but as full-fledged members of the Western literary community.

For French Canada, the question of modernism is somewhat more complex. Chronologically, the formal rebelliousness and thematic irreverence that we associate with this movement did not appear on any extensive scale until the 1960s, when both French Canadian literature and culture underwent a series of profound and often violent changes. Aesthetically, however, the seeds of a new literature had been sown as early as 1898 when, with poems like "Moines en défilade," Emile Nelligan began to participate in the "Ecole Littéraire de Montréal," which promoted new trends in literature during the early years of the twentieth century. Although Nelligan was not a radical innovator of poetic forms, his language and his images were singularly new, and it is here that his importance lies. Combining the formal perfection of the parnassians with the evocative power of the symbolists as Darío had done a few years earlier, Nelligan established himself as French Canada's first great poet.

In comparison to English Canada, it is clear that French Canada was much less concerned with following the new literature that was appearing in such twentieth-century literary centers as Paris, London, Berlin, and New York. Of all the American cultures, in fact, the modernism of French Canada seems the least revolutionary. Indeed, save for Nelligan, Paul Morin, Robert Choquette, and Hector de Saint-Denys-Garneau, modernism as a viable movement can hardly be said to have existed at all in the French Canada of the early twentieth century. When in the 1960s the revolt against provincialism and orthodoxy did occur, it did so with a vengeance, however. One could thus argue that the real flowering of French Canadian modernism is best studied as a cultural and artistic phenomenon of the 1960s and 1970s, even though its roots are in the first two or three decades of the twentieth century.

The final American culture to be discussed in terms of this second variety of American modernism is the United States. Like that of its neighbors to the north, the literary history of the United States does not show a movement or period known as modernism. Nevertheless, between 1900 and 1930 the United States produced a number of distinctly modernistic writers, a few of whom, T. S. Eliot, William Faulkner, Gertrude Stein, and the earlier Walt Whitman, for example, would become greatly influential within the intensely international movement that modernism rapidly became. The "new" poetry in the United States is often said to date from 1912 and the appearance of Harriet Monroe's magazine, *Poetry: A Magazine of Verse*, or from 1915 and the appearance (in *Poetry*) of Eliot's "Love Song of J. Alfred Prufrock," a poem that did for modernism something akin to what Wordsworth's *Lyrical Ballads* had done for European romanticism. Like their counterparts in Spanish America, Brazil, and Canada, the early modernists of the United States sought a new poetic language, one which would be thoroughly "American" and, free from the artificial conventionality of "proper poetry," could become colloquial, direct, and full of unusual, concrete, often mechanistic images. With this in mind, Ezra Pound, Hilda Doolittle, and others formed around 1912 a new school of poetry, Imagism, which though rather short-lived had considerable influence in the United States and in Canada, where it attracted the attention of such early modernists as Dorothy Livesay and Raymond Knister.

The modernist poetry of writers like Pound and Eliot was, however, substantially different from the modernism of Carl Sandburg, William Carlos Williams, Vachel Lindsay, Robert Frost, and E. A. Robinson, poets who also stressed the essential Americanism, linguistic and thematic, of their work. In contrast to these writers, who emphasized the American landscape, language, and questions of social, ethical, and historical significance, Pound and Eliot began to develop a second kind of "new" poetry for the United States, one that, as we can see in Pound's *Cantos* or in Eliot's *Waste Land*, is distinctly international rather than national in its focus, tone, diction, and allusions.

This dualism parallels similar developments in English Canada and Brazil, where, ironically, the forces of change that characterize modernism everywhere were used to discover and nurture nationalistic issues. The same can be seen to apply to the modernismo of Rubén Darío and his followers in Spanish America. While Darío's modernism was essentially an amalgam of the best features of parnassianism and symbolism, he, like Emile Nelligan, broke new ground, especially with the strikingly original images and themes he developed. Darío, however, even more than Nelligan, succeeded in establishing once and for all the linguistic validity of Spanish America, a struggle also undertaken by many other American writers, such as Mário de Andrade, Frost, Robinson, Williams, Sandburg, William Faulkner, Knister, Stringer, and Livesay.

Beyond the validation of "American" Spanish that Darío's modernism achieved, however, was another important development: the open advocacy of a strong and vigorous New Worldism,[1] a sense of life, in both its positive and negative aspects, as it was lived in the New World. Besides Darío, other promoters of this recognition of New World existence include Peru's José Santos Chocano and Uruguay's José Enrique Rodó, whose *Ariel* (1900) contrasts the essential virtues of Spanish American culture with those of the United States. A similar strain of New Worldism can be seen in the work of the French Canadian poet Robert Choquette, whose *Metropolitan Museum* (1931) in particular generates its own unique sense of Americanism. Robinson, Frost, Williams, Lindsay, and Sandburg also joined with other New World artists and thinkers in wanting to call attention to the nature of that experience.

The two-fold development of modernism in the United States also parallels the Brazilian and Canadian experience in that while both cultures produced their own brands of Americanism (or New Worldism), they also generated a kind of modernism that is consciously international, one that rejects what were then construed as the too-narrow boundaries of literary nationalism. In the United States, as we have seen, this latter type of modernism is best exemplified in the work of writers like Pound and Eliot, while in Canada it appears in the work of the Montreal Group and writers Kennedy, Smith, and Klein, who wanted to establish the validity of Canadian literature by internationalizing it.

In summary, then, one can say that regardless of the degree to which it existed as an officially defined movement or period, New World modernism is unified by three common features. First, having benefited materially and commercially from the same war that had been so cataclysmic for the Europeans, the cultures of the New World tended to view modernism in terms more of cultural progress and development than cultural devastation. Increased material prosperity and a new adoration of machines and technology led to a cultivation of new poetic images and diction and to a sense that the future was, on balance, full of promise. This tendency was more pronounced in the work of the nationalistic modernists than in that of the internationalists, however, whose artistic and philosophical orientation often led them back to an Old World wracked by the Great War. The material prosperity of the 1920s led throughout the Americas not only to a new literature and art but to a new and elevated status for them among the established literary cultures. With so many New World writers like Wyndham Lewis, Gertrude Stein, Ernest Hemingway, Huidobro, Borges, Malfatti, and Oswald de Andrade living and working among the European avant-garde, the new ideas about literature and art were very quickly transplanted to American soil, the result of which was to achieve a greater international recognition of New World art than had hitherto been the case.

A second common characteristic of New World modernism is typified in Ezra Pound's dictum that artists of his time had "to make it new," a belief that seemed to justify precisely what the several New World cultures had been doing for hundreds of years, that is, forging new identities. It is in this context especially that the need for an authentic American language was felt most acutely.[2] New languages, which would generate the new images and convey the new themes, were sorely needed to express the realities of the rapidly evolving American experience, one that looked both backward and forward and that was suddenly possessed of both national and international perspectives. As an international phenomenon, literary modernism came at a favorable moment for the Americas, which after World War I stood ready to assert themselves on many different fronts. Culturally and artistically, the time was right "to make it new," and the American modernists, recognizing the propitiousness of the moment, forged ahead.

The third common feature of American modernism is its distinctive sociological dimension, its special political consciousness. While it may be true that the American modernists were not as overtly political as some European modernists were (Thomas Mann, for example), it would be absurd to think that works like the anthology *New Provinces*, Pound's *Cantos*, Eliot's *Waste Land*, Huidobro's *Altazor*, and Andrade's *Hallucinated City* lacked social relevance. Throughout the Americas, from the work of the Montreal Group to that of the Spanish American vanguardists, there was a strong affirmation of cultural identity, a sense that newness was not only acceptable but necessary. Additionally, there was a recognition that daring modernist literature, like that of the later Livesay, Klein, Nicanor Parra, Alfonsina Storni, Vallejo, Neruda, Andrade, Stein, and Eliot, could be politically aware as well as aesthetically valid. This entwining of modernist art and politics would have far-reaching implications.

One of the most interesting of the early American modernists is Emile Nelligan, who, in his passion for melodic and synesthetic verse, represents for French Canadian poetry what Rubén Darío represents to Spanish American poetry. Nelligan, a true *poète maudit* who introduced French parnassianism and symbolism into the staid corpus of French Canadian literature, is best considered as a transition writer, similar in this respect to Rimbaud or Baudelaire. Much of Nelligan's work represents a definite break with the kind of literature that preceded him in French Canada, but it cannot be considered fully modernist in spirit and form. Rather, in poems like "La passante," "Rêve d'artiste," "Beauté cruelle," "Mon âme," "Un poète," "Gretchen la pâle," "La vierge noire," "Musiques funèbres," "Les corbeaux," "La romance du vin," and "Le vaisseau d'or," Nelligan shows himself to be essentially a symbolist in the tradition of Verlaine, Mallarmé, Musset, and Poe, yet sensitive to the new developments in language use, form, and theme.

Dedicated to what we might call the craft of poetry rather than to the evocation of exclusively Canadian themes and forms, Nelligan proved that French Canadian poetry did not have to be narrowly provincial or rigidly orthodox to be good. Indeed, Nelligan can be regarded as something of a radical in that he successfully challenged the established critical concepts of "proper" French Canadian poetry. Some of his poems, like "Rêve d'artiste," "Mon âme," and "Un poète," are symbolist in theme while attaining a parnassianlike perfection of form and image. Others, like "Musiques funèbres" and "Les corbeaux," show a striking new use of almost hallucinatory imagery, a kind of poetic creativeness that suggests surrealism, a later-developing movement of central importance to the modernists. "Les corbeaux" ("The Ravens"), a despairing sonnet that like "Musiques funèbres" seems to express Nelligan's own rapidly disintegrating sense of self, is dominated by surrealistic images of a wastelandlike soul, the futility of the artist's endeavor in a crass world, and the violent destruction of a sensitive human consciousness:

> In my heart I thought I saw a host of ravens
> Invading a secret wasteland with their dismal flights,
> Noble ravens who came from celebrated mountains
> And were passing by moonlight and torchlights.
>
> Mournfully, like hovering in circles above graves
> And then detecting a feast of zebra carcasses,
> They were soaring to the cold shudder of my bones,
> Tearing my flesh into morsels with their beaks.
>
> .　　.　　.　　.　　.　　.　　.　　.　　.
>
> Chaotically, with thrusts of their beaks piercing
> My soul, a mutilated carrion that in the matter of days,
> These old ravens will devour completely.[3]

Nelligan's best work, which includes "Rêve d'artiste," "La passante," "Beauté cruelle," and "Le vaisseau d'or," shows, as with Darío, a continuing effort to perfect harmony and form while simultaneously creating original images that had not been seen before in French Canadian poetry. Modernistic in its intense subjectivity and its focus on the anguished psychology of the artist who must live and work within a stultified and stultifying social setting, Nelligan's pioneering poetry paves the way for later, more radical experimentation in form and structure, language and imagery, and thematics.

One of the most important of these later French Canadian modernists is Robert Choquette, whose lyrical yet epical "hymne à la civilisation américaine,"[4] *Metropolitan Museum*, ranks as one of the high points of French Canadian modernism. For some four hundred Alexandrine and free-verse lines, Choquette, recasting Eliot's "mythic method," panoramically contrasts disillusioned twentieth-century existence with that of earlier ages. Choquette's setting in *Metropolitan Museum* is the modern city, whose shapes and forms underscore modern humankind's disillusioned spirit. "Je suis l'Homme Moderne," he writes at the beginning of his poem, "aux villes jusqu'aux nues!"[5] Then, invoking the standard images of high modernism, those of crass materialism, technology, the wasteland, exile, isolation, and the self-conscious artist, Choquette ends his poem as Eliot ends *The Waste Land*, by asking how worthy our twentieth-century society can be if we, as youthful Americans, fail to regenerate the impoverished spirit of our age.

A third French Canadian modernist, credited by the French critic Samuel de Sacy with having initiated modern poetry in French Canada,[6] is Hector de Saint-Denys-Garneau, the poems of whose "Esquisses en plein air" (1935) are often original in form as well as theme. Frequently working like Huidobro, without periods and commas, and reproached as Eliot was with "The Love Song of J. Alfred Prufrock" for not having written "poetry" at all,[7] Saint-Denys-Garneau was especially innovative in his forms, images, and symbols. He openly challenged the orthodoxy of French Canadian poetry by radically alternating his line lengths and, like Choquette, by mixing classical alexandrines with lines of a single word. This deliberate departure from standard poetic form and structuring was not undertaken for cosmetic effect, however. Saint-Denys-Garneau, a modernist in spirit as well as form, was seeking to revivify his language, to create new images for a new time, and to control them (and through them the emotion and tone of the poem) through such free-verse functions as line length, disrupted rhythm patterns, syntax, and stanza structure. One experiences this new and imagistic approach to poetic structuring in such works as "Bird Cage" and "Willows," poems of precisely the kind of symbiotic integration of meaning, rhythm, and structure that we always associate with good modernist poetry.[8]

Another modernistic aspect of Saint-Denys-Garneau's work is its affrontery—what Irving Howe calls the "shocking" or "perverse" quality characteristic of modernist art.[9] Intensely cultural in its context, this "shocking" dimension is the driving force in "Il nous est arrivé des aventures":

Arse-kissers, bootlickers, bowers and scrapers,
Who renounce longwindedly and with perfect composure,
Having nothing to renounce.

This is a country of little creatures to be stepped on
You cannot see them because they're dead
But you'd like to boot them in the bum
And see them underground for the sake of the beauty of unpeopled space.[10]

Reminiscent of Mário de Andrade's *Hallucinated City* (in particular, "Ode to the Bourgeois Gentleman") and Eliot's "The Hollow Men," this poem clearly expresses the merging of sociopolitical awareness, thematic iconoclasm, and technical innovation that typifies modernism in the Americas.

A final feature of Saint-Denys-Garneau's poetry is its occasional coupling of an intense poetic self-consciousness with an equally intense metacritical stance. "Each and All" manifests these characteristics quite vividly:

> Each and all, all and each, interchangeable things
> A pair of words
> Symbols
> Of the unutterable identity
> Where the whole poem can assume the light
>
> .   .   .   .
>
> Each and all reversible
> And often I could do nothing for this alteration
> But couple you together.[11]

We see here the inventive alternation of line length and the gradual focusing of the reader's attention on a single, unadorned image, often expressed in only a word or two. Active here, too, is what might now be regarded as a poststructuralist concern over the arbitrary and unstable relationship between language and human identity, between reality and language, and between the writer, the reader, and the meaning of a text.

Though one hesitates to call Saint-Denys-Garneau a great poet, there can be no doubt that he was a powerful revitalizing force within the isolated, parochial world of French Canadian literature. Technically and, to a lesser degree, thematically, Saint-Denys-Garneau can rightly be regarded as the modernist emancipator of French Canadian verse.

A similar liberation of English Canadian literature had been under way for several years. Although by the mid to late 1920s the leading members of the cosmopolitan Montreal Group, Smith, Scott, Kennedy, and Klein, had determined "to create a Canadian literature worthy of comparison with the new literature emanating from abroad,"[12] these writers nevertheless effected a new literary nationalism. Paralleling what happened in Brazil, this new impulse tended (as in Smith's poem "Lonely Land") to merge more traditional kinds of nationalism with the new international forms used so effectively by artists like Pound, Eliot, and James Joyce.

The political dimension of English Canadian modernism is also clearly evident in the writers of the Montreal Group, who, after 1929 and the advent of the Great Depression, began to write material that was more openly critical of the abuses and injustices of the capitalist system. This late-1920s literature, however, sometimes lacked the formal experimentation and daring use of language that we associate with high modernism. One concludes, therefore, that as a technically and thematically renovating force English Canadian modernism had a relatively long life, from the publication of Arthur Stringer's early attempts to cultivate free verse through the 1930s and into the 1940s and 1950s, at least insofar as the influences of the Montreal Group were concerned.

As Munroe Beattie has noted, Stringer's landmark volume of verse (*Open Water*, 1914) included a preface that amounts to a manifesto of English Canadian modernism.[13] Arguing that the new English Canadian poet must express the attitudes of a new age, Stringer said that this could be done only by rejecting the exhausted and outmoded themes and forms of the past. A new language was needed also to reflect what was most uniquely Canadian about the poem's characters and their Canadian identity. Yet despite Stringer's admirable attempt to create a new poetry for English Canada, many of the sixty poems of *Open Water* fall short of generating the kind of unity, rhythm, and impetus essential to good free verse.[14]

An English Canadian poet of the modernist era who was a more successful practitioner of free verse was Raymond Knister. Closely attentive to then-current avant-garde poetics, Knister united formal imagination (often, as in "The Hawk," in the imagist tradition of Ezra Pound and Amy Lowell) with scenes of farm life in Ontario. The result was poetry that successfully combined the technical experimentation of modernism with subject matter that was at once intensely Canadian and universal. Full of spare, often stark imagery and characterized by an unadorned diction, poems like "Quiet Snow," "Snowfall," "The Hawk," and "The Plowman" come alive for the reader with a maximum of economy and clarity. The effect of Knister's best poems, as with Williams's "The Red Wheelbarrow" or Pound's "In a Station at the Metro," is to focus intensely on a single image and thereby generate a mood or evoke a particular sensation. In "The Hawk," for example, Knister writes a twelve-line free-verse poem that, without directly mentioning it, describes a hawk seen soaring against the vastness of the open sky:

> Across the bristled and sallow fields,
> The speckled stubble of cut clover,
> Wades your shadow.
>
> Or against a grimy and tattered
> Sky
> You plunge.[15]

Another of Knister's poems, "The Motor: A Fragment," focuses on the image of a single car roaring down a deserted country road. The car, itself a powerful symbol of the mechanization of modern life, is depicted in futuristic images of speed and power that stand in stark contrast to those of the countryside:

> Down, down the slope,
> To flow in effortless speed,
> To break, to slacken,
> Leashed power that gives me joy.
>
> .　　.　　.　　.　　.　　.　　.
>
> Past the huge wheat-fields
> Dry-smelling and toasting.
> Up the long hill in a burst
> Of splendid speed,
> Unleashed power, that gives me joy.[16]

Although, as with "The Plowman," "Peach Buds," "The Colt," and "The Hawk," many of Knister's best efforts have a rural setting, he also wrote several first-rate poems with an urban setting. "On a Skyscraper," for example, mixes images of darkness, death, and hunger, linking the modern urban condition to discontent and disillusionment and imbuing the poem with a subtle social dimension.

A final poet who represents early English Canadian modernism is Dorothy Livesay, who like Knister was significantly influenced by the imagists. Her 1928 collection, *Green Pitcher*, contains several short, powerful poems that evoke the direct, concrete sense of experience that the imagists prized so highly. Of these "Autumn," "Reality," "Such Silence," and "Fire and Reason" are particularly striking. Later imagist poems, like "In the Street" and "Green Rain" (both from *Signpost*, 1932), show an elevated level of sophistication, while other selections from this same collection, "Blindness," "Perversity," and "The Difference," for example, express a powerful sense of female sexuality.

"Reality," one of Livesay's most concentrated poems, is also a vivid example of the new Canadian poetry of the 1920s:

> Encased in the hard, bright shell of my dream,
> How sudden now to wake
> And find . . .
> The wind still crying in the naked trees,
> Myself alone, within a narrow bed.[17]

Written with a similar economy of style and simplicity is "Fire and Reason," one of Livesay's most anthologized pieces:

> I cannot shut out the night—
> Nor its sharp clarity.
>
> The many blinds we draw,
> You and I,
> The many fires we light
> Can never quite obliterate
>
> .　.　.　.　.　.
>
> The last, unsolved finality
> Of night.[18]

While "Reality" expresses through its spare imagery the acute self-consciousness, internalization, and isolation we associate with modernist poetry, "Fire and Reason," through its splintering of lines and stanzas into separate images, reflects modernism's concern for the multiple and often paradoxical dimensions of human existence.

An even more decisive and definitive break from Canada's poetic provincialism would come in 1936 with the publication of *New Provinces*, a collection of poems by A. J. M. Smith, F. R. Scott, E. J. Pratt, A. M. Klein, Leo Kennedy, and Robert Finch. These poets, who collectively constituted the Montreal Group (which, by 1936, had established itself as Canada's avant-garde), disparaged the nationalism of the earlier modernists and championed what they considered to be a necessary and entirely healthy internationalization of Canadian literature. As A. J. M. Smith, the nominal leader of the group, suggested in a letter to F. R. Scott, modern Canadian literature had to be conscious of its position in time as well as in space, be aware of new developments in poetry in other countries, be receptive to new kinds of poetic material, language, and images, and recognize that it did not have to be nationalistic to be good.[19]

The iconoclastic tone of Smith's 1936 "rejected preface," which in its contentiousness is similar to Mário de Andrade's preface to *Hallucinated City*, underscores the position of the Montreal Group toward the Canadian poetry that had been written before their time, a poetry, according to Smith, characterized by the themes of love ("idealized, sanctified, and inflated") and nature ("humanized, endowed with feeling and made sentimental").[20] Smith said that in general Canadian poetry tended toward rhymes that, while "definite" and "mechanically correct," were also "obvious" and "commonplace."[21] Worst of

all, charged Smith, Canadian poetry had been long characterized by a preference for form over content and by a fatal lack of the intellectual seriousness and
complexity that are the earmarks of good poetry everywhere. As Smith and the
other members of the Montreal Group (including the Toronto poets E. J. Pratt
and Robert Finch) saw it, it was their duty to change all this. To a great extent
they succeeded, and one can justifiably argue that *New Provinces* ushered in a
new age for Canadian poetry, paralleled in Brazil by Andrade's *Hallucinated
City* (1922), in the United States by Eliot's "Love Song of J. Alfred Prufrock"
(1915), in French Canada by Saint-Denys-Garneau's "Esquisses en plein air"
(1935), and in Spanish America by Huidobro's *El espejo de agua* (1916).

Several of the poems in *New Provinces*, such as "The Lonely Land," "The
Creek," "News of the Phoenix," and "Trees in Ice," became models of what
English Canadian modernism would be like. Scott's "Trees in Ice" (which, like
some of the work of Saint-Denys-Garneau, Huidobro, and e. e. cummings, eschews orthodox capitalization and punctuation) shows clearly his provocative
experimentation with poetic structuring, diction, and imagery:

> lean fingers of black ice
> steal the sun's drawn fire
> to make a burning of a barren bush
>
> underneath
>   from
>   still
>   branch
>   and
>   arm
>   flakes
>   of
>   light
>   fall
>   fall
>   fleck-
>   ing
>   the
>   dark
>   white
>   snow[22]

Scott's poem, unmistakably modernistic in form, language, and perspective, also calls for alternate readings, one along a "normal" or horizontal axis, the other along a vertical axis. The images themselves, presented in isolation, shorn of all sentimentalism yet linked to form a controlling image (of ice-covered trees), impart to the poem a fragmented spatial quality that parallels Picasso's cubist experiments and Stravinsky's atonal *Le sacre du printemps*.

Written in a similar vein is Smith's "The Creek":

> Stones
> still wet with cold black earth,
> roots, whips of roots
> and wisps of straw,
> green soaked crushed leaves
> mud-soiled where hoof has touched them,
> twisted grass
> and hairs of herbs
> that lip the ledge of the stream's edge.[23]

Working as if from the modernist premise set forth by Archibald MacLeish ("Ars Poetica") that "a poem should not mean / But be," Smith describes "The Creek" as an example of imagist poetry, as an objective and impersonal art form that exists by and for itself, "unconcerned with anything save its own existence."[24] The modernist breakthrough achieved by *New Provinces* would, especially in the case of Smith, exert a profound influence on generations of English Canadian poets. In doing so, this seminal work highlights a pattern of development that parallels the evolution of modernism in the other American cultures.

One of these cultures, the United States, is like Canada in that while it does not possess a definite literary period known as "modernism," it very definitely does possess modernist writers, some of whom, Stein, Pound, Faulkner, Hemingway, and Eliot, for example, would become major international figures. The influence of Eliot's poem *The Waste Land* was pervasive, its central image of the sterile wasteland coming to epitomize what artists in many lands felt about "modern" (that is, post–World War I) existence. *The Waste Land* was profoundly concerned with social conditions, including ethical questions, but these were only indirectly discernible, submerged in a complex web of allusions, ironies, and interlocking levels of interpretation. When, at the end, the narrator of the poem declares, "I sat upon the shore / Fishing, with the arid plain behind me / Shall I at least set my lands in order?" the reader clearly hears the poem's call for a new awareness linking the need for individual moral action with social good.

Pillars of high modernism in the Western tradition, *The Waste Land* and Pound's *Cantos* represent for the United States the kind of literary internationalization that we see in *New Provinces* and the Montreal Group. In both English Canada and the United States there are, in spirit if not in literary history, two modernist movements, then: one basically nationalistic, stressing language, regions, landscapes, and types; the other basically international, stressing universal themes, motifs, and myths.

This same basic dialectic, moreover, is characteristic of modernism's development throughout the Americas, whether it be in French Canada (where it can be seen in the evolution from Nelligan to Saint-Denys-Garneau), in Spanish America (where it moves from Darío to Huidobro to Borges), or in Brazil (where it can be said to range from Malfatti and Oswald de Andrade to the "Tropicalismo" popular music movement of the 1970s and 1980s). Brazil, however, is unique among the five American cultures studied here in the degree that it strove, creatively and theoretically, to integrate the national impulse with the international. Similar attempts were made by individual poets in the United States, like Hart Crane (*The Bridge*) and William Carlos Williams (*Paterson*), but nowhere was the attempt at union quite so pervasive or so successful as it was in Brazil. In the United States, then, the two strains of modernism remained essentially separate, with the nationalistically inclined writers like Robinson, Williams, Frost, Vachel Lindsay, and Sandburg at one end of the spectrum and the internationalists like Pound, Stein, and Eliot at the other.

But if the new poetry of the United States dates from the years between 1912 (when Harriet Monroe began to publish *Poetry: A Magazine of Verse*) and 1915 (when *Poetry* published Eliot's "Love Song of J. Alfred Prufrock"), the new narrative must surely date from 1909 and the publication of Gertrude Stein's *Three Lives*. Undertaking radical experiments with the writing of prose fiction, Stein linked William James's theories on mental "flow," or "stream of consciousness," with new ideas about "automatic writing," fragmented syntax, and "primitive" psychology (à la Picasso) to produce a very different kind of narrative; as in *Three Lives*, the metaphoric *Tender Buttons* (1914), and the more metonymic *The Making of Americans* (1924), this narrative was basically nonrepresentational and strove to achieve what Stein herself called a "continuous present."

Composed of three stories, *Three Lives* is characterized by a precise prose that emphasizes the present participle, eschews descriptions of background and setting, and disrupts the normative patterns of grammar and syntax. Utilizing a simple vocabulary, Stein tries to make the language of her text a reflection of the process of consciousness itself. Influenced possibly by Picasso's landmark painting *Les Demoiselles d'Avignon* (1907), *Three Lives* ushered in a new kind of fiction writing.

The second story in *Three Lives*, "Melanctha," focuses on the inner life and gradual self-discovery of a young black woman. Unconventional in its structuring, style, and subject matter, "Melanctha" may also have been the first literary work from the United States to deal with a black character without condescension or derision.[25] The story of Melanctha Herbert and her love affair with Jeff Campbell broke new ground with its subject matter, its form, and its style:

> Jeff Campbell was so angry now in him, because he had begged Melanctha always to be honest to him. Jeff could stand it in her not to love him, he could not stand it in her not to be honest to him.
>
> Jeff Campbell went home from where Melanctha had not met him, and he was sore and full of anger in him.[26]

Using unsophisticated diction, repetition, unconventional punctuation, and jumbled syntax, Stein tries to reproduce the ebb and flow of an unlettered mind. By setting her two main characters in an explosive social environment where sexism, racism, and issues of sexuality pose problems, Stein also achieves the dual perspective characteristic of modernist literature: its sense of the mental self existing simultaneously in both inner (or psychological) and outer (or social) contexts.

In a later work, *Tender Buttons*, Stein undertakes even more radical experiments with her prose. Indeed, in terms of narrative theory, the gulf that separates *Three Lives* and *Tender Buttons* is considerable. Whereas the earlier work, for all of its considerable innovativeness, remained recognizably novelistic in its presentation of a story, the later work, more metaphoric, transforms itself into poetry. As David Lodge suggests, parts of *Tender Buttons* read like surrealist lyrics or dadaist "word heaps."[27] Stein's evolution from *Three Lives* to *Tender Buttons* illustrates what Roman Jakobson had in mind when he suggests that the metonymic is closer to prose, which forwards itself largely by means of contiguity, while the metaphoric, which stresses similarity and substitution, hews closer to poetry.[28] Arguing that a fundamental stylistic feature of modernist prose is its calculated merging of the metonymic and metaphoric modes of expression, Lodge cites Stein's work as exemplary of the shift away from the "old" writing and toward the "new," "poetic," or "modernistic."[29] As we see in "Sausages," "Butter," and "Celery," it is through the free association of images

which generate, react to, and substitute for one another and the selective breaking of lines into single images and clusters of images that Stein forces the
reader to "see" (and thereby "understand") things in new and different ways.

Phenomenological in their interaction with the reader, the fluid, cubist collage texts of *Tender Buttons* take on a new and self-sustaining objectivity at the
same time that they require the reader to recognize the process of becoming
newly aware of objects in the world. With *Tender Buttons*, Stein brings to a climax her efforts to establish the double narrative perspective—a mind simultaneously conscious of its own arcane self-reflection and its place in the outer
world of "things"—that she had begun to experiment with in *Three Lives*.

Among the many New World artists who, like Stein, came to Europe in the
early decades of the twentieth century to write, paint, and study was the Chilean
poet Vicente Huidobro. Huidobro, "the first Latin American to play an active
role in the French avant-garde,"[30] traveled to Paris in 1916 and quickly made
the acquaintance of Pierre Reverdy, the editor of the influential avant-garde
journal *Nord-Sud*. While in Europe Huidobro also came to know Robert
Delaunay, Hans Arp, Jacques Lipchitz, Fernand Léger, Juan Gris, and Pablo
Picasso, who eventually painted Huidobro's portrait. Like Apollinaire, with
whom he also worked on *Nord-Sud*, Huidobro began to experiment with formally unusual poems, works that Apollinaire would later call *calligrammes*.
Often writing in a fractured French (which, according to Huidobro, lent a certain "charm" to his compositions), Huidobro called these early works painted-
poems. Visually striking, painted-poems like "Tour Eiffel," "Marine," "Un
astre a perdu son chemin," and "Moulin" deliberately challenged the reader to
decipher their several levels of meaning. Anticipating the work of the con-
cretists, a poem like "Moulin," for example, underscores its "meaning" with its
form; that is, the form of the poem—that of a mill—parallels the ordinary de-
notations of the poem's key word, *moulin*, or mill. Existing both spatially and
temporally, poems like "Téléphone," "Moulin," and "Tour Eiffel" come alive
for the reader in ways that were tantamount to a declaration of war against orthodox or bourgeois notions of what was properly poetic and what was not.

Huidobro, like Ezra Pound, had an urgent sense of the need for artists of his
time to "make it new," to create what had never existed before, and in "Ars
poetica," included in *El espejo de agua* (1916), he made specific his concepts of
the new poetry and the new poet:

> Let poetry be like a key
> Opening a thousand doors.

. . . . .

Invent new worlds and watch your word;
The adjective, when it doesn't give life, kills it.

. . . .

The poet is a little God.[31]

Embodying Huidobro's theory of "creationism," the not altogether novel idea that words themselves bring realities into being (it recalls the Pre-Columbian concept of the word), "Ars poetica" also demonstrates the self-sufficiency of the modernist work of art as well as its stress on newness and originality, the use of spare and unadorned language, and the simultaneity that artists like Picasso, Marcel Duchamp, Virginia Woolf, and Joyce saw as most accurately reflecting the fragmented, discontented, and interiorized modern world.

Although several of Huidobro's early poems are fine examples of modernism's enthusiasm for formal innovation and striking imagery, *Altazor: Or the Parachute Voyage*, published in 1931, remains his masterpiece. The title itself, a portmanteau word combining *alto*, high, and *azor*, hawk, reflects Huidobro's penchant for both visual and verbal pyrotechnics. The language and imagery of *Altazor* are intensely modernistic (and even postmodernistic) for the poem is really about language itself, especially its need to constantly reinvent itself. Thematically, the poem describes the flight, or eternal fall, of the poem's "I," the same artist-as-protagonist figure used so effectively by other modernists, including Eliot, Joyce, Thomas Mann, and Luigi Pirandello. The poem's final canto shows the poet's language disintegrating into an unintelligible flow of isolated, fragmented letters and phonemes:

ivarisa tarirá
Campanudio lalalí
Auriciento auronida
Lalaí
Io ia
i i i o
Ai a i ai a i i i i o ia[32]

As if to suggest something about the modernist vision of the poet's place in society, the language that brings *Altazor* to a close is broken up and shorn of its normal denotative meaning. With its value as a medium of social discourse and interaction denied, *Altazor*'s closing lines consist of semantic units that do not permit any easy or orthodox transmission of thought. Exemplifying one of modernism's seminal themes, the language of the poem, including that of the artist, fails here to send and receive coherent messages. With *Altazor* and the breakdown of even the poet's language, the ultimate kind of modernist isolation results.

Altazor is also modernistic in its themes and its mythic foundation. Like *Ulysses* and *The Waste Land, Altazor* establishes a structural and thematic dichotomy between the barren "now" of the poem and a more fecund past. The Icarus legend, for example (in addition to that of the biblical Fall), is ironically replayed in *Altazor*. Here, however, the heroic flyer seeking to touch the sun is replaced by a parachutist falling, perhaps eternally, through an unconscious and uncaring universe. As in *The Waste Land*, the "I" of *Altazor* is both self-aware and socially aware, conscious of the desperate need to regenerate and rejustify twentieth-century existence. Altazor, the poet-as-hawk-as-parachutist, is the epitome of the poet as "little God" that Huidobro speaks of in his "Ars poetica"; the "little God" he most resembles—that he personifies—is Prometheus,[33] the Titan who stole fire from the gods and brought it to humankind. Here, Altazor/Prometheus utilizes liberated words (poetry) instead of fire, but the intended result is the same—the liberation of human beings. Through his use of language and metaphor Huidobro succeeds in *Altazor* in creating a "transubstantiated" poetry that transforms or transubstantiates mere language into a sacred entity, poetry. Consciously influenced by an Aymara Indian poet,[34] Huidobro saw the modern poet as a shaman whose skillful use of words could create new and better worlds. Thus, Huidobro also invokes the ancient myth of the poet as seer and magically endowed engenderer, a creature able to bring reality into being by naming it.

Structurally and thematically integrated into the heart of *Altazor*'s essentially mythic base is the poem's controlling image, that of the mill. Occurring at about the midway point, the mill, more than any other of Huidobro's modernistically mechanistic imagery, stands in relation to wheat as the poet does in relation to language; that is, both wheat and language must be processed before they are suitable for human consumption. Just as bread is created from wheat, so too, Huidobro suggests, the poet creates poetry (another kind of sustenance) from language.

One might argue that *Altazor*, composed between 1919 and 1931, is, formally, the epic poem of modernism. Mythic in its structural moorings, conceived on a grand scale, and dealing with a theme of heroic proportions, *Altazor* does for modernist poetry what *Finnegans Wake* does for modernist narrative and *Six Characters in Search of an Author* does for modernist drama. Again reflecting the integrally modernist theme of the artist in society, the epic hero of *Altazor* is the poet, a semidivine being (like Icarus and Prometheus) who must teach people how to communicate with themselves and each other.

The final American culture in which modernism existed as a clearly defined literary movement is that of Brazil, which like the United States had seen many of its artists travel to Europe during the early decades of the twentieth century to study and work. Long influenced by French culture, Brazil was receptive to avant-garde European influences, yet it was able to receive these influences without losing its own sense of cultural identity.

Brazilian modernismo dates from 1922, the Semana de Arte Moderna to roughly World War II. Its appearance as a new, iconoclastic, and renovating force touching all areas of Brazilian art and culture had at least seven definite precursors: Oswald de Andrade, Brazilian modernism's *enfant terrible*, returned to Brazil in 1912 from a sojourn in Europe, enthusiastically preaching the virtues of Italian Futurism; Victor Brecheret had gone to France to study the new sculpture with Rodin; in 1913 Brazil hosted its first modern art exhibition (an event that, in its cultural impact, parallels the 1913 Armory Show in the United States); Anita Malfatti returned in 1914 from Berlin to exhibit her expressionistic art (later she would promote Cubism as well); in 1915 Heitor Villa-Lobos composed his *Danses africaines*, a breakthrough piece of modernist music; Mário de Andrade's "Trianon Manifesto" of 1921 called for an artistic revolution in Brazil that would adhere to modernist principles; and, finally, the rambunctious Modern Art Week was held in São Paulo, February 13–17, 1922.

As elsewhere, modernism in Brazil elicited an outraged response from the artistic and intellectual establishment, which was not well disposed toward the kind of radical innovation proposed by the advocates of the new art. Nevertheless, the liberating force of modernism reached immediately into all aspects of Brazilian life and transformed Brazilian culture in ways both profound and lasting. The cultural effects of modernism were greater in Brazil perhaps, in scale, scope, and profundity, than anywhere else in the Americas, with the possible exception of the United States, whose modernist experience closely parallels that of Brazil. As in the United States, for example, modernism did for Brazilian literature what it had taken two modernist rebellions to do for Spanish American literature: it established the validity of the national tongue, and it nationalized (and simultaneously internationalized) the national literature.

The Brazilian modernists, led in theory and often in practice by Mário de Andrade, strove to create art that was authentically nationalistic and that would express what was unique about the multifaceted Brazilian experience. This seemingly paradoxical goal, to produce an authentic national art by means of liberating international forms and techniques, produced extraordinarily eclectic works of art. Some of these, like Emiliano Di Cavalcanti's Brazilianized expressionist drawings, *Fantoches da méia-noite* (1921), Mário de Andrade's

Hallucinated City (1922), Heitor Villa-Lobos's *Chôros* (1926), and Oswald de Andrade's mythic rhapsode, *Macunaíma* (1926), were destined to become classics of twentieth-century Brazilian art. Villa-Lobos's *Chôros*, for example, shows the Brazilian composer bringing Stravinsky's influence to bear on the composition of Brazilian folk music, while Oswald de Andrade's infamous "cannibalistic" journal, the *Revista de antropofagia* (1928), wryly suggests that Brazilian culture had historically first ingested its influences, both foreign and domestic, before assimilating them in the production of something new.[35]

In examining the historical development of Brazilian modernism, one sees that while the Modern Art Week had a bombshell-like effect on Brazilian culture, the seeds of the rebellion had been sown more than ten years earlier. Nevertheless, one can still look at the publication in 1922 of Mário de Andrade's *Hallucinated City* as the single event that heralded the arrival of the new poetry in Brazil. The impact of the poem was immediate. The formally challenging, linguistically daring, and thematically shocking poems of *Hallucinated City* were violently attacked as not being poetry at all. Representative of the sharply antibourgeois tenor of the book is "Ode to the Bourgeois Gentleman," a poem that epitomizes the aggressively iconoclastic stance of early Brazilian modernism:

> I insult the bourgeois! The money-grabbing bourgeois,
> the bourgeois-bourgeois!
> The well-made digestion of São Paulo!
> The man-belly! The man-buttocks!
> The man who being French, Brazilian, Italian,
> is always a cautious little take-your-time![36]

Epitomizing the usage of free verse that is generically so closely identified with modernism, but allowing for an occasional rhyme (of both assonance and consonance), "Ode to the Bourgeois Gentleman" openly attacks the materialism and philistine values of Paulista society. Using the classical form of the ode for modernistically satiric purposes, Andrade's diction is calculatedly gross, insulting, and irreverent.

Thematically, too, "Ode to the Bourgeois Gentleman" takes an unambiguously antagonistic position with respect to the mores of the bourgeoisie. Here, as in other works, like the four "Landscape" poems and "The Moral Fibrature of the Ipiranga," the bourgeoisie represents the stale status quo; it is an unthinking, hypocritical social class that resists all progress and growth save that which supports cultural orthodoxy. It receives an extra measure of sociopolitical censure in "The Moral Fibrature of the Ipiranga," an ironic "profane oratorio" in which the "Green-Gilt Youths," who represent the force of change (and who in their invocation of crucifixion imagery also suggest that the artist's role in society is similar to that of Christ), are overwhelmed, then figuratively crucified by bourgeois conventionality and materialism.

The "Landscape" poems, which collectively form the core of *Hallucinated City*, echo both Eliot and Apollinaire in that a self-conscious and reflective "I" tours a modern urban setting, one that is simultaneously local and cosmic, national and international. As in Apollinaire's "Zone" and Eliot's *Prufrock*, the rhythms of the "Landscape" poems reflect the movement of a person walking and thinking. Less intensely personal than *Prufrock* yet more nationalistic than most of Huidobro's work or the poems of *New Provinces*, the "Landscape" pieces recall the work of Saint-Denys-Garneau in that, though distinctly modernistic in language, form, and imagery, they are clearly linked to a specific culture and time.

Another example of this same phenomenon is the "Very Interesting Preface" that Andrade wrote as a foreword for *Hallucinated City*. Both it and Smith's rejected preface to *New Provinces* are satirical attacks on conventionality in poetry and formal statements of what the poetics of modernism should be in their respective cultures. Both decry the stagnant poetry of their time, and both call for a new poetry for a new age. They differ, however, on the question of nationalism. For Smith and his colleagues in the Montreal Group, nationalistic sentiments were anathema; the new poetry had to be international in context. For Andrade, however, images of and references to São Paulo in particular and Brazil in general were put to use not as examples of a narrow provincialism but as founts of subject matter wherein poetry could join the local with the universal, the individual with the type, the national with the international. Like the Futurist Marinetti, Mário de Andrade recognized the power of the liberated (and therefore liberating) word, especially that of the vernacular. And like other modernists from Eliot to Huidobro, Andrade puts the noise and smell of the modern world's machinery at the heart of his new poetic vision.

Like Amy Lowell, Andrade was critically aware of how polyphonic verse, working in consort with melodic and harmonic verse, could be utilized to create the modernist effect of simultaneity.[37] Paralleling in literature the effect of simultaneous visual movement achieved by Duchamp's *Nude Descending a Staircase*, the twenty-two poems of *Hallucinated City* work together to produce a "hallucinated" or kaleidoscopic vision that, brought to life through the surrealistic imagery of the poet's reflective mind, derives from an intensely Brazilian language that generates a series of striking metaphors and tropes.

For all that *Hallucinated City* is rightly credited by literary historians as being the breakthrough text of Brazilian modernism, however, two works by Oswald de Andrade, *The Sentimental Memoirs of João Miramar* (1923) and *Seraphim Grosse Pointe* (1933), are establishing themselves not merely as pillars of Brazilian modernism but as milestones of modernism in general. Recalling the early work of John Dos Passos, Faulkner, and, especially, Stein, the 1923 narrative (a satirical Bildungsroman) challenged accepted definitions of the novel as a form by deliberately tangling its syntax, by splintering its narrative sequences into brief, telegraphic chapters, and by playing with what Saussure had a few years earlier called the arbitrary and differential functions of words as signifiers and signifieds. The result was a text that, widely condemned at the time as "obscene trash," was an open assault on everything Brazilian culture and society held to be sacred. A challenge even to the phallogocentric power structure of Brazilian society, *The Sentimental Memoirs of João Miramar* can, in the context of poststructuralist theory and criticism, be seen as a narrative far ahead of its time.

Andrade's second work went even further with his decentering challenge. Moving from the disruption of syntax and diction that characterizes the *Memoirs*, Andrade created in *Seraphim Grosse Pointe* one of the most extraordinary and yet least-known narratives of the early twentieth century. A parodic entwining of both metonymic and metaphoric modes of discourse, structured metafictionally like cubist collage, *Seraphim* questions its own validity, its coherence as a work of art, and the nature of its relation to other realities, including sociopolitical ones. Subtly matriarchal in its utopian spirit,[38] *Seraphim* reflects the reading its author had done on James G. Frazer, Lucien Lévy-Bruhl, Sigmund Freud, and Karl Marx. In addition, *Seraphim* epitomizes Claude Lévi-Strauss's concept of *bricolage* and Mikhail Bakhtin's "carnivalization," both of which, in structuralist and poststructuralist thought, underscore *Seraphim*'s fragmentary, seemingly random structuring. Rivaled in the Americas only by Stein's *Three Lives* and *Tender Buttons*, Oswald de Andrade's *Sentimental Memoirs of João Miramar* and *Seraphim Grosse Pointe* deserve more attention by readers interested in the development of twentieth-century narrative and narrative theory.

Whether as a clearly defined movement or as a loosely defined set of attitudes, modernism existed as a powerful renovating force in the Americas. Related to romanticism in its emphasis on the individual and on the need to discover an authentic national identity, modernism tended less to stress the kind of cultural emancipation advocated by Emerson in *The American Scholar* and by Andrés Bello in his "Ode" than a kind of cultural maturity, a national coming of age that would produce literature (and other art forms) worthy of serious consideration within the world community. More a sign of an increasing cultural sophistication than of the establishment of a culture (which by this time had been accomplished, if not widely recognized), modernism saw the Americas move definitively into the international arena. Evolving within a powerful network of influences both internal and external in nature (and that still need to be studied in detail), the literatures of English and French Canada, the United States, Spanish America, and Brazil developed along axes that were both national and international. The result was a distinctively new literature, avantgarde in its forms, techniques, and imagery but uniquely American. From the publication of Darío's *Azul* in 1888 to the appearance of *New Provinces* in 1936, American modernism produced some of the most fascinating literary texts of the time. Just as the cultures of the New World had come of age, so too had their literatures.

7

In Quest of an American Identity

* * * * * * * * * * * *

Arguably the ur-theme of American literature, the quest for identity is not only a common thread running through all the European-based cultures of the New World, it is endemic to them. Although most of the early explorers saw themselves essentially as Europeans who, once their conquest of the New World was complete, would return to Europe, those who chose to stay and settle soon began to feel that they were somehow different from the people they had left behind in the Old World. This early sense of difference was heightened when the first generation of American-born children of Europeans began to appear. These children would struggle with the question of identity in ways both more complex and more compelling than those experienced by their parents. It is here, in this generation, that we see the gulf between the Old World and the New suddenly grow much larger.

As they matured, these new Americans began to feel less and less European and more and more something else. The problem was what this "something else" was. What did it mean, culturally and politically, to have been born in New France, New Spain, or New England? Gradually, these first-generation new Americans came to realize that though they shared the language of their European heritage, they were not easily accepted into it. Like the Mexican playwright Ruiz de Alarcón, many artists and intellectuals of this period realized that they were often disparaged by Old World culture because of their New World birthright. The problem of identity thus became sharply focused well before the close of the sixteenth century: if we in the Americas were not European, what were we? What did it mean to be Canadian, Mexican, Brazilian, or Caribbean? Since no cultural identity was immediately available to this first generation of new Americans, one would have to be created, and it is here that one of American literature's most seminal themes begins to appear.

It is difficult to deal with the question of American identity. On the one hand, it is so pervasively a part of the conquest, colonization, and development of the New World that it naturally demands our attention. On the other hand, it is so complex an issue, and one perhaps infinitely divisible, that it defies our attempts to organize it. My intention here is not to show how the quest for identity has developed historically through the literary history of the Americas but to call attention to the issue itself, central to any thorough understanding of the American experience. I hope to compare the ways the quest for identity was perceived early in the development of the American cultures with the ways the same theme was perceived later, after a degree of cultural self-affirmation had been achieved. Approaching the problem in this manner, one can divide the works that deal with this subject into two broad categories: those of an overtly cultural or sociopolitical orientation and those of a more private or personalized bent.

One of the earliest New World writers to generate a uniquely American sense of identity was Inca Garcilaso de la Vega. The son of a Spanish conquistador and an Incan princess, Inca Garcilaso secured both a fine European education and a substantial reputation as a scholar in the Spanish city of Córdoba, where he resided. Although Garcilaso was schooled in the European tradition, this experience never displaced his love and admiration for his Incan heritage, a fact clearly reflected in his masterpiece, *The Royal Commentaries* (1, 1609; 2, 1617).

The *Commentaries*, a historical and mythic recreation of the brilliant Incan Empire and the Spanish conquest, allowed Garcilaso to praise both his mother's cultural heritage and that of his father. An example of oral history at its finest, *The Royal Commentaries* is simultaneously an in-depth portrait of a newly born American culture's double heritage and a poignant autobiographical account of the author's own sense of self. Sharply self-conscious of his style and sometimes consciously critical of both his Indian and his European progenitors, Inca Garcilaso has with good reason been described as the "founding father" of Spanish American literature.[1]

Farther to the north and east, another early newcomer to the New World was also discovering and defining a new cultural identity, this time in New France.

Marc Lescarbot (c. 1570–1642) was a Parisian lawyer who, disgusted with the corruption of his Old World society, came to Canada as the Spanish and Portuguese had come earlier to Central and South America, in search of an edenic paradise. One of Lescarbot's earliest poems, "Adieu à la France," conveys his not uncommon sense of the New World as a haven from the decadence and injustice of the Old. In other poems, however, like "La défaite des sauvages armouchiquois," Lescarbot describes the violent conflict between the early French settlers and the indigenous people they encountered. Like Inca Garcilaso de la Vega but with less subtlety and lacking the former's intimate understanding of the cultural war that characterized the conquest, Lescarbot was instrumental in establishing an early sense of cultural identity for New France.[2]

A third early American writer to generate an unmistakable sense of New Worldism is the Mexican poet, dramatist, and essayist Sor Juana Inés de la Cruz. Born in 1651, Juana de Asbaje (her real name) became a nun in 1667, a biographical fact that has served primarily to increase the mystery that surrounds her life. Monegal describes Sor Juana as the New World's first great poet.[3] More than that, she is the first writer and thinker of the New World to compare favorably with the best European minds of the time. A prodigious intellectual, Sor Juana was deeply aware of current European trends in poetry and art. The Spanish masters Francisco Gómez y Quevedo and Luis de Góngora were important influences on her work, a fact clearly seen in her masterpiece, "First Dream," a long metaphysical and philosophical poem that ranks as one of the greatest achievements of its time. Another poem by Sor Juana, the sonnet "Divine Rose," artfully evokes the Baroque theme of the transitory nature of human life:

> Divine rose, . . . in a pleasant garden,
>
> .　 .　 .　 .　 .　 .　 .　 .
>
> How haughty in thy pomp, presumptuous
> and proud, thou dost disdain the threat of death,
> and then, dismayed and humbled, showest forth
>
> thy perishable being's withered marks!
> Thus with learned death and ignorant life
> living thou dost deceive and dying teach.[4]

Sor Juana was also a staunch defender of intellectual freedom (a theme we see developed in her "apologetic" letter to the bishop of Puebla) and of women's rights, which we learn from her incisive roundel "Foolish Men":

Foolish men, who accuse women without reason, without seeing that you are yourselves the cause of the very thing that you blame!

.   .   .   .

With foolish presumption, you wish to find her whom you seek Thaïs when you attempt her and Lucretia when you possess her.

.   .   .   .

Who is the more in fault in an erring passion, she who falls through entreaty, or he who entreats her to fall?

Or which is the more to blame, although both do ill, she who sins for pay or he who pays for sinning?[5]

Sor Juana, who like Anne Bradstreet was called "the Tenth Muse,"[6] was one of the greatest poets of her age, rivaled in the Americas only by Edward Taylor and seen in Europe as a highly original reaction to Quevedo and Góngora as well as a metaphysical poet worthy of comparison with Donne.

A fourth early New World writer to express an early sense of Americanism was the Brazilian poet Gregório de Matos (c. 1623–1696). Like Lescarbot, Matos was a lawyer whose verses utilize many New World words, themes, and expressions. So pronounced is this tendency in Matos' work, which he sang while wandering through the streets of Bahia, strumming a guitar fashioned from a gourd, that he is commonly credited with having founded a distinctly Brazilian national literature, one expressed in the language and culture not of Portugal, the European homeland, but of Brazil, its colony.

Called the "Bôca do Inferno" ("Mouth of Hell") because of his caustic wit and sometimes vitriolic satires, Matos, like his Peruvian counterpart Juan del Valle y Caviedes, also composed deeply moving religious poetry, lyrical poetry, and love poetry (of both an erotic and a spiritual nature). Exemplifying his satirical work is a poem in which Matos chastises his city, Bahia, of which he says, "Of two f's as I see it, / is this city composed, / one fraud, the other fornication."[7] In the tradition of François Villon and like Lescarbot and Valle y Caviedes, Matos freely mixed classical poetic forms and motifs with the language, themes, and characters of the New World. In so doing, he established himself as one of the New World's most original and refreshing early poetic voices.

When we seek the first signs of an authentic English Canadian consciousness, we are led to consider the work of Frances Brooke (English Canada's first novelist), Henry Alline, Joseph Howe, and Oliver Goldsmith. Goldsmith's "Rising Village" and Howe's "Acadia" are ambitious poems that attempt to deal

with the startling newness of the New World adventure. Goldsmith, "the first
native-born Canadian poet to receive critical attention,"[8] hoped in "Rising Village" to contrast the decline of the Old World with the rise of the New World.
Sounding once again the basic theme of the Americas as a Garden of Eden,
Goldsmith concludes his poem by interpreting the future greatness of the New
World in terms of the specific virtues of Nova Scotia (Acadia), which is presented as a commodious extension of England's best features.

> Then blest Acadia! ever may thy name,
> Like hers [Britain's], be graven on the rolls of fame;
>
> . . . .
>
> So may thy years increase, thy glories rise,
> To be the wonder of the Western skies;
> And bliss and peace encircle all thy shore,
> Till empires rise and sink, on earth, no more.[9]

Goldsmith's enthusiasm for his particular New World culture is not unlike
the *ufanismo*, or exaggerated boastfulness, of early Brazilian writers like Rocha
Pita, who could also wax hyperbolic about the virtues, real and imagined, of his
country:

> In no other region are the heavens more serene or the dawn more beau-
> tiful; in no other hemisphere does the sun have such gilded rays or noc-
> turnal reflections that are more brilliant; the waters, . . . are the purest that
> there are; the short of the matter is; Brazil, where the mighty rivers rise
> and flow, is an earthly paradise.[10]

What is lacking in both "Rising Village" and Howe's "Acadia" is the degree
of Americanized language and imagery that we find in Lescarbot's best work
and, especially, in that of Inca Garcilaso, Sor Juana, and Gregório de Matos. As
we see in "Rising Village," Goldsmith's optimistic vision of Nova Scotia was
still rather closely tied to Britain, to the Old World. The failure to separate
more decisively from Britain's cultural hegemony would delay the emancipation
of English Canadian literature for generations to come.

This crucial question of cultural emancipation is seen in a new perspective
when considered in terms of Spanish America and the United States. While
one can reasonably argue that English and French Canada have developed as
culturally unique entities only in the twentieth century, Spanish America and
the United States separated themselves from the Old World, politically if not so
much culturally, much earlier and in a more militant and irrevocable fashion.

And Brazil's cultural evolution falls somewhere in between: Brazil did not suffer a war in order to win independence from its European home country, and its development of a national consciousness has been relatively orderly.

The consequences of an abrupt rupturing of ties with the Old World can be clearly seen in Spanish America, which up to the early years of the nineteenth century had enjoyed the cultural and political unity that comes with being a relatively successful colonial society. By 1824, however, the wars for independence had been essentially concluded, and Spanish America suddenly found itself free of Spanish rule. But with the political stability afforded by Spanish rule gone, the region fell into the chaos of civil war and a seemingly endless struggle among caudillos, or local strongmen, for political control. This Balkanization of Spanish America, which lasted through most of the nineteenth century, represented a crisis of continental proportions for those Spanish Americans who wanted to bring about cultural and political unity for South America.

Among these progressive thinkers was the Venezuelan Andrés Bello, who spent most of his adult life trying to integrate the disparate cultures of Spanish America into a cohesive whole. Bello's "American Odes," for example, stressed once again the quintessentially American theme of the New World as an edenic escape from the decadence and corruption of the Old. A kind of New World Virgil, Bello also extolled the virtues of peace, cooperation, and honest agrarian labor. Incorporating all these themes, Bello's best-known poem, "Ode to the Agriculture of the Torrid Zone," is a long, elegant work filled with images and metaphors that reflect the agricultural fertility of the New World and extol the physical grandeur of the American landscape:

> Hail fecund zone,
>
> .   .   .   .
> . . . thou givest
> the grape to the seething cask,
>
> .   .   .   .   .   .
> and flocks go without number
> graying thy verdure, from the plain
> that has the horizon for its edge,
> as far as the uplifted mountain
> of inaccessible and everwhite snow.[11]

In the second half of the poem, Bello changes his focus from the flora, fauna, and geography of the Americas to the human and therefore political realm:

> But if, just as thy soil
> yields, oh fertile zone, to no other soil,
> and as it has been the special care of Nature,
> so would it were of thy indolent inhabitant!
>
> .   .   .   .
>
> Citizen soldier,
> cast aside the livery of war;
>
> .   .   .   .   .   .
>
> Oh, young nations, who raise
> above the astonished occident
> your head girt with early laurels!
> Honor the field, honor the simple life
> of the farmer, and his frugal plainness.
> Thus liberty will have in you
> a perpetual dwelling,
> ambition a restraint and law a temple.[12]

In stressing the physiocratic centrality of agriculture and the supposed virtues of agrarian life in the development of Spanish American culture, Bello was sounding a note that would reverberate throughout the Americas: in French Canada (where veneration of rural existence would become a powerful tradition), in English Canada, in Brazil, and in the United States.

In the United States, one might seek the earliest indications of a new and different cultural awareness in the works of such writers as Anne Bradstreet, Edward Taylor, Cotton Mather, and Jonathan Edwards (as preachers the latter two afford an interesting comparison with Bartolomé de Las Casas, representing Spanish America, and Antônio Vieira, of Brazil). Or, conversely, one might argue that a definite sense of the United States as a unique cultural entity does not appear until later, in the work of Benjamin Franklin. Still again, however, one could take the position that it is St. Jean de Crèvecoeur who marks the point of transition, since he was a European (French) nobleman whose first experience with the New World was in Canada, as a lieutenant in Montcalm's ill-fated army.

Crèvecoeur came to the United States around 1759, bought a farm a short distance north of New York City, and married a woman from the United States. An admirer of Rousseau and a product of French romanticism, Crèvecoeur thought he had found in the United States the kind of idealized agrarian nationalism he had been searching for, a classless society of smallholding farmers in close harmony with the benevolent nature that Bello had touted in his "Ode to the Agriculture of the Torrid Zone." In his popular and widely circulated "Letters from an American Farmer," Crèvecoeur tries to define what it meant to be an American, that is, a person living in the United States. In the letter entitled "What Is an American?" he writes:

> Here are no aristocratical families, no courts, no kings, no bishops, no ecclesiastical dominion, no invisible power giving to a few a very visible one; no great manufacturers employing thousands, no great refinements of luxury. The rich and poor are not so far removed from each other as they are in Europe. Some few towns excepted, we are all tillers of the earth, from Nova Scotia to West Florida.[13]

Later in this same "letter," Crèvecoeur places the social, political, and economic flexibility of the New World in sharp contrast to what he considers the rigidity and decadence of the Old:

> A European, when he first arrives, seems limited in his intentions, as well as in his views; but he very suddenly alters his scale; two hundred miles formerly appeared a very great distance, it is now but a trifle; he no sooner breathes our air than he forms schemes, and embarks in designs he never would have thought of in his own country. . . . Thus Europeans become Americans.[14]

Crèvecoeur thus concretizes the nascent sense of Americanism that appears in the writings of so many early inhabitants of the New World. From Inca Garcilaso and Gregório Matos to Marc Lescarbot and from Oliver Goldsmith to St. Jean de Crèvecoeur, an awareness of becoming a new person with a new life in a new land became a fundamental theme of early American literature.

But the theme of an emergent New World identity is by no means limited to sociopolitical works appearing early in the development of the Americas. Poems, dramas, and, after a time, novels (which were banned in colonial Spanish America) have dealt with this theme from the beginning of New World culture up to the present day. In the nineteenth century, for example, there appeared several novels from different American republics that dealt with the issue of cultural identity by showing citizens of the New World in direct conflict with those of the Old.

Prototypical of this deliberately contrastive approach to New World/Old World relations was the work of Henry James, who wrote a series of novels focusing on precisely this subject and for whom this theme was of singular importance.[15] By James's time the United States had definitively asserted its political independence from England and was self-consciously trying to emancipate itself culturally as well.

This dual process of political and cultural liberation was also being played out in Spanish America, which suffered through several wars of independence, and Brazil, where political independence had been secured without recourse to bloody revolution. There is one great difference between what took place in Latin America and in the United States during the nineteenth century, however; in Brazil and Spanish America, colonial rule had been in effect for approximately four hundred years. The result was that colonialism, or a colonial mentality, would weigh heavily on cultural expression for a very long time. Beginning with Gregório de Matos, Andrés Bello, and a few others, the quest for an authentic and unique Latin American identity emerged early on as a real and vital issue for the writers and artists of Spanish America and Brazil. In the United States, where the war for independence was over before the end of the eighteenth century, there was, after the "Romantic Flowering" and the generation of Nathaniel Hawthorne, Ralph Waldo Emerson, Herman Melville, and Henry Thoreau, an increasingly robust sense of national identity, a sentiment epitomized in Barlow's epic *The Columbiad*. Although this theme is first outlined by Emerson in his *American Scholar* speech and given free expression in Whitman's *Leaves of Grass*, it remained for Henry James, in *The American, The Europeans, Daisy Miller,* and *The Ambassadors*, to bring the cultural identity of the New World into sharp contrast with that of the Old.

Other American writers would also take up this theme. In Canada, for example, this comparison of the Old World with the New plays a central role in several novels written by Sara Jeannette Duncan. *An American Girl in London* (1891), for example, focuses, as does James's *The Wings of the Dove*, on the adventures of an American woman from Chicago who is pursued by avaricious Englishmen. In *Those Delightful Americans* (1902), which, less cynical, is slightly reminiscent of James's *The Europeans*, Duncan tells the amusing story of an English woman's discovery of American high society. Other of Duncan's efforts that developed this international theme include what is widely regarded as her masterpiece, *The Imperialist* (1904), and *Cousin Cinderella; or, A Canadian Girl in London* (1908), also considered one of her better works. The latter tale, especially, offers an interesting thematic comparison with other nineteenth-century New World novels, including James's *The American*, Alberto Blest Gana's *Los Transplantados*, and *Les anciens Canadiens*.[16]

Often described as a historical romance rather than a novel per se, *Les anciens Canadiens* was written by Philippe-Joseph Aubert de Gaspé, the father of Philippe-Ignace-François Aubert de Gaspé, who was the author of the work generally credited with being French Canada's first novel, *L'influence d'un livre* (1837). *Les anciens Canadiens* is a loosely connected collection of scenes, events, and customs of French Canadian life toward the end of the French reign in Canada. The scenes of daily life involving the idealized d'Haberville family and its manor were quite possibly based on the author's nostalgic memories of his experiences as a seigneur in Québec. The primary characters are Jules d'Haberville, the dutiful son of a French Canadian seigneur, and Archibald Cameron, the scion of a Scot who died fighting the British at Culloden. These two young men, both of them brave and generous, find themselves on opposite sides of the conflict when England and France go to war over the control of Canada. Archie, who has accepted a commission in the British army, is unexpectedly sent from Europe to Canada to join the fighting. His first assignment, which revolts him, is to burn strategically important French Canadian farms and estates; one of them is the d'Haberville manor where for many years he had been treated as a natural son. Bitterly resentful of these orders, Archie resolves to warn the d'Haberville family and help them to safety. During the decisive battle between Montcalm and Wolfe on the Plains of Abraham Archie saves the life of Jules, although angry words are exchanged between the erstwhile best friends. After the war, Archie returns to live with the ruined d'Haberville family, and he helps them to regain some of what had been lost in the English takeover. The political rift that had split Archie and Jules is slowly bridged, though it is never forgotten by either.

An important plot twist coming in the final few chapters of the romance concerns the suddenly developing love affair between Jules's strong-willed sister, Blanche, and Archie. When Archie asks Blanche to marry him, she refuses, saying:

> "You offend me, Captain de Lochiel! You have not considered the cruelty of the offer you are making me! Is it now you make me such a proposal, when the flames that you and yours have lighted in my unhappy country are hardly yet extinguished?" [17]

Fiercely loyal to French Canada, Blanche remains true to her decision not to wed Archie, even though she loves him and in spite of her brother's intervention on Archie's behalf. Although it occurs unexpectedly and late in the novel, after the violent political schism between English and French Canada had settled into an attenuated and embittering cultural conflict, the categoric and clearheaded rejection of Archie by Blanche is important to *Les anciens Canadiens* because it symbolizes the refusal of French Canada to capitulate further to English Canada. Thus if the subject matter of this romance is an idealized look at a cultural past lost forever, its theme, a more pointedly political issue, could be interpreted as French Canada's refusal to be assimilated into English Canada. Put another way, the real theme of *Les anciens Canadiens* is an affirmation of what it means, culturally and politically, to maintain a French Canadian identity in the face of an overwhelming English Canadian presence.

Yet as if realizing that to end his narrative with Blanche's refusal to marry Archie would only suggest an ever-greater and more rancorous segregation of English and French Canada, Gaspé builds one final plot surprise into his narrative's structure. In the final chapter, Jules d'Haberville, the son of the seigneur, marries not an English Canadian woman but an English woman. This event, wholly unexpected, offers a dual perspective on the key issue of French Canadian identity: its ever more intimate relationship with English Canada and its now strained relationship with France, which the narrator of *Les anciens Canadiens* says "had abandoned her Canadian children." [18] It is Blanche who (recalling, in reverse fashion, Mexico's Doña Marina) in the final pages manages to express both the need to develop a future Canada in which the English and French cultures are harmoniously integrated and the need to maintain the integrity of French Canadian cultural identity. As Blanche puts it:

> "It is natural and even desirable that the French and English in Canada, having now one country and the same laws, should forget their ancient hostility and enter into the most intimate relationships; but I am not the one to set the example." [19]

A classic of Canadian literature, *Les anciens Canadiens* offers both a nostalgic look at French Canada's pre-1759 seigneurial society and a glance at the future, when, thoroughly integrated into the larger Canadian identity, French Canada will begin its ongoing struggle to retain its cultural uniqueness.

A work that, in pursuing this same theme of New World identity contrasted with that of the Old, also mixes elements of the romance with the more realistic techniques of the novel proper is Henry James's *The American* (1877). More centrally international than *Les anciens Canadiens*, which only tangentially confronts the issue of cultural identity in an international perspective, *The American* was the first of James's full-length works to address what would become one of his most definitive themes: the uneasy and perhaps ultimately irreconcilable relationship between European and American identity. Yet just as Gaspé had idealized the French Canadian seigneur, so too does James offer an idealized version of an American man of the mid nineteenth century, a self-made man from a land where "everything was being made over and 'made new.'"[20] Even the name of James's protagonist, Christopher Newman, is charged with mythic and symbolic force; epitomizing the "new man" (and anticipating the "new woman") who would inevitably emerge from Christopher Columbus's "discovery" of the New World, Christopher Newman comes to life here as the ingenuous American who seems slightly out of place among the crafty Europeans.[21]

But for all its mythmaking, romance, and melodrama, *The American*, like *The Ambassadors*, is basically ironic: first, because its protagonist sails eastward across the Atlantic not to discover Europe but to rediscover and conquer it; second, because he is a common man from a democratically organized society who goes in quest of aristocrats; and third, because he is wronged by the very people who profess to uphold the highest levels of moral conduct and behavior. In general terms, then, the conflict of the work rests on a clash of cultures; specifically, however, it rests upon the suitability of Newman, an American, as a prospective husband for an aristocratic French woman, Claire de Cintré.

James presents Newman as a wealthy entrepreneur who had made his fortune during the Civil War, a man whose "sole aim in life had been to make money."[22] In his thirty-fifth year, however, Newman begins to suspect that there may be more to life than making money, and he goes to Europe in hopes of discovering what this something more might be. Revealing his innate acquisitiveness and yet speaking with candor and honesty, Newman declares to an acquaintance, "I have come to see Europe, to get the best out of it I can. I want to see all the great things, and do what the clever people do."[23]

As a literary character, however, Newman is more than a type; he is a fairly complex character who, if he does not change a great deal, is possessed of some paradoxical qualities. For all his candor and honesty, for example, he can also be shrewd and calculating. And although he is acutely aware of wanting to improve himself as a person, he is also profoundly materialistic, wanting, as he puts it, to buy or otherwise own things, to possess the best available, whether it be a painting, an article of clothing, or a person (as with Claire de Cintré). Sounding like a mid nineteenth-century yuppie, Newman "believed that Europe was made for him, and not he for Europe. . . . The world, to his sense, was a great bazaar, where one might stroll about and purchase handsome things."[24]

Throughout his narrative, James sets up situations in which European social codes of conduct and morality are contrasted with their American counterparts. One of James's best minor characters, the narrow-minded Babcock, provides a foil for Newman's genuine but rather aggressive appreciation of the finer things European culture has to offer. Speaking of Reverend Babcock, the novel's narrative voice notes:

> Mr. Babcock's moral malaise, I am afraid, lay deeper than where any definition of mine can reach it. He mistrusted the European temperament, he suffered from the European climate, he hated the European dinner-hour; European life seemed to him unscrupulous and impure.[25]

Another minor character, who like Babcock also functions as a foil to Newman, is Mr. Tristram, a vacuous but monied American expatriate living in Paris. Unlike Babcock, who sees the United States as a paragon of morality and virtue, Tristram sees it as hopelessly vulgar and utterly unworthy of any serious regard whatever. The views of both Babcock and Tristram are extreme and therefore distorted, and Newman rejects them both, underscoring his essential open-mindedness and his capacity for self-scrutiny.

The American advances the New World/Old World contrast far beyond its decidedly marginalized role in *Les anciens Canadiens*. Although the French Canadian romance unquestionably touches upon the internationalist theme, it is not the work's thematic focal point, as it is in *The American*. Nevertheless, in *Les anciens Canadiens* as in *The American*, it is the Old World that fails the New; in one, France abandons its American colony while in the other the French aristocracy proves itself to be less moral than, ironically, an American commoner. Finally, both *Les anciens Canadiens* and *The American* imply that their respective cultures have unique identities that, while maintaining some ties with Europe, must continue to develop.

Alberto Blest Gana, another New World writer to pursue this theme, is generally regarded as Spanish America's outstanding realist, a writer who, deeply influenced by Balzac and Stendhal, attempted to compose his own *comédie humaine* of Chilean life and customs. But living abroad in France for some fifty years as the Chilean minister to France, Blest Gana also saw firsthand what happened when, fatuously pursuing what they believed to be higher forms of cultural expression, Chilean émigrés came to Paris in the hope of marrying or buying into the world of the French aristocracy.

Written under the sign of French realism, Blest Gana's great study of this subject is *Los Transplantados* (1904). Its realistic objectivity aside, *Los Trans-*

plantados constitutes a sharp satire of the nouveau-riche Chilean Canalejas family, "the transplanted ones," who unctuously throw themselves at the Parisians and other titled Europeans in an attempt to gain admittance to their social circles. The Europeans, portrayed by Blest Gana as living otiose and decadent lives (a fact that, ironically, the Chileans fail to realize), haughtily disdain and disparage the American newcomers, even coining a new word, *rastaquouères*, with which to ridicule them. Oblivious to the contempt with which the Europeans view them, and feeling culturally inferior, these Chilean *rastaquouères* are concerned not with learning to appreciate the finer things of European culture (as Christopher Newman seemed intent on doing) but merely with gaining access to Parisian high society.

A powerful force for all the players in this game is money; for both James and Blest Gana, the issue of personal wealth was of crucial importance because more than anything else, money had a chance of bringing about what the Americans wanted. In *The American*, Christopher Newman was viewed as a possible son-in-law by Claire de Cintré's mother, the narrowly aristocratic Madame Bellegarde, not because he was an honorable person but because he was wealthy and therefore a source of income for the old French family. (The Bellegardes, of course, had not worked for their money for several generations.)

In *Los Transplantados* the question of whose motivations are noble and whose are not is not quite so clearly posed. Although the Chilean émigrés are for the most part portrayed as shameless in their bid to gain entry into the Parisian salons, the Europeans are at the same time shown to be vain, self-serving, and cruelly exploitive. Their interest in taking advantage of the Chileans' financial status is apparent early in the novel, when two empty-headed young Chilean women, Dolores and Milagritos, are eagerly hoping to be introduced into the right circles of Parisian society:

> . . . the count had explained to Varielle-Landry . . . that the two "rastá" were very rich.
>
> "And all set to give it away on charity, right? This is an open purse, my friend. They're capable of committing base acts because the duchess invites them to her dances."[26]

As in James's *American*, then, the question of material wealth is a crucial one for Blest Gana and *Los Transplantados*. In both novels, each of which liberally mixes melodrama with the techniques of realism, it is the now-impecunious Old World nobility that recognizes the existence of the New only because it possesses wealth.

The key difference between the novels rests on the nature of their protagonists, Christopher Newman, a self-made American financier, and Mercedes Canalejas, the daughter of a wealthy and socially ambitious Chilean family; while Newman is shown to be largely in control of his destiny, Mercedes is
not. She is forced by her socially ambitious family to marry a now-impoverished
and cynical European prince and to reject her real love, the student Patricio.
Overwhelmed on her wedding night by the mistake she has made (or that she
has been forced to make), Mercedes (unlike Isabel Archer, who in James's *Portrait of a Lady* makes a similar mistake) rather melodramatically commits suicide. Newman also fails to get what he wants, the hand of Claire de Cintré in
marriage, although because of the generosity of his spirit he decides against
taking revenge on the Bellegarde family.

The primary thematic difference between the two novels is that while Blest
Gana's real intention seems to be to question the materialistic and superficial
values of a particular type of Latin American social group, caustically represented by the ostentatious Canalejas family, James's main intent is to throw into
contrastive relief the value systems of the United States and Europe. For all his
material wealth, Newman is still not satisfied with who and what he is, an intelligent man who understands there are things in life more valuable than money.
The Canalejas family does not understand this, and their failure to distinguish
between what is precious in life and what is not becomes the target of Blest
Gana's attack. The real complicating factor in *Los Transplantados*, therefore, is
that while later generations of Chileans would seek an identity in Paris, their
ancestors had forged their identity by waging a war of revolution against the
Spanish. As Blest Gana bitterly demonstrates, it is a cruel irony that Chileans
should so unctuously seek a French yoke after their forebears had shed so much
blood in freeing themselves from a Spanish one.

Known as the Balzac of Spanish America, Blest Gana does not so much contrast the New World with the Old (as James does) as he castigates the shallow
materialism of Chile's nouveau riche. Implicit in his criticism, however, is a
comparison of Old World society with that of the New, a comparison, moreover, suggesting that while the former may have become decadent and cynically
parasitic, the latter commits an even greater error in slavishly copying it and
prizing its meretricious values so unquestioningly.

Another writer who has described the cultural clash that occurs when New
World characters are placed in an Old World milieu is Canada's Sara Jeannette
Duncan. Of Duncan's many novels, three, as we have seen, treat this theme of
New World/Old World relations: *An American Girl in London, The Imperialist,*
and *Cousin Cinderella; or, A Canadian Girl in London.*

Cousin Cinderella, which takes place in London, resembles Blest Gana's *Los Transplantados* in that a pair of New World characters, a Canadian brother and sister, struggle to win social acceptance for themselves and for their country from the Europeans. Unlike the Chilean work, however, *Cousin Cinderella*, written in a lighter and much less angry tone, does not attack the integrity of Canadian culture, as Blest Gana does the materialistic culture of the "transplanted" Chileans. The Canadian work, like *The Imperialist* a first-rate piece of fiction writing, does not suffer from the heavy-handedness that detracts from the prolix *Los Transplantados*. In this respect, it resembles James's *American*, although it is a more comically entertaining read.

One difference between *The American*, however, and Duncan's novels is that for the Canadian writer the sense of cultural identity that permeates each work is linked to a strong sense of a still-present colonialism, to a sense that Canada is not really Canada but "English" Canada, a North American outpost of the Old World home country. Thus Duncan raises the persistent question of whether a distinctly Canadian identity does indeed exist, an issue that was also taken up at about the same time by the so-called Confederation Poets, said to constitute the first distinctly Canadian group of writers in Canadian literary history.[27] Unlike the Confederation Poets, who drew a good deal of their essential imagery and thematics from depictions of Canadian nature, Duncan labored to awaken a distinctively Canadian sense of self and of Canada's place in the world.

In *The Imperialist*, for example, the main character, Lorne Murchison, is an ardent imperialist. He advocates a political philosophy that requires people to choose whether they wish to be independent Canadians or "English" Canadians, that is, subjects of the British Empire in the European tradition. As the novel makes clear, however, Canada's future is not bound up solely with England; it also involves the United States, a fact of Canadian life not lost on Murchison. He argues:

> If we would preserve ourselves as a nation, it has become our business, not only to reject American overtures in favor of our own great England, but to keenly watch and actively resist American influence, as it already threatens us through the common channels of life and energy.[28]

Later, in the novel's climactic scene, Murchison lays out in dramatic form the consequences of the political decision Canada must make, a decision that will determine the nature of Canada's future identity. As much concerned with the economic and sociopolitical influence of the United States as with Canada's traditional ties to Great Britain, Murchison's imperialism would preserve Canada's British heritage, temper the hegemony of the United States, and, in so doing, locate a middle ground for Canada, one that, according to Murchison, would see Canada eventually grow to be "the centre of the Empire."[29]

Duncan's novel is identifiably Canadian in ways other than in the realm of national politics, however. *The Imperialist* is also a penetrating study of small-town Canadian life, in which religion and politics come to dominate all other forms of social intercourse. The novel's fictional town, Elgin, is full of characters who, like Octavius Milburn, are politically, culturally, and economically conscious of what it means to be Canadian, a subject of the British Empire yet living in close proximity to the ever more influential United States.

The novel's narrator, who underscores the cultural and political ebb and flow inherent in the plot structure by noting that "we are here at the making of a nation,"[30] takes pains to offer an extensive description of Elgin, its inhabitants, and their customs. The effect of this is to establish a uniquely Canadian milieu for the novel, one that gives the reader a solid feel for the life and times of a small southern Ontario town at the turn of the century. Even the language of the place becomes a point of contention, since what is presented as Elgin's supposedly correct English accent is contrasted with what is felt to be the corrupting "American" way of speaking.

Yet while *Cousin Cinderella*, like *The American* and *Los Transplantados*, depicts the efforts of New World citizens to deal with Old World social customs, *The Imperialist* takes up the internationalist theme by staying home, as James does in *The Europeans*. Set in Canada, *The Imperialist* makes a convincing case for the inevitable emergence of a postcolonial national consciousness, one that sees not just Europe but also the United States as a potentially overwhelming presence. As in *Los Transplantados*, the fundamental conflict is not so much between Canada and England (or Scotland) but between the several differing views about Canadian national identity held by the citizens of Elgin themselves. The fact that Lorne Murchison loses the political election he had hoped so ardently to win strongly suggests that Canada's future lies with cultural and political independence and not as a part—not even the most important part (as Murchison believes will eventually be the case)—of the British Empire.

In contrast to both *Los Transplantados* and *The Imperialist*, *The American* reflects a society that, for all its newness and uncertainty, has decisively broken with Europe. The United States that produces Christopher Newman does not obsequiously seek European acceptance, as do the Chileans in *Los Transplantados*, nor does it reflect an intensely nationalistic struggle to identify itself that we see portrayed in *The Imperialist*. *Cousin Cinderella*, on the other hand, is more akin to *The American* because in both there is a sense (one felt more sharply in *The American*) that for better or worse the New World society had already developed a separate identity. Though perhaps not yet fully mature, the New World cultures depicted here are no longer the wholly dependent children of Europe.

This same theme of the New World in contact and conflict with Old World society also assumes importance in Brazilian literature. Perhaps because of Brazil's cultural diversity, its size, and above all its comparatively steady political development, the theme of identity can be clearly traced throughout the development of Brazilian literature. Indeed, almost any work of Brazilian literature can be said to relate in some way to this most fundamental of American themes.

Nevertheless, there is one book, a novel published in the same year (1902) as Duncan's *Those Delightful Americans*, that crystallizes virtually everything this bedrock theme has meant for Brazilian literature. This work, *Canaã* (*Canaan*) by Graça Aranha, is a symbolically rendered thesis novel that concerns itself with the effects of miscegenation on Brazil's multiracial population and with the relationship between human beings and their natural environment. *Canaan*'s plot structure derives from a running debate between the novel's two chief characters, a pair of German immigrants who have come to Brazil seeking a new life. One of these, Milkau, is a pantheistic idealist who believes in universal peace, love, and harmony and who argues that because of its size, its racial diversity, and the fertility of its land, Brazil is destined to become "Canaan," the long-sought land of milk and honey. Milkau's companion, Lentz, is of another mind, however; like Nietzsche, he believes in the viability of the individual will, in force, and in violence.[31] Echoing several turn-of-the-century racial theories (including those of Joseph Gobineau), he also espouses the essentially racist position that Europeans are destined to wrest control of Brazil from the Brazilians, who because of their racially mixed heritage are, according to many European racial "scientists" like Gobineau, Gustave Le Bon, and Georges Vacher de Lapouge, regressing to a state of "barbarism."

For all that their positions differ, Milkau and Lentz both envision Brazil as the promised land. Milkau especially argues that Brazil will become the "new Canaan," but he contends that this will never happen unless the New World can shake itself free from the debilitating social, racial, and political prejudices that have infected the Old World for so long. In the novel's rather ponderous allegorical conclusion, Milkau also realizes that the establishment of the promised land will not be in his time, that it will come about only for some future generation.

Another interesting feature of *Canaan* and its handling of the theme of national identity is that, as with Canada and *The Imperialist*, the novel's basic conflict presents itself as being a function of Brazil's long-standing cultural ties with Europe and the increasingly powerful economic hegemony of its giant American neighbor, the United States: "And what good will the United States do us? They will always be our boss. This continent is destined to be the prey of beasts." [32]

The key question of national identity is thus raised in *Canaan* much in the same context as it is in *The Imperialist*. Well along in their national development yet not so confident of their identities as Christopher Newman shows the United States to be in *The American*, the Canada of *The Imperialist* and the Brazil of *Canaan* are struggling more to refine a sense of cultural identity than to compare themselves with the Europeans; the struggle merely to establish a national identity is largely over.

Graça Aranha, the author of *Canaan*, is also less critical of Brazilian society than Blest Gana is of his Chilean émigrés in *Los Transplantados*. Both Aranha and Sara Jeannette Duncan tend to be honestly and constructively critical rather than abusive of the national situation, and their works are thereby strengthened in their depictions of New World cultures on the verge of developing authentic identities. In contrasting the greatness of Chile's pioneering past with the decadence of his novel's present, Blest Gana seems to suggest that a strong sense of Chilean identity is still a long way off. The philosophical debate between Milkau, who believes that "history is nothing but a record of the fusion of races," and Lentz, who sees "alighting on the land of Brazil, . . . the black eagle of Germany," and who maintains that Brazil ultimately "will be conquered by the armies of Europe," [33] is never resolved, underscoring Milkau's final realization that Brazil's growth into the land of milk and honey is still an undecided issue.

This conflict of interests does not appear so sharply in *The Imperialist, Cousin Cinderella,* or *The American,* works in which the New World societies in question had already gained a more secure sense of identity. In *Canaan,* which also deals with the need more to create a national identity than, as we see in *The American,* to cope with the established existence of a powerful one, there is not so much a sense of newness as there is a sense of potential, of a hoped-for growth into a definable and admirable culture.

As evidenced by the work of writers as distinct as Amy Tan (Chinese-American), Manuel Puig (Spanish American), Robertson Davies (English Canadian), V. S. Naipaul (Caribbean), Louise Erdrich (Native American),

Bernice Zamora (Chicana), and Clarice Lispector (Brazilian), the evolution of the theme of identity in Inter-American literature continues unabated. One might argue that, given the inherent plurality of American culture, this is necessarily so. As vital now in the closing decades of the twentieth century as it has ever been, the quest for identity emerges as a hallmark of New World literature. Throughout the Americas, as witnessed in works as diverse as Naipaul's *The Mimic Men* and Zamora's *Restless Serpents*, cultural groups hitherto little heard from are laboring to define themselves in an abundance of novels, poems, and dramas.

One of the most interesting cultures involved in this process is French Canada, which has since the 1960s been undergoing a social and political renaissance of profound significance. Many writers, often connected to the separatist movement or associated with the journal *Parti Pris*, have dedicated themselves and their art to a radical reformation of French Canadian society. This frankly revolutionary linkage of social change and literary art has produced several powerful new interpretations of French Canadian identity. Sometimes utilizing joual, the nonstandard French spoken by many French Canadians, works like Réjean Ducharme's *St. Lawrence Blues*, Jacques Godbout's *The Knife on the Table*, Hubert Aquin's *Prochain épisode*, and Claude Jasmin's *Ethel and the Terrorist* are manifestations of both what the new French Canadian novel is like and how experimental literature can be effectively put to the task of social change. A crucial element in the artistic dimension of the separatist camp has had to do with the honing of a sharply defined sense of French Canadian identity, and it was in these works, as well as Marie-Claire Blais's *Mad Shadows* and *A Season in the Life of Emmanuel*, Anne Hébert's *The Torrent* and *Silent Rooms*, Claire Martin's *In an Iron Glove*, and Roch Carrier's *La Guerre, Yes Sir!*, that a new, militant sense of social self-awareness was first given shape and direction. The extraordinary achievement of French Canadian literature during the 1960s and 1970s constitutes in both quality and quantity one of the most singular developments in twentieth-century American literature.

Another American culture in which, since World War II, political reform and social consciousness have been mixed with technical innovation and experimentation is Spanish America, which since the 1930s has been producing some of Western literature's most stimulating narrative, poetry, and theater. Writers like Marta Lynch, Pablo Neruda, Maria Luisa Bombal, Silvina Ocampo, Jorge Luis Borges, Octavio Paz, Demetrio Aguilera-Malta, Alejo Carpentier, Nicolás Guillén, Gabriel García Márquez, Julio Cortázar, Elena Poniatowska, Elena Garro, Juan Rulfo, and Carlos Fuentes have explored the question of human identity both in political terms and in intensely subjective and psychological ways. In Fuentes' *The Death of Artemio Cruz* and *The Old Gringo*, Paz's *The Labyrinth of Solitude*, Neruda's *Residence on Earth* and *The General Song*, Carpentier's *Explosion in a Cathedral* and *The Harp and the Shadow*, Márquez's *One Hundred Years of Solitude*, Eduardo Galeano's *Memory of Fire*, and Isabel Allende's *The House of the Spirits*, highly individualized human identities are merged with larger cultural, political, and historical issues. Galeano's work, a marvelous trilogy of epic proportions, attempts to create an integrated history of the entire New World, incorporating the experiences of Native Americans, Europeans, African slaves, and others into a vast cultural panorama structured in strict chronological order. Like its French Canadian counterparts, much of twentieth-century Spanish American literature possesses a vital political dimension, one that rests almost invariably on a call for both political liberation and cultural self-assertion. The new novels of French Canada and Spanish America are especially expressive of this tendency and merit a thorough comparative study.

Often fuzzily identified with Spanish America and lost under the vague rubric of "Latin American" literature, the literature of Brazil has, as we see with the 1989 publication of João Ubaldo Ribeiro's *An Invincible Memory* and Nélida Piñon's *The Republic of Dreams*, also continued to cultivate actively the theme of identity. In Brazil, where the new literature of the twentieth century derives largely from its powerful and eclectic modernist movement, works like Mário de Andrade's *Macunaíma* (a nationalistically mythic narrative that uses Brazilian slang as joual is used in French Canada), Cassiano Ricardo's *Martim Cererê*, João Guimarães Rosa's *Sagarana* and *The Devil to Pay in the Backlands*, Clarice Lispector's *The Stream of Life* and *The Hour of the Star*, and Nélida Piñon's *House of Passion* all merge the myriad aspects of personal identity with those of political, cultural, or human identity.

In the United States, too, the poetry, prose, and drama of the twentieth century have seen an expansion of the theme of identity. Cultural groups not traditionally well represented in literature—women, Jews, Native Americans, African-Americans, Chinese-Americans, Hispanics, and other cultural minorities—have found eloquent and moving voices to tell their stories. Works of African-American literature, like the poems of Langston Hughes, Richard Wright's *Native Son*, Ralph Ellison's *Invisible Man*, and Baldwin's *Notes of a Native Son*, are paralleled in Brazil by the poems of Jorge de Lima, Solano Trindade, and João da Cruz e Sousa, the dramas of Pedro Bloch and Abdias do Nascimento, and the narratives of Jorge Amado and Lima Barreto, among many others. Spanish American literature, too, has shown an overt concern for black African, or Afro-Caribbean, culture, a salient feature of many of the poems of Nicolás Guillén, Luis Palés Matos, and Candelario Obeso, among others. Reflecting the cultural mosaic of the late twentieth-century United States are such diverse works as *The Adventures of Augie March* by Saul Bellow (who was born in Lachine, Québec),[34] Leslie Marmon Silko's *Ceremony*, Luis Valdez's "Bernabe" (and the Chicano Theater), Lorna Dee Cervantes' *Emplumada*, and Amy Tan's *The Joy Luck Club*, works in which the problems and aspirations of non-WASP groups are given powerful expression.

Many of these cultural subgroups are represented in the literatures of other American republics, as their art is by no means the exclusive domain of the United States. In Canada, for example, there is a strong tradition of Jewish writers, a tradition as potent and influential as it is in the United States. One of the best of the Jewish-Canadian writers is Mordecai Richler, whose *St. Urbain's Horseman*, *The Apprenticeship of Duddy Kravitz*, *The Incomparable Atuk*, and *Solomon Gursky Was Here* (which would seem to have been influenced by Márquez's *One Hundred Years of Solitude*) all involve the entwined questions of Canadian and Jewish identity. The story of Duddy Kravitz makes for an interesting comparison with Bellow's *Adventures of Augie March*, while *The Incomparable Atuk* satirizes the vacuous but corrupting power of pop culture as it is manufactured and exported from the United States, a theme also explored by such Brazilian writers as Rubem Braga, Sergio Sant'Anna, Luiz Vilela, and, especially, Roberto Drummond.

The twentieth century has also seen a marked increase in the number of American women writers, many of whom, like Canada's Margaret Laurence, Margaret Atwood, Alice Munro, Mavis Gallant, Claire Martin, Marie-Claire Blais, Gabrielle Roy, and Anne Hébert, are beginning to enjoy substantial international reputations. The best of these authors' works, like Laurence's *The Stone Angel* and *The Diviners*, Atwood's *The Journals of Susanna Moodie, Two-Headed Poems, The Edible Woman*, and *Lady Oracle*, Munro's *Lives of Girls and Women*, and Gallant's *Home Truths* and *In Transit*, involve the reader not merely in a quest to discover what it means to be female or even a Canadian female but what it means to be human.[35]

This same thematic extrapolation from the sexual, cultural, and political condition of the individual to the universal is also found among a number of fine contemporary women writers in Brazil, a group headed by the late Clarice Lispector and including Nélida Piñon, Lygia Fagundes Telles, Lya Luft, Sônia Coutinho, Márcia Denser, Helena Parente Cunha, Bruna Lombardi, and Myriam Campello, among many others.

Outstanding women writers have also begun to emerge in the Caribbean and in Spanish America, where authors like Maryse Condé, Simone Schwarz-Bart, Marie-Thérèse Colimon, Griselda Gambaro, Blanca Varela, Isabel Allende, Idea Vileriño, and Luisa Valenzuela have initiated a second, female literary explosion and have thereby begun to transform late twentieth-century Spanish American literature.

The theme of identity is endemic to New World literature. Although it is true that almost any work of American poetry, prose, or drama can in some sense be said to exemplify a quest for identity, the real vitality of this theme stems from a fundamental feature of the New World culture: the emphasis on development or change, on becoming viable, culturally, politically, or individually. A sense of mutability, of flux and progress, pervades New World consciousness and makes process rather than culmination the most revealing metaphor. This abiding concern over "becoming something" turns up again and again in the literatures of the New World. From Canada to Argentina and from Rio to New York, American writers have continued to find the deceptively simple question, Who are we? to be one of enormous potential. For all their differences, the nations and cultures of the Americas are united by their passion for answering this most basic of questions.

8

Regionalism as a Shaping Force

* * * * * * * * * *

In literature, regionalism is generally thought of as the kind of writing that, by means of its characters, style, and themes, faithfully reproduces the history, speech habits, manners, and attitudes of a particular time and place. Regionalist writing is therefore characterized by a strong correlation between its subject matter and the defining characteristics of the region the text purports to recreate. A convenient yardstick of a work's regionalist qualities has traditionally been to ask whether the work could be placed in another setting without serious distortion or loss of significance. If it cannot be so moved, then one is probably dealing with a work that is genuinely regionalist in nature.

The twentieth century has seen the emergence of another variety of regionalism, one that, without neglecting a detailed and verisimilar treatment of a local scene, attains levels of universal significance. This latter kind of regionalism, which might be called deep regionalism, stresses the connection between the local or particular and the general or universal. Deep regionalism, then, is not a rejection of the earlier type but a refinement and, above all, an extension of it that links local events with the larger human experience. The difference between the two is essentially one of degree and intent, in that deep regionalism is more consciously committed to revealing the universal truths inherent in a mimetically portrayed local scene.

As a literary force, regionalism has played a vital role in the evolution of New World literature. Because of the vast and varied geography of the Americas, there has been a marked tendency for differing regions to emerge, develop, and become highly individualized through their history, culture, and literature. One can, for example, speak of the novel of the prairies, of the mountain areas, of the cities, of the land, of the jungles, and of the polar regions. Although of course sociopolitical and cultural divisions have always played an important role in the development of New World literature, the variety of the New World's geography has had an at least equal and perhaps even greater impact on the ways American arts and letters have evolved. As one reads New World literature, it becomes clear that the regionalist affinities between particular texts (and nations) outweigh the political disjunctions that separate them. As the works discussed in this chapter will show, the powerful and often problematic relationship between human beings and their sense of place is remarkably universal, whether the setting be Canada (either French or English), the United States, a Spanish American nation, the Caribbean, or Brazil. Although the political differences, which are real and often divisive, figure prominently in certain of these works, their common bond—the sense of place that they share—cannot be ignored.

Consequently, if it is difficult to speak meaningfully of that mythical beast known variously as the great Canadian—or American, or Brazilian—novel, one can, in the American context, speak confidently of great regionalist novels. Put another way, it is clear that when we look at the historical development of New World literature we can see different regions producing their own unique masterpieces, texts which capture the essence of a specific geographic locale or social stratum rather than express a comprehensive political abstraction. In the Americas, then, if there are few great national or nationalistic novels, there are many outstanding regionalist works, for which the geographic and cultural diversity of the New World is not an obstacle but an inspiration. Indeed, there are so many fine pieces of regionalist literature in the Americas that one is led to describe regionalism as a characterizing feature of New World writing. American authors as different as Margaret Laurence, Alice Munro, Sarah Orne Jewett, Mark Twain, Willa Cather, Sinclair Ross, Stephen Leacock, Margaret Hutchison, Marie-Claire Blais, Roch Carrier, V. S. Naipaul, Derek Walcott, Ricardo Güiraldes, Juan Rulfo, Jorge Amado, and Guimarães Rosa are linked by a regionalist approach to literature.

In the category of regionalist writing that labors to reproduce the speech, customs, history, folklore, attitudes, and beliefs of a specific region, one could cite many works, including those of the "local-color" writing movement in the United States during the last two or three decades of the nineteenth century and the similar *costumbrismo* movement of Spanish America. This kind of writing has been a staple of New World literature from the beginning. From the

arctic reaches of northern Canada to the Great Plains, and from city neighbor-
hoods to the wind-swept barrens of Tierra del Fuego, New World writers have
scrupulously tried to describe not only the differing flora and fauna to be found
in these regions but the unique realities of their human cultures as well.

A prime example of this first variety of New World regionalist writing is
Frances Brooke's *The History of Emily Montague* (1769), a work often cited as
Canada's first novel.[1] Epistolary in form, *Emily Montague* is significantly regionalist for several reasons: it offers an extensive commentary on the unusual aspects of the Canadian climate; it features Canadian scenery; it discusses the
"nature" of Québecois Canadians (their culture, customs, and language); and it
addresses the special issue of the two Canadas, one French, the other English.
Set in Québec during the 1760s, *Emily Montague* also touches on other dimensions of Canadian life, including the weather, taxation, political representation,
religion, and Indians. The novel's regional ties to the Canada of this era are so
strong, in fact, that (invoking our rule of thumb) one cannot imagine it as existing beyond its distinctly Canadian environment.

Of the harsh weather, always a staple of Canadian literature, one letter-writer
notes, for example: "Adieu! I can no more: the ink freezes as I take it from the
standish to the paper, though close to a large stove. Don't expect me to write
again till May; one's faculties are absolutely congealed this weather."[2] The author of this letter, and one of the most witty and spirited presences in the novel,
is Arabella Fermor, an early prototype of the "learned coquette" and a possible
double for the author.[3] Though English by birth, Arabella, commenting freely
on a wide range of topics, emerges as the character who, by adopting a variety
of tones and self-conscious postures, shows the reader most vividly what life
and times are like in Québec during the years following the French defeat on
the Plains of Abraham in 1759.

While the Canadian climate is so pervasive a theme in *Emily Montague* that
virtually all the characters comment on it, Brooke does not neglect the other
aspects of the work's intensely regionalist underpinnings. For example, Arabella's
father, William, discusses at one point what he takes to be the "indolence" of
the French Canadians and by extension the supposed inferiority of their entire
culture. Reflecting the prevailing attitude of British superiority, Fermor decries
even the religion of the French Canadians, whom he believes to be "extremely
bigoted" and slothful. Fermor concludes by suggesting that the Canadians and
their culture—their region—will be vastly "improved" by continued English
rule. Fermor, moreover (to whom it falls to discuss the political realities of Canada), appears to have a vision of a unified Canada, made up of two cultures (one

superior to the other) but held together chiefly by the dominance of English culture and the English language. Concerned as it is, then, with the particularities of Canada's manners and customs, its geography, scenery, and climate, its character types, and its sense of identity as a New World unification of two hitherto antagonistic European cultures, *The History of Emily Montague* is an early and engagingly successful example of regionalism in the English Canadian novel.

Another major English Canadian work that derives much of its lasting appeal from its regionalism is Thomas Chandler Haliburton's *The Clockmaker; or the Sayings and Doings of Samuel Slick, of Slickville* (1836). *The Clockmaker* established Haliburton's reputation as a sharp-eyed satirist and commentator on the social scene in his native Nova Scotia. An immediate success, it was later translated into French and German, a fact which explains how Haliburton came to enjoy a considerable following on both sides of the Atlantic. However, as Northrop Frye has noted, Haliburton saw himself more as a Nova Scotian than as a Canadian,[4] reflecting an authorial sense of identity decidedly more regionalistic than nationalistic in nature.

Haliburton's satiric purpose, then, was closely tied to a strong sense of local identity, for he wished, by contrasting the economic aggressiveness of Sam Slick, a Yankee peddler of wooden clocks, to the lethargy of his fellow Nova Scotians, the "Bluenoses," to show how though "Nova Scotia . . . had nothing to learn politically from the States, . . . it had a lot to learn economically."[5] Written by a conservative Nova Scotian, *The Clockmaker* is interesting in part because it offers the reader two comparative perspectives: one involves the political and economic virtues and vices of Nova Scotia compared with the United States, while the other focuses on the contrast between the vigorous New World cultures represented by Canada and the United States, cultures which, Haliburton suggests, England failed to appreciate in any serious fashion.

The result is a funny and thought-provoking text, in which Sam Slick, the prototypical Yankee, offers up an endless stream of witty observations not only about the "gullible Bluenoses"[6] but about the sometimes dubious behavior of his compatriots in the United States as well. *The Clockmaker*, like *Emily Montague*, is the kind of regional work in which a shrewd, observant, and candid outsider comes into a relatively closed society and, by becoming involved with its people, can offer a penetrating firsthand commentary on it.

Typically, each section, written primarily in the form of lively and clever dialogue, begins with some minor event and ends with some social, political, or moral observation, one immediately relevant to the local situation but enriched by a degree of universal applicability as well. In the second sketch, for example, Slick, who has just made a handsome profit on a sale by shrewdly preying on the vanity and selfishness of a local Bluenose, explains his theory of selling to his companion:

"That," said the Clockmaker, . . . "I call 'human natur' . . . We can do without any article of luxury we have never had, but . . . it is not in human natur' to surrender it voluntarily. Of fifteen thousand sold by myself and my partners in this Province, twelve thousand were left in this manner; and only ten clocks were ever returned. . . . We trust to soft sawder to get them into the house, and to human natur' that they never come out of it."[7]

As we see in this quotation, one especially notable aspect of *The Clockmaker*'s regionalism is Haliburton's use of the vernacular. Working through his characters' dialogues, with language that reflects both the vocabulary and rhythms of Nova Scotian speech and the linguistic peculiarities of Yankee speech, Haliburton roots his work in the tongue of a particular region, encompassing not only Nova Scotia but, crossing a political boundary, New England as well. As the indefatigable Sam breezily says:

"It makes me so kinder wamblecropt when I think on it that I'm afeerd to venture on matrimony at all. I have seed some Bluenoses properly bit, you may depend. You've seed a boy slidin' on a most beautiful smooth piece of ice, ha'n't you, larfin', and hoopin', and hallooin' like one possessed, when presently sowse he goes in, head over ears?"[8]

Like Frances Brooke's William Fermor, who criticized the "indolence" of the French Canadians, Slick points out the "apathy" of the Bluenoses, typically by contrasting the "slothful" Nova Scotians with the "energetic Americans." As Frye observes, "Sam Slick is at his best when he's describing the country and its customs, and he's at his best often enough to bring Nova Scotia in the 1830s really to life."[9]

Another Haliburton work, *The Old Judge; or, Life in a Colony* (1849), offers even more local-color description of life and times in Nova Scotia. Not satirical, as *The Clockmaker* was, *The Old Judge* offers an essentially sympathetic and at times nostalgic treatment of Haliburton's home region; it differs essentially from *The Clockmaker* in its noncritical evocation of a place and time and in its extensive utilization of Nova Scotia's folklore and legends. Like Washington Irving in this regard, Haliburton here mixes sensitive description of the area's natural beauties and climate with realistic depictions of places, morals, and manners and with local history, including tales of buried treasure, violence, and witches.

Like English Canada and the rest of its American neighbors, French Canada, too, has produced its share of first-rate regionalist literature. Among the classics by writers from Québec, a distinct region within the larger political entity of Canada, are Antoine Gérin-Lajoie's *Jean Rivard* (1862), Louis Hémon's *Maria Chapdelaine* (1913), and Félix-Antoine Savard's *Boss of the River* (1937). As Margaret Atwood has observed, the struggle of Québec to survive has given its case a special significance,[10] integrally linked, as we shall see, to both categories of regionalism under consideration here.

Two of Québec's outstanding early twentieth-century novels are Albert Laberge's *La Scouine* (*Bitter Bread*) and Germaine Guèvremont's *The Outlander*. These works, which offer radically contrasting treatments of life in rural Québec, are regionalist because, in their different ways, they attempt realistic reproductions of life for the farm people of Québec and for the inhabitants of its small, isolated rural communities.

Laberge's *Bitter Bread*, like *Emily Montague*, *The Clockmaker*, and *The Old Judge*, belongs to the category of regionalist works in which a universalist dimension is not stressed or extensively developed. Though his short but sharply etched novel was published in 1918, Laberge is often credited with being a pioneering Canadian naturalist writer.[11] Given the harshly deterministic view of life presented in *Bitter Bread*, it is easy enough to understand why this pessimistic, uncompromising novel could be considered an example of naturalism. But other of its most salient features, its meticulous attention to mimetic description, for example, and its effective use of character types, imagery, and thematics, could also reasonably lead one to consider *Bitter Bread* as an essentially realistic novel, realism having arrived very late in French Canada.[12]

Set in the farming region of Beauharnois during the first half of the nineteenth century, *Bitter Bread* tells the bleak story of Paulina Deschamps and her family, who are unceasingly brutalized by the harsh agricultural existence they seek to coax from the land—which itself becomes a kind of indifferently malevolent character in the novel. In the history of French Canadian literature, *Bitter Bread* stands out as the earliest narrative to challenge the bucolic myth of rural happiness, morality, and beauty that had developed within the literature of French Canada. This early romanticized orientation to rural life, characterized (as in *Maria Chapdelaine* and *Jean Rivard*) by unquestioning loyalty to the land, the local culture, and the Catholic church, was inherently and aggressively regionalist. Though it challenges these conventional attitudes with a grimly fatalistic view of the grinding poverty and isolation that characterize human existence in its rural setting, *Bitter Bread* remains intensely regionalist and thus, as with Haliburton's *Clockmaker*, not narrow but intensely vivid and concrete. Of the human effect of the agricultural disasters that are an immutable part of rural existence, Laberge writes:

> Anthrax had reduced the herds terribly. . . . The farmers went about worried and depressed, at the dismal thought of their rapidly approaching payments. . . . It was as if the region had become a huge charnel house, a pile of rot and corruption.[13]

Later, again suggesting how even the climate seems to conspire against the farmers, Laberge laconically observes:

> The harvest had been under way for a month, but hardly any work had been accomplished due to the continuous rain. . . . All the farmers' efforts were paralyzed, and a feeling of discouragement was creeping over them. One man had hanged himself in a moment of depression. The uselessness of work and hard labor was evident.[14]

The region's violently divided political life is also touched on, albeit with a bit of sardonic humor:

> It was election day. The Conservatives (Bleus) and the Liberals (Rouges) were battling for power; the population was divided in two camps absolutely split down the middle. All the English-speaking people were Conservatives without exception, while the French Canadians were Liberals for the most part. . . . Three toughs were guarding the passage leading to the poll. As Deschamps approached, these brave lads began to laugh, and the biggest of the three greeted him by saying,
> "What d'ya want, bloody pea soup?"
> A tremendous punch on the jaw was Deschamps' answer.[15]

Laberge is also regionalist in his presentation of the decisive role the church plays in this poor, isolated, and agriculturally based region. As a French Canadian writer, however, he is unusual in that he offers us a powerfully negative picture of the Catholic church, its ideas, sociopolitical positions, and representatives. Indeed, it is precisely in the context of the church and the people it purports to serve that the title of the English translation shows its significance, the word "bitter" referring to the bread made regularly by the Deschamps family. Always marked with the sign of a cross, the bread ironically and inevitably turns out to be heavy, sour, and bitter. This bread, as a symbol of the blighted, misguided, and repressed lives these people lead, becomes the novel's central image.

Bitter Bread succeeds brilliantly as an example of regionalist narrative. Using a series of short sketches or vignettes, Laberge creates an intense portrait of a place, a time, and a way of life, a portrait that with its many crude, violent, and hostile features captures in powerful fashion the essence of human existence in this unsparing region.

Another regionalist work that focuses on the harshness of nineteenth-century rural existence is Hamlin Garland's *Main-Travelled Roads* (1891), a collection of austere stories about life on the dreary pioneer farms of Iowa, Wisconsin, and the Dakotas during the 1860s and 1870s. Like those of *Bitter Bread*, the tales of *Main-Travelled Roads* are short but poignant snapshots of the homesteaders' struggles merely to survive, struggles waged ceaselessly against a land that was fertile but unforgiving and against an exploitive economic system that they could neither control nor understand. For both Garland and Laberge, the brutalization of life that results from these circumstances forms the basis of their regionalism as well as their strong sense of determinism. The difference between them is that for Garland, an avid student of Charles Darwin, Hippolyte Taine, and Herbert Spencer, this determinism is derived from an all-too-real system, one fully explainable—and therefore rectifiable—in terms of then-current social, political, and economic conditions. For Laberge and *Bitter Bread*, however, this same sense of determinism was both more amorphous than in *Main-Travelled Roads* and less a matter that could be changed by social reform.

As Mark Schorer has noted, one of the principal defects of Garland's narratives is his tendency to give his stories a "schoolmasterish tone, as if he is instructing some uninformed person in the anthropology of the frontier, lecturing him on sociological injustices while showing lantern slides of picturesque native habits."[16] Though Schorer's comment rightly takes note of Garland's occasionally heavy-handed dogmatism, it also calls attention to two of Garland's strengths as a fiction writer: his scrupulous attention to realistic detail and, surprisingly, his capacity for lyrical description. In "Up the Coulee," for example, Garland merges a mimetically accurate descriptiveness early in the story with what unexpectedly becomes a poetic and impressionistic rendering later on:

> It was magically, mystically beautiful over all this squalor and toil and bitterness, from five till seven—a moving hour. Again the falling sun

streamed in broad banners across the valleys; again the blue mist lay far down the coulee over the river.[17]

If Laberge is more relentless in wielding his realistic prose, Garland at least occasionally reaches similar levels of excellence, especially when, as above, he merges his own brand of realistic local-color detail with the revealing impressions these scenes make upon his narrators and his rough, inarticulate characters.

Both Laberge and Garland also show the role religion plays in their respective regions. The Catholicism of Laberge's community, however, receives greater and more constant play than does the dour and repressive Puritanism of Garland's people. The Catholic religion, operating out of its own state of siege within otherwise-Protestant Canada, plays a more vital role in the lives of Laberge's men and women than does Garland's Puritanism, which is present only as a scarcely acknowledged sociopolitical force, one which teaches people to accept unquestioningly their poor lot in life and to work ever harder. Laberge is more critical than Garland of the church's dominant role in the lives of his characters. For the French Canadian writer, the Catholic church is much more a living institution than is Puritanism or even the Protestant church itself, yet in neither *Bitter Bread* nor *Main-Travelled Roads* is religion presented as a progressive or enlightening force.

More than anything else, it is the authors' attitudes about the relationship between the land and the people who farm it that form the most striking bond between these works. Although both Laberge and Garland generate moments of bitter humor in their narratives, on balance these are texts that depict nineteenth-century farm life as an existence dominated by cultural and economic deprivation, grinding and relentless physical labor, and deep, numbing despair. Although both writers, especially Garland, can show the beauty of the land, the narratives center on the dehumanizing demands it makes on the people who would struggle with it. For both Laberge and Garland the land remains an indomitable and eternal adversary, relentless in its demands, while the puny humans who cultivate it come and go.

As one expects in regionalist literature, much of *Bitter Bread* and *Main-Travelled Roads* is devoted to the reproduction of regional speech habits. Laberge narrates more than Garland, whose dialogue-rich works are authentic reproductions of nineteenth-century "middle border" speech. Laberge does not neglect the speech habits of his region, however, and even in translation something of the original flavor comes through. Less laconic than the characters of *Bitter Bread*, those of *Main-Travelled Roads* say things that crystallize the uniqueness of their region's dialect, an ungrammatical admixture of English, German, and Swedish:

> "Dew tell! I wanto know!" exclaimed granny. "Wal I never! An, you're my little Willy boy who ust 'o be in my class. Well! Well! W'y, Pa, ain't he growed tall! Growed handsome, tew. I ust 'o think he was a dretful humly boy." [18]

Although Garland, along with Bret Harte, George Washington Cable, Sarah Orne Jewett, Willa Cather, and Charles Waddell Chesnutt, is chiefly remembered as an American regionalist, he seems on balance closer to his French Canadian counterpart Laberge than he is to these other writers from his own nation. Like Laberge, Garland was unconventionally critical in his literary approach to the depiction of rural life in his region, and both he and Laberge shattered the myth of rural existence as pastoral paradise by showing how isolated, brutalizing, and deterministic it really was. Though possessed of differing degrees of artistic skill, both Garland and Laberge prove how powerful regional literature can be.

The literature of Central and South America, like that of North America, also enjoys a long history of exceptional regionalist writing. With its many and varied environments (both human and physical), Latin America has produced a plethora of high-quality novels, short stories, poems, and dramas, some of which rank as masterpieces. With first poetry and then narrative leading the way, Latin American literature during the early twentieth century began to shed its cultural isolation and gain an increasingly international audience. The gradual integration of Latin American literature into the mainstream of Western literature was, in fact, achieved largely on the strength of a socially aware and politically involved regionalist literature. The novel, always closely tied to the prevailing social scene, was an especially potent force in bringing this change about. Indeed, many regionalist novels, written primarily during the first three decades of the twentieth century, have established themselves as classics of Latin American literature.

In Spanish America, works like Mariano Azuela's *The Underdogs* (1916), Gregorio López y Fuentes's *The Indian* (1935), Jorge Icaza's *Huasipungo* (1934), José Rubén Romero's *The Useless Life of Pito Pérez* (1938), José Eustasio Rivera's *The Vortex* (1924), Rómulo Gallegos's *Doña Bárbara* (1929), and Ricardo Güiraldes' *Don Segundo Sombra* (1926) are among the most enduring examples of regionalist literature ever produced. It is no exaggeration to say that it is within its great tradition of regionalist letters, and especially the novel, that Spanish

American literature began to discover its authenticity, to find its voice, and to assert its independence.

Although describing *The Vortex* as "the prototype of the new regionalist novel of the '20s," the critic Jean Franco also declares that "the greatest regional novel of this century is *Don Segundo Sombra*." [19] In truth, each of these novels offers ample evidence of why regionalism has long been so powerful a force in the literary development of Spanish America. While *The Vortex* is a realistically detailed yet hallucinatory novel in which the New World jungle, personified in a decidedly unromanticized fashion, overwhelms people and drives them to madness and death, *Don Segundo Sombra*, a Bildungsroman of the pampas, or Argentine plains,[20] realistically recreates the character of gaucho life while also managing to idealize it, to raise it to the level of an American myth or archetype. Indeed, as Franco notes, "the pattern which *Don Segundo Sombra* recalls is that of *Huckleberry Finn* rather than any European archetype. Here, as in *Huckleberry Finn*, we are confronted with a male world, one in which women, towns, officials of any kind, represent a threat." [21]

Like the other regionalists we have examined, Güiraldes imbues his text with the unique diction, speech rhythms, and customs of the gaucho world. Freely mixing words with intensely regional connotations, such as *tero* (a night bird of the pampas), *maté* (a strong tea) and *ombú* (the only tree native to the pampas) with words like "bridle," "lassos," and "poncho," for the things a gaucho uses in his daily routine, Güiraldes linguistically imparts a strong sense of a particular place. As in the case of other regionalist writers, like Haliburton, Laberge, and Garland, one cannot change the language of *Don Segundo Sombra* without incurring a serious distortion of the text's primary effect.

Yet the singular feature of *Don Segundo Sombra* is that, like all great works of art, it transcends the local to attain the universal. For all its careful recreation of the life of the gauchos, Güiraldes' work achieves mythic proportions. In this sense, it is a good example of the power and effectiveness of good regional literature, its ability to tap the universal by rooting its story in the local.

Another powerful example is José Eustasio Rivera's 1924 masterpiece, *La Vorágine* (*The Vortex*). In contrast to *Don Segundo Sombra*, *The Vortex* is not about gaining a mature sense of self and life but about how puny and insignificant human beings are in the face of the primeval New World jungle, a hostile, uncontrollable environment that first seduces and then destroys. The novel's protagonist, a city man nurtured on romanticized views of the New World, is thrown into a violent confrontation with the jungle that ultimately strips him of his veneer of civilization and renders him as savage as the natural world that engulfs him. Casting it in overwhelming and destructive terms, Rivera vividly brings the jungle to life in his novel, transforming it ultimately into the most important character in the work. More than Brooke, Laberge, Garland, or Güiraldes, Rivera makes the natural environment of his region the dominant force in the narrative. Indeed, when the focus of *The Vortex* moves away from the jungle, the novel degenerates into an undistinguished mélange of illicit love, economic exploitation, and violence; when, however, it concentrates on the dangerous presence of the jungle, as it does most of the time, *The Vortex* becomes a powerful demonstration of regionalism's special ability to bring to life the realities of existence that define unique regions and ethnic groups.

Brazil, a major part of what we mean when we speak of Latin America, has also had a long and important tradition of regionalism in its literary history. Like Canada and the United States, Brazil is a single large nation made up of distinctive regions. And in Brazil, as in Canada, the United States, and Spanish America, regionalism can be seen as the connecting link between romanticism and realism. Brazilian regionalism, moreover, which Samuel Putnam views as embodying Brazil's search for its "grass roots" identity,[22] possesses a pronounced kind of social consciousness, one that, as in Canada, the United States, and Spanish America, imbues it with a unique energy and commitment. Indeed, it is what we might term the political dimension of regionalism, its ability to mirror those social, geographic, linguistic, and cultural aspects of a nation's existence, that gives it its special character, that provides the most viable perspective from which to view the importance of the regionalist movement to literature throughout the Americas.

In Brazil, then, as in Spanish America, regionalist literature early on deliberately merged politics and local color, and works like Bernardo Guimarães' *The Hermit of Muquem* (1869) and *The Slave Girl Isaura* (1875),[23] Franklin Távora's *O Cabeleira* (1876), *The Backwoodsman* (1878), and *Laurenço* (1881), Escragnolle Taunay's *The Retreat from Laguna* (1871) and *Inocência* (1872), and Domingos Olímpio's *Luzia-Homem* (1903) have established themselves as classics of Brazilian literature. These texts, like the later novels of Jorge Amado, José Lins do Rêgo, Rachel de Queiróz, and Graciliano Ramos, show how from its inception Brazilian regionalism has blended political awareness into the realistic novel of manners.[24]

When in the 1876 preface to *O Cabeleira* (its subject an infamous backlands bandit), Távora wrote what can be regarded as Brazil's regionalist manifesto, he opened the way for a deluge of local and regionalist works. Developing through the 1870s and 1880s into a kind of national polemic on the nature of creative writing, regionalism came to have a revolutionary impact on Brazilian literature, which had long been dominated by the artificialities and inauthenticities of romanticism.

Ironically, however, it was a love story, *Inocência*, that became one of Brazilian regionalism's most important early works. Described as an idyl,[25] *Inocência* offers the reader a sober and realistically depicted love story shorn of the sentimentalism and passion that often characterize the romantic mode. Like *Main-Travelled Roads* and *Bitter Bread*, *Inocência* reflects the isolation, monotony, and backwardness that characterize the region it faithfully depicts. In a certain sense, because of the way it presents backlands culture and habits, *Inocência* is, like *Main-Travelled Roads*, a protest novel. Yet while Garland's work calls into question the economic inequities of some vast "system," Taunay's novel has a more limited focus, the rigidly determined gender roles men and women are forced to accept within this region. Also explored is the region's generally closed attitude toward outsiders, a prominent emphasis in *Bitter Bread* and only somewhat less important in *Main-Travelled Roads*.

With the exception of *Don Segundo Sombra*, all of the works so far examined exemplify our first definition of literary regionalism, that is, a kind of writing in which the author deliberately attempts to reproduce the natural environment, the character types, the attitudes, customs, beliefs, and speech habits of a particular region. The emphasis of such works is on faithful reproduction of a special place, of its people, and of its history. In short, a successful regionalist work of this type should leave the reader feeling that she or he recognizes what is unique and distinctive about a certain locale. There is little or nothing in such a work that is designed to lead the reader to considerations on a more universal plane; indeed, were the local-color dimension of such works eliminated, very little would remain. Finely crafted though they may be, as in the case of *Bitter Bread*, they are limited to a single frame of reference, to a single dimension.

As suggested earlier, however, there is a second category of regionalist literature, one that in contrast to the first variety stresses both the local and the universal, the latter deriving from the former. Works of this category, though perhaps fewer in number, include some of the New World's greatest literary achievements. New World masters like William Faulkner, Sherwood Anderson, Willa Cather, Juan Rulfo, Gabriel García Márquez, Luisa Valenzuela, Anne Hébert, Jacques Godbout, Gabrielle Roy, Margaret Laurence, Margaret Hutchison, Alice Munro, Mordecai Richler, Machado de Assis, Nélida Piñon, and Guimarães Rosa all succeed in capturing not only the manifold realities of the local places described but the humanizing force of the universal dimension that exists within these places as well. Laurence's fictional Manawaka, Márquez's Macondo, Faulkner's Yoknapatawpha, and Machado's Rio de Janeiro all exist as realistically portrayed locales at the same time that they come to life as places populated by characters (often local types) who in their hopes, fears, and struggles also play out the timeless human experience.

The works selected for closer examination here, Sinclair Ross's *As for Me and My House* (1941), Jacques Godbout's *Hail Galarneau* (1967), Herman Melville's *Moby-Dick* (1851), João Guimarães Rosa's *The Devil to Pay in the Backlands* (1956), and Juan Rulfo's *Pedro Páramo* (1956), all succeed in different ways in this powerful merger of the local and the universal, in showing how the one resonates within the other.

Described by Hugo McPherson as "one of the most finished works that Canada has produced," [26] Ross's *As for Me and My House* offers a prototypical blending of the two modes of regionalistic fiction, the local and the universal. As with all successful works of deep regionalism, *As for Me and My House* generates its appeal primarily by developing characters and themes that are inextricably bound up in a particular environment. Typical of the second category of regionalism, however, Ross's novel consistently transcends the local to confront issues of universal human significance.

The theme of Ross's work is the failure of the artist in a society whose values are hypocritical and materialistic. Although the novel's main character is ostensibly Philip Bentley, a frustrated artist who ekes out a subsistence existence for his family as a small-town preacher, *As for Me and My House* is narrated in diary form by Mrs. Bentley (whom the reader never knows except as "Mrs. Bentley"), whose own frustration and pain mirror and deflect those of her husband. These narrative threads generate and sustain a quadruple perspective: the painful drama of Philip Bentley himself; his wife's anguished commentary on her husband's dilemma; her poignant comments about her own degenerating situation; and, finally, the reader's response to each of the Bentleys' separate self-revelations, to their wretched cultural predicament, and to the harsh physical and psychological environment of the small Saskatchewan town in which they live. Ironically named Horizon, this town full of intolerance, narrow-minded bigotry, and hypocrisy is powerfully realized both as a "real" place and as a "timeless image of spiritual travail." [27]

The artistic excellence of *As for Me and My House* lies in Ross's ability to entwine what is authentic and unique about life in a small Canadian prairie town during the depression years with the eternal frustrations and hopes of the human spirit. Although life in Horizon unquestionably exacerbates their personal agony, the Bentleys' struggle is with garnering a modicum of dignity in their lives, with being able to gain a sense of authentic identity, satisfaction, and personal worth. The Bentleys could be removed from *As for Me and My House* in a way that Arabella Fermor or Sam Slick could not be removed from their stories without distorting the aesthetic integrity of the texts in which they appear.

Yet though the Bentleys, with their universal personal conflicts, would be just as unhappy in another time and place, Ross takes pains to merge the particularities of their status with the solitude, hypocrisy, and isolation that are peculiar to Horizon. For example, Mrs. Bentley writes of her husband, the epitome of the frustrated artist manqué: "I wish I could reach him, but it's like the wilderness outside of night and sky and prairie, with this one little spot of Horizon hung up lost in its immensity. He's as lost, and alone." [28]

Culturally and spiritually, Horizon (and all places like it) is a wilderness, and, as befits a book about the wilderness, Ross emphasizes the severity of its climate: the wind (which is the work's dominant motif), the sun, the endless cycles of wet and dry weather, the dust, the heat, and the cold all recur so often that they impart a relentless sense of aridity and stasis.

Although Philip Bentley represents the human version of this environmental harshness, his wife, the novel's chief narrative voice, who herself once had high artistic aspirations (to be a concert pianist), also suffers from the cultural and human wasteland that Horizon is. As she writes, late in the novel, wondering what is happening to her and her husband:

> I don't know what the outcome's going to be. . . . I feel old and spent tonight. . . . I catch myself staring into space, answering at random. I dread the nights. I dread getting up to start another day. There's no escape. I feel as if I were slowly turning to lead. [29]

The Bentleys' conflict is paralleled in a more restricted rural way by both Hamlin Garland and Albert Laberge in their works. For the Bentleys, however, the problem is not Horizon but any place that is like Horizon, a place that, in its suffocating conformity and rigid conventionality, blunts the kind of human growth and creativity that they seek. A poignant study of one of the human condition's most profound impulses, the urge to grow and develop, *As for Me and My House* succeeds brilliantly because its author melds, by means of realistic regional description and sensitive psychological portraiture, an evocation of a particular place at a particular time with a subtle depiction of what is timeless and universal about the human experience.

Another outstanding twentieth-century Canadian novel, Jacques Godbout's *Hail Galarneau*, also utilizes the motif of the frustrated artist to achieve the same moving blend of the local and the universal. An important difference between the two works, however, is that while *As for Me and My House* is basically dark and somber, *Hail Galarneau* is light and comical. Both texts have ambiguous conclusions that suggest guarded or skeptical optimism in relation to the futures of the characters portrayed. As the Bentleys' novel ends, they are thinking about leaving the church, which Philip can no longer even pretend to support, and opening a bookshop in a larger, more cosmopolitan town; *Hail Galarneau* ends with its protagonist, the sardonic antihero François Galarneau, becoming an artist, a writer who chooses to deal with life as it is, with all its failings, frustrations, and shortcomings.

Yet in spite of what appears to be a conventional happy ending, Galarneau's thoughts at the conclusion suggest that his decision is less felicitous than forced upon him by his realization that he has no other choice than to accept his fate, to do the best he can in an unfair and unjust world, and to laugh, perhaps angrily, about it. As he mordantly notes, "Happiness is like mayonnaise. It can turn bad for no reason at all. Life is never really simple." [30]

It is perhaps not quite proper to call Galarneau an artist in the same sense that Philip Bentley wanted to be an artist, however. Galarneau is less the artistically driven writer than he is a "scribbler" who, as he grills burgers and hot dogs at his L'Ile-Perrot stand, jots down on paper "poetic" fragments, random thoughts about himself and his French Canadian culture. A self-conscious and comically ironic narrator, Galarneau says, wryly: "When I grill my hot dogs I dream that they're priests sizzling at the stake. I make my revolutions in the grease-drain of my stove, and it works every time. I always win, I control the referendums." [31]

Written as a novel within a novel, *Hail Galarneau* criticizes and confirms various characteristics, attitudes, and dimensions of French Canadian culture, including the regionalist division within modern Québec itself into worldly, revolutionary urban centers and conservative, tradition-oriented rural areas. A kind of amateur ethnographer, Galarneau makes sarcastic but revealing observations about life in twentieth-century Québec. Eventually, these show him to be a disenchanted French Canadian "Everyman," a nobody whose struggles to survive in a complex and alien world reflect the struggle of little people everywhere. Acutely cognizant of who and what he is, "Le Roi du Hot Dog" (who watches American television and suspects his life is really controlled by two ubiquitous generals, General Electric and General Motors) emerges not just as a modern French Canadian but as the prototypical survivor who throughout history has managed to endure the wars and cultural conflicts more influential people generate.

Increasingly frustrated by the innumerable forces that work on him, by his inability to feel free, to be an individual, Galarneau eventually decides to have a wall built around him and his burger stand. Painfully aware of his ever-increasing psychic deformation, he says, "I'm shrivelling like a boiled hot dog forgotten at the bottom of the pot."[32] Yet when he reaches this point of despair, Galarneau tries to understand better how he feels by writing himself a letter, in which he speaks not only for himself but for all humanity: "It seems to me, if I may say so, that the only weak point in your solution of going into retreat is that while the wall indeed protects you it also isolates you."[33]

If Galarneau's self-imposed isolation is construed allegorically as an act of extreme separatism, his subsequent decision to become more of a "scribbler," "to replace the concrete wall by a paper one, a wall of words,"[34] is a brave and humane act of social integration and self-affirmation. Missing his customers, loutish though they often were, Galarneau finally realizes that he, a college dropout, can best express himself through a combination of nonexploitive, honest work, acceptance of the world as it is, and the use of the self-affirming act of writing to show how much better life might be if only people behaved differently.

Hail Galarneau is written partly in joual, a popular, nonstandard form of French cultivated especially from 1964 to the mid-1970s by a number of politically conscious Québec writers whose best work featured French Canadian images, characters, and political issues, such as Québec separatism and the pervasive influence of the culture of the United States in Canada. Despite this particularity, the book achieves a universal resonance.

Two other masterpieces of New World literature, Herman Melville's *Moby-Dick* and João Guimarães Rosa's *The Devil to Pay in the Backlands*, similarly achieve a powerfully affective union of the local and the universal. Written at different times and coming from different cultures, these works have many points in common: both involve a real quest as well as a symbolic one; both deal with the inscrutable mixture of good and evil in life; both demonstrate what the genre of the anatomy can look like in narrative fiction; and both are great adventure stories. Other similarities include the presence of a (possibly) demonic pact, a prose style that is conspicuously poetic, the use of narrators who are survivors of the conflict they narrate, and a distinctly epic stature to the action. Finally, *Moby-Dick* and *The Devil to Pay in the Backlands* both utilize a controlling yet ambiguous symbol to weld the entire text together—for Melville's work, the white whale, for Rosa the *sertão*, or backlands, of the state of Minas Gerais.

In *Moby-Dick* the whale, a part of nature, assumes a different significance for the several men who pursue it. Ahab, who senses the malevolence of the universe in Moby-Dick, vengefully seeks his destruction, while Starbuck, a devout

Quaker, insists that he is nothing more than "a dumb brute," an unthinking creature upon which it is madness and blasphemy to seek vengeance. Dominated by the figure of Ahab, *Moby-Dick* develops into a mythic study of good versus evil, a theme that is recast and replayed in *The Devil to Pay in the Backlands*.

Like *Moby-Dick*, *The Devil to Pay in the Backlands* rests on a single symbol which is inextricably bound up in the basic issue raised by both works—the ambiguous nature of existence. For Rosa, this central symbol is not a living creature but a region, the wild backlands of Minas Gerais, a microcosm of the world. Rosa's *sertão*, then, functions symbolically like Melville's whale, presenting human existence as an undecipherable interweaving of good and evil, a tangled web of events, motivations, and interpretations. Rosa's narrator, an ex-*jagunço*, or backlands gunman, makes this crucial point about the confusing nature of human existence early in the novel. Using a plant found in the *sertão* to serve as his example, Riobaldo, the narrator, says to his Marlowe-like interlocutor:

> Look here: in the same ground, and with branches and leaves of the same shape, doesn't the sweet cassava, which we eat, grow and the bitter cassava, which kills? Now the strange thing is that the sweet cassava can turn poisonous—why, I don't know. . . . But the other, the bitter cassava, sometimes changes too, and for no reason turns sweet and edible. . . . Everything is and isn't.[35]

A fully dramatized and self-conscious narrator/protagonist, Riobaldo refers again and again to the *sertão* as a mysterious "oceanlike expanse"[36] in which (as in life) appearances are deceiving and nothing can be trusted to be what it seems. In such a setting, vast, unknowable, and certainly inescapable, the human creature senses the precariousness and eternal mutability of existence. A recurring comment by Riobaldo becomes a key motif in the novel: "Living is a very dangerous business."[37] Ahab, one feels, would have understood what Riobaldo meant.

Melville generates a powerful sense of ambiguity in regard to the whale's symbolism. Moby-Dick, like the *sertão*, is as significant and as manifold as nature itself and, again like nature, both the whale and the backlands can be "paradoxically benign and malevolent, nourishing and destructive."[38] While Rosa focuses on the unpredictable mutations of the cassava plant to illustrate the uncertainty of life in the *sertão* and elsewhere, Melville, moving from the narrow regionalism of a whaling voyage to the universal, expresses the mystery of the human experience by focusing on the whale's paradoxical white color:

It was the whiteness of the whale that above all things appalled me. . . . Is it that by its indefiniteness it shadows forth the heartless voids and immensities of the universe, and thus stabs us from behind with the thought of annihilation, when beholding the white depths of the milky way?[39]

Recalling the timelessness of François Galarneau's wry observation that life, like mayonnaise, can suddenly go bad, Rosa's *sertão* and Melville's white whale establish themselves not merely as essential and integral aspects of particular regions and ways of life but as timeless symbols of the impenetrable enigma that is life.

Although *Moby-Dick* and *The Devil to Pay in the Backlands* have several features in common, they differ on several issues, too. Rosa's saga, for example, features a single narrator who remains in firm (if self-questioning) control of his narrative from beginning to end. Equipped with as much firsthand knowledge and experience about his story as Ishmael is, Riobaldo is much more self-consciously dubious about his ability to decipher what really happened in his life than is his more confident counterpart in *Moby-Dick*. Another key difference is that Ahab is a more tragic hero than Riobaldo, whose story is more mythic than tragic, more ironic than heroic, and ultimately more human than symbolic. Finally, while the crew of Ahab's *Pequod* has a parallel in Riobaldo's *jagunço* gang (the pitching backside of a backlands pony not being all that different from the rolling quarterdeck of a New England whaler), Riobaldo's vast *sertão* is not unlike Melville's ocean, for both are full of danger, contradiction, and confusion yet have to be crossed and recrossed in the living of life, which is not only "a very dangerous business" but an unfathomable one as well.

Another point of comparison between the two works has to do with the issue of diabolical possession, which at least one critic believes to be the real theme of Rosa's epic masterpiece.[40] Whether it is the basic theme of *The Devil to Pay in the Backlands* or a crucial motif that enhances the confusion of good and evil in life, the issue of possible demonic possession plays a fundamental role in the novel's structuring.

In *Moby-Dick* the same issue is present, though much less overtly. It derives largely from Ahab's oddly intimate relationship with Fedallah, the Parsee who, descended from "a race notorious for a certain diabolism of subtlety, and by some honest white mariners supposed to be the paid spies and secret confidential agents on the water of the devil,"[41] becomes Ahab's personal harpooner. In both works, then, there is the suggestion that the protagonists, reared in nominally Christian environments, make a pact with the devil in order to accomplish their respective goals, which, driven by vengeance, also turn out to be surprisingly similar. The meaning of the final struggle is much less a problem for Ahab than it is for Riobaldo, who, greatly changed by the events he relates to an unknown listener, lives to experience a new and even more maddening quest—that of understanding, of knowledge, of certainty.

The key difference in terms of vengeance, however, is that while Ahab seeks an ultimately deforming personal vengeance against another living creature (and in so doing challenges the rule of God),[42] Riobaldo, initially seeking to avenge the murder of one of his comrades, comes gradually to be motivated by a more saving social and perhaps even matriarchal vision, that of a *sertão* existing under the sign of peace and the rule of law and order. The texts imply that while Ahab's quest for vengeance damns him, Riobaldo's quest, ultimately directed toward a larger social good, redeems him.

The deep regionalism that distinguishes so much New World literature has also flourished in twentieth-century Spanish America, a part of the literary world long renowned for its regionalist art. Of the many modern Spanish American texts to achieve a universal scope by digging deep into the particular, as in *As for Me and My House*, *The Devil to Pay in the Backlands*, and *Moby-Dick*, Juan Rulfo's *Pedro Páramo* ranks among the best. Written in short, interlocking fragments that represent the voices of people dead and gone, *Pedro Páramo* tells the story of the destruction wrought by a Mexican cacique, or boss, on himself and those around him. Indeed, the word *páramo*, "desert" or "wasteland," is precisely what the novel's titular protagonist, Pedro Páramo, has created. Influenced perhaps by Faulkner's works, including *As I Lay Dying*, *Pedro Páramo* shows how one powerful man's selfishness and tyranny have created a kind of death in life for those who survive him. A dark, complex, and pessimistic work, *Pedro Páramo* is both quintessentially Mexican in its treatment of the cacique theme and universal in its depiction of the ruination that accompanies a life—or a culture—that sanctions greed, exploitation, and violence. As John Brushwood sees it, in *Pedro Páramo* "the universal human reality discovered by the author also contributes to the Mexican act of self-discovery."[43] By brilliantly baring the heart of the Mexican tragedy he presents here, Rulfo, like Faulkner, simultaneously speaks about the eternal conflicts of the human condition.

Pedro Páramo is also similar in some respects to Ross's *As for Me and My House*. Like the Canadian work (and in a sense like *Moby-Dick* and *The Devil to Pay in the Backlands*), *Pedro Páramo* is based on the motif of the quest. But while the Bentleys sought to escape the deadening lives they led in a small prairie town, Juan Preciado, a kind of ironic and ill-fated prodigal son, searches for his father, Pedro Páramo, who had long ago disappeared. Páramo, he learns, has died, as he himself eventually does, gradually smothered by the suffocating weight that the dead past exerts on the living present.

A significant difference here is that while *As for Me and My House* ends on a guardedly optimistic note, with the suggestion that the Bentleys are going to leave the church and their town, *Pedro Páramo* ends on a note of utter defeat. No one will ever escape the village of Comala (and the ruinous influence of men like Pedro Páramo), though others, like the Bentleys, may manage to escape the narrowness and rigid conventionality of Horizon. It is, moreover, the uniquely Mexican version of *caciquismo* (captured in the portrait of Páramo himself) that fatally infects Comala; Horizon, though bigoted and suspicious of imagination, intellectual growth, and new ways of doing things, is situated in a culture where characters like Pedro Páramo are less common.

Both Comala and Horizon are carefully depicted as being isolated, far from urban centers of culture and refinement. The central image of the empty rail-road line running off into the wind-swept distance is often invoked by Ross and serves to stress the tremendous distance, physical as well as psychological, that separates Horizon from more progressive places. Rulfo, like Ross, also utilizes images of distance and space and dust, death, and decay to underscore the isolation of Comala and the people in it. Always at the center of this isolation and decay is Pedro Páramo himself, a man "who was alone, like a tree trunk beginning to rot away inside." [44] The Bentleys, too, are portrayed as being alone, each lost within her or his own bitter and frustrated world, but the text implies that if they can escape from Horizon they may ultimately pull together again, to achieve the kind of loving human union that Páramo, for all his power, can never attain.

Like other great regionalist writers, Ross and Rulfo skillfully weave aspects of the natural and human environments into their characterizations. Rulfo, for example, enveloping his narrative in an oppressive and ominous atmosphere, writes: "It was in the dog-days, when the hot August wind is poisoned by the rotten smell of the saponaria. . . . The heat shimmered on the plain like a transparent lake." [45] Like Ross, Rulfo is adept at suggesting not just the physical isolation of his novel's setting but its psychological desolation as well. As his narrator, Juan Preciado, says of Comala:

Now I was here in this silent village. I heard the sound of my footsteps on the fieldstones that paved the streets. A hollow sound, echoing against the walls.

I was walking down the main street, past the empty houses with their broken doors and their weeds. . . . There weren't any children playing. . . . I wasn't used to silence, with my head so full of noises and voices.[46]

Horizon, of course, even during the Great Depression is a more viable town than the moribund Comala. But in both places there is a sense that the atmosphere, geophysical as well as sociopolitical, suffocates people, that the oppressive mores and codes of conduct ensure that life there will be stunted and blighted. Literally and metaphorically, both Ross and Rulfo entwine the deadened existence of their protagonists with the nature of their settings.

As we have seen, *As for Me and My House, Hail Galarneau, Moby-Dick, The Devil to Pay in the Backlands*, and *Pedro Páramo* are all based on the motif of the quest; each of the very different protagonists of these novels seeks something, and in seeking it he or she reveals both a specific regional situation and a timeless human impulse. It is precisely this dimension of regionalism, its capacity to stress the uniquely local while simultaneously embodying the universal, that has made it such a potent and enduring force in the development of New World literature.

The Americas encompass a geography that is extraordinarily varied. When one adds to these natural differences the ethnic multiplicity of the New World and its radically different systems of social, political, and economic development, it becomes clear why regionalism has historically played such a powerful role in the evolution of letters in North, Central, and South America. In a certain sense, of course, all writers are regionalists because all literature is about someone somewhere. Yet the greatest writers of the New World, among them Willa Cather, William Faulkner, Emily Dickinson, Margaret Laurence, Alice Munro, Sinclair Ross, Gabrielle Roy, Jacques Godbout, João Guimarães Rosa, Nélida Piñon, Luisa Valenzuela, and Juan Rulfo, go far beyond the narrow category of local color to achieve powerful and affective statements about the eternal human condition. Long a vital dimension of New World literature, regionalism continues to offer the people of the Americas a way of highlighting their cultural differences while at the same time permitting us to see our common bonds.

Solitude

9

The Evolution of

an American Literary

* * * * * * * * * * Motif

The evolution of solitude as a motif of New World literature is both logical and ironic: logical because one could reasonably expect it, given the cultural diversity and geographic isolation of the Americas, and ironic because one would not expect the frustration and paralysis associated with this theme to develop in cultures so self-consciously concerned with their own making and remaking. The development of this motif also seems to be a result both of the tumult of the twentieth century and of the gradual demise of the myth of the New World as an edenic paradise. In the literature of the United States the latter element has been given form as the "failure of the American Dream," and failure is understood more often than not in materialistic rather than idealistic terms. In other parts of the New World, we have similar examples of failure, though in these often "less-developed" areas it is more frequently not the failure of a dream so much as it is the failure of the social, political, and economic systems that could make the dream reality.

Though traditionally said to be more flexible than European society, the New World has not been uniformly paradisiacal in the opportunities it affords people. As our own history shows us, the social, political, and economic realities of the New World have rarely been able to measure up to the expectations that people have had of them. The result, as we see in one of Inter-American literature's most powerful themes, is a sharp sense of disillusionment, of the failure of things to be as good as they could be, to be as good as they should be.

Implicit in the works that express this sense of disenchantment is the belief that, at bottom (and harking back to Columbus's letters and reports), the New World has always been more real as an ideal than as a material reality. A corollary to this basic belief is that given the ideal context in which the Americas have long been envisioned by people elsewhere, we in the Americas can never be satisfied with anything less than perfect societies. To accept an imperfect status quo by saying that "this is the way things are" is lamely to betray the highest principle of the American experience, which is to seek always to make things better. By substituting materialism for idealism and pragmatism for justice, we debase the aspirations of all who have labored to make the New World a place of equal opportunity for everyone. Closely related to the positive and exciting quest for identity, then, the evolution of solitude as an identifiable motif of American literature has a traceable history, one in which the disillusionment and disenchantment of the American experience are recast in terms that show not only what has gone wrong but why.

Often anguished, occasionally despairing, but virtually never nihilistic, works like Gabrielle Roy's *The Tin Flute*, Anne Hébert's *The Torrent*, Saint-Denys-Garneau's *Les Solitudes*, Marie-Claire Blais' *L'ange de la solitude*, Hubert Aquin's *Prochain épisode*, Hugh MacLennan's *The Two Solitudes*, Claude Jasmin's *Ethel and the Terrorist*, Malcolm Lowry's *Under the Volcano*, Margaret Laurence's *A Jest of God*, William Faulkner's *Absalom, Absalom!*, Ralph Ellison's *Invisible Man*, N. Scott Momaday's *House Made of Dawn* and *The Ancient Child*, Gabriel García Márquez's *One Hundred Years of Solitude*, Octavio Paz's *The Labyrinth of Solitude*, Carlos Fuentes' *The Old Gringo*, Machado de Assis's *Esau and Jacob*, Dalton Trevisan's *The Vampire of Curitiba*, Rachel de Queiróz's *The Three Marias*, and Clarice Lispector's *The Hour of the Star* show that as a literary motif American solitude possesses distinctively cultural, historical, and psychological dimensions which, as we shall now see, animate some of the New World's most powerful works of literature.

Considered a classic of Canadian literature and a work that in many respects can be considered the prototypical expression of American solitude is Hugh MacLennan's 1945 novel, *The Two Solitudes*. As the title suggests, *The Two Solitudes* takes up the issue of the "two Canadas," one French and one English, and, through the interplay of its characters, shows not only the forces that separate and estrange them but (recalling *Les anciens Canadiens*) how they might ultimately be reconciled as well. The plot of *The Two Solitudes*, as many critics have noted, really generates two different novels: one is dominated by the struggle between the wealthy, progressive French Canadian aristocrat Athanase Tallard and the poor, conservative parish priest, Father Beaubien (who stubbornly opposes change), while the other is dominated by one of Tallard's sons, Paul, and his marriage to Heather Methuen, a marriage that symbolizes the union of the two Canadas. In contrast to the bitter conflict between Tallard and Beaubien, which, in laying bare the inner sociopolitical tensions of Québec as well as its uneasy relationship with English Canada, has the inevitability of Greek tragedy, the relationship between Paul and Heather, and their symbolic significance for Canadian unity, seems pale and contrived.

Early in the novel, Tallard (who has been reflecting on how, long before, the French court at Versailles had sealed New France's doom by failing to colonize and fortify it, as La Salle and others had advised) begins to dream about how he would modernize life in his small, rural, and poor Québec locale: "He knew what he wanted here: the factory would become the foundation of the parish, lifting the living standards, wiping out debts, keeping the people in their homes where they had been born, giving everyone a chance. . . . It would be a revolution, and he would be the one to plan and control it."[1]

Summing up the old antagonisms between English and French Canada and pinpointing the internal conflicts within Québec itself, Tallard realizes that "changes were certain to come. . . . They would either come from the outside, from the English and Americans as they were coming now, or they would come from French-Canadians like himself."[2] In making these plans, Tallard's fatal error is in thinking that he, wealthy, educated, and progressive, could manipulate the poorly educated but fanatically determined Father Beaubien, who "had begun to think of Athanase as the embodiment of all the forces of materialism which threatened French-Canada, and his own parish in particular."[3] The two antagonists become locked into unreconcilable positions that in their immutability reflect the "two solitudes" of Canadian culture, the two cultures that obstinately resist cooperation with each other.

The central irony in the struggle between Tallard and Beaubien over Québec's future is that after Tallard risks everything he has—his fortune as well as his cultural identity—to bring a factory and jobs to Saint-Marc, he is betrayed by a ruthless English Canadian financier, McQueen, who sees that Athanase's usefulness to him is finished when he is excommunicated and made a pariah by the unyielding Beaubien. Realizing that by becoming formally ostracized by the parish Tallard is of no further use to him, McQueen goes to the bishop to complete his scheme. Suggesting that for the hierarchy of the Catholic church money is more powerful and important than morality or the ideals of a parish priest, McQueen's deal with the bishop ironically undercuts both Beaubien and Tallard.

This devastating turn of events proves to be fatal for Tallard, whose death brings the first part of the novel to a close. Although he is reconciled with his church before he expires, Tallard's demise poignantly underscores the complex solitude in which French and English Canada coexist, a solitude that because of the generations of enmity and mistrust involved amounts to a potentially ruinous isolationism.

Though the novel might well have ended here, with the problem of the two Canadian solitudes powerfully etched, it does not; rather, it begins to focus on the growing rift between the siblings, Paul and Marius, the latter a militantly Anglophobic advocate of Québec separatism who stands in opposition to Paul, who with Heather offers a unified vision of Canada. As John Yardley, an important secondary character and the grandfather of Heather, believes, Paul and Heather together represent the "New Canada," proud of both its French and English heritages.

Heather's pretentious and narrow-minded mother, Janet Methuen, raises two objections to the proposed marriage of Paul and Heather: the first is radical, that "it was most undesirable for mixed marriages to occur between French and English families,"[4] while the second, an expression of class-conscious snobbery, is that Paul is "not Heather's kind at all. He's worked in garages and he's been a professional hockey player. . . . Why, he was even an ordinary seaman."[5] Set in the novel's larger context, Janet Methuen's objections suggest how heavily the deeds and attitudes of past generations weigh on present and future generations, how powerfully and insidiously the events of the past affect what we think and do in the present. This reality contributes directly to the near inviolability of the solitudes that have enveloped the two Canadas. (And as we shall see, this same theme, the corruption of the present by the crimes of the past, also contributes decisively to the motif of solitude in other major works of American literature, most notably Faulkner's *Absalom, Absalom!*, Machado de Assis's *Dom Casmurro*, and García Márquez's *One Hundred Years of Solitude*.)

The novel ends with the marriage of Paul and Heather, the reconciliation of Heather and her mother, and with Canada—both its English and French elements—poised on the brink of World War II. The novel's concluding lines imply that war, first World War I and now World War II, had, ironically, brought the two Canadas closer together, that war had helped break down the barriers between them. Crucial in the final scene is the image of French and English Canada as being "like oil and alcohol in the same bottle," an image that implies not an easy, rapid, or harmonious breakdown of the two solitudes but one that would be hard, slow, and charged with controversy. However, because "the bottle had not been broken yet,"[6] MacLennan's concluding image also suggests that Canada's two solitudes might yet be reconciled. The motif of solitude thus emerges as part of the larger issue of identity, which MacLennan shows to be an ongoing process rather than a definitive end result.

Another classic Canadian novel, Gabrielle Roy's *Bonheur d'occasion* (*The Tin Flute*),[7] also addresses the issue of solitude, this time from a cultural perspective that, unlike *The Two Solitudes*, is limited to that of French Canada. *The Tin Flute* deals with the vicissitudes of a Montreal slum family locked in the solitude of poverty. Set in a part of pre–World War II Montreal known as Saint-Henri, a district isolated from the rest of the city by its economic status, *The Tin Flute* focuses on the struggle of the Lacasse family to survive, a struggle that as in *The Two Solitudes* is ironically made somewhat easier when the impoverished husbands, fathers, and brothers of Saint-Henri find new incomes for their families by enlisting in the army.

More than MacLennan, however, Roy questions the morality and justice of a social system that can bring a very modest prosperity to poor people only by paying them to go off and fight a "European" war. This situation, keenly sensed by Florentine and, especially, Emmanuel, two of the novel's major characters, contributes to the oppressive sense not merely of solitude and isolation but of rejection and exploitation.

Their lives locked in the solitude of destitution, the members of the Lacasse family, barely held together by the mother's frugality and Florentine's meager income from her dime-store job, struggle against the economic deprivation and psychological alienation that threaten to disintegrate them. The poverty that has engulfed the Lacasse family gives the lie to the old myth of the New World as an earthly paradise, and Roy's grimly realistic novel can be read as a cry of protest against the injustices of a socioeconomic system that benefits one group at the expense of another.

Representing both the present and the future and desperate to escape her suffocating environment, Florentine offers herself to a man, Jean Lévesque, in the blind hope that love can somehow save her from the slow agony of her death in life. This theme, later to be handled brilliantly by Malcolm Lowry in *Under the Volcano* and by Clarice Lispector in *The Apple in the Dark* and *The Hour of the Star*, comes to be a major force in *The Tin Flute*. What Florentine, unlike the reader, does not recognize, however, is that the man at whose feet she is throwing herself is incapable of helping anyone; already rendered utterly selfish and exploitive by the solitude of his own poverty, Lévesque, an orphan, reflects on what a woman like Florentine means to him: "She was his poverty, his solitude, his dreary childhood, his lonely youth; she was everything he had hated and denied."[8]

Of the characters who use love as a weapon with which they hope to shatter the solitude that envelops their lives, only Florentine's mother, Rose-Anna, and Emmanuel Létourneau, an idealistic and selfless young man who, enamored of Florentine, becomes her fiancé after Lévesque abandons her, are able to wield it unselfishly. Even Florentine ultimately fails to do this; so diminished is she at the end of the novel by her solitude, loneliness, and disillusionment that she marries Emmanuel, whom she does not love but to whom she is grateful for loving her. The corruption of her once-innocent character by the poverty of her life is made painfully evident in the novel's closing scene, in which Florentine selfishly thinks: "Yes, a new life was beginning for them all. . . . Good gracious, she was rich! . . . At heart she rejoiced at the course of events, for without the war where would they all be?" [9] The redemptive force of love is thus blunted in *The Tin Flute* by the multiple assaults of an overwhelming poverty that not only separates people but isolates them by fostering their selfishness.

Because the perverting of Jean Lévesque early in the novel is paralleled by Florentine's slightly more disguised degeneration late in the novel, the reader of *The Tin Flute* is left with the strong impression that, as Márquez shows in *One Hundred Years of Solitude*, as Faulkner shows in *Absalom, Absalom!*, and as Lispector shows in *The Hour of the Star*, there is a cyclicality of oppression at work here, one that in its relentless twisting of human lives and values is passed on from generation to generation. Just as Rose-Anna is told by her mother that things will not be any better for her than they were for her mother, so too does Rose-Anna represent for her daughter, Florentine, the kind of stunted life that must be avoided. Florentine, a sensitive young woman, is painfully aware that she does not want to lead the kind of life her mother has led. But, as *The Tin Flute* makes clear, her tragedy is that she cannot escape the psychologically crippling weight of generations of exploitation.

Locked profoundly in the solitude of their poverty, Jean Lévesque and Florentine Lacasse have physical intimacy but fail to achieve any sort of spiritual relationship. Lost in the solitude of noncommunication, they come to see selfishness—itself a form of social solitude—as the only worthy principle on which to base one's life. Though the past weighs heavily on the events depicted in MacLennan's *The Two Solitudes*, its pernicious force is more poignantly felt in *The Tin Flute*, where, as in the Macondo of *One Hundred Years of Solitude*, there is the implication that the cultural solitude of French Canada is virtually impenetrable, that the oppressive weight of the past is too great to throw off.

A work that attempts to depict the militant overthrow of the cultural, psychological, political, and economic solitude in which French Canada has been forced to exist is Hubert Aquin's powerful 1965 novel, *Prochain épisode*, a work that, ironically, is as much about stasis, paralysis, and the failure of revolution as it is about the need for revolution. One of many excellent French Canadian novels published in the mid-1960s, *Prochain épisode* is a complex, incisively political work that functions, according to Ronald Sutherland, on at least three levels: as a dramatic spy story, as the personal confession of an avowed terrorist, and as a symbolic commentary on contemporary Québec's struggle to achieve identity and independence.[10] Although *Prochain épisode* is initially presented as the metafictional attempt of a jailed Québecois separatist to recapture his former commitment and sense of purpose by writing a novel, the reader's attention is quickly riveted upon the tormented and obsessive main character of the narrator's story, an ardent revolutionary ordered to assassinate a certain H. de Heutz. This relatively simple plot structure grows increasingly elaborate, however, as the narrator begins more and more to identify with his intended victim, a development that can be read as a symbolic representation of the tangled and all too often rancorous relationship between English Canada and Québec.

It is on this latter level of interpretation, which gives a deeper resonance to the other two, that the reader senses the extent of modern-day Québec's solitude and the degree to which its past as a subservient minority culture weighs oppressively upon its restive present. But, as the terrorist-protagonist of *Prochain épisode* shows, the problem in all this is uncertainty: uncertainty about whom in Québec society he can safely love and whom he should hate as his enemy; uncertainty as to when he should act; uncertainty as to exactly what action he should take; and, most crucial to the novel's theme, uncertainty as to the effects of the actions contemplated. Like Hamlet, the self-conscious narrator of *Prochain épisode* is beset by doubts. Mesmerized by his intended victim's tale, which has the suggestion of fratricide about it, and paralyzed by the thought that the woman he loves (a woman he identifies with his love for the separatist revolution) might also be his victim's mistress, the protagonist is unable to act.

This mysterious woman is of crucial importance for the novel because it is largely through her intimate relationship with the narrator (and, perhaps, with the narrator's target) that the reader senses just how complex modern Québec's situation really is: if the "blond woman" the protagonist loves is a lover of both the revolution and of Québec's status quo (she is suspected of having had an affair with the protagonist's intended victim, who has been designated an "enemy" of the revolution), then the question of how to proceed with the revolution is suddenly much more confused, personally and politically, than it had seemed earlier. Painfully aware of the mistake he may have made in not executing H. de Heutz and of the uncertainty and doubt that led him to spare his intended victim, the narrator/protagonist agonizes over what has happened and what it all means, to him and to Québec: "When the battles are over, the revolution will continue; only then will I perhaps have time to finish this book and to kill H. de Heutz once and for all. . . . That will be the end of my story."[11]

The solitude of Québec, which is presented as though on the verge of full-scale civil war, remains externally intact in *Prochain épisode*. Internally, however, where the forces of its unchanging past are colliding ever more violently with the forces of its rapidly changing present, the question is not so much whether Québec will break out of its cultural solitude but of how it will do so. It thus remains an issue for the "next episode," one which will have profound significance not only for Canada as a whole but for the rest of the Americas as well.

William Faulkner's *Absalom, Absalom!* is another work that shows how the past can affect the present. Rooting the universal in the local, Faulkner develops the motif of solitude in this famous 1936 novel in such a way that it becomes a metaphor for the physical, spiritual, and psychological isolation of women and men everywhere. Set in the fictional Yoknapatawpha, Mississippi, in the early nineteenth century, *Absalom, Absalom!* tells the story of Thomas Sutpen, who, having been wronged, feels justified in committing a series of crimes that perpetuate a pattern of human rejection and vengeance and produce tragic consequences for many others, including Sutpen's own descendants. Thus, the story is not so much about Sutpen as it is about the effects of his life on other people, some of whom are generations removed.

The novel's four primary narrators, each of whom can be seen as a victim of Sutpen's crimes, tell highly imperfect versions about the meaning of the web of events that connects them to each other and to Sutpen, himself a victim of a baser aspect of the human condition: our indifference to the welfare of others. For Faulkner as for Machado de Assis, it is human indifference that produces the solitude that grips his characters. Epitomizing this problem is one of the four principal narrators, Rosa Coldfield, who as a child had been treated so indifferently by her family that her life became devoid of love, the one force that for Faulkner (as for Machado) can break the solitude that imprisons and twists people. Rosa, now an old woman, describes her early years as being enveloped in a "warped and spartan solitude" which taught her little besides how to fear and shun the world around her.[12]

Yet, as Rosa's words show, the damage done by the loveless solitude of her childhood years was not merely the result of her own stunted existence; just as she had been ignored and denied love, so too would she retreat into selfish self-absorption and reject the very people she desperately needs to love and to be loved by. In short, and in a way that typifies the fundamental problem in *Absalom, Absalom!*, the wrong that was done to Rosa is perpetuated by similar crimes through future generations. In Faulkner's world, which is at once intensely local and expansively universal, the victims all too often become victimizers.

Rosa Coldfield is not the only character in *Absalom, Absalom!* to exist in a state of solitude. Thomas Sutpen himself, who lived in the "masculine solitude" [13] of one accustomed to bending people to his will, suffered (though he was not aware of it) from "that solitude of contempt and distrust which success brings to him who gained it because he was strong instead of merely lucky." [14] Sutpen, desiring a male heir to the dynasty he hopes to build, asks the then twenty-one-year-old Rosa to prove herself a suitable wife by bearing a male child before they marry. Sutpen's debasing proposal lies at the heart of Faulkner's novel.

Rosa, though offended by the profound indecency of what Sutpen wants, is desperate enough for love that she knows she is not far from acquiescing to his demand. The great injustice that Sutpen does Rosa therefore does not rest on an issue of outraged puritanical sexuality but on a deeper moral issue: the callous disregard of one human being by another. What Sutpen proposes to Rosa offends her primarily because what he wants reduces her to chattel, to the status of a thing, a possession that before being "bought" must prove its utility. Rosa comes to understand this when she recalls how he "spoke the bold outrageous words exactly as if he were consulting with Jones or with some other man about a bitch dog or a cow or mare." [15]

By showing how future generations struggle to understand the meaning of Sutpen's life and its relationship to their own lives, Faulkner describes a unique brand of American solitude, one that calls into serious question not only the myth of the New World as an earthly paradise but, in a more nationalistic context, the myth of the rugged individualist that is so much a part of the New World's cultural development.

As did Gabrielle Roy in *The Tin Flute*, Faulkner, through Thomas Sutpen, leads his reader to ask whether the end ever justifies the means. By giving free rein to personal ambition, unrestrained individualism, and the quest for power, do we not imprison ourselves in a kind of moral solitude? Like Absalom in the biblical story of King David, from which Faulkner draws the title of his novel, Sutpen rises to a position of great power before he falls, leaving his descendants to ponder his downfall and, above all, to expiate the guilt they feel because of his crimes.

Illustrative of the tragic entanglement of lives is Henry Sutpen, a descendant of Thomas Sutpen and the murderer of a man named Charles Bon. Bon, the reader discovers, was the child of Thomas Sutpen and a Haitian woman, Eulalia Bon, who was abandoned by Sutpen upon his discovery that she was the product of an earlier miscegenous union. The central mystery of *Absalom, Absalom!* revolves around this murder: why did Henry Sutpen murder Charles Bon after some five years of friendship? Only in the final pages of the novel, when Quentin Compson III, a later descendant of the family, and his Canadian roommate at Harvard, Shreve McCannon, begin to reconstruct all that has happened to the Sutpen clan, does Faulkner reveal the key to the puzzling murder: Charles Bon had "Negro blood" in his veins.

Ironically, however, the reader, seeing through Bon's eyes, suddenly realizes that while Henry Sutpen could out of his love and admiration of Bon accept the incestuous marriage of Bon, his half-brother, and his sister, Judith Sutpen, he could not accept a racially mixed marriage. As Charles Bon says to Henry Sutpen, moments before the latter kills him, "So it's the miscegenation, not the incest, which you cant bear." [16] In killing Charles Bon, who along with his mother had been rejected by Thomas Sutpen, his father, Henry Sutpen plays out once again the central theme of *Absalom, Absalom!*, the ruinous effects of one human's rejection of another.

Using the Old South as a metaphor for the entire human experience, Faulkner focuses on the tragic effect of slavery upon both the people who lived it and those who descend from it. Through four generations of Sutpens, the theme of the abuse of one person by another, and the revenge this abuse inevitably begets, is played out repeatedly. The final effect is not merely that Sutpen's story symbolizes the experience of the South within the United States but that it symbolizes what is most essential in the human condition. As Faulkner shows, solitude is, ironically, a condition of the powerful as well as the weak, for the violator becomes as isolated as the violated.

A very similar kind of solitude is developed in *One Hundred Years of Solitude*, written by the Nobel Prize–winning Colombian author, Gabriel García Márquez. Márquez, whose work has often been compared to Faulkner's, creates in this extraordinary 1967 novel a fictional world, Macondo, that resembles Faulkner's Yoknapatawpha in several ways: both locales are isolated; they are pervaded by a kind of fatalistic sadness; they exist in an atmosphere of abandonment; and, finally, in both the present is largely ruled by the past. And, again like Faulkner, Márquez is a mythic writer who sees time as a circular force, who develops his narrative around a single theme (the isolation of a place and the people who inhabit it), and who creates characters (replete with genealogical charts) so intensely involved with each other that their relationships become incestuous. There are other similarities as well: both novels involve the fall of a family; out of very particular places, both develop the universal theme of abandonment and rejection; and both use a lushly poetic and metaphoric style.

But for all these similarities, there are substantial differences as well: Márquez's narrative is both funnier and more compassionate toward its characters; it is also more fatalistic than Faulkner's work (because it suggests that human solitude is utterly inescapable); and, finally, Márquez's world, brought vividly to life through his magical realism, is decidedly more fabulous than Faulkner's more mimetically rendered world. Although it is as locked in its solitude as Yoknapatawpha is, Macondo is also an enchanted place where priests levitate, where a girl can be so pure and innocent that one day while hanging sheets up to dry she suddenly ascends to heaven, where it can rain nonstop for four years, eleven months, and two days, where dead men return as lonely ghosts, and where a plague of insomnia can make everyone forget what things are called and what they are used for. Márquez, unlike Faulkner, also shows the reader how Macondo came to be and how it was settled by José Arcadio Buendía and his wife, Ursula, the New World Adam-and-Eve progenitors of the Buendía family, whose epic rise and fall the narrative chronicles through five generations. In a sense, José Arcadio, a dreamer and an idealist always fascinated by the unknown, and Ursula, the epitome of level-headed (if gender-dictated) endurance, are the only two characters in the novel, for all the others can be seen simply as variations on the strengths and weaknesses of these two.

The founding of Macondo, which occurs early in the narrative, underscores the enchanted quality of the tale and revives the venerable theme of the New World as the Garden of Eden. Moving through the region's unknown but extraordinary terrain, José Arcadio, Ursula, and their party felt that they had plunged deep into the biblical primeval forest: "The men on the expedition felt overwhelmed by their most ancient memories in that paradise of dampness and silence, going back to before original sin."[17] Hemmed in by the wilderness, they unexpectedly encounter an ancient Spanish galleon, whose "whole structure seemed to occupy its own space, one of solitude and oblivion, protected from the vices of time and the habits of the birds."[18] Macondo is thus founded in a place "protected from the vices of time," a place whose reality is from the beginning a matter of "solitude and oblivion."

In the course of a few pages, Márquez's narration establishes the atmosphere not just of wonder and enchantment in Macondo but, more significant, of isolation and impenetrable solitude. Structurally, these pages are also decisive, for it is here, at the very genesis of Macondo, that the reader is apprised of what is to be Macondo's ultimate fate, its eventual descent into "oblivion." Some 360 pages later, at the very moment this descent begins, a descendant of José Arcadio and Ursula cracks the code of the mysterious parchments that predict the fall of Macondo—which, though magical for a time, would ultimately be "exiled from the memory of men."[19] By giving his story this structural circularity, Márquez implies that escape from the solitude and oblivion of places like Macondo is impossible, that "races condemned to one hundred years of solitude did not have a second opportunity on earth."[20]

Márquez is more absolute about the imprisoning power of Macondo's solitude than Faulkner is of Yoknapatawpha's. Although the Sutpen clan and the Buendías come to the same end—oblivion—they do so for different reasons: the Buendías fail because they are fated to, because they are already condemned to a certain period of time in a certain place, but the Sutpens fail, in contrast, because they will not change their way of life based on selfishness, exploitation, rejection, and, inevitably, revenge. Both Márquez and Faulkner use the motif of solitude to symbolize the entire human condition: Márquez by suggesting that the Buendías, like people everywhere, have only a limited time on earth and Faulkner by stressing that the important thing is the question of choice in our decisions about how we live out our lives, about what we do and why. If Márquez's solitude is essentially historical, then Faulkner's can be said to be fundamentally moral.

As is appropriate for a motif, the word "solitude" occurs repeatedly in *One Hundred Years of Solitude*, as it does in *The Tin Flute* and *Absalom, Absalom!*. Colonel Aureliano Buendía (who organized thirty-two armed rebellions and lost them all) is like Rosa Coldfield and Florentine Lacasse in that the solitude of his early years ensured that he would later languish in another kind of solitude, one replete with sociopolitical implications but still characterized by personal loneliness and isolation. And Colonel Buendía, who, painfully conscious of his condition, would never "break the hard shell of his solitude," would engender seventeen sons, each of whom had his father's "solitary air."[21]

There is, however, in both *Absalom, Absalom!* and *One Hundred Years of Solitude* a pervasive sense of inevitability not found in *The Two Solitudes*, *The Tin Flute*, or *Prochain épisode*. Both Faulkner and Márquez stress humankind's insignificance in time and in so doing emphasize the eventual oblivion that is our fate. A character like Thomas Sutpen, as much a tragic hero as a monster, struggles mightily against this fate, trying always to "make that scratch, that undying mark on the blank face of the oblivion to which we are all doomed,"[22] while the Buendías accept their fate much more stoically. Yet if *Absalom, Ab-*

salom! often has the flavor of classical Greek tragedy, *One Hundred Years of Solitude* seems more of a black comedy, a wryly comic farce in which the human condition is treated more with sardonic resignation and fatalism than with hubris.

An additional dimension of this point, one which illuminates a basic difference in the way these two works deal with the motif of solitude, has to do with the nature and development of the central characters. Thomas Sutpen, for example, is really two very different people: one, the older Sutpen, dominates the story and holds it together through time; the other, the young Sutpen, experiences at the age of fifteen the cruel rejection that the older Sutpen will repeatedly inflict upon others.

In *One Hundred Years of Solitude*, on the other hand, which has no single character of the stature of Thomas Sutpen, the several generations of the Buendía family coalesce to replicate the strengths, weaknesses, manias, and idiosyncrasies of the original pair, Ursula and José Arcadio. In their own way, the descendants of the founding couple are as tied to their progenitors as Sutpen's descendants are to him. The difference is that while there are two Sutpens, there is only one category of Buendías, and all of them overwhelmingly resemble not the older Sutpen (the one who is strong, aloof, and implacable in his power and solitude) but the younger one, the callow boy who, powerless, vulnerable, and in need of love, was rejected by a status- and race-conscious mountain family. Culturally, psychologically, and politically, the Buendías come to life not as the victors, one of whom Thomas Sutpen ruthlessly becomes, but as the vanquished, like Sutpen the forsaken child. Márquez's novel, moreover, reverberates with political overtones; on one level Macondo is a metaphor for all of Latin America, which except for the exploitation of its natural resources has largely been ignored. Macondo's complex solitude, then, is not just "marvelous" but political, cultural, and historical as well, a product of its having been rejected by the rest of the world.

Márquez uses two devices to show the reader the nature of Macondo's solitude: the first is the character of the ageless gypsy magician, Melquíades, who introduces strange and wonderful "inventions" like ice, magnets, telescopes, and magnifying glasses to the credulous inhabitants of Macondo; the second is the intrusion of a railroad into Macondo, a technological "advancement" that also brings the gringos—the banana plantation entrepreneurs—and, finally, terrible violence and bloodshed. The train's symbolic function is to show how the outer world of "civilized" and "progressive" societies finally shatters the hermetic solitude and isolation of Macondo.

Almost immediately, however, the people of Macondo realize that those who come with the railroad have come not to help but to exploit. Carefully segregating themselves in an armed camp surrounded by an electrified fence, the gringos set about transforming Macondo not into what its inhabitants want it to be (and what it once was), a paradise free of want and strife, but into an ill-paid supplier of raw materials for factories in the United States. As Colonel Aureliano Buendía ruefully announces one day to no one in particular, "Look at the mess we've gotten ourselves into . . . just because we invited a gringo to eat some bananas."[23] The conflict between the owners of the banana plantation and the workers finally leads to a strike for higher wages and better working conditions, but it is violently crushed with great loss of life. The entire episode is summarily denied in the official reports, suggesting that in such cases the lies of the exploiters are more powerful than the truths of the exploited. The experience of Macondo with the train (technological "progress") and the official denial of any wrongdoing serve as metaphors of the history of the United States' involvement in Latin America. As Márquez suggests, this history is bitterly ironic in view of the fact that we are—or should be—New World allies, not adversaries.

The politically charged theme of the ever-greater cultural, political, and economic influence that the United States exerts on its New World neighbors turns up with increasing frequency in New World literature, especially that of the twentieth century. In works as diverse as *The Imperialist, Hail Galarneau, Canaan*, and *One Hundred Years of Solitude*, the United States is depicted both as a powerful though often misguided friend and as a frankly dangerous problem, a culture whose own vanity and isolationism have too often rendered it indifferent to the needs of its New World neighbors.

In addition to its pungent political dimension, *One Hundred Years of Solitude* differs stylistically from *Absalom, Absalom!* in that it is largely a narrated story rather than a novel in dialogue. The various senses of solitude established by the several first-person narrators of *Absalom, Absalom!* have an immediacy and power that are not present in the more resigned and fatalistically detached sense of solitude established by the omniscient third-person voice that dominates *One Hundred Years of Solitude*. Yet this latter work's more objective tone is itself a brilliant technical achievement by which Márquez can suggest just how pervasive Macondo's solitude really is and how, in fact, it cannot be overcome.

Although both novels rely heavily on biblical symbolism and imagery, their conclusions, which spring directly from their texts' differing points of view, show some significant differences. In *Absalom, Absalom!*, Quentin shouts in the cold, dark air of a Harvard dorm room that he doesn't hate the South, while at the end of *One Hundred Years of Solitude* Aureliano Babilonia, the last of his line, has just deciphered the parchments (given him by Melquíades) that explain the origin and fall of the house of Buendía. Both novels conclude with a character's realization of the meaning of all that has happened, though Quentin's personal anguish stands in sharp contrast to Aureliano Babilonia's fatalistic acceptance. In each case, however, the essence of New World solitude—a function of historical, political, and cultural forces—is definitively established.

Three other New World novels that develop the motif of solitude in a less cultural and more psychological fashion are Clarice Lispector's *The Apple in the Dark* (1961) and *The Hour of the Star* (1977) and Malcolm Lowry's *Under the Volcano* (1947). Of these three works, *Under the Volcano* and *The Hour of the Star* link the motif of solitude to a certain culture, to a particular place and time. Lowry's work, indeed, contrasts two disparate aspects of the American experience with solitude: the cool, sparsely populated and pristine forests of Canada and the hot, densely populated, and corrupt Mexican city of Quauhnahuac during the late 1930s, while Lispector's metafictive 1977 text speaks to the "two Brazils," the rich one and the poor one, and, like *The Tin Flute*, to the psychological solitude imposed by poverty.

While the essential despair or solitude of *Under the Volcano*'s protagonist is to some degree a reflection of European political events during the years of the Third Reich and the Spanish Civil War, Lispector's earlier work, *The Apple in the Dark*, is in contrast to *The Hour of the Star* much less concerned with specific political or social circumstances. Yet for the Lispector of the 1961 narrative, the drama of human existence can be seen as a function of phallogocentrism, of a male-dominated sociopolitical system that, in its rigid assignment of gender-based identities, effectively isolates and cripples everyone involved, men as well as women. Lispector's solitude in *The Apple in the Dark* is therefore more philosophic—especially in a poststructural sense—than is that of Lowry, who, more than Lispector, is concerned with showing the impact of international politics on individual lives.

Although there are many differences between them, Lowry and Lispector both make the motif of solitude a central feature of their respective works; both writers depict the personal struggle between our human need for love and for our equally strong need for privacy (a form of solitude); and, finally, both develop what might be termed the solitude of stasis, of the inability to act or to get beyond a paralyzing confusion over what action to take.

Of the first category, the solitude of individual existence, Lowry and Lispector offer a great many examples, most of which deal with the loneliness and isolation of the human condition and with the failure of both love and language to bridge the gap between our isolated existences. Both authors focus primarily on a single character who, ironically, is surrounded by others who in their own ways are either trying to reach the protagonist or to be reached.

Although the protagonist of *The Apple in the Dark*, a very ordinary middle-class man named Martim, is described by the narrative voice as being "in the heart of Brazil," [24] Brazil is not nearly as important to his story as Geoffrey Firmin's Mexico is to his, and this constitutes an important difference between the two texts. Building her text lyrically rather than mimetically, allowing waste-land imagery and the images of darkness and silence to dominate, and narrating as if she were inside Martim's mind, Lispector describes her protagonist as slowly coming to a realization about the nature of his condition: "Open-mouthed, he looked around himself, because certain gestures had become terrifying in the solitude." [25]

Geoffrey Firmin, the British consul of *Under the Volcano*, comes to a similar understanding about the tragic essence of his condition, though he does so much later in his story. As Lowry describes it: "The Consul, with a slow burning pain of apprehension, felt again how lonely he was, that all around him . . . stretched a solitude like the wilderness of grey heaving Atlantic." [26] Firmin realizes that he is at least as attracted to his own impenetrable solitude as he is to Yvonne, his former wife and the woman he still loves.

The problem of love in human relationships is thus developed by both Lowry and Lispector as the single most crucial element in their characters' struggles to break down the solitude that imprisons them. When Firmin, finally lost in despair, asks to be delivered from the "dreadful tyranny of self," [27] he is expressing the crux of his dilemma. Martim, in a less courageous and hence less affecting fashion, struggles in his own myopic way with a similar problem:

> Since Ermelinda had never told him that she had loved him up to the point of making it a life Martim did not know that he himself was the man not loved now, nor did he understand that she had stopped loving him. But as if she were imploring him for a truth more merciful than reality, he pleaded desperately for the cause of someone else.[28]

The ambivalent pull of love, generously toward another but also selfishly toward oneself, thus plays a critical role in the development of both Firmin and Martim, both of whom struggle against love even while they realize that love is the only thing that can save them.

The essential difference between Martim and Firmin can be seen as one of perspicacity; Geoffrey Firmin, an honest and sensitive intellectual, understands his situation only too well, even to the point of realizing that he is his own worst enemy, his own agent of destruction. When we meet him, Firmin has consciously decided to stop his self-deception and confront the terror of his situation, which, as the text develops, is shown to rest on one point: Firmin's refusal to act, even to save himself. Firmin's tragic flaw, then, is not ignorance but knowledge, and self-knowledge in particular. As the text makes evident, many of Firmin's final hours are spent thinking about Yvonne and the love that in spite of their divorce they still feel for each other. But theirs is a doomed love, one that each of them has abandoned in favor of something else: for Yvonne, the chance to lead a more stable, less ruinous life by dissociating herself from her increasingly alienated and disintegrating mate and for Firmin, the opportunity to indulge his love of self, a condition that propels him ever more rapidly toward self-destruction.

Though it too is profoundly bound up in the ambivalences and contradictions of love, Martim's predicament differs considerably from that of Geoffrey Firmin. This thematic difference is reflected in the respective styles of the two novels. While *Under the Volcano* is subjective, intense, and tightly orchestrated, *The Apple in the Dark* is objective, endlessly raciocinative, and plotless. Lispector's poststructuralist approach to narrative style and structuring gives to Martim's experience with love a very different cast, one that is basically rational rather than emotive. Because of Martim's limited understanding of what is happening to him, his love is also fraught with misconceptions and misrepresentations, problems, the text shows us, inherent in language itself.

Like Firmin, then, but in a more muddled fashion, Martim experiences the ambivalence of love. But whereas Firmin, a man hopelessly and compulsively alienated from everything and everyone around him, including those who love him, has already opted to continue with the anguish of his self-imposed exile, Martim, a less tragic figure, eventually gives up his quest for authentic existence in favor of the inauthentic, unsatisfying, but safe existence allotted to him by the gender-conscious society he had earlier lashed out against. So it is that at the end of his novel Martim, a timorous and willing male victim, is docilely led back into the crippling but stable society he had once fled. His flat, nontragic fate stands in sharp contrast to the pointless murder of Firmin. Lowry's is a conclusion that, richly symbolic of the ethical malaise of twentieth-century society, presents Firmin in the tragic mode. Martim, on the other hand a "prisoner of a ring of words,"[29] is the quintessential poststructuralist hero, sensitive to (if not clearly understanding) the deforming demands made by a phallogocentric system but—like the women around him—unable to break free of it.

Although the solitude of Geoffrey Firmin and Martim is (its sociopolitical overtones notwithstanding) essentially private and psychological in nature, it nevertheless possesses a dimension related to the theme of the New World as failed paradise. It is in this context that the cultures of Mexico, with its corruption and fascist police, and Canada, which here provides an almost utopian contrast to Mexico, come to life. But beyond this intra–New World comparison of cultures and attitudes, Lowry, more than Lispector, offers a new interpretation of the New World considered as Eden. One of his secondary characters, a Frenchman, M. Laruelle, ponders his own conduct in Mexico, for him an "Earthly Paradise": "Yet in the Earthly Paradise, what had he done? He had made few friends. He had acquired a Mexican mistress with whom he quarrelled, and numerous beautiful Mayan idols he would be unable to take out of the country." [30] Later literally described as Eden, Mexico leads Firmin to make an acridly ironic comparison between Mexico and the biblical Garden of Eden:

> "Did you know, Quincey, I've often wondered whether there isn't more in the old legend of the Garden of Eden, and so on, than meets the eye. What if Adam wasn't really banished from the place at all? . . . Or perhaps, . . . Adam was the first property owner and God, the first agrarian, a kind of Cárdenas, in fact—tee hee!—kicked him out. Eh?" [31]

Implicit in Firmin's comparison is a view of Firmin himself as Adam. Like Adam, Firmin pays a price for tasting of the fruit of the tree of knowledge and, as with Adam, love played a role in his downfall, just as it might in his regeneration. And, finally, Firmin like Adam is painfully conscious of having to go on living and suffering, condemned to a personal hell of isolation and agony. The private solitude of Firmin, the British consul, is thus linked metaphorically to the failure of the New World to live up to the paradisiacal myths that had over several centuries been promulgated about it. Far from being edenic, Firmin's Mexico, a New World reflection of what was happening politically in Europe during the late 1930s and early 1940s, was in actuality a hellhole, in which the fatally flawed Geoffrey Firmin could do no better than choose to self-destruct.

Martim, too, is a kind of Adam (albeit an ironic one, since he flees from his seemingly edenic society), and so it is that an apple, the popularly accepted fruit of the tree of knowledge, comes to play a key symbolic role in his story. This is especially apparent in the closing section of the novel ("The Apple in the Dark"), when Martim, anxiously trying to expiate the guilt he bears for having tried (in a confused and desultory fashion) to establish a somehow free and authentic existence, is seeking to be punished and then forgiven for having committed what he had formerly viewed as his liberating crime: "In the name of

God, I'm only waiting for you to know what you're doing. Because I, my son, I am only hungry. And I have that clumsy way of reaching for an apple in the dark—and trying not to drop it." [32] Overall, Martim's story, including his pathetic relationships with Ermelinda and Vitória, the women who run the farm he stumbles upon, can be taken as a sad parable of what life in a phallogocentric system is like.

Unlike Lowry, Lispector makes no explicit connection between the setting of her novel—Brazil—and the New World. Central to Lispector's development of her novel's atmosphere, however, is an abundance of wasteland imagery. One might argue that this permeating barrenness underscores the isolation and solitude of its New World characters. Yet while this is undoubtedly a valid critical statement about the text, and although it could therefore be read as an anti-utopian novel about the failure of the New World as a Garden of Eden, Lispector (*The Hour of the Star* excepted) never makes this connection as pointedly as Lowry does. Thematically, then, *The Apple in the Dark* deals with what are essentially poststructuralist relationships among language, gender, and being, while *Under the Volcano*, with its numerous references to the Spanish Civil War and to fascist governments, develops more around the depiction of Geoffrey Firmin's sociopolitical consciousness.

Firmin, like Martim, hardly exists except as a flow of consciousness, as a pattern of self-reflection and divagation. One major difference in the psychological development of these two characters is that while Firmin's story is, except for flashbacks, limited to a few chronological hours, Martim's story, unrelentingly interiorized, runs over a much longer stretch of chronological time. But Martim's story parallels Firmin's in that it too rests on the two levels of language use, our silent inner thought-flow and our spoken language; Martim, like Firmin, exists primarily in the ebb and flow of his private and often duplicitous thought process. Although it may at any time be penetrated by the language and therefore the existence of someone else, this inner reality, established and maintained by the instability and elusiveness of language itself, becomes Martim's primary ground as a literary character. The conscious contemplation of language and its ontological reliability, features which figure more prominently in *The Apple in the Dark* and *The Hour of the Star* than in *Under the Volcano*, are therefore viewed by both Lowry and Lispector as the means by which the consciousness of the protagonist can best be presented. But for Martim as for Firmin, this intense presentation of consciousness can be simultaneously cause and symptom of each character's inability to act.

The solitude and isolation generated by Martim's inner musings about the uncertainties of language, being, and truth are much more dispassionately presented than are those in *Under the Volcano*, where they inexorably lead to Firmin's violent destruction. While Martim, in what might be termed a passive action, allows events to happen to him in such a way that society assumes responsibility for his existence, Firmin remains true to his deeply alienated self, his desperately guarded isolation, even when his refusal to act, even "passively," results in his death at the hands of the corrupt, fascistic police, the same social group to whom Martim so obsequiously capitulates. If Firmin steadfastly refuses to play the role of the active, aggressive hero, Martim, gradually worn down by fear and responsibility, becomes a dutifully repentant citizen, humbly seeking readmission into the immorality and amorality of social existence. While the one cannot allow himself to act in a conventionally heroic fashion, the other cannot resist the security that comes with asking others to act on him. In each case, however, a state of profound solitude is created and each character finds himself utterly alone at the conclusion of his narrative.

Though no one would argue that the motif of solitude is in any way the special province of New World literature, the texts under consideration here do show that solitude continues to exist as an issue of special significance for New World artists. Manifesting very definite historical, cultural, and psychological dimensions and bringing into contrast not only the New World/Old World dichotomy but a new and critically self-reflective intra-American perspective as well, the sense of solitude estabished in works like *The Tin Flute, Prochain épisode, The Two Solitudes, Absalom, Absalom!, One Hundred Years of Solitude, Under the Volcano, The Apple in the Dark,* and *The Hour of the Star* is demonstrably American, one which binds the Americas together by focusing on how we relate to ourselves, to each other, and to the rest of the world. As writers like MacLennan, Laurence, Roy, Blais, Aquin, Faulkner, García Márquez, Allende, Lowry, Lispector, Piñon, and many others make clear, we in the Americas are united not only by history, circumstance, and geography but also by our common sense of solitude, by our sense of cultural isolation and failure. Less relevant to what we have been than to what we need to become, the motif of solitude offers a disturbing view of the New World experience.

10

* * * * * * * * * *

The Conflict between Civilization and Barbarism

Another of New World literature's most definitive themes, the conflict between civilization and barbarism (often portrayed in terms of the wilderness and its inhabitants), can also be traced back to the arrival of the Europeans. Perhaps only the cultures of the Pre-Columbian peoples, who attempted to live in harmony with nature, have succeeded in avoiding a sense of antagonism between the human realm and its natural counterpart. Since 1492, however, American literature has manifested this theme to the extent that it can now be said to constitute a defining feature of life and letters in the New World. When the Europeans began to arrive, they found themselves everywhere having to deal with an often hostile natural environment as well as its inhabitants, a rancorous situation that was itself a reflection of an even more fundamental dichotomy in the Americas, the interests of the Old World versus those of the New. This deep-seated sense of conflict between civilization and the "barbarous" wilderness has developed into a basic feature of New World literature, manifesting itself at different times and in different forms and coming to symbolize our passion for progress, development, and expansion as well as our still-ambivalent relationship with the environment and with ourselves.

One particular dimension of this theme, a supposed contrast between the corruption of human society and the edenic innocence of "natural" life in the American wilderness, shows that what the educated European mind thought must be true about the New World experience proved not always to be the case. The American version of the *bon sauvage* turned out on occasion to be just as rapacious and cruel as his Old World counterpart, the "civilized man." Still, from the outset the New World was seen by the Europeans as a place of innocence, a place free from the prejudices and vices that had long plagued their own societies. This idealized attitude would change, however, rather quickly.

But if it changed, it did not disappear. Rather, it evolved into a number of different forms and concepts, one of which, the idea that American culture was split between its "civilizing" attributes and its "natural" or "barbarous" ones, would, nearly five hundred years later, emerge as a staple of American literature. In the process of pushing west, whether in Canada, the United States, Brazil, or Spanish America (where the issue is more muddled), the "civilizing" forces of the east (and of the eastern cities) were pitted against the wild, "uncivilized" forces of nature, of the wilderness. Throughout the Americas, images of the frontier or the garrison are commonplace, as are those that reflect another of American literature's most endemic themes, the hybrid culture that, neither totally "cultured" nor totally "barbaric," struggles to define itself. Closely related to the quest for identity, the theme of conflict between civilization and barbarism, or the wilderness, has been a constant in New World literature, present in the Americas from the early exploration chronicles up to the present day. From the northernmost reaches of Canada to the tip of Argentina, the expansion of the Americas has produced a wealth of poems, dramas, and narratives that intrinsically or extrinsically address this integral New World conflict.

An early classic of English Canadian fiction that takes up this issue is Susanna Moodie's *Roughing It in the Bush; or Forest Life in Canada* (1852). A genteel member of nineteenth-century England's middle class, Moodie offers in her entertaining work a series of lively autobiographical sketches of life in the Canadian wilderness (Ontario) of the 1830s. Although ostensibly written to warn other people not to do what she and her husband had done—give up a comfortable urban culture for a "wild" one—Moodie's often slyly humorous narrative suggests a profound fascination with wilderness life and illustrates her ability to adapt to it, to unlearn what her romanticized European education had taught her to expect. Moodie's distinctly ambivalent attitude about "the bush," an attitude that Margaret Atwood believes is quintessentially Canadian,[1] is made even more compelling for the reader because of the author's implicit (and sometimes explicit) comparison of life there with city life, the latter functioning as an emblem of civilization's supposed virtues. Placing herself at the center of her narrative, Moodie (like her older sister, Catharine Parr Traill, whose 1836 book, *Backwoods of Canada*, also chronicles a pioneer's experiences) manages to be both clinically objective and subtly subjective in her recounting of what her life, that of an urbane Englishwoman, was like in the Canadian wilds, where one's "civilized" expectations were rarely realized.

Another canonical nineteenth-century English Canadian work to deal with the conflict between the wilderness and civilization is Major John Richardson's *Wacousta* (1832), an engrossing gothic romance that strikes what Northrop Frye has called "a tone of deep terror in regard to nature."[2] Developing largely through flashbacks and the use of intense descriptions of nature as both terrifying and balsamic, *Wacousta* takes place in and around Fort Detroit during Pontiac's rebellion in 1763. Often compared to the Leatherstocking Tales of Cooper,[3] *Wacousta* is the epitome of the work that develops its central conflict from the antagonism between civilization, here represented (ironically enough) by an army garrison, and the wilderness, peopled by "savages."

The action of *Wacousta*, which labors under an often-stilted dialogue, reflects a state of mind as well as a place, and this is crucial to the work's surprisingly poetic effect. Nightmarish and at times even surreal, *Wacousta* splits itself between a structural polarity: the "civilized" world of the British soldiers inside the fort and the "wilderness" world of the Indians and the surrounding primeval, sinister forest. The text's conflict becomes more complex when, at the conclusion, the reader learns that the dreaded "devilish savage," Wacousta, is really a former British officer, Sir Reginald Morton, who has joined the Indian world because of a wrong done him in Europe by his erstwhile comrade-in-arms, Charles De Haldimar, the officer now in charge of the garrison. If Morton thus represents both worlds, civilization and nature (though he has forsaken one for the other), De Haldimar, the reader senses (recalling Moodie), feels an unsettling psychological attraction to the wilderness as well. In spite of being repelled by what he sees as its inherent savagery, De Haldimar is at the same time attracted to its sensuousness and primitivism.

Wacousta's controlled ambivalence about who is morally right or wrong in the struggle between the "rational" forces of the garrison troops and the "irrational savagery" of Wacousta and his forces suggests that Morton and De Haldimar might symbolize the new and confused psychology of the citizen of the Old World who comes to the New World not for a tour of duty but (like Martim, of

Iracema) to stay, to forge a new existence. Created largely of psychological and cultural tensions, *Wacousta* can be read as a metaphor for the problematic struggle to unify two dissimilar but not unrelated ways of life, a struggle that as in *Iracema* epitomizes the entire New World experience. Artificially imposed on a natural or wilderness state, the garrison and the rigid military sense of order that goes with it are but an intermediary step, one is led to believe, along the road that at some future point will lead to a symbiotic synthesis of the wilderness and civilization.

A slightly different approach to this theme appears in two twentieth-century works, Margaret Atwood's *Surfacing* (1972) and William Faulkner's *The Bear* (1942). In these narratives the protagonist, who comes from a civilization that is felt to be corruptingly materialistic, profane, and violent, undertakes a literal and psychological journey of self-discovery and regeneration in the untrammeled wilderness. Like *Wacousta*, these works depict the wilderness as a formidable place, inimical to the ways of the civilized world. The difference, however, is that Richardson blurs the boundary between "civilized" and "barbarous" behavior (and therefore between civilization and the wilderness) more than Atwood and Faulkner do. For these latter writers, whose works are set in the twentieth century, when technology is thought to control or dominate nature, the wilderness requires a different way of life, a different set of values. In *Wacousta* the text (with its 1763 setting) generates not a clear-cut choice between civilization and nature but an ambiguous and uneasy merging of the two.

All three novels are powerfully psychological, however, in that each deals with a highly interiorized struggle to create and sustain an authentic identity, a struggle that takes place within the mind of the protagonist. Atwood's hero, an unnamed woman, fits this pattern more neatly than Faulkner's main character, who is less urbane, less analytical, and less decisive. The protagonist of *Surfacing*, shown early in the narrative to be vaguely dissatisfied with the successful city life she is leading, decides to undertake a search for her missing botanist father in the wilds of northern Québec. Led ever deeper into the wilderness in her search, the narrator comes to realize that she is also searching for herself, a theme that dominates the latter half of the novel. The wilderness, for the narrator both a physical place and a conceptual construct, requires that she change as she enters more deeply into it, that she adopt new ways of seeing, thinking, and being. By having the protagonist regress geographically and psychologically to a more "primitive" state, one ultimately accompanied by a physical transformation as well, Atwood suggests that her hero needs a new sense of identity, based on the realization that human beings do not control or dominate nature but participate in it, as parts of it.

It is interesting to note that although *Surfacing*'s narrator does discover that her materialistic urban existence has been largely a fraud and that she needs to reconnect with her "primitive" roots, she at no point believes she can remain in the wilderness. Such a conclusion to this lyrical and symbolic novel would be too simplisitic. Atwood chooses instead to show her protagonist passing through an intensely private process of self-discovery and then, after the ecstasy of rebirth has ebbed, realizing that she cannot physically survive in the wilderness, that her proper state is the social one created by other men and women. The novel ends as the narrator is rather dubiously making plans to return to society, the text implying that she is a radically changed person. Her final self-conscious remarks suggest, however, that there is no reason to be confident that her future back in human society will necessarily be happy or rewarding. Indeed, like *Wacousta*, *Surfacing* suggests that the ways of civilized and primitive existence are or can be intertwined and that we, as the thinking animal whose realities are determined by words, must learn to recognize and maintain some sort of mutually sustaining balance between these two worlds.

The conclusion of *Surfacing* achieves what Atwood herself has called a "kind of harmony with the world," one that merges the narrator's sense of self with both the primitive forces of the wilderness and the realities of her twentieth-century urban existence.[4] Because the novel's development is structured around two poles, the wilderness and civilization, it is the narrator's self-critical consciousness that charts the ebb and flow of the basic conflict. Thus the path of the narrator's naturalist father, who split his family's time between "the city and the bush,"[5] is eventually replicated by the narrator herself, who says, reflecting on her metamorphosis by the wilderness, "It's too late, I no longer have a name. I tried for all those years to be civilized but I'm not and I'm through pretending."[6] Seeking her father in the Québec bush but discovering herself, the narrator of *Surfacing* is in quest of a new existence, one which will harmoniously reconcile the best features of civilization with those of the wilderness.

Like Atwood in *Surfacing*, Faulkner in *The Bear* sharply contrasts life in civilization with life in the wilderness. In both novels a strong sense of opposition is implied, though this feature is more sharply stressed by Faulkner than by Atwood. Both writers develop the conflict by means of certain key images and symbols: for Faulkner, it is the old bear, a mythic beast that epitomizes all that is free and majestic in nature, while Atwood used several images, including a frog, a loon, Indian gods, and a sacred lake. Each of these images is contrasted with the relentlessly destructive incursions of twentieth-century humankind, whose overweening belief in machines and what they can do has led us to think we are the rulers of the natural world. As the omniscient narrator says, referring to the boy who becomes the novella's protagonist:

> He was sixteen. For six years now he had been a man's hunter. For six years now he had heard the best of all talking. It was of the wilderness, the big woods, bigger and older than any recorded document:—of white man fatuous enough to believe he had bought any fragment of it.[7]

Like Atwood, Faulkner sets up a situation in which there exists a powerful antagonism between civilization and the wilderness. Unlike *Surfacing*, however, where this conflict does not immediately appear, *The Bear* draws the lines of battle almost from the outset. Speaking of the sacred nature of the struggle and of the humans involved, the narrative voice of *The Bear* declares:

> It was of the men, not white nor black nor red but men, hunters, with the will and hardihood to endure and the humility and skill to survive, and the dogs and the bear and deer juxtaposed and reliefed against it, ordered and compelled by and within the wilderness in the ancient and unremitting contest according to the ancient and immitigable rules which voided all regrets and brooked no quarter.[8]

Faulkner stresses the fact that his main characters, Sam Fathers and his protégé, Ike, are not random agents of death and destruction but hunters, men who in the context of the story have almost priestly duties to perform in relation to the sanctity of the wilderness and its creatures.

On the other hand, Atwood's characters, both female and male, are more thoroughly urbanized. More important, they show themselves to be considerably more tainted and misled by their urban existence. With the exception of Boon, Faulkner's characters are portrayed as at least sensing the sacred significance of the wilderness and, in appreciating its laws, they seem at least partially at home in it. Atwood's characters, in contrast, are idle, shallow interlopers, men and women who, both victims and victimizers, are wholly out of place in the wilderness. Only Atwood's narrator is capable of sensing through her contact with the wilderness what has become imbalanced and false in her life and of doing something about it.

As a consequence, both Faulkner and Atwood weave their narratives around the struggles of their protagonists to develop a code of existence, a way of life that does not violate what for each of them is an essentially religious conversion via the wilderness. For both the narrator of *Surfacing* and Ike, in *The Bear*, a natural existence is contrasted with a social one. Both characters, moreover, are faced at the end of their stories with the perhaps impossible task of reconciling the two modes of existence. Just as Ike fails to repudiate the guilt he feels for the slavery-related crimes his ancestors had committed, so too does the narrator of *Surfacing* doubt both the durability of her conversion in an acquisitive urban world and her ability to effect a change in any part of that society. While Ike is a kind of acolyte who participates humbly in a semiannual hunting trip in the wilderness, Atwood's narrator is an outsider, yet one whose way of life, though largely alien to the ways of the forest, still allows her to retain enough sensitivity, courage, and honest self-awareness to respond to her regenerating encounter with nature. Though they approach it from different perspectives, Ike and the narrator of *Surfacing* are similar in their positive responses to the wilderness.

A crucial moment for both characters in their deeply personal, even mystical union with the wilderness comes when both realize that, in order to bridge the gulf that separates the urban from the wilderness world, they must divest themselves of something. For Ike, the pivotal act is the discarding of his gun, watch, and compass, for it is only after he has done this that he is permitted to see the bear, an archetypical creature which "ran in his knowledge before he ever saw it." [9]

Atwood's protagonist similarly enters into the sanctity of the wilderness by giving up something she too had previously thought important. In her case, it is her clothing, the trappings of her vain urban existence, and the ring of her lover. As she says, growing more conscious of her conversion:

> I slip the ring from my left hand, non-husband, he is the next thing I must discard finally, and drop it into the fire, altar, it may not melt but it will at least be purified, the blood will burn off. [10]

Then, as if completing a wilderness baptism, a transformation into a more primitive kind of animal, the narrator's stream of consciousness declares:

> I have to clear a space. . . . I leave, carrying one of the . . . blankets with me, I will need it until the fur grows. . . . I . . . step into the water and lie down. When every part of me is wet I take off my clothes, peeling them away from my flesh like wallpaper. . . . Inshore a loon: it lowers its head, then lifts it again and calls. It sees me but it ignores me, accepts me as part of the land. [11]

Just as the narrator seems now to exist with the loon as an equal, and not as a threat, so too does Ike see the bear, in a brotherly way, immediately after he lays aside his gun, watch, and compass:

> . . . the bush, the compass and the watch glinting where a ray of sunlight touched them. Then he saw the bear. . . . It was . . . looking at him. . . . It . . . looked back at him across one shoulder. Then it was gone . . . sank back into the wilderness.[12]

Standing in sharp and poignant contrast to the sense of communion and harmony that characterizes the scenes in which Ike and Atwood's narrator accept—and are accepted by—the loon and the bear is the debasing sense of possessiveness and power that emanates from certain of the secondary characters. The illusion that humans ever possess anything in nature is best symbolized in *The Bear* by Boon, the insensitive and violent character who, surrounded by squirrels as the text concludes, yells, "Get out of here! Dont touch them! Dont touch a one of them! They're mine!"[13] Boon's pathos suggests that in Faulkner's narrative the basic dichotomy is between the world of nature and those human beings who believe that they are the rulers of nature, that nature is to do with as they please.

Atwood sets up a similar contrast in *Surfacing*, though here the question of possession does not involve the human animal and nature but a more social issue—the relationship between men and women. In *Surfacing*, the narrator's quest for self-discovery necessarily involves self-liberation; her rejection of a social system based on power and the subjugation and exploitation of one sex by another implies her decision to cease being possessed, sexually, psychologically, or culturally, by men. Just as Faulkner makes use of a secondary character, Boon, to highlight the clash between civilization and the wilderness, so too does Atwood utilize two of her minor characters, the unhappy couple, David and Anna, to dramatize what is wrong when one person attempts to possess or control another. Both David, a pretentious boor, and Anna, shallow and submissive, are victims of a social structure in which one sex is allowed (and even encouraged) to dominate the other.

At the core of Atwood's feminism in *Surfacing* is the suggestion that the problem is neither men in general nor even individual men like the obnoxious David (who, though he would never be able to understand why or how, is just as surely a victim, though one on a higher rung of the social pecking order, as Anna, who sees herself obliged to endure David's abuse, is). The problem, rather, is that the human society reflected in *Surfacing* has become so distorted in its value systems that it victimizes almost everyone, men as well as women. By corrupting a few with the lure of power, the seductive but false belief that we should possess things and people, human society has become a perversion, one that all honest, sensitive, and compassionate human beings would seek either to reject or to change. To dramatize this situation is the role of *Surfacing*'s narrator, a woman who has been victimized, who realizes what the real problem is, and who, having undergone a personal awakening, also recognizes the difficulties that face her as she contemplates a return to society. It is worthwhile to note that Atwood depicts Joe, the narrator's former and perhaps future lover, as a victim too, a human being as damaged by society as the narrator is. The question implicit in the conclusion is whether these two victims can learn to work together as equals in the struggle to reform their lives and their society.

Ike and the narrator of *Surfacing* are similar in that it is only when they are in the wilderness that they realize the oneness of all life. Ike sees that the social prejudices that separate whites and nonwhites, for example, in "civilized" society are simply irrelevant to life in the woods, where desirable qualities have nothing to do with one's racial heritage. *Surfacing*'s narrator comes to a similar realization, except that what is so terribly wrong in her world is not the racial question but the distorted relationships between men and women. Ike's attempt to repudiate the crimes of his grandfather, who had fathered a child by his own daughter, and of his society, which did nothing to discourage such dehumanizing conduct, reflects both the racism and the sexism of his culture. *Surfacing* develops the question of female/male relations by showing one woman's rejection of her spurious social existence, one sharply contrasted, as Ike's is, with the nature of wilderness existence.

Finally, both Ike and the narrator of *Surfacing* envision their futures as constituting not merely new lives but as utopias, as new worlds in which all people could live together harmoniously. Both *Surfacing* and *The Bear*, then, make use of the venerable theme of the New World as an edenic place where people can begin again and where the mistakes of the past can be corrected. Yet in contrast to Ike, who speaks categorically in part 4 of trying to live a new and more just life, Atwood's narrator speaks only obliquely of her ability to create a new life for herself back in civilization. While Ike appears doomed to failure in his attempt to live in human society by the codes of conduct he learned in the wilderness, Atwood's narrator, a late twentieth-century woman with more options open to her, has a better chance to succeed. In each case, however, the future of our human existence seems to hang, symbolically, in the balance. Racially, sexually, and every other way, Atwood and Faulkner seem to be saying, we must work together for our mutual benefit rather than work separately to dominate, possess, or control each other. When Atwood's narrator says, "This above all, to refuse to be a victim," [14] one can almost imagine Ike responding, "Yes, but how? And how to refuse to be a victimizer in a society that encourages both?"

A different treatment of the wilderness/civilization theme is provided by Georges Bugnet in *La fôret* (*The Forest*, 1935), in which nature takes on an openly adversarial position toward the humans in the story. Nature, portrayed as an awesome, uncompromising, and irresistible force, emerges as the true protagonist of the work, the all-pervading presence that, as in Rivera's *Vortex*, holds it together and determines its outcome.

The Forest involves a simple conflict: a young French couple, Roger and Louise Bourgoin, have come to Canada seeking wealth and prosperity so that after a few years they can return to France and live in luxury the rest of their days. Their mistake lies in their utter lack of understanding about what the wilderness is really like. In attempting to dominate nature rather than become part of it (as Ike and the narrator of *Surfacing* do), they encounter only failure, frustration, and death. Louise, the more urbane and cultured of the two, is surprisingly also the one who, like Susanna Moodie, senses from the outset the perils of the New World wilderness:

> "It scares me, Roger."
> "What does?"
> "The forest. We shouldn't have settled so far away from civilization." [15]

As the story progresses, Louise's instinctive fear of the forest grows in ironic contrast to her husband's fatal belief that the forest, which he sees rather romantically as beautiful and "challenging," is there for them to exploit, to use for their own ends. Gradually, the forest becomes an almost malevolent presence, for Louise "a mute and sinister force, crouched in the shade, lying in wait for its prey." [16]

Ineluctably, the forest begins to degenerate not only Louise but Roger, even, ironically, while he thinks he is becoming more and more its master (as happens to the protagonist in *The Vortex*). Symbolizing the future of human life in the wilderness, a son is born to the couple; his birth initially serves to mollify Louise's trepidations about their prospects for survival in the wilderness:

> You, Savage Country, who made everything so hard for me, take a look at this one. He's one of Yours. . . . You're shaping him invisibly, as I am. . . . If we must raise him together through the years, don't be my enemy. [17]

Increasingly, the child becomes his mother's sole reason for living, and when he dies in an accident, Louise's world dies as well.

The Forest concludes on a note of human pain and failure; both Louise, who had sensed throughout the novel that she and her husband were hopelessly out of place in the wilderness, and Roger, who had been unable to adapt to the ways of the forest, come to realize that the primeval American wilderness has beaten them, that it has thwarted all their plans and left them with nothing, not even a clear understanding of how and why they had been defeated.

> "What could we ever have expected from this land? What would it have done to you? And what would it have done to me? After breaking us, heart and soul, don't you see that it would only stop when it had claimed your body and mine?" [18]

Bugnet's *Forest* differs from Faulkner's *Bear* and Atwood's *Surfacing* primarily because in the French Canadian work neither of the two major characters ever comes to accept, as Ike and Atwood's narrator do, the eternal and inexorable laws of the wilderness. Moreover, Roger and Louise leave their wilderness experience already defeated. Because they have learned nothing from the wilderness, except that it is a harsh and implacable antagonist and that it can kill, they will never be able even to attempt to live by a more enlightened code of conduct among the "civilized" world of humans, to which they too return.

The sense of failure in *The Forest*, then, is different from the sense of failure, expressed or implied, that pervades the closing pages of *The Bear* and *Surfacing*. For Bugnet, the tragedy is that the humans involved fail to understand that they must live in harmony with nature, that they cannot hope to possess it or control it, and that they must accept it on its own terms. Because Roger and Louise never comprehend this, they are doomed; they will return to Europe never understanding what has happened to them or why. For Moodie, Ike, and the protagonist of *Surfacing*, failure is more complex, involving their ability or inability to apply the profound truths they learned in the wilderness to their future lives as urban, social beings.

In their concern with questions of race relations and relationships between women and men, *The Bear* and *Surfacing* link the wilderness to civilization in ways that do not figure prominently in *The Forest*. Bugnet's novel, however, is exceptional in showing how the New World wilderness can be portrayed as a powerful and intractable protagonist. If *The Bear* and, especially, *Surfacing* suggest that the codes of the wilderness can be adapted to the needs of the social human world, *The Forest* suggests just as forcefully that this process of adaptation is by no means guaranteed, that some people may be incapable of understanding the issues involved, and that civilization and the wilderness will remain poised in an adversarial stance.

An interesting variation on this theme of nature and its problematic relationship to civilization can be found in other classics of French Canadian literature such as Antoine Gérin-Lajoie's highly influential *Jean Rivard, le défricheur* (1862), its sequel, *Jean Rivard: Economiste* (1864), and Louis Hémon's *Maria Chapdelaine* (1914). While *Jean Rivard, le défricheur*, a kind of physiocratic thesis novel, was written specifically to extol the virtues of agriculture and country life over those of city life, the more sophisticated *Maria Chapdelaine*, which is set in Québec's rural Lac Saint-Jean region, is in one sense simply the story of a farmer's struggle to wrest a living from the land.

By studying the development of the protagonist, Maria Chapdelaine, however, one can interpret this exceptional novel of the land (a form richly cultivated throughout the Americas) as a French Canadian cultural parable in which human beings, though suffering hardship, setbacks, and even death at the hands of the wilderness they are trying to farm, eventually come humbly to accept nature. Maria, who has lost the great love of her life, François Paradis, to a blizzard, chooses to marry the habitant farmer, Eutrope Gagnon, rather than the materially wealthy but culturally traitorous Lorenzo Surprenant (who has emigrated to Lowell, Massachusetts, to work in the textile factories). In so doing, she symbolically reaffirms a certain kind of culture for French Canada, one that equates nature (in all its forms) with God and both of these to the supposed moral supremacy of Québec's rural Catholic culture. It is ironic that, through a Christmas-time snowstorm, it is malevolent nature that kills François Paradis, a descendant of *coureurs de bois* who had lived his entire life in harmony with nature. In its metaphoric function, however, the death of Paradis suggests that although French Canadians like Maria may possess an essentially romantic view of nature, not dissimilar to that held by Roger Bourgoin in *The Forest*, eventually, in order to preserve their "race" and their habitant way of life, they must choose farming over the life of a forest adventurer.[19]

But overshadowing all these plot twists and symbolic choices is the omnipresent force of nature, dominating everything in the novel, including Maria. An effective stylistic feature of the novel is the way Hémon's nature imagery vacillates between the positive and the negative, a movement that reflects Maria's own evolving sense of nature as possessing both a destructive presence and a constructive one. When, for example, at the beginning of the novel her love for Paradis begins to bloom, Maria conceives of nature as fruitful and beautiful, as an almost-human life force. Later, when Paradis perishes in the storm, Maria, now devastated and feeling betrayed, views nature as a fierce, threatening, evil force, an implacable enemy of human life. This attitude, which parallels the basic conflict in *The Forest* and *The Vortex*, evolves into a humbler and more accepting sense of nature, expressed in the nurturing imagery at the end of the novel when Maria becomes reconciled both to her future as Gagnon's wife and to nature. With the gentle spring rains evoking rebirth and renewal, Maria, having made peace with herself, her lot in life, and nature itself (with which she is now closely identified), is content:

> Throughout the hours of the night Maria moved not; with hands folded in her lap, patient of spirit and without bitterness, yet dreaming a little wistfully of the far-off wonders her eyes would never behold and of the land wherein she was bidden to live with its store of sorrowful memories.[20]

More literarily sophisticated than *The Forest*, *Maria Chapdelaine* also differs from Bugnet's novel in that it comes to emphasize that women and men can reconcile themselves and their ways of life with nature. Hémon (like Gérin-Lajoie before him) also advocates a simple, agrarian, Catholic mythos, one that coincides with what he seems to have felt was—and should be—French Canada's proper mode of existence.

Like *The Bear* and *Surfacing*, *Maria Chapdelaine* structurally reflects the physical and psychological movement of a character into a state of accord with nature. This condition effects a change in the character, who, having experienced this change, reenters the social world of men and women. Within this movement, there are two essential differences, however: first, both *The Bear* and *Surfacing* show their characters having to leave the wilderness for an urban way of life (while Maria will remain on a wilderness farm) and, second, both *The Bear* and *Surfacing* imply that it will be difficult if not impossible to live in human society on the strength of what was learned in the wilderness. Maria, who has resolved (perhaps too submissively) to remain on a farm (an intermediate point between the city and the wilderness), seems more than Ike or the narrator of *Surfacing* destined to succeed with her chosen life, more able to harmonize the ways of the wilderness with those of human society.

Other canonical New World texts that develop this seminal American theme are Rudy Wiebe's *The Scorched-Wood People* (1977), Yves Thériault's *Agaguk* (1958) and *Ashini* (1960), Euclides da Cunha's *Os Sertões* (*Rebellion in the Backlands*, 1902), Domingo Faustino Sarmiento's *Facundo* (1845), and Mark Twain's *Huckleberry Finn* (1884). Although these works, classics of their respective national literatures, differ markedly in form and style, all involve a demonstration of the basic conflict between civilization and barbarism. Wiebe's novel, for example, a singular example of revisionist historical fiction,[21] casts this conflict in terms of Louis Riel's "barbarous" 1885 Métis uprising against the "civilized" white government of Prime Minister John Macdonald. Da Cunha's epic narrative, *Rebellion in the Backlands*, is similar to *The Scorched-Wood People* in that both works (one fiction, the other nonfiction) depict the bloody efforts of fledgling national governments to quell what they perceived as mutinous insurrections threatening to rend the fragile fabric of national unity. In addition, both center dramatically on charismatic, even messianic historical characters (Louis Riel and Antônio Maciel), and both suggest that though atrocities were committed by both sides, the greater moral wrongs were committed, ironically, by the supposedly civilized forces of the national government, the political entity that determined to civilize their "barbarous" dissident elements at bayonet point.

Although there are many other similarities between these two works, there are some revealing differences as well. *The Scorched-Wood People*, for example, a novel, gives greater scope and importance to its protagonist, Louis Riel. Antônio Maciel, the leader of Brazil's so-called Canudos Rebellion (1896–1897), plays a relatively minor role in *Rebellion in the Backlands*, a nonfiction work that because of its many novelistic and cinematic features reads as if it were fiction. Yet while Wiebe develops Riel both as an individual centrally involved in the conflict and as an articulate and idealized spokesperson for his people, the disparaged Métis, da Cunha develops Maciel only as a type, as the epitome of the Brazilian *sertanejo*, or backlander. The eventual exhumation and decapitation of Maciel's corpse by the supposedly civilized government forces symbolize da Cunha's basic point: that while the Canudos war may have been initially perceived by progressive, urban southern Brazil as a clear-cut conflict between a handful of backlands fanatics, driven by a maniacal leader espousing an explosive mixture of religion and politics, and the forces of an enlightened modern nation, it very quickly degenerated into an apocalyptic death struggle that reduced everyone involved to unimagined levels of barbarism. With his trenchantly ironic style expressing his true sentiments about this debasing conflict, da Cunha describes, at the conclusion of his work, the disinterment of the rebel leader:

> They carefully disinterred the body, precious relic that it was—the sole prize, the only spoils of war this conflict had to offer! . . . They photo-

graphed it afterward and drew up an affidavit in due form, certifying its identity; for the entire nation must be thoroughly convinced that at last this terrible foe had been done away with.[22]

Wiebe, too, makes clear his own opinions about the Northwest Rebellions and about the punishment meted out to the captured Louis Riel; while Macdonald would grant a general amnesty to the other Métis insurrectionists, Riel, their leader and inspiration, would be hanged. Wiebe's position on this issue is succinctly expressed when, in an exchange between two of the combatants at the very end of the novel, we read, in regard to Riel's execution:

"They were right, they had to hang him, yes. They were right."

"What?" Crozier tilted across the table, half-standing. "They were right?"

"Sure. All his life he tried to show how the government was destroying us in the West. He got away from them once, to the States, so he could fight them again, but he wouldn't run this time. You know why, you know? . . . So his body on the end of that rope would prove forever how Canada destroyed us!"[23]

As is apparent in this concluding scene, it is Wiebe's intention to cast Riel in the role of a martyr, a religious visionary whose political leadership of the outcast and "barbarous" Métis people placed him in fatal opposition to the expansionism of the "civilized" Ottawa government. When da Cunha, in the concluding line of his narrative, memorializes the significance of events such as those of the Canudos war by speaking of the "acts of madness and crimes on the part of nations,"[24] he is echoing a sentiment expressed by Wiebe in regard to the symbolic significance of Louis Riel and the Métis rebellions:

"You think Riel is finished? . . . We'll remember. A hundred years and whites still won't know what to do with him. The smart whites will say, . . . it's judicial murder; Riel was mad. But it wasn't, and he wasn't mad. There's no white country can hold a man with a vision like Riel, with people like us who would understand it and believe it, and follow. Canada couldn't handle that, not Ontario, and not Quebec."[25]

Both Wiebe and da Cunha therefore conclude their narratives by linking the historical record, the terrible civil wars waged by two progressive "civilized" governments against two small and supposedly "barbarous" groups within their own societies, with the future of these societies. Implicit in both conclusions, consequently, is the argument that the governments of both Brazil and Canada need to become more just and less prejudiced, a condition that will not be met unless education—for all concerned—is given a higher priority than in the past. This crucial point, though indirectly present in virtually all of what Riel advocates about the relationship between the Métis and the rest of Canadian society, is explicitly expressed by da Cunha:

> It was plain that the Canudos Campaign must have a higher objective than the stupid and inglorious one of merely wiping out a backlands settlement. There was a more serious enemy to be combatted, in a warfare of a slower and more worthy kind. This entire campaign would be a crime, a futile and barbarous one, if we were not to take advantage of the paths opened by the artillery, by following up our cannon with a constant, stubborn, and persistent campaign of education, with the object of drawing these rude and backward fellow-countrymen of ours into the current of our times and our own national life.[26]

Another dimension of this relationship, the degree to which the Métis and the *sertanejos* represent some fundamental and therefore legitimate part of their respective countries, is also given considerable attention by both Wiebe and da Cunha. Wiebe deftly makes the crucial point about the cultural authenticity of the Métis by allowing Riel to summarize, during his trial, the background and evolution of the Métis. Stressing both the political stability and integrity of the Métis as well as their contributions to the welfare of the rest of Canada, Riel justifies the existence of his people:

> "The new yet in their own way civilized Métis people had been formed on true concepts of public liberty and equity, they had peacefully traded with the Hudson's Bay Company, prevented the horrible Indian wars and savagery that had been perpetrated again and again in the United States; and they had rightly resisted Canada laying hands on their country. At gun-point they demanded justice when they were about to be robbed of the future they had created for themselves. . . . Was it just that a greater people destroy a smaller people's leaders, tear from them their country? Humanity answers no. . . . The Government of Ottawa is guilty of conscienceless sacrilege towards the Métis!"[27]

Da Cunha makes this point as well. Speaking on behalf of his own "civilized" Brazil, he notes, sardonically:

We ourselves are but little in advance of our rude and backward fellow-countrymen. The latter, at least, were logical. Isolated in space and time, the jagunço, being an ethnic anachronism, could do only what he did do—that is, combat, and combat in a terrible fashion, the nation which, after having cast him off for three centuries almost, suddenly sought to raise him to our own state of enlightenment at the point of the bayonet, revealing to him the brilliancy of our civilization in the blinding flash of cannons.[28]

Although da Cunha makes no effort to argue, as Riel does in regard to the Métis, that the *sertanejos*, the "bedrock" of their nation, have contributed anything to the development of progressive southern Brazil (indeed his point is that the two Brazils were virtual strangers to each other), he does, like Wiebe, stress that politically, culturally, and morally it is incumbent upon any truly civilized government to help all its citizens to escape the plagues of ignorance, fanaticism, and poverty.

Written in prose styles that avail themselves of the techniques of both realism and symbolism, *The Scorched-Wood People* and *Rebellion in the Backlands* are powerful examples of how central the theme of the conflict between civilization and barbarism is to the American experience. Ironically challenging the concepts of their respective cultures in regard to who is "civilized" and who is "barbaric" or "savage," Wiebe and da Cunha demonstrate why this issue is second only to the issue of identity in its significance to the cultural and literary development of the New World.

Another singular New World text, Domingo Faustino Sarmiento's *Facundo*, is the prototype of this fundamental theme. Like *The Scorched-Wood People* and *Rebellion in the Backlands*, *Facundo* seeks to link the theme of conflict between civilization and barbarism to the political question of governance: how shall the powerful within a culture rule those who do not have political potency? What political principles are involved and what rights, legal as well as human, are maintained, created, or, in some cases, denied? Also like *The Scorched-Wood People* and *Rebellion in the Backlands*, *Facundo* is a hybrid work, one that freely mixes the modes of fiction and nonfiction. Less dramatic and ironic than da Cunha's epic, *Facundo* is nevertheless similar to it in stressing the crucial influence that the environment, physical as well as human, exerts on the people of a certain place, in this case, Argentina. Like da Cunha, Sarmiento sets up a sharp dichotomy between Argentina's "civilized" culture, that of the city of Buenos Aires, and its "barbarous" culture, embodied in the pampas and the gauchos who rule it.

Sarmiento's thesis is that at the time of his writing the gaucho culture of the pampas had almost fatally retarded Argentina's growth into a modern nation. He extends this proposition into other, interrelated struggles within Argentine society—struggles between the Old World and the New, between despotism and democracy, and between ignorance and education or enlightenment. Deeply influenced by Benjamin Franklin's *Autobiography* as well as by Comte's positivism, Sarmiento presented the gauchos as the embodiments of all the dark, destructive forces that were tearing Argentina apart during the nineteenth century. Although later in life Sarmiento would modify these views a bit, conceding that the cities had not produced all that was positive in Argentina and that the gauchos had not produced all that was negative, *Facundo* portrays the Argentina of the future as having to make a clearly delineated choice: would it be for the barbarism of the pampas and the gauchos or the civilization of the cities, particularly Buenos Aires? Of this conflict Sarmiento writes, "There were, before 1810, in the Argentine Republic, two distinct, rival and incompatible societies, two diverse civilizations: one, Spanish, European, cultured; the other, barbarous, American, almost indigenous."[29]

By focusing his study on the background and life of a particular gaucho leader, Juan Facundo Quiroga, Sarmiento sought also to attack the bloody dictatorship of Juan Manuel Rosas, a tyrant who had used the gauchos as a form of repressive secret police. By linking Rosas to Quiroga and by linking the two of them to the pampas culture that spawned them, Sarmiento could write that:

in Facundo Quiroga, ultimately triumphant everywhere, we see the campaign against the cities, which are dominated by him in their spirit, government and civilization, and the formation, finally, of the central, single and despotic government of Juan Manuel Rosas, who drives into cultured Buenos Aires the gaucho's knife and who, in so doing, destroys the work of centuries, of civilization itself, its laws and liberties.[30]

Like da Cunha, Sarmiento succeeded brilliantly in evoking the dubious effect the land and its gaucho culture had on the people who lived there. Of the influence of the pampas, he would write:

The life of the pampas, therefore, had developed the gaucho's physical faculties and none of those relating to intelligence. His moral character was resistant to his habit of triumphing over obstacles and over the power of Nature itself; he was strong, haughty and energetic.[31]

Yet while da Cunha and Sarmiento both stress the decisive impact that the physical environment had on human lives, it is da Cunha who more effectively connects the tragic events at Canudos to his sociological and climatological analysis of Brazil's isolated and forgotten *sertão*. Unlike *Rebellion in the Backlands*, *Facundo* does not have an event like the war at Canudos to give the narrative a sharp sense of tension and climax, a fact which helps explain why *Rebellion in the Backlands* reads more like fiction than *Facundo* does. Yet *The Scorched-Wood People*, which like *Rebellion in the Backlands* makes structural use of an organized war and its decisive battle (Batoche), goes a step beyond da Cunha's work in dramatizing the events it depicts. But where Wiebe uses (and often revises) the facts of history to write fiction, da Cunha uses the devices of fiction (dramatic structuring, point of view, dialogue, irony, and characterization, for example) to write nonfiction. Sarmiento, though certainly aware of the techniques of fiction available to him, hews closer to a nonfictionalized mode of writing, amplified nevertheless with its own brand of drama, irony, and pathos. Though they differ in their modes of narration (*Rebellion in the Backlands* and *The Scorched-Wood People* are most similar), these three classics of New World literature have one major factor in common: each of them develops the theme of civilization versus barbarism by focusing on a single historical figure who incarnates the various ways in which this fundamental conflict festered environmentally, culturally, and politically in his society.

Offering an interesting variation on this same basic theme are Mark Twain's *Huckleberry Finn* and Yves Thériault's *Agaguk*, works which suggest that the idea of a clear-cut dichotomy between civilization and barbarism may be spurious and that the reality of human existence inevitably involves both.

Huckleberry Finn, widely acknowledged to be a masterwork of American literature, is structured around two poles: the river, associated with the idyllic, harmonious innocence that only nature is thought to afford, and the shore, associated with violence, cruelty, and sham—the human realm. As the novel proceeds, Huck's psychological development as the narrator and protagonist is directly tied to his physical movement back and forth between these two poles.

Thériault's *Agaguk*, a twentieth-century French Canadian novel that casts the civilization/barbarism theme in terms of the "primitive" hero versus the group and the individual against society,[32] develops not in a clearly polarized fashion but with regard to the hero's sense of self as an individual and, crucially, to his relationship to his wife. Aside from the basic theme of conflict between civilization and barbarism, these two works have several other features in com-

mon: both involve complex heroes who reject their respective societies and undergo profound changes in their outlook; both confront the possibility that even
the would-be Eden of the New World has deception, violence, and death in it;
and both succeed in merging the realistically described local scene with issues
of larger, even universal scope.

Of the several differences between these works, two stand out: the reasons
why Huck and Agaguk change and the ways in which they react to the realities
of "white," or "civilized," society. Huck, who is both the naive narrator of his
story and the principal player in it, changes, as Richard Chase notes, primarily
in the sense that "he comes to adopt" through his relationship to Jim, a runaway
slave he befriends, "a morality based on New Testament ethic rather than the
convention of his time and place."[33] Experiencing the rites of initiation into
manhood, Huck's evolution as a character gives the novel its backbone. The
brutality, treachery, and deceitfulness of the life that he had experienced along
the river transform him. From a youthful innocent, a child of nature, he becomes a wily and skeptical adult, a hardened but not hardhearted man who
chooses at the end of his story to deal with the evil and wickedness of human
society by shunning it, by asserting his self-reliant individualism. Even when he
learns that were he to come back into society he could enjoy a financial windfall,
Huck chooses to remain free and unfettered by the restrictions of civilized life.
As he says, "I reckon I got to light out for the territory ahead of the rest, because Aunt Sally she's going to adopt me and sivilize me, and I can't stand it. I
been there before."[34] By removing himself from society, Huck chooses, ironically, what he takes to be the more civilized life of nature, symbolized in the
mysterious and mythic river.

Huck's great river, and the idyllic raft-life he and his comrades had known
while traveling on it, is, like Melville's whale and Rosa's *sertão*, an ambiguous
symbol of nature, full of death as well as life. Huck, like Agaguk, epitomizes the
individual at odds with the group. In a sense, *Huckleberry Finn* ends where
Agaguk begins, that is, with the hero rejecting his society and its dubious values
to set out on his own.

Agaguk, more of a "primitive"[35] hero than the naive Huck, opens his novel
by separating himself not only from his Eskimo society, which he believes has
become corrupt through the pernicious influence of "white" society, but from
his own father, Ramook, who as chief is held to be primarily responsible for the
decline of his people. The reader learns that Agaguk and "his woman," Iriook,
will "make a new beginning"[36] based presumably on older, better ways of doing
things. Later in the novel, Agaguk like Huck has a chance to return to society.

To go back to it, however, means for Agaguk that he would have to give up what he prized most of all—his freedom as an individual: "A man does not become chief so young in the tribes. The honor was attractive. But it meant a return to life in the village. Agaguk did not want to lose what he had, . . . the peace, the isolation, the liberty to decide his own movements."[37] When Huck, at the end of his novel, declares that he has to "light out for the territory ahead of the rest" because Aunt Sally was going to "sivilize" him, a prospect he could not face, he expresses a sentiment that Agaguk would have easily understood.

Although it is more obvious in Agaguk's case, both Huck and Agaguk undergo profound character transformations. For Agaguk, though, in contrast to Huck, this transformation is brought about by a woman, Iriook, who gradually emerges as a powerful and compelling character,[38] at least the equal of Agaguk himself. (For all her virtues—virtues which Huck, in his innately moral way, recognizes—Aunt Sally does not change Huck very much.) Yet, ironically, Iriook is portrayed as one whose beliefs are more consistent with those of white culture than with traditional Eskimo or Inuit culture. At first an anomalous presence, Iriook emerges as a unique character, able to span both cultures by taking the best each has to offer and creating a new kind of person, in harmony with the positive features of each culture but not crippled by its many negative features. The reason for Iriook's success in transforming Agaguk is that she is able to grow and develop without threatening her mate's sense of self. Indeed, Agaguk comes not only to accept but to appreciate and even to prize her transformation from chattel to companion.

To underscore the ever-greater social equality between Iriook and Agaguk (who, crucially, is able to recognize and value how strong and, when need be, assertive his wife is), Thériault utilizes scenes of intense sexuality to show that sex need not be a divisive act of aggression that perpetuates the domination of one sex by the other. Indeed, by casting Iriook as the more sexually adventurous of the pair, Thériault implies that for couples who wish to please each other (as Iriook and Agaguk do), sex can be a force to draw people together while helping them to grow and develop as healthy individuals. Unlike *Huckleberry Finn*, which is open to criticism as a misogynistic tale of male bonding, or life in the "fraternity of men," *Agaguk* suggests that human fulfillment comes from a loving union, as sexual as it is political and psychological, between woman and man. For Thériault, the mutually satisfying sexual life of Agaguk and Iriook, in which Iriook is often the initiator and innovator, is linked to the vital forces of the wilderness, the nonsocial domain in which they, like Huck Finn, choose to live.

By merging the theme of the individual who is in conflict with the group with the theme of civilization versus nature, *Huckleberry Finn* and *Agaguk* both imply that the human experience is basically one of choice and change. Less violent than Agaguk is, at least initially, Huck is like Agaguk in his capacity to observe and learn. What Huck learns, in what Wallace Stegner calls his "moral development," [39] is that he prefers the existence he associates with nature, symbolized by his life on the river, over the supposedly "sivilized" life of human existence symbolized, ironically, by the lynchings, murders, and lies of the river towns. In *Agaguk*, which lacks the dichotomy of the river/shore structuring, Thériault presents Agaguk as a "primitive" being capable of terrible violence and even murder. But beyond this, as his complex relationship with Iriook develops, he emerges as a man who can learn to behave in less barbaric ways.

For both Twain and Thériault, then, there is irony in the fact that it is only their "primitive" or antisocial rebel heroes who are capable of truly civilized existence. While Huck, interpreted as the isolated hero who will be forever incapable of coming to terms with either women or human society in general, is last seen setting out alone into the wilderness, Agaguk, transformed by the love and good sense of a woman into a gentler man, is led at the end of his novel to accept the birth of a daughter, a weak and dependent creature the new "civilized" Agaguk will not kill, as the old, "savage" Agaguk would have done.

So while both *Huckleberry Finn* and *Agaguk* cultivate the conflict between civilization and nature, only *Agaguk* (recalling Atwood's *Surfacing*) suggests that the hero must not only learn from the wilderness but return with this precious knowledge to society, which exists at its most important level in the mutually supportive relationship between a woman and a man. It is here, in this potentially life-giving and life-affirming relationship, that the most constructive forces of the "primitive" world will be blended, to the benefit of all, with the most constructive forces of "civilization." The result will be a new kind of existence, one built upon the best qualities and features of these two hitherto antithetical modes of existence.

Afterword

* * * * * * * * * *

Although the study of Inter-American or New World literature must, at this writing, still be regarded as something of an anomaly in the larger academic community, it has rapidly been gaining acceptance in a number of prestigious professional organizations, prominent among which are the International Comparative Literature Association (which, in 1982, focused on Inter-American literary relations), the American Comparative Literature Association, and the Modern Language Association.

It is interesting to note, however, that within the Americas it is the United States that has been most laggardly in embracing a significant Inter-American consciousness. In spite of—or perhaps because of—its long-standing political and economic hegemony, the United States is only now beginning to appreciate the cultural contributions of its hemispheric neighbors. This is an entirely salubrious development and it augurs well for the future.

In Canada, on the other hand, and in Latin America, the situation is quite different. Still too often regarded as minor or marginal literatures (that is, as literatures not widely recognized in an international context), the novels, stories, poems, and dramas of these countries have long been judged not only against European models but against those of the United States as well. Unfortunately, the result of this process has been a kind of inferiority complex, a nagging fear by authors that their work might not measure up or, worse, that even if it were first-rate it might not, because of its place of origin, receive the kind of international attention it deserved. Although this situation has been improving somewhat in recent years, with breakthroughs by writers like Borges, Márquez, Atwood, Munro, and Davies leading the way, many New World cultures—conspicuous among which are French Canada and Brazil—have not yet received the recognition they merit. It is my hope that *Rediscovering the New World* will help begin to correct this problem.

Literarily speaking, the rediscovery of New World literature in a comparative context opens up vast new possibilities for research and inquiry, some of which, in addition to the issues dealt with in the current work, include the following: the nature of colonial letters, the development of American romanticism (or any other literary movement), the historical evolution of literary genres in the New World, the impact of immigrant literature, patterns of influence and reception, and the seemingly endless thematic comparisons that present themselves. As scholars deal with these and other issues, the study of Inter-American literature will eventually shed its current uncertain status and take its proper place as yet another useful approach to our better appreciation of world literature. It is toward this end that I have devoted my efforts.

Notes

* * * * * * * * * *

I. THE PRE-COLUMBIAN ERA

1. Ursula K. Le Guin, "Above All Keep the Tale Going," review of Paula Gunn Allen, *Spider Woman's Granddaughters* (Boston: Beacon, 1989), *New York Times Book Review*, May 14, 1989, p. 15.

2. Luis Valdez and Stan Steiner, eds., *Aztlan: An Anthology of Mexican-American Literature* (New York: Vintage, 1972), p. xvii.

3. *American Indian Prose and Poetry*, ed. and intro. Margot Astrov (New York: Capricorn, 1962), pp. 3–17.

4. Ibid., p. 3.

5. Ibid.

6. Ibid., pp. 31–38.

7. Frances Densmore, *Chippewa Music 2*, Smithsonian Institution, U.S. Bureau of American Ethnology Bulletin 53 (Washington, D.C., 1913), pp. 247–50.

8. Astrov, *American Indian Prose and Poetry*, p. 46.

9. Ibid., p. 47.

10. Paula Gunn Allen, introduction to *Spider Woman's Granddaughters*, pp. 1–25; see also Le Guin's brief comment on this point in her review of this work, p. 15.

11. Astrov, *American Indian Prose and Poetry*, pp. 3, 19–22.

12. Karl Kroeber, "The Wolf Comes: Indian Poetry and Linguistic Criticism," in *Smoothing the Ground*, Brian Swann, ed. (Berkeley: University of California Press, 1983), pp. 98–111; see also Karl Kroeber, "Deconstructionist Criticism and American Indian Literatures," *Boundary 2* 7, no. 3 (1979), pp. 73–89.

13. Cited by Astrov, *American Indian Prose and Poetry*, p. 23.

14. C. Daryll Forde, *Ethnography of the Yuma Indians*, University of California Publications in American Archaeology and Ethnology, vol. 28, no. 4 (Berkeley, 1931), p. 190; see also Astrov, *American Indian Prose and Poetry*, p. 265.

15. Dennis Tedlock, "The Question of Translation and Literary Criticism: On the Translation of Style in Oral Literature," in Swann, *Smoothing the Ground*, pp. 57–77.

16. Francis LaFlésche, *The Osage Tribe*, 39th Annual Report of the Bureau of American Ethnology (Washington, D.C., 1925), pp. 634–35. See also Astrov, *American Indian Prose and Poetry*, p. 100.

17. LaFlésche, *The Osage Tribe*, pp. 634–35.

18. Astrov, *American Indian Prose and Poetry*, p. 46.

19. Daniel G. Brinton, *Essays of an Americanist* (Philadelphia, 1890), p. 292; reprinted in Astrov, *American Indian Prose and Poetry*, p. 109.

20. Alice Fletcher and Francis LaFlésche, *The Omaha Tribe*, 27th Annual Report of the Bureau of American Ethnology (Washington, D.C., 1911), p. 475; see also Astrov, *American Indian Prose and Poetry*, p. 133.

21. Brinton, *Essays of an Americanist*, p. 292.

22. Daniel G. Brinton, *Ancient Náhuatl Poetry*, vol. 7 (Philadelphia: Library of Aboriginal American Literature, 1887), p. 123, and Astrov, *American Indian Prose and Poetry*, pp. 314–15.

23. Irene Nicholson, *Firefly in the Night* (London: Faber, 1959), p. 95.

24. Ibid.

25. Astrov, *American Indian Prose and Poetry*, p. 315.

26. Valdez and Steiner, *Aztlan*, p. xix.

27. Nicholson, *Firefly in the Night*, pp. 132–33.

28. Ibid., p. 132; see also Brinton, *Ancient Náhuatl Poetry*, pp. 45–47. Brinton's version of this poem, which is accompanied by its original form in Náhuatl, differs somewhat from Nicholson's version.

29. Astrov, *American Indian Prose and Poetry*, p. 329.

30. Ibid., pp. 341–42; the translation from Quechua into English was by Miguel Mossi (*Lafone Quevedo*, 1892, p. 339), whose work provided the basis for P. Ainsworth Means's version (*Ancient Civilization of the Andes* [New York: Scribner's, 1931], p. 437).

31. See Raoul d'Harcourt and Marie d'Harcourt, *La musique des Incas et ses survivances*, 2 vols. (Paris: P. Geuthner, 1925).

32. Astrov, *American Indian Prose and Poetry*, p. 48.

33. Robert Lowrie, *The Religion of the Crow Indians*, Smithsonian Institution, American Museum of Natural History Anthropological Papers, vol. 4, pt. 1 (Washington, D.C., 1922), p. 25; Astrov, *American Indian Prose and Poetry*, p. 48.

34. Astrov, *American Indian Prose and Poetry*, p. 48.

35. Densmore, *Chippewa Music 2*, pp. 113–14, and Astrov, *American Indian Prose and Poetry*, p. 49.

36. Astrov, *American Indian Prose and Poetry*, p. 49.

37. Ibid., p. 196.

38. Ibid., p. 240.

39. Ibid., p. 242.

40. Hubert Bancroft, *The Native Races of the Pacific States*, vol. 3 (San Francisco: A. L. Bancroft, 1886), p. 42.

41. Sylvanus G. Morley, foreword to *Popol Vuh*, by Delia Goetz and Sylvanus G.

Morley, from the translations of Adrián Recinos (Norman: University of Oklahoma Press, 1950), p. ix.

42. Abraham Arias-Larreta, *Pre-Columbian Literatures* (Kansas City: Editorial Indoamérica, 1967), p. 100.

43. Goetz and Morley, *Popol Vuh*, pp. 81–82.

44. Abraham Arias-Larreta, *Pre-Columbian Literary Masterpieces* (Kansas City: Editorial Indoamérica, 1967), p. 63, n. 7.

45. José Cid Pérez and Dolores Martí de Cid, *Teatro indio precolombino* (Avila: Aguilar, 1964), p. 320.

46. Arias-Larreta, *Pre-Columbian Literary Masterpieces*, p. 88.

47. Ibid., p. 90.

48. Miguel León-Portilla, *Pre-Columbian Literatures of Mexico*, trans. Grace Lobanov and Miguel León-Portilla (Norman: University of Oklahoma Press, 1969), p. 105.

49. Cid Pérez and Martí de Cid, *Teatro indio precolombino*, p. 211.

50. León-Portilla, *Pre-Columbian Literatures of Mexico*, p. 106.

51. Paul Zolbrod, *Diné Bahané* (Albuquerque: University of New Mexico Press, 1984).

52. Octavio Paz, *Seven Voices*, ed. Rita Guibert (New York: Vintage, 1973), pp. 243–44.

2. THE NARRATIVES OF DISCOVERY AND CONQUEST

1. Emir Rodríguez Monegal and Thomas Colchie, eds., *The Borzoi Anthology of Latin American Literature*, vol. 1 (New York: Knopf, 1977), p. 1. Hereafter, *Borzoi Anthology*.

2. James A. Williamson, ed., *The Cabot Voyages and Bristol Discoveries* (Cambridge: Cambridge University Press, 1962), pp. 24–25, 207, 209–10; see also L. A. Vigneras, "The Cape Breton Landfall: 1494 or 1497?" *Canadian Historical Review* 38 (1957), pp. 219–28.

3. *Journal and Other Documents on the Life and Voyages of Christopher Columbus*, trans. and ed. Samuel Eliot Morison (New York: Heritage, 1963), pp. 64–66.

4. Ibid., p. 180.

5. *Borzoi Anthology*, vol. 1, p. 4.

6. Ibid., pp. 4–5.

7. Ibid., p. 5.

8. The issue of colonization is of decisive importance for the history of the Americas. If the French, for example, had colonized the New World according to the plans advocated by such men as Champlain and La Salle, French and not English would probably be the main language of North America today.

9. Williamson, *The Cabot Voyages and Bristol Discoveries*, p. 210.

10. *Borzoi Anthology*, vol. 1, p. 13.

11. Ibid., p. 12.

12. *The Voyages of Jacques Cartier*, translations, notes, and appendixes by H. P. Bigger (Ottawa: F. A. Ackland, 1924), pp. 22, 6.

13. Ibid., pp. 22–23.

14. Ibid., p. 201; see also pp. 221, 225, 264, and 298.

15. John Smith, *A True Relation of Occurrences and Accidents in Virginia*, ed. E. Arbor, intro. A. G. Bradley (Edinburgh: J. Grant, 1910), p. 5.

16. Ibid., p. xvii.

17. Ibid., p. 84.

18. Illustrative of this all-too-frequent tendency to convert the aboriginal American to Christianity on pain of death is a story related by Alistair Cooke in his book *America*. As Cooke relates it, a native king who would not renounce his religion was about to be burned at the stake as an unrepentant pagan. As he felt the first flames bite at his body, he was offered the rite of baptism one final time. He refused again, saying he feared that if he accepted baptism, he might go to heaven and meet there only Christians. Alistair Cooke, *America* (New York: Knopf, 1974), p. 36.

19. Victor G. Hopwood, "Explorers by Land to 1867," in Carl F. Klinck, gen. ed., *A Literary History of Canada*, 2d ed., vol. 1 (Toronto: University of Toronto Press, 1976), p. 21.

20. David Galloway, "The Voyagers," in Klinck, *A Literary History of Canada*, vol. 1, pp. 5–7.

21. Margaret Atwood, *Survival: A Thematic Guide to Canadian Literature* (Toronto: Anansi, 1972), pp. 31–32.

22. Captain John Franklin, *A Narrative of a Journey to the Shores of the Polar Sea* (Rutland, Vt.: Charles E. Tuttle, 1970), p. xix.

23. Ibid., p. 217.

24. Ibid.

25. Ibid., p. 279.

26. Ibid., p. 299.

27. Ibid., pp. 400–401.

28. Ibid., pp. 438–39.

29. Ibid., p. 450.

30. Ibid., p. 451.

31. Ibid., p. 454.

32. Ibid.

33. Ibid., p. 455.

34. Ibid., pp. 455–56.

35. Ibid., p. 458.

36. Ibid., p. 468.

37. Ibid., p. 494.

38. Bernal Díaz del Castillo, *True History of the Conquest of New Spain*, trans. and intro. J. M. Cohen (New York: Penguin, 1963).

39. *Borzoi Anthology*, vol. 1, p. 39.

40. Ibid.

41. Díaz, *True History of the Conquest of New Spain*, p. 14.

42. Ibid., p. 87.

43. Ibid., p. 214.

44. Ibid., p. 216.
45. Ibid., p. 229.
46. Ibid., p. 242.
47. Ibid., p. 244.
48. Ibid., p. 289.
49. Ibid., p. 294.
50. Ibid., p. 303.
51. Ibid., p. 371.

3. THE NEW WORLD EPIC

1. Brazil has produced a number of national epics and epical poems. Some of these are Cláudio Manuel da Costa's *Vila Rica* (1773), Santa Rita Durão's *Caramurú* (1781), and Bento Teixeira Pinto's *Prosopopéia* (1601). Epics from Spanish America are many (perhaps owing to the number of different nations) and include works as diverse as Ricardo Güiraldes' *Don Segundo Sombra* (1926) and Pedro de Oña's *The Arauco Tamed* (1596), which was written in response to *The Araucaniad* of Ercilla y Zúñiga and which defended Ercilla's commanding officer and antagonist, Don García Hurtado de Mendoza. The United States too has produced several epics or epical works, including Longfellow's *Hiawatha*, Whitman's *Leaves of Grass*, Bénet's *John Brown's Body*, Pound's *Cantos*, and Crane's *The Bridge*. The Aztec, Mayan, and Incan people all possessed bodies of literature, oral in nature, that many critics believe to have generated epics or epical works as well.

2. Excepting the imperfectly preserved and consequently little-understood Aztec, Mayan, and Incan epics, the Iroquois folk epic *The Dekanawida* is the outstanding exception to this general tendency.

3. C. M. Bowra, *From Virgil to Milton* (London: Macmillan, 1965), p. 1.

4. Thomas E. Sanders and Walter W. Peek, *The Literature of the American Indian* (Beverly Hills: Glencoe, 1973), p. 193.

5. Curiously enough, even Marxist theory, via Friedrich Engels' and Karl Marx's research on Lewis Henry Morgan's *The League of the Ho-de-no-sau-nee, or Iroquois* (1851), has been influenced by the Iroquois Great Law. See Sanders and Peek, *The Literature of the American Indian*, p. 190.

6. Charles Maxwell Lancaster and Paul Thomas Manchester give a useful historical account of the poem's reception and influence in their introduction to Alonso de Ercilla y Zúñiga, *The Araucaniad*, trans. Lancaster and Manchester (Nashville: Vanderbilt University Press, 1945), pp. 9–25.

7. Enrique Anderson Imbert and Eugenio Florit, *Literatura hispanoamericana* (New York: Holt, Rinehart and Winston, 1960), pp. 78–79.

8. *Borzoi Anthology*, vol. 1, p. 63.

9. Marcelino Menéndez y Pelayo, in *Historia de la poesía hispanoamericana* (Madrid: Consejo Superior de Investigaciones Científicas, 1948), disagrees with my assessment (p. 229).

10. See the introduction to *The Uruguay*, trans. Sir Richard F. Burton, edited with notes, introduction, and bibliography by Frederick C. H. Garcia and Edward F. Stanton (Berkeley: University of California Press, 1982), pp. 1–38.

11. Samuel Putnam, *Marvelous Journey: A Survey of Four Centuries of Brazilian Writing* (New York: Knopf, 1948), pp. 83–86.

12. Cacambo is also the name of Voltaire's Indian in *Candide*. For a more detailed account of the influence Voltaire may have had on da Gama, see Frederick C. H. Garcia, "Richard Francis Burton and Basílio da Gama: The Translator and the Poet," *Luso-Brazilian Review* 12, no. 1 (Summer 1975), pp. 37–38 and p. 55, n. 15. See also p. 9, n. 13, in the introduction to *The Uruguay*.

13. *The Uruguay*, p. 63.

14. Ibid.

15. *The Columbiad*, in *The Works of Joel Barlow*, intro. W. K. Bottorff and A. L. Ford (Gainesville: Scholars' Facsimiles and Reprints, 1970). Burton, the translator of da Gama's *Uruguay*, knew about Barlow's poem and comments comparatively on it (*The Uruguay*, p. 110).

16. A. L. Ford, *Joel Barlow* (New York: Twayne, 1971), p. 64.

17. Ibid., p. 67.

18. E. J. Pratt, *Towards the Last Spike* (Toronto: Macmillan, 1952). Pratt, an excellent narrative poet, wrote an earlier narrative poem, *Brébeuf and His Brethren* (1940), that could in a more limited way (it deals with the Jesuit settlement of Québec) also be considered a national epic. According to Northrop Frye, English Canada possesses a strong narrative tradition in its poetry, with Pratt one of its finest practitioners. See Northrop Frye, *The Bush Garden: Essays on the Canadian Imagination* (Toronto: Anansi, 1971), pp. 145–55.

19. Frye, *The Bush Garden*, p. 11. For more comments on the epicality of *Towards the Last Spike*, see Paul West, "Ethos and Epic: Aspects of Contemporary Canadian Poetry," *Canadian Literature* 4 (Spring 1960), pp. 7–17 (reprinted in Eli Mandel, ed., *The Contexts of Canadian Criticism* [Chicago: University of Chicago Press, 1971], pp. 206–15); Dorothy Livesay, "The Documentary Poem: A Canadian Genre," in Mandel, pp. 267–81; *E. J. Pratt on His Life and Poetry*, ed. Susan Gingell (Toronto: University of Toronto Press, 1983), pp. 144–53; and Margaret Atwood, *Survival*, pp. 172–73.

20. Pratt, *Towards the Last Spike*, pp. 2, 28.

21. Ibid., p. 40.

22. Frye, *The Bush Garden*, p. 11.

23. Other French Canadian works of an epical or epic nature are Robert Choquette's *Metropolitan Museum*, Marc Lescarbot's "La défaite des sauvages armouchiquois," and the approximately fifteen books by Maurice Constantin-Weyer that are often grouped together as "l'épopée canadienne." One of Lescarbot's most significant legacies is that he seems to have been the first writer in French to have suggested that the New World could be more desirable than the Old, indeed, that it could be an escape from it.

24. See David Hayne, "Louis Fréchette," in *Canada's Past and Present*, ed. Robert MacDougall, 5th series (Toronto: University of Toronto Press, 1965), p. 120.

25. Pratt, *Towards the Last Spike*, p. 32.

26. Ibid., p. 25.

27. See Garcia and Stanton, introduction, *The Uruguay*, p. 2.

28. Ercilla, *The Araucaniad*, p. 46.

29. Ibid., p. 27.

30. Ibid., pp. 142–43.

31. Da Gama, *The Uruguay*, p. 69.

32. Barlow, *The Columbiad*, p. 636.

33. Though still generally regarded as an epic poem, *The Uruguay* has inspired critics to note its several nonepic features: its essential lyricism, its limited plot, its less than heroic action, its blank verse, and its generally anticlassical stance.

34. Antônio Cândido, "O ritmo do mundo," *Minas Gerais Suplemento Literário* (September 7, 1968), p. 4.

35. *The Dekanawida*, in Sanders and Peek, *The Literature of the American Indian*, p. 196. Seth Newhouse, an Onondaga Indian, was instrumental in the translation and transcription of the poem from the traditional oral form.

36. Ibid.

37. Ibid., p. 207.

38. Pratt, *Towards the Last Spike*, p. 50.

39. *The Dekanawida*, p. 196.

40. Ercilla, *The Araucaniad*, p. 213.

41. Eponamon, an Araucanian devil.

42. Ercilla, *The Araucaniad*, p. 98.

43. Ibid.

44. Garcia and Stanton, introduction, *The Uruguay*, p. 12.

45. Ibid., pp. 74–75.

46. Ibid., pp. 78–82.

47. Barlow, *The Columbiad*, pp. 419–20.

48. Barlow, too, relies extensively on personification. For example, in book 6 he personifies Cruelty. In book 8, he prophetically presents Slavery as both a blight on the greatness of America and a potentially ruinous cancer.

49. For Pratt's own comments on why the creature is female, see Gingell, *E. J. Pratt on His Life and Poetry*, pp. 147–48.

50. Pratt, *Towards the Last Spike*, pp. 29–30.

51. Barlow, *The Columbiad*, p. 568.

52. Hayne, "Louis Fréchette," p. 120.

53. Ibid.

54. *The Dekanawida*, p. 193.

55. Ibid.

56. Pratt, *Towards the Last Spike*, p. 52.

57. Lancaster and Manchester, introduction to Ercilla, *The Araucaniad*, p. 10.

58. Ibid., p. 146.

59. Ibid., p. 317.

60. Ibid., p. 318.

4. THE THEME OF MISCEGENATION

1. Octavio Paz, *The Labyrinth of Solitude*, trans. Lysander Kemp (New York: Grove, 1961), pp. 65–88.

2. E. Bradford Burns, *A History of Brazil*, 2d ed. (New York: Columbia University Press, 1980), pp. 43–44.

3. Putnam, *Marvelous Journey*, pp. 7–10.

4. Bartolomé de Las Casas was among the first European-born intellectuals to protest the exploitation of the American Indians and the atrocities being committed against them. There is an interesting parallel on this point between de Las Casas and Antônio Vieira, who waged a similar campaign in Brazil against the abuse of the Indians.

5. A partial list of works that deal with this theme would include *La bourrasque* (*The Half-Breed* in the U.S.; *A Martyr's Folly* in Canada), *Napoléon, Vers l'ouest* (*Towards the West*), and *Un homme se penche sur son passé* (*A Man Scans His Past*) by Maurice Constantin-Weyer, Esteban Echeverría's *La cautiva*, Helen Hunt Jackson's *Ramona*, Frei José de Santa Rita Durão's *Caramurú*, Manuel de Jesús Galván's *Enriquillo*, Mark Twain's *The Tragedy of Pudd'nhead Wilson*, Inca Garcilaso de la Vega's *The Royal Commentaries*, Lydia Maria Child's *A Romance of the Republic* and *Hobomok*, Miguel Angel Asturias' *Mulata*, Duke Redbird's *We Are Métis*, Maria Campbell's *Half-Breed*, Francisco Arriví's *Vejigantes*, Abdias do Nascimento's *Anjo Negro*, Celestino Gorostiza's *El color de nuestra piel*, Adolfo Caminha's *Bom-Crioulho* (*The Black Man and the Cabin Boy*), Catharine Maria Sedgwick's *Hope Leslie*, Carson McCullers' *The Member of the Wedding*, James Fenimore Cooper's *The Wept of Wish-Ton-Wish*, Cirilo Villaverde's *Cecilia Valdés*, Lionel Adolphe Grouix's *L'appel de la race*, Walt Whitman's *The Half-Breed and Other Stories*, Antônio Callado's *Quarup*, and Aluísio Azevedo's *O mulato* and *O cortiço*.

6. James Baldwin, *Another Country* (New York: Dell, 1962), p. 24.

7. Ibid.

8. Ibid., p. 25.

9. Ibid., p. 287.

10. Archanjo, a fictional character, is based on a real person; see Maria Luisa Nunes, "The Preservation of African Culture in Brazilian Society: The Novels of Jorge Amado," *Luso-Brazilian Review* 10, no. 1 (June 1973), pp. 86–101.

11. Jorge Amado, *Tent of Miracles*, trans. Barbara Shelby (New York: Bard/Avon, 1971), p. 12.

12. Ibid., p. 92.

13. Ibid., p. 293.

14. Ibid., p. 298.

15. These "Manawaka" novels, which recall Faulkner's Yoknapatawpha, Márquez's Macondo, and José Lins de Rego's Santa Rosa, are *The Stone Angel* (1961), *A Jest of God* (1966), *The Fire-Dwellers* (1969), and *The Diviners* (1974).

16. Margaret Laurence, *The Diviners* (Toronto: McClelland and Stewart, 1974), p. 225.

17. Ibid., p. 287.

18. Georges Bugnet, *Nipsya*, trans. Constance Davies Woodrow (New York: Louis Carrier, 1929), p. 259.

19. Ibid., p. 285.

20. Ibid., p. 286.

21. Putnam, *Marvelous Journey*, p. 142.

22. Isaac Goldberg, *Brazilian Literature* (New York: Knopf, 1922), p. 95.

23. David Miller Driver, *The Indian in Brazilian Literature* (New York: Hispanic Institute, 1942), p. 106.

24. Leslie Fiedler, *Love and Death in the American Novel* (New York: Criterion, 1960), p. 205.

25. Putnam, *Marvelous Journey*, p. 143.

26. José de Alencar, *O Guarani*, 8th ed. (São Paulo: Edições Melhoramentos, 1960).

27. Robert E. Spiller, *The Cycle of American Literature: An Essay in Historical Criticism* (New York: Free Press, 1955), p. 33.

28. José de Alencar, *Iracema, the Honey-Lips, a Legend of Brazil*, trans. Isabel Burton (London: Bickers, 1886; reprint New York: H. Fertig, 1976).

29. Erico Veríssimo, *Brazilian Literature* (New York: Macmillan, 1945), p. 49.

30. Driver, *The Indian in Brazilian Literature*, pp. 106–7.

31. Ibid., pp. 101–4.

32. Ibid., p. 106.

33. Fiedler, *Love and Death in the American Novel*, p. 202.

34. Lydia Maria Child, *Hobomok and Other Writings on Indians*, ed. and intro. Carolyn L. Karcher (New Brunswick: Rutgers University Press, 1986). Several of Child's other works, including the stories "The Indian Wife," "The Quadroons," and "Slavery's Pleasant Homes" and the novel *A Romance of the Republic* (1867), also deal with the themes of gender relations and miscegenation. An interesting variation on the theme of the noble savage as a woman can be found in Catharine Maria Sedgwick's *Hope Leslie* (1827).

35. Karcher, in her introduction to *Hobomok*, p. xxxv.

36. Ibid., pp. xxxiv–xxxv.

37. Jean Franco, *Spanish-American Literature* (Cambridge: Cambridge University Press, 1969), p. 85.

38. Ibid., p. 86.

39. *Borzoi Anthology*, vol. 1, pp. 66–67.

5. REFINING THE NEW WORLD NOVEL: HENRY JAMES AND MACHADO DE ASSIS

1. *American Poetry and Prose*, pt. 2, 5th ed., ed. Norman Foerster, Norman S. Grabo, Russel B. Nye, E. Fred Carlisle, and Robert Falk (Boston: Houghton Mifflin, 1977), p. 898.

2. Helen Caldwell, *The Brazilian Othello of Machado de Assis* (Berkeley: University of California Press, 1960), p. 1.

3. Machado de Assis, *Epitaph of a Small Winner*, trans. William Grossman (New York: Noonday Press, 1952), p. 17.

4. Ibid., p. 223.

5. Ibid., p. 188.

6. Putnam, *Marvelous Journey*, p. 178.

7. Massaud Moisés has discussed this time-oriented, pre-Proustian aspect of Machado's work in his *Machado de Assis: "Ressureição" and "A mão e a luva"* (São Paulo: Editora Cultrix, 1968), p. 20.

8. Helen Caldwell, *Machado de Assis: The Brazilian Master and His Novels* (Berkeley: University of California Press, 1970), and Paul B. Dixon, *Retired Dreams* (West Lafayette, Ind.: Purdue University Press, 1989).

9. Earl E. Fitz, *Machado de Assis* (Boston: Twayne, 1989), pp. 36–46.

10. Henry James, *The Ambassadors*, intro. Lem Edd (Boston: Houghton Mifflin, 1960), p. x.

11. Ibid., p. 137.

12. Robert Spiller, *The Cycle of American Literature* (New York: Free Press, 1955), p. 136.

13. Caldwell, *The Brazilian Othello of Machado de Assis*, pp. 150–60.

14. Spiller, *The Cycle of American Literature*, p. 137.

15. Henry James, "The Art of Fiction," in *The Future of the Novel*, ed. Leon Edel (New York: Vintage, 1956), pp. 3–27.

16. Fitz, *Machado de Assis*, pp. 100–106.

17. Machado de Assis, *Obra completa*, trans. Earl Fitz, organized by Afrânio Coutinho (Rio de Janeiro: Editôra José Aguilar, 1962), vol. 1, p. 196.

18. However much Machado may have disliked naturalism, he occasionally made use of some of its techniques; see Fitz, *Machado de Assis*, pp. 103–6.

19. Henry James, "Nana," in Edel, *The Future of the Novel*, p. 96.

20. Machado, *Obra completa*, vol. 3, pp. 905–6.

21. Henry James, "The Art of Fiction," in *The Great Critics*, ed. James Harry Smith and Edd Winfield Parks, 3rd ed. (New York: Norton, 1951), p. 661.

22. Mary McCarthy, *Ideas and the Novel* (New York: Harcourt, Brace, Jovanovich, 1981).

23. See Earl Fitz, "The Influence of Machado de Assis on John Barth's *The Floating Opera*," *Comparatist* 10 (May 1986), pp. 56–66.

24. John Barth, letter to the author, April 3, 1984.

6. THE FIVE (SIX?) FACES OF AMERICAN MODERNISM

1. Arturo Torres-Ríoseco, *The Epic of Latin American Literature*, rev. ed. (New York: Oxford University Press, 1946), pp. 86–132.

2. Marine Leland, "Québec Literature in Its American Context," in *The Canadian Imagination*, ed. David Staines (Cambridge: Harvard University Press, 1977), pp. 188–225. See also David Haberly, "The Search for a National Language: A Problem in the Comparative History of Postcolonial Literatures," *Comparative Literature Studies* 11, no. 1 (March 1974), pp. 85–97.

3. Emile Nelligan, "Les corbeaux," in Sharman Stanic, "French Canada Studies: The Dimensions of Emile Nelligan," M.A. thesis, Pennsylvania State University, 1973, p. 72. Trans. unknown; possibly Stanic.

4. Gérard Tougas, *Histoire de la littérature canadienne-française* (Paris: Presses Universitaires de France, 1960), p. 112.

5. Robert Choquette, *Metropolitan Museum*, in *Poèmes choisés* (Ottawa: Editions Fides, 1970), pp. 61–62.

6. Samuel de Sacy, cited in *The Complete Poems of Saint-Denys-Garneau*, trans. and intro. John Glassco (Canada: Oberon Press, 1975), p. 8.

7. Ibid., p. 7.

8. Ibid., p. 14.

9. Irving Howe, "The Idea of the Modern," in *Literary Modernism*, ed. and intro. Howe (New York: Fawcett, 1967), pp. 11–40.

10. Glassco, *The Complete Poems of Saint-Denys-Garneau*, p. 139.

11. Ibid., p. 95.

12. Desmond Pacey, "The Writer and His Public: 1920–1960," in Klinck, *The Literary History of Canada*, vol. 2, p. 8.

13. Munroe Beattie, "Poetry: 1920–1935," in Klinck, *The Literary History of Canada*, vol. 2, p. 236.

14. Ibid.

15. *The Collected Poems of Raymond Knister*, ed. and intro. Dorothy Livesay (Toronto: Ryerson, 1949), p. 27.

16. Ibid., p. 37.

17. Dorothy Livesay, "Reality," in *Collected Poems: The Two Seasons* (Toronto: McGraw-Hill Ryerson, 1972), p. 9.

18. *The Selected Poems of Dorothy Livesay (1926–1956)*, ed. Desmond Pacey (Toronto: Ryerson, 1957), p. 6.

19. *New Provinces* (1936), ed. Douglas Lochhead, intro. M. Gnarowski (Toronto: University of Toronto Press, 1976), p. xii. Smith's stinging indictment of the work of earlier Canadian poets was eventually rejected in favor of a new, shorter, and less harsh preface by F. R. Scott (in collaboration with Smith).

20. Ibid., p. xxvii.

21. Ibid.

22. Ibid., p. 71.

23. Ibid.

24. Ibid., p. xxx.

25. Carl Van Vechten, introduction to Gertrude Stein, *Three Lives* (New York: Modern Library, 1933), p. x.

26. Ibid., p. 190.

27. David Lodge, "The Language of Modernist Fiction: Metaphor and Metonymy," in *Modernism*, ed. Malcolm Bradbury and James McFarlane (London: Penguin, 1976), pp. 481–96.

28. Roman Jakobson, "Two Aspects of Language and Two Aspects of Aphasic Disturbances," in Roman Jakobson and Morris Halle, *Fundamentals of Language* (Hague: Gravenhage, Mouton, 1956), pp. 55–82.

29. Lodge, "The Language of Modernist Fiction," pp. 486–89.

30. *Borzoi Anthology*, vol. 2, p. 576.

31. Vicente Huidobro, *The Selected Poetry of Vicente Huidobro*, trans. and intro. David M. Guss (New York: New Directions, 1981), p. 3.

32. Ibid., p. 159.

33. Ibid., pp. xviii–xix.

34. Ibid., p. xviii.

35. During the early 1500s, a Portuguese bishop named, incredibly, Sardinha was captured and eaten by cannibals.

36. Mário de Andrade, *Hallucinated City*, trans. and intro. Jack E. Tomlins (Nashville: Vanderbilt University Press, 1968), p. 37.

37. Ibid., pp. xi–xviii.

38. Haroldo de Campos, "*Seraphim*: A Great Nonbook," afterword to *Seraphim Grosse Pointe*, trans. Kenneth D. Jackson and Albert Bork (Austin: New Latin Quarter Editions, 1979), pp. 113–31.

7. IN QUEST OF AN AMERICAN IDENTITY

1. *Borzoi Anthology*, vol. 1, p. 67.

2. Lescarbot's "Le Théâtre de Neptune" (1606), which mixed native characters, words, and terms with classical poetic conventions, may have been North America's first non-native, nondidactic theatrical performance. The Spanish and Portuguese priests had earlier utilized religious dramas in their attempts to convert the Indians they encountered, but their theater was designed to proselytize rather than to entertain. "Les muses de la Nouvelle France" (1609) clearly expresses support for further exploration and colonization of the New World, an idea also expressed in his monumental *Histoire de la Nouvelle France* (1609, 1611–1612, 1617–1618), for which Lescarbot is justly famous. See *Histoire de la Nouvelle France*, vol. 1 (Paris: I. Millot, 1609); see also University Microfilm, American Culture Series, reel 3, no. 22 (Ann Arbor, 1941); also published as *History of New France*, trans. W. L. Grant and intro. H. P. Biggar (New York: Greenwood, 1968).

3. *Borzoi Anthology*, vol. 1, p. 96.

4. Sor Juana Inés de la Cruz, "Divine Rose," in *An Anthology of Mexican Poetry*, ed. Octavio Paz and trans. Samuel Beckett (Bloomington: Indiana University Press, 1958), pp. 85–86.

5. Sor Juana Inés de la Cruz, "Foolish Men," in *Some Spanish American Poets*, trans. Alice Stone Blackwell (Philadelphia: University of Philadelphia Press, 1937), p. 150.

6. For an excellent comparative discussion of Sor Juana and Anne Bradstreet as poets, see A. Owen Aldridge's *Early American Literature* (Princeton: Princeton University Press, 1982), pp. 25–52.

7. Gregório de Matos, "The Poet Defines His City," *Borzoi Anthology*, vol. 1, p. 142.

8. Catherine M. McLay, ed., *Canadian Literature* (Toronto: McClelland and Stewart, 1974), p. 67.

9. Ibid., p. 72.

10. Rocha Pita, *História da América Portuguesa* (1730), cited in Putnam, *Marvelous Journey*, p. 75.

11. Andrés Bello, "Ode to the Agriculture of the Torrid Zone," *Borzoi Anthology*, vol. 1, p. 201.

12. Ibid., pp. 202–3.

13. St. Jean de Crèvecoeur, "What Is an American?" in Foerster et al., *American Poetry and Prose*, pt. 1, p. 276.

14. Ibid., p. 287.

15. These include *The American* (1877), *Daisy Miller* (1878), *The Europeans* (1879), *The Portrait of a Lady* (1881), *The Wings of the Dove* (1902), *The Ambassadors* (1903), and *The Golden Bowl* (1904).

16. Two other French Canadian works that touch on this issue are Arsène Bessette's *Le débutant* (1914), a novel in which French Canada's narrow conservatism and parochialism are criticized and set in contrast to the United States, to which the protagonist ultimately emigrates, and Leo-Paul Desrosier's 1931 novel, *Nord-Sud*, which examines the plight of Québecois young people forced by lack of opportunity to leave their home and seek a better life in the gold fields of California.

17. Philippe-Joseph Aubert de Gaspé, *The Canadians of Old*, trans. Charles G. D. Roberts (New York: Appleton, 1890), p. 245 (later, in 1905, reissued as *Cameron of Lochiel*).

18. Ibid., p. 167.

19. Ibid., p. 273.

20. Leon Edel, afterword to Henry James, *The American* (New York: New American Library, 1963), p. 326.

21. Ibid., pp. 327–31.

22. Ibid., p. 21.

23. Ibid., p. 22.

24. Ibid., p. 58.

25. Ibid., p. 61.

26. Alberto Blest Gana, *Los Transplantados* (Paris: Garnier, 1911), vol. 1, p. 10. Trans. for this volume by the author.

27. For a good discussion of this point, see W. J. Keith's "Archibald Lampman," in *Profiles in Canadian Literature*, ed. Jeffrey M. Heath, vol. 1 (Toronto: Dundurn, 1980), pp. 17–24.

28. Sara Jeannette Duncan, *The Imperialist* (Toronto: McClelland and Stewart, 1961), p. 232.

29. Ibid., p. 229.

30. Ibid., p. 47.

31. Claude Hulet, *Brazilian Literature* (Washington, D.C.: Georgetown University Press, 1974), vol. 2, p. 207.

32. Graça Aranha, *Canaan*, trans. Joaquin Mariano Lorente (Boston: Four Seas, 1920), pp. 198–99.

33. Ibid., pp. 296, 109, 297.

34. The name Lachine has an ironic history, one that reminds us of the false hopes held by the early explorers of North America. Failing to find China, as he was confident he would, La Salle is said to have bitterly given the name Lachine (China) to the place.

35. Atwood's *Two-Headed Poems* gets directly at the problem of Canadian identity by suggesting, metaphorically, that Canada is a two-headed creature, one head representing French Canada and the other English Canada. Gallant's *Home Truths* explores the problems of Canadian identity by having her characters reflect on the nature of their political and psychological existence while residing abroad, that is, outside Canada but conscious of it.

8. REGIONALISM AS A SHAPING FORCE

1. Desmond Pacey, "The First Canadian Novel," *Dalhousie Review* 26, no. 2 (July 1946), pp. 143–50.

2. Frances Brooke, *The History of Emily Montague*, vol. 1 (New York: Garland, 1947), pp. 214–15.

3. Linda Shohet, "An Essay on *The History of Emily Montague*," in *The Canadian Novel*, ed. John Moss (Toronto: New Canada Publications, 1980), vol. 1, pp. 28–34.

4. Northrop Frye, "Haliburton: Mask and Ego," in Moss, *The Canadian Novel*, vol. 1, pp. 40–44.

5. Ibid., p. 42.

6. Thomas H. Raddall, "Haliburton: A Lasting Impression," in Moss, *The Canadian Novel*, vol. 1, pp. 37–39.

7. Thomas C. Haliburton, *Sam Slick*, ed. Ray Palmer Baker (New York: George H. Doran, 1923), pp. 39–40.

8. Ibid., pp. 56–57.

9. Frye, "Haliburton," p. 43.

10. Atwood, *Survival*, pp. 213–31.

11. Conrad Dion, foreword to Albert Laberge, *Bitter Bread*, trans. Dion (Toronto: Harvest House, 1977), [p. 3].

12. Gérard Tougas, *A History of French-Canadian Literature*, trans. Alta Lind Cook (Toronto: Ryerson, 1966), p. 8.

13. Laberge, *Bitter Bread*, p. 41.

14. Ibid., p. 69.

15. Ibid., pp. 65–66.

16. Mark Schorer, afterword to Hamlin Garland, *Main-Travelled Roads* (New York: New American Library, 1962), p. 262.

17. Ibid., p. 78.

18. Ibid., p. 40.

19. Jean Franco, *An Introduction to Spanish-American Literature* (Cambridge: Cambridge University Press, 1969), pp. 208, 222.

20. Ibid., p. 225.

21. Ibid.

22. Putnam, *Marvelous Journey*, p. 154.

23. *The Slave Girl Isaura* makes an interesting comparison to *Uncle Tom's Cabin* (1851), as do Gertrudis Gómez de Avellaneda's *Sab* (1841) and Cirilo Villaverde's *Cecilia Valdés* (1839), a novel that indicts the institution of slavery while combining, like Faulkner in *Absalom, Absalom!*, the issues of miscegenation and incest.

24. Putnam, *Marvelous Journey*, pp. 152–60.

25. Ibid., p. 159.

26. Hugo McPherson, "Fiction (1940–1960)," in Klinck, *A Literary History of Canada*, vol. 2, p. 218.

27. Ibid., p. 217.

28. Sinclair Ross, *As for Me and My House* (Toronto: McClelland and Stewart, 1957), p. 25.

29. Ibid., p. 140.

30. Jacques Godbout, *Hail Galarneau*, trans. Alan Brown (Don Mills, Ontario: Longman Canada, 1970), p. 80.

31. Ibid., pp. 25–26.

32. Ibid., p. 106.

33. Ibid., pp. 107–8.

34. Ibid., p. 113.

35. João Guimarães Rosa, *The Devil to Pay in the Backlands*, trans. James L. Taylor and Harriet de Onis (New York: Knopf, 1971), pp. 6–7.

36. Ibid., p. 487.

37. Ibid., p. 6 passim.

38. Richard Chase, *The American Novel and Its Traditions* (Baltimore: Johns Hopkins University Press, 1957), p. 110.

39. Herman Melville, *Moby-Dick* (New York: Modern Library, 1950), pp. 187, 194–95.

40. Emir Rodríguez Monegal, "The Contemporary Brazilian Novel," in *Fiction in Several Languages*, ed. Henri Peyre (Boston: Beacon, 1968), p. 11.

41. Melville, *Moby-Dick*, p. 216.

42. Spiller, *The Cycle of American Literature*, p. 68.

43. John Brushwood, *Mexico in Its Novel* (Austin: University of Texas Press, 1966), p. 34.

44. Juan Rulfo, *Pedro Páramo*, trans. Lysander Kemp (New York: Grove, 1959), p. 107.

45. Ibid., pp. 1–2.
46. Ibid., pp. 5–6.

9. SOLITUDE: THE EVOLUTION OF AN AMERICAN LITERARY MOTIF

1. Hugh MacLennan, *The Two Solitudes* (Toronto: Macmillan, 1978), pp. 100–01.
2. Ibid., p. 78.
3. Ibid., p. 138.
4. Ibid., p. 344.
5. Ibid.
6. Ibid., pp. 411–12.
7. The English translation of Roy's original title misses the sense of momentary and tawdry good fortune suggested in the original French, a sense that, for the people of the novel, life is a cheap and fleeting affair. Thus the original title ironically underscores the psychosocial solitude of the characters' debased condition.
8. Gabrielle Roy, *The Tin Flute*, trans. Hannah Josephson (New York: Reynal and Hitchcock, 1947), p. 167.
9. Ibid., p. 315.
10. Ronald Sutherland, intro. to Hubert Aquin, *Prochain épisode*, trans. Penny Williams (Toronto: McClelland and Stewart, 1967), pp. v–vii.
11. Ibid., pp. 124–25.
12. William Faulkner, *Absalom, Absalom!* (New York: Modern Library, 1964), p. 140.
13. Ibid., p. 39.
14. Ibid., p. 103.
15. Ibid., p. 168.
16. Ibid., p. 356.
17. Gabriel García Márquez, *One Hundred Years of Solitude*, trans. Gregory Rabassa (New York: Avon, 1970), p. 20.
18. Ibid., p. 21.
19. Ibid., p. 383.
20. Ibid.
21. Ibid., pp. 163, 204.
22. Faulkner, *Absalom, Absalom!*, p. 129.
23. Márquez, *One Hundred Years of Solitude*, p. 215.
24. Clarice Lispector, *The Apple in the Dark*, trans. Gregory Rabassa (New York: Knopf, 1967), p. 11.
25. Ibid., p. 17.
26. Malcolm Lowry, *Under the Volcano* (New York: New American Library, 1966), p. 391.
27. Ibid., p. 319.
28. Lispector, *The Apple in the Dark*, pp. 210–11.
29. Ibid., p. 37.

30. Lowry, *Under the Volcano*, p. 36.

31. Ibid., p. 161.

32. Lispector, *The Apple in the Dark*, p. 361.

10. THE CONFLICT BETWEEN CIVILIZATION AND BARBARISM

1. Margaret Atwood, *The Journals of Susanna Moodie* (Toronto: Oxford University Press, 1970).

2. Frye, *The Bush Garden*, p. 225.

3. Michael Hurley, "*Wacousta*: The Borders of Nightmare," in Moss, *The Canadian Novel*, vol. 2, pp. 60–69. For a note about Richardson's debt to Cooper, see Robert Lecker, "Patterns of Deception in *Wacousta*," in Moss, *The Canadian Novel*, vol. 2, pp. 47–59.

4. Catherine McLay, "The Divided Self: Theme and Pattern in *Surfacing*," in Moss, *The Canadian Novel*, vol. 1, p. 44.

5. Margaret Atwood, *Surfacing* (New York: Fawcett Popular Library, 1972), p. 68.

6. Ibid., p. 198.

7. William Faulkner, *The Bear*, in *Three Famous Short Novels* (New York: Vintage, 1961), pp. 185–86.

8. Ibid., p. 186.

9. Ibid., p. 187.

10. Atwood, *Surfacing*, p. 207.

11. Ibid., p. 208.

12. Faulkner, *The Bear*, p. 202.

13. Ibid., p. 316.

14. Atwood, *Surfacing*, p. 222.

15. Georges Bugnet, *The Forest*, trans. David Carpenter (Montreal: Harvest House, 1976), p. 9.

16. Ibid., p. 49.

17. Ibid., pp. 107–8.

18. Ibid., p. 165.

19. Jeanette Urbas, *From Thirty Acres to Modern Times: The Story of French-Canadian Literature* (Toronto: McGraw-Hill Ryerson, 1976), p. 12.

20. Louis Hémon, *Maria Chapdelaine*, trans. W. H. Blake (New York: Modern Library, 1934), p. 284.

21. Alan Dueck, "Rudy Wiebe's Approach to Historical Fiction: A Study of *The Temptation of Big Bear* and *The Scorched-Wood People*," in Moss, *The Canadian Novel*, vol. 1, pp. 182–200.

22. Euclides da Cunha, *Rebellion in the Backlands*, trans. Samuel Putnam (Chicago: University of Chicago Press, 1975), p. 476.

23. Rudy Wiebe, *The Scorched-Wood People* (Toronto: McClelland and Stewart, 1977), pp. 350–51.

24. Da Cunha, *Rebellion in the Backlands*, p. 476.

25. Wiebe, *The Scorched-Wood People*, p. 351.

26. Da Cunha, *Rebellion in the Backlands*, p. 408.

27. Wiebe, *The Scorched-Wood People*, p. 335.

28. Da Cunha, *Rebellion in the Backlands*, p. 464.

29. Domingo Faustino Sarmiento, *Facundo* (Mexico City: Editorial Navarro, 1958), p. 85. Trans. for this volume by the author.

30. Ibid., p. 86.

31. Ibid., p. 52.

32. Urbas, *From Thirty Acres to Modern Times*, p. 76.

33. Chase, *The American Novel and Its Traditions*, p. 145.

34. Mark Twain, *The Adventures of Huckleberry Finn* (New York: Dell, 1960), p. 351.

35. Urbas, *From Thirty Acres to Modern Times*, pp. 76–84.

36. Yves Thériault, *Agaguk*, trans. Mirian Chapin (Toronto: Ryerson, 1963), p. 4.

37. Ibid., p. 203.

38. Urbas, *From Thirty Acres to Modern Times*, pp. 78–79.

39. Wallace Stegner, introduction to Mark Twain, *The Adventures of Huckleberry Finn*, p. 13.

Selected Bibliography

* * * * * * * * * * * * *

Adams, Mildred. "Literary Criticism in Spanish America." *Comparative Literature Studies* 1, no. 3 (1964), pp. 217–29.

Adams, Percy G. "The Discovery of America and European Renaissance Literature." *Comparative Literature Studies* 13, no. 2 (June 1976), pp. 100–115.

Aldridge, A. Owen. *Early American Literature: A Comparatist Approach*. Princeton: Princeton University Press, 1982. Primarily concerned with the literatures of the United States and Spanish America; a good comparative study of Sor Juana Inés de la Cruz and Anne Bradstreet.

———. "The Enlightenment in the Americas." *Proceedings of the Seventh Congress of the ICLA* (1973), vol. 1, pp. 59–67.

———. "From Sterne to Machado de Assis." In *The Winged Skull*, edited by A. H. Cash, pp. 170–85. London: Methuen, 1971.

———, ed. *The Ibero-American Enlightenment*. Urbana: University of Illinois Press, 1971.

———. "The Influences of Thomas Paine in the United States, England, France, Germany, and South America." *Proceedings of the Second Congress of the ICLA*, Werner P. Friederich, ed., vol. 2, pp. 369–83. Chapel Hill: University of North Carolina Press, 1959.

Alegría, Fernando. *Walt Whitman en Hispanoamérica*. Mexico City: Fondo de Cultura Económica, 1954.

Anderson, Arthur J. O. "Aztec Hymns of Life and Love." *New Scholar* 8 (1982), pp. 1–74.

Astrov, Margot, ed. *American Indian Prose and Poetry*. New York: Capricorn, 1946.

Atwood, Margaret. *Survival: A Thematic Guide to Canadian Literature*. Toronto: Anansi, 1972. In the main, English and French Canadian literature; some references to the United States.

Barth, John. "The Literature of Exhaustion." *Atlantic*, August 1967, pp. 29–34. Lauds the renovating narratives of Borges.

———. "The Literature of Replenishment." *Atlantic*, January 1980, pp. 65–71. Praises the work of Márquez and, to a degree, Cortázar, in terms of postmodernism.

Barton, Richard L. *Ties That Blind in Canadian/American Relations: The Politics of News Discourse*. Hillsdale, N.J.: Lawrence Erlbaum, 1990.

Bayard, Caroline. *The New Poetics in Canada and Quebec*. Toronto: University of Toronto Press, 1989. Focuses on avant-garde poetics in English and French Canada; also discusses Brazilian concretist poetry.

———. *Out-Posts*. Erin, Ont.: Press Porcépic, 1978. Interviews with and commentaries on eight major Canadian poets, including Carl Birney, Nicole Brossard, and Raoul Duguay.

Beaty, Jerome, and J. Paul Hunter, eds. *New Worlds of Literature*. New York: Norton, 1989. An anthology rich in work by Canadian, Caribbean, and nonmainstream writers from the United States, especially ethnic minorities.

Bell-Villada, Gene H. "Functional Criticism." *Review* 23 (1979), pp. 79–81. Review of Alfred J. MacAdam, *Modern Latin American Narratives*, and Gordon Brotherston, *The Emergence of the Latin American Novel*; notes the "Latin American penchant for 'satire' and the U.S. taste for 'realism.'"

———. "Lit. Crit. in Latin America, or the Advantages of Underdevelopment." *American Book Review* 5, no. 6 (September–October 1983), pp. 4–5.

———. "Two Americas, Two World Views, and a Widening Gap." *Monthly Review* 34 (October 1982), pp. 37–43.

Bennett, Maurice J. "The Detective Fiction of Poe and Borges." *Comparative Literature* 35, no. 3 (Winter 1983), pp. 262–75.

Bernucci, Leo. *Historia de un malentendido: Un estudio transtextual de "La Guerra del Fin del Mundo."* New York: Peter Lang, 1989. Studies the influence of da Cunha's *Os Sertões* on the Vargas Llosa novel.

Bierhorst, John. *Cantares mexicanos: Songs of the Aztecs*. Translated from the Náhuatl by John Bierhorst. Stanford: Stanford University Press, 1985.

Blodgett, E. D. "Canadian as Comparative Literature." *Canadian Review of Comparative Literature/Revue Canadienne de Littérature Comparée* 6, no. 2 (Spring 1979), pp. 127–30. Hereafter abbreviated *CRCL/RCLC*.

———. "The Canadian Literatures in a Comparative Perspective." *Essays on Canadian Writing*, no. 15 (Summer 1979), pp. 5–24. An excellent study; highly recommended.

———. "Cold Pastorals: A Prolegomenon." *CRCL/RCLC* 6, no. 2 (Spring 1979), pp. 166–94. Compares Grove, Roy, Bugnet, Moodie, Gérin-Lajoie, Blais, and Cohen; argues that the pastoral is "one of the dominant patterns of the Canadian novel."

Bolton, Herbert E. "The Epic of Greater America." *American Historical Review* 38, no. 3 (April 1933), pp. 448–74. A noted historian's call for an integrated, interAmerican approach to New World affairs; for some fifteen years, the author taught "The History of the Americas," a course embodying this viewpoint, at the University of California.

Borges, Jorge Luis. "Nathaniel Hawthorne." In *Other Inquisitions*, translated by Ruth L. C. Simms, pp. 47–65. Austin: University of Texas Press, 1964. In calling attention to Hawthorne's enthusiasm for allegory and dreamlike narratives and to his belief in the primacy of imaginative art over a mimetically rendered recreation of physical reality (that is, realism), Borges here seems to offer the fascinating possibility that—through his influential admiration for the North American's creative genius—Nathaniel Hawthorne may actually have had a powerful influence on the development of the "New Narrative" that Borges would introduce into Spanish American literature. At the very least, one could say that the critical ideas behind Borges' praise for Hawthorne are consistent with those expressed in two of the Argentine writer's most important essays, "La postulación de la realidad" and "El arte narrativo y la magia," the latter study relying heavily on Poe's only novel, *The Narrative of A. Gordon Pym* (1838). Thus one could also argue that Poe had an influence on Borges' theory about the aesthetic superiority of magical narratives over realistic ones.

———. "Note on Walt Whitman." In *Other Inquisitions*, translated by Ruth L. C. Simms, pp. 66–72. Austin: University of Texas Press, 1964.

Bourque, Paul-André. "L'américanité du roman québecois." *Etudes Littéraires* 8, no. 1 (April 1975), pp. 9–19.

Brakel, Arthur. "Ambiguity and Enigma in Art: The Case of Henry James and Machado de Assis." *Comparative Literature Studies* 19, no. 4 (Winter 1982), pp. 442–49.

Brault, Gerard. "The Franco-Americans of New England." *Mid-Atlantic Journal of Canadian Studies* 1, no. 1 (Spring 1986), pp. 5–28.

Brotherston, Gordon. *Image of the New World: The American Continent Portrayed in Native Texts*. London: Thames and Hudson, 1979.

———. Introduction to *José Enrique Rodó: Ariel*, ed. Brotherston, p. 14. Cambridge: Cambridge University Press, 1967. Discusses Rodó's views on the significance of Poe, Longfellow, and Whitman to Spanish America.

———. "*Ubirajara, Hiawatha, Cumandá*: National Virtue from American Indian Literature." *Comparative Literature Studies* 9, no. 3 (September 1972), pp. 243–52. Examines the notion of a national literature deriving from indigenous sources as exemplified in works by Mera, Longfellow, and Alencar.

Bruce-Novoa, Juan. "Pluralism vs. Nationalism: U.S. Literature." *Council on National Literatures/Quarterly World Report* 6, nos. 1–2 (January–April 1983), pp. 13–18.

Bruner, Charlotte. "The Meaning of Caliban in Black Literature Today." *Comparative Literature Studies* 13, no. 3 (September 1976), pp. 240–53.

Carpentier, Alejo. "Una carta de Melville." "Letra y solfa" [Carpentier's daily column], *El Nacional* (Caracas), June 8, 1954, p. 30.

———. "Confidencias de Faulkner." "Letra y solfa," *El Nacional*, July 21, 1956, p. 16.

———. "Un discurso de Aimé Césaire." "Letra y solfa," *El Nacional*, May 18, 1956, p. 16.

———. "Herman Melville y la América Latina." "Letra y solfa," *El Nacional*, February 4, 1955, p. 32.

———. "Revelación de Melville." "Letra y solfa," *El Nacional*, September 30, 1951.

———. "Los sertones." "Letra y solfa," *El Nacional*, September 8, 1951, p. 12. Discusses da Cunha's *Os Sertões*.

Carr, Pat, and Gingerich, Willard. "The Vagina Dentata Motif in Náhuatl and Pueblo Mythic Narratives: A Comparative Study." *New Scholar* 8 (1982), pp. 85–101.

Carvalho, Joaquim de, ed. *Panorama das literaturas das Américas, de 1900 a atualidade.* 4 vols. Nova Lisboa, Angola: Edição do Município de Nova Lisboa, 1958–1963.

Chapman, Arnold. "Pampas and Big Woods: Heroic Initiation in Güiraldes and Faulkner." *Comparative Literature* 11, no. 1 (Winter 1959), pp. 61–77.

———. *The Spanish American Reception of U.S. Fiction, 1920–1940.* Berkeley: University of California Press, 1966. Issues of translation, influence and reception.

Chevigny, Bell Gale. "'Insatiable Unease': Melville and Carpentier and the Search for an American Hermeneutic." In *Reinventing the Americas*, Chevigny and Laguardia, eds., pp. 34–59. An excellent study.

———, and Gari Laguardia, eds. *Reinventing the Americas: Comparative Studies of Literature of the United States and Spanish America.* Cambridge: Cambridge University Press, 1986. An interesting and useful introduction; several excellent essays.

Christ, Ronald, ed. "Focus: The U.S." *Review* 17 (Spring 1976), pp. 7–95. A collection of pieces by Spanish Americans and a few Brazilians on different aspects of U.S. literature and culture; Borges on Melville's "Bartleby," Cortázar on Poe, Fuentes on Styron, and Drummond de Andrade on Charlie Chaplin.

Cisneros-Lavaller, Alberto. "Old Wine in New Bottles: An Essay on the Study of Inter-American Relations." *New Scholar* 8 (1982), pp. 267–88. A survey of sociopolitical relations between Latin America and the United States.

Coleman, Alexander. "Introductory Note." *Review '69*, pp. 7–10. A brief but useful discussion of the reception of Latin American literature in the U.S. of the 1960s.

Collin, W. E. *The White Savannahs.* Toronto: Macmillan, 1936. Discusses English Canadian modernism, myth criticism, and issues of influence and reception; examines the importance of Eliot.

Collmer, Robert G. "When 'Word' Meets 'Palabra': Crossing the Border with Literature." *Proceedings of the Comparative Literature Symposium* 6 (1973), pp. 153–64. Lubbock: Texas Tech University, 1973.

Cox, Harvey. *The Secular City.* Harmondsworth: Pelican, 1968.

David, Jack, and Ronald Lecker, eds. *Essays on Canadian Writing*, no. 15 (Summer 1979). Erin, Ont.: Porcupine's Quill.

Davis, Mary E. "The Haunted Voice: Echoes of William Faulkner in García Márquez, Fuentes, and Vargas Llosa." *World Literature Today* 59, no. 4 (Autumn 1985), pp. 531–35.

———. "The Town That Was an Open Wound." *Comparative Literature Studies* 23, no. 1 (Spring 1986), pp. 24–43. Márquez and Faulkner.

Dean, James Seay. "Upon These Banks and Shoals of Time: Herman Melville's

Whale, João Guimarães Rosa's Crocodile." *Luso-Brazilian Review* 20, no. 2 (Winter 1983), pp. 198–212.

Diehl, Digby. "Conversación con Edward Albee." *Casa de las Américas: Revista Bimestral* 4, no. 24 (January–April 1964), pp. 88–98. Albee believes that while South American writers would like to have close relations with North American writers, they are "fifty to seventy-five years behind the United States" in finding their "natural, authentic voice."

Dimić, Milan V. "Aspects of American and Canadian Gothicism." *Proceedings of the Seventh Congress of the ICLA* (1973), vol. 1, pp. 143–49.

———. "Towards a Methodology of Comparative Canadian Studies/A la recherche d'une méthodologie en études comparées canadiennes." *CRCL/RCLC* 6, no. 2 (Spring 1979), pp. 115–17, and (by other authors) pp. 117–30. Highly recommended.

Donoso, José. *The Boom in Spanish American Literature*. Translated by Gregory Kolovakos. New York: Columbia University Press, 1971. Outlines the growth of communication between the hitherto isolated Spanish American writers and, to a lesser degree, the increasing involvement during the 1960s of writers and artists from the United States in literary developments in Spanish America.

Dorfman, Ariel. *The Empire's Old Clothes: What the Lone Ranger, Babar, and Other Innocent Heroes Do to Our Minds*. New York: Pantheon, 1983.

———. *Imaginación y violencia en América*. Santiago: Editorial Universitaria, S.A., 1970.

———. *Reader's nuestros que estás en la tierra: Ensayos sobre el imperialismo cultural*. Mexico City: Nueva Imagen, 1980.

Dorfman, Ariel, and Armand Mattelart. *Para leer al pato Donald*. Havana: Editorial de Ciencias Sociales, 1974.

Dorsinville, Max. "The Myth of the Negro in the Literatures of the Americas." *Proceedings of the Seventh Congress of the ICLA* (1973), vol. 1, pp. 351–53.

Driver, David Miller. *The Indian in Brazilian Literature*. New York: Hispanic Institute, 1942. Offers several comments on the Indian as portrayed in Brazil, Spanish America, and the United States; discusses the relationship between Cooper and Alencar.

Edinger, Catarina. "Machismo and Androgyny in Mid-Nineteenth-Century Brazilian and American Novels." *Comparative Literature Studies* 27, no. 2 (June 1990), pp. 124–39.

Englekirk, John E. *Edgar Allan Poe in Hispanic Literature*. New York: Instituto de las Españas en los Estados Unidos, 1934.

———. *A literatura norteamericana no Brasil*. Mexico City: N.p., 1950. Brazilian reception of such U.S. writers as Franklin, Cooper, Stowe, Longfellow, Poe, Emerson, Whitman, Dos Passos, and others.

Erdoes, Richard, and Alfonso Ortiz, eds. *American Indian Myths and Legends*. New York: Pantheon, 1984.

Fernández, Pablo Armando. "Dreams of Two Americas." In *Reinventing the Americas*, Chevigny and Laguardia, eds., pp. 122–36.

Feuser, Willfried. "Littérature négro américaine et négritude." *Proceedings of the Seventh Congress of the ICLA* 1 (1973), pp. 339–47.

Finley, J. B. *Life among the Indians.* Cincinnati: Cranston and Stowe, 1857. One of the earliest authors to speak of "the great battle-fields between barbarism and civilization" in regard to white settlers and the Indians.

Fitz, Earl E. "The Black Poetry of Jorge de Lima and Nicolás Guillén: A Comparative Study." *Inti*, no. 4 (Fall 1976), pp. 76–84.

———. "Caracterização e a visão fenomenológica nos romances de Clarice Lispector e Djuna Barnes." *Travessia* 14, no. 2 (1987), pp. 136–47.

———. "The First Inter-American Novels: Some Choices and Some Comments." *Comparative Literature Studies* 22, no. 3 (Fall 1985), pp. 361–76.

———. "Gregôrio de Matos and Juan del Valle y Caviedes: Two Baroque Poets in Colonial Spanish and Portuguese America." *Inti*, nos. 5–6 (Spring–Fall 1977), pp. 143–50.

———. "The Influence of Machado de Assis on John Barth's *The Floating Opera.*" *Comparatist* 10 (May 1986), pp. 56–66.

———. "Is There a Latin American Literature? The Comparatist's Dilemma." *Council on National Literatures/Quarterly World Report* 4, no. 2 (April 1981), pp. 5–8.

———. "John Barth's Brazilian Connection." *New World* 2, nos. 1–2 (1987), pp. 123–38.

———. *Machado de Assis.* Boston: Twayne, 1989. See esp. pp. 10–22, 136–39. Chapter 2 is devoted to placing Machado in international and Inter-American contexts.

———. "Macondo, Yoknapatawpha y Santa Rosa: Una interpretación comparativa de tres perspectivas regionalistas." *Humanidades* (Bucaramanga, Colombia) 2, no. 1 (September 1982), pp. 47–60.

———. "Old World Roots/New World Realities: A Comparatist Looks at the Growth of Literature in North and South America." *Council on National Literatures/Quarterly World Report* 3, no. 3 (July 1980), pp. 8–11.

———. "Translation as Political Act: The Creation and Exportation of Canada through Its Literature." *Mid-Atlantic Journal of Canadian Studies* 1, no. 1 (Spring 1986), pp. 31–39.

———. "The Vox Populi of John Steinbeck and Jorge Amado." *Prismal/Cabral* (University of Maryland), Regina Egel, ed. Forthcoming.

———. "Whither Inter-American Literature?" *CRCL/RCLC.* Forthcoming.

Foster, David William. "Varieties of Urban Colloquiality in the Contemporary Latin American and American Novel." *World Literature Today* 59, no. 4 (Autumn 1985), pp. 556–60.

Franco, Jean. *An Introduction to Spanish-American Literature.* Cambridge: Cambridge University Press, 1969. Makes mention of—but does not discuss—Poe's influence on the Spanish American "modernistas" and on the stories of Horacio Quiroga, pp. 147, 157, 217, 221, and 300; a number of other possible North American influences are also mentioned.

Frye, Northrop. *The Bush Garden: Essays on the Canadian Imagination.* Toronto: Anansi, 1971.

Galinsky, Hans. *The Transit of Civilization: From Europe to America: Essays in Honor of Hans Galinsky*. Edited by Winfried Herget and Karl Ortseifen. Tübingen: Narr, 1986.

Genovese, Eugene. *The World the Slaveholders Made*. New York: Vintage, 1971. Offers comparative evaluations of slavery in the United States and Latin America.

Giguère, Richard. "Un cas pratique." *CRCL/RCLC* 6, no. 2 (Spring 1979), pp. 123–27.

Gill, Anne. "*Dom Casmurro* and *Lolita*: Machado among the Metafictionists." *Luso-Brazilian Review* 24, no. 1 (Summer 1987), pp. 17–26. Compares Machado de Assis to Nabokov.

González de la Garza, Mauricio. *Walt Whitman: Racista, imperialista, anti-Mexicano*. Mexico City: Colección Málaga, 1971.

Grace, Sherrill E. *Regression and Apocalypse*. Toronto: University of Toronto, 1989. Studies in Canadian and American expressionist fiction and drama; compares O'Neill, Voaden, Lowry, Ellison, Barnes, and Watson.

Guillén, Claudio. "Distant Relations: French, Anglo-American, Hispanic." *World Literature Today* 59, no. 4 (Autumn 1985), pp. 503–7.

Haberly, David. "The Search for a National Language: A Problem in the Comparative History of Postcolonial Literatures." *Comparative Literature Studies* 11, no. 1 (March 1974), pp. 85–97.

Haly, Richard. "Poetics of the Aztecs." *New Scholar*, new series, vol. 10 (1986), pp. 85–133.

Harss, Luis. *Into the Mainstream*. New York: Harper and Row, 1967. Interviews with Latin American authors; some influences discussed.

Hartz, Louis, with contributions by Kenneth D. McRae et al. *The Founding of New Societies*. New York: Harcourt, Brace, 1964. See esp. Hartz, "A Theory of the Development of the New Societies," pp. 1–122, and Richard M. Morse, "The Heritage of Latin America," pp. 123–77.

Hayne, David M. "Les grandes options de la littérature canadienne-française." In *Littérature canadienne-française: Conférences*, edited by J. A. de Sève, pp. 1–10. Montreal: Les Presses de l'Université de Montréal, 1969.

———. "Literary Movements in Canada." *CRCL/RCLC* 6, no. 2 (Spring 1979), pp. 121–23.

———, Antoine Sirois, and Jean Vigneault, comps. "Preliminary Bibliography of Comparative Canadian Literature (English-Canadian and French-Canadian): Ninth Supplement, 1983–84." *CRCL/RCLC* 12, no. 3 (September 1985), pp. 462–68. *CRCL/RCLC* should be routinely reviewed for its earlier and ongoing reviews of these very useful bibliographies.

Head, Harold. *Canada in Us Now*. Toronto: NC Press, 1976. Black Canadian literature and poetics.

International Comparative Literature Association. *Inter-American Literary Relations*. Vol. 3, *Proceedings of the Tenth Congress of the ICLA* (1982), ed. M. J. Valdés. New York: New York University, 1985. A basic resource text; excellent studies.

———. *Proceedings of the Seventh Congress of the ICLA* (1973), M. V. Dimic and

E. Kushner, eds. Vol. 1, 1979, "Literatures of America: Dependence, Independence, Interdependence," pp. 5–559. A treasure trove of Inter-American and New World essays.

Irby, James E. "La influencia de William Faulkner en cuatro narradores hispanoamericanos." M.A. thesis, Universidad Nacional Autónoma de México, 1956. Treats Revueltas, Onetti, Rulfo, and Novás.

Jaenen, Cornelius J. *Friend and Foe: Aspects of French-Amerindian Cultural Contact in the Sixteenth and Seventeenth Centuries*. Toronto: McClelland and Stewart, 1976.

Jehlen, Myra. *American Incarnation: The Infinite Spirit of Man and Its Continent*. Cambridge: Harvard University Press, 1986. Compares the ways Jefferson and Sarmiento viewed nature, the landscape, and the wilderness; argues that Jefferson could accommodate nature in his vision but that Sarmiento, seeing nature as an alien force, could not.

Jones, D. G. *Butterfly on Rock*. Toronto: University of Toronto Press, 1970. Examines both English and French Canadian works.

Kazin, Alfred. *On Native Grounds*. New York: Doubleday, 1956.

Kline, Marcia. *Beyond the Land Itself*. Cambridge: Harvard University Press, 1970. Argues that there are important differences between "American" and English Canadian literature; examines differing attitudes about the land and the concept of the wilderness; compares Cooper and Richardson.

Kroeber, Karl. "Deconstructionist Criticism and American Indian Literature." *Boundary 2* 7, no. 3 (Spring 1979), pp. 73–92.

———, ed. *Traditional Literatures of the American Indian: Texts and Interpretations*. Lincoln: University of Nebraska Press, 1981.

Kröller, Eva-Marie. "Comparative Canadian Literature: Notes on Its Definition and Method." *CRCL/RCLC* 6, no. 2 (Spring 1979), pp. 139–50. An excellent theoretical study of the comparative method as applied to Canadian literature.

———. "Walter Scott in America, English Canada, and Québec: A Comparison." *CRCL/RCLC* 7 (Winter 1980), pp. 32–46.

Krupat, Arnold. "An Approach to Native American Texts." *Critical Inquiry* 9, no. 2 (December 1982), pp. 323–38.

———. "Native American Literature." In *Canons*, edited by Robert von Hallberg, pp. 309–38. Chicago: University of Chicago Press, 1984.

Kulin, Katalin. "Reasons and Characteristics of Faulkner's Influence on Juan Carlos Onetti, Juan Rulfo and Gabriel García Márquez." *Proceedings of the Seventh Congress of the ICLA* (1973), vol. 1, pp. 277–80.

Kutzinsky, Vera M. *Against the American Grain*. Baltimore: Johns Hopkins University Press, 1987. Myth and history in William Carlos Williams, Jay Wright, and Nicolás Guillén.

La Bossière, Camille R. *The Dark Age of Enlightenment: An Essay on Québec Literature*. Fredericton, N.B.: York Press, 1980.

Laguardia, Gari. "Digesting Modernismo: Peristalsis and Poetic Paternity in Vallejo." Forthcoming. Argues that Whitman's influence allowed Vallejo to escape the "preciousness" of modernismo.

————. "Marvelous Realism/Marvelous Criticism." In *Reinventing the Americas*, Chevigny and Laguardia, eds., pp. 298–318. A discussion of current trends in literary theory and criticism as they apply to literary relations between the United States and Spanish America.

Lareau, Edmund. *Histoire da la littérature canadienne*. Montreal: Lovell, 1874. Perhaps the first Canadian literary history to discuss both the English and French Canadian traditions.

Larsen, Neil. "Latin America: The View from Comparative Literature." *Ideologies and Literature* 4, no. 16 (May–June 1983), pp. 144–48. Brief comment on certain methodological problems inherent in a comparative approach to "Latin American" literature, which unfortunately is referred to almost entirely in terms of Spanish American authors and texts.

Latin American Literary Review 14, no. 27 (January–June 1986). A special issue devoted to a discussion of Brazilian literature in a comparative context.

Leal, Luis. "Native and Foreign Influences in Contemporary Mexican Fiction: A Search for Identity." In *Tradition and Renewal*, edited by Merlin H. Forster, pp. 102–28. Urbana: University of Illinois Press, 1974.

Lecker, Robert, Jack David, and Peter O'Brien, eds. *An Introduction to Literature: British, American, Canadian*. New York: Harper and Row, 1987.

Leland, Marine. "Québec Literature in Its American Context." In *The Canadian Imagination*, Staines, ed., pp. 188–225.

Le Moine, J. M. *Maple Leaves*. Québec: Demers, 1894. A survey of highlights from English and French Canadian letters.

Levin, Harry. "Literature and Cultural Identity." *Comparative Literature Studies* 10, no. 2 (June 1973), pp. 139–56. Criteria for the evaluation of ethnic literature.

Levine, Susan F., and Stuart Levine. "Poe and Fuentes: The Reader's Prerogatives." *Comparative Literature* 36, no. 1 (Winter 1984), pp. 34–53.

Levitas, Gloria, ed. *American Indian Prose and Poetry*. New York: Putnam, 1974.

Lipset, Seymour Martin. *Continental Divide: The Values and Institutions of the United States and Canada*. New York: Routledge, 1990.

MacAdam, Alfred J. *Modern Latin American Narratives: The Dreams of Reason*. Chicago: University of Chicago Press, 1977. Spanish American and Brazilian literature; argues that "there is no Latin American novel . . . but there is a Latin American satire."

————. *Textual Confrontations: Comparative Readings in Latin American Literature*. Chicago: University of Chicago Press, 1987. Discusses Latin American literature in international and, to a lesser degree, Inter-American contexts.

MacLeish, Archibald. "Remarks on the Occasion of the Dedication of the Hispanic Room in the Library of Congress," October 12, 1939. Excerpted in Torres-Ríoseco, *The Epic of Latin American Literature*, p. 6.

Marcotte, Gilles. *Une littérature qui se fait*. Montreal: H.M.H., 1962.

Marinello, Juan. "Americanismo y cubanismo literarios." In Juan Marinello, *Ensayos*, pp. 45–60. Havana: Editorial Arte y Literatura, 1977.

Martí, José. *The America of José Martí*. Translated by Juan de Onís and with an intro-

duction by Federico de Onís. New York: Noonday Press, 1954. See especially
"Emerson," pp. 216–38; "The Poet, Walt Whitman," pp. 239–58; "The Other
America," pp. 2–135; and "Aboriginal American Authors," pp. 193–97.

————. *Our America*. Translated by Elinor Randall. New York: Monthly Review, 1977.

————. "El poeta Walt Whitman." In *José Martí: Letras Fieras*, edited by Roberto
Retamar, pp. 494–506. Havana: Editorial Letras Cubanas, 1981.

————. "Walt Whitman." Translated by Luis Baralt. In *Martí on the U.S.A.*, edited by
José Martí, pp. 3–16. Carbondale: Southern Illinois University Press, 1966.

McClendon, Carmen Chaves. "A Rose for Rosalina: From Yoknapatawpha to *Opera
dos Mortos*." *Comparative Literature Studies* 19, no. 4 (Winter 1982), pp. 450–58.

McCormick, John O. "Notes on a Comparative American Literary History." *Comparative Literature Studies* 5, no. 2 (June 1968), pp. 167–79.

McLuhan, Marshall. "Canada: The Borderline Case." In *The Canadian Imagination*,
Staines, ed., pp. 226–48. Compares Canada and the United States in terms of cultural identity.

McMurray, David Arthur. "The Theme of the Negro in the Literature of the Americas: Some Brief Remarks." *Proceedings of the Seventh Congress of the ICLA* (1973),
vol. 1, pp. 349–50.

Merivale, Patricia. "Neo-Modernism in the Canadian Artist-Parable: Hubert Aquin
and Brian Moore." *CRCL/RCLC* 6, no. 2 (Spring 1979), pp. 195–205.

Mezei, Kathy. "Lampman and Nelligan: Dream Landscapes." *CRCL/RCLC* 6, no. 2
(Spring 1979), pp. 151–65.

Milton, John R., ed. *The American Indian Speaks*. Vermillion: University of South Dakota Press, 1969.

Modern Language Association of America. *The Impact of Latin American Literature on
Writing in the United States*. Papers of a special session of the MLA convention,
December 1984, Gene Bell-Villada, chair.

Moisán, Clément. *L'âge de la littérature canadienne*. Montreal: H.M.H., 1969. A good
survey of selected writers, critics, and trends in both French and English Canada;
underscores the importance of comparative literary studies to Canada.

————. *Poésie des frontières—études comparées des poésies canadienne et québecoise*. Victoria,
B.C.: Press Porcépic, 1979. Comparison of English and French Canadian frontier poetry.

————. *A Poetry of Frontiers: Comparative Studies in Quebec/Canadian Literature*. Translated by George Lang and Linda Weber. Edited by Sharon Sterling. Toronto: Press
Porcépic, 1983.

————. "Quelques Propositions." *CRCL/RCLC* 6, no. 2 (Spring 1979), pp. 117–19.

Monegal, Emir Rodríguez. "Carnaval, Antropofagía, Parodia." *Revista iberoamericana*
45, nos. 108–9 (1979), pp. 401–12. An application of the theories of Bakhtin and
Kristeva to Spanish American and Brazilian literature; stresses parody as a fundamental aspect of Latin American writing.

————. "A Game of Shifting Mirrors: The New Latin American Novel and the North
American Novel." *Proceedings of the Seventh Congress of the ICLA* (1973), vol. 1, 1979,
pp. 269–75. Largely a survey of influences between Latin American and U.S. nar-

rativists; stresses Faulkner's vast influence and the importance of Borges, especially his presence in Pynchon's *The Crying of Lot 49*, *V.*, and *Gravity's Rainbow*.

————. "The Integration of Latin American Literatures." *Proceedings of the Eighth Congress of the ICLA* (1976), Béla Köpeczi and György M. Vajda, eds., vol. 2, 1980, pp. 111–16. Brazilian and Spanish American literature; argues that as of 1976 there is still no "integrated" "Latin American" literature or culture.

————. *Narradores de esta América II*. Buenos Aires: Alfa, 1974.

————. "The New Latin American Literature in the USA." *Review '68*, pp. 3–13. A succinct assessment of Latin American literature's reception in the United States of the 1960s; notes the deep cultural bias against Latin American literature and culture that has long pervaded the view from the U.S.

————. "The New Latin American Novelists." In *The Triquarterly Anthology of Contemporary Latin American Literature*, edited by José Donoso and William Henkin, pp. 9–28. New York: Dutton, 1969. Influences and receptions.

————, and Thomas Colchie, eds. *The Borzoi Anthology of Latin American Literature*. 2 vols. New York: Knopf, 1977. The methodology and orientation of this work are synchronically comparative and examine the literatures of Brazil, Spanish America, and, to a degree, the United States.

Monteiro, George. "Emily Dickinson's Brazilian Poems." *Revista Inter-Americana de Bibliografía* 22, no. 4 (October–December 1972), pp. 404–10.

Moss, John. *A Reader's Guide to the Canadian Novel*. Toronto: McClelland, 1981.

————, ed. *The Canadian Novel*. 2 vols. Toronto: New Canada Publications, 1980.

Mullen, Edward J. "European and North American Writers in *Contemporáneos*." *Comparative Literature Studies* 8, no. 4 (December 1971), pp. 338–48. A survey of the reception of foreign authors by the editors of the vanguard Mexican journal *Contemporáneos*, 1928–1931.

————. "The Literary Reputation of Langston Hughes in the Hispanic World." *Comparative Literature Studies* 13, no. 3 (September 1976), pp. 254–69.

Neruda, Pablo. "Comienzo por invocar a Walt Whitman." In *Incitación al nixonicidio y alabanza de la revolución chilena*. Edited by Pablo Neruda. Santiago: Empresa Editora Nacional Quimantu, 1973.

New Scholar 10 (1986), "Voices of the First America: Text and Context in the New World." This issue includes essays by many scholars on various aspects of Pre-Columbian literature; highly recommended. See also vol. 5, no. 2 (1978); vol. 6 (1977); and vol. 8 (1982).

The New Worlds of Literature (motion picture). Great Neck, N.Y.: Salzburg Enterprises, 1976. Fantastic images of the New World—Amazons, cities of gold, human monstrosities, fountains of youth, etc.—held by European conquerors.

Northey, Margot. *The Haunted Wilderness: The Gothic and Grotesque in Canadian Fiction*. Toronto: University of Toronto Press, 1976. English and French Canadian texts compared.

Núñez, Estuardo. "Franklin en Hispanoamérica." *Cuadernos Americanos* 88, no. 4 (July–August 1956), pp. 155–68.

————. "Herman Melville en la América Latina." *Cuadernos Americanos* 68, no. 2

(March–April 1953), pp. 209–21. Studies the sources of "Benito Cereno" in
Amasa Delano's voyage narratives.

———. "Literatura comparada en Hispanoamérica." *Comparative Literature Studies* 1,
no. 1 (1964), pp. 41–45.

———. "El poeta Chocano en Nueva York." *Cuadernos Americanos* 75, no. 3
(May–June 1954), pp. 292–98.

Oberhelman, Harley D. "William Faulkner's Reception in Spanish America." *American Hispanist* 3, no. 26 (April 1979), pp. 13–17.

Onís, José de. "Messianic Nationalism in the Literature of the Americas: Melville and
the Hispanic World." *Proceedings of the Fourth Congress of the ICLA* (1966), edited by
François Jost, vol. 1, pp. 229–36.

Paz, Octavio. *The Labyrinth of Solitude*. Translated by Lysander Kemp. New York:
Grove, 1961. Compares the culture of Mexico to that of the United States.

———. "A Literature of Foundations." Translated by Lysander Kemp. In *The Triquarterly Anthology of Latin American Literature*. Edited by José Donoso and William
Henkin, pp. 2–8. New York: Dutton, 1969.

———. *The Other Mexico*. Translated by Lysander Kemp. New York: Grove, 1972.

———. "Reflections: Mexico and the United States." *New Yorker*, September 17,
1979, pp. 136–53.

Pearce, Roy Harvey. *The Savages of America: A Study of the Indian and the Idea of Civilization*. Rev. ed. Baltimore: Johns Hopkins University Press, 1965.

Peavler, Terry J. "Guillermo Cabrera Infante's Debt to Ernest Hemingway." *Hispania*
62, no. 3 (May–September 1979), pp. 289–96.

Peixoto, Afrânio. "American Social and Literary Influences in Brazil." In *Books Abroad*
9, no. 2 (Spring 1935), pp. 127–29. See also the preceding installment: *Books
Abroad* 9, no. 1 (Winter 1935), pp. 3–5.

Pierce, Lorne. *An Outline of Canadian Literature*. Montreal: Carrier, 1927. Discusses
both English and French Canadian literature; Canada's first Anglophone literary history.

Purdy, A. W., ed. *The New Romans: Candid Canadian Opinions of the United States*.
Edmonton: Hurtig, 1968.

Putnam, Samuel. *Marvelous Journey: A Survey of Four Centuries of Brazilian Writing*.
New York: Knopf, 1948. Rich in comparisons between the literatures of Brazil and
the United States.

Rabassa, Gregory. "A Comparative Look at the Literatures of Spanish America and
Brazil: The Dangers of Deception." In *Ibero-American Letters in a Comparative Perspective*, edited by W. T. Zyla and W. M. Aycock, pp. 119–32. Lubbock: Texas Tech
University, 1978.

Ramsey, Jarold. *Reading the Fire: Essays in the Traditional Indian Literatures of the Far
West*. Lincoln: University of Nebraska Press, 1983. Places Native American literature in a mainstream context.

Retamar, Roberto Fernández. *Apuntes para una teoría literaria hispanoamericana*. Mexico
City: Nuestro Tiempo, 1975.

———. *Caliban: Notes toward a Discussion of Culture in Our America.* Translated by Lynn Garafola, David Arthur McMurray, and Robert Márquez. *Massachusetts Review* 15, nos. 1–2 (Winter–Spring 1974), pp. 7–72.

Riddel, Joseph. "Decentering the Image: The 'Project' of 'American' Poetics?" In *Textual Strategies: Perspectives in Post-Structuralist Literature,* edited by Josué V. Harrari, pp. 322–58. Ithaca: Cornell University Press, 1979.

Robles, Mercedes. "La presencia de *The Wild Palms* de William Faulkner en *Punta de Rieles* de Manuel Rojas." *Revista Iberoamericana* 45, nos. 108–9 (July–December 1979), pp. 563–71.

Rodó, José Enrique. *Ariel.* Translated by F. J. Stimson. Boston: Houghton Mifflin, 1922. Contrasts what he believes is the "materialism" of the United States with the "idealism" of Latin America.

Roy, Camille. *Manuel d'histoire de la littérature canadienne de langue française.* 8th ed. Montreal: Beauchemin, 1940. One of the earliest French Canadian literary histories to incorporate comparative comments on English Canadian literature.

———. *Nous origines littéraires.* Québec: L'Action Sociale, 1909.

Rudnyćkyj, J. B. "Canadian and Argentine-Brasilian Novels on Ukrainian Pioneers." *Proceedings of the Seventh Congress of the ICLA,* vol. 1 (1973), pp. 295–99.

Ruland, Richard, ed. *The Native Muse: Theories of American Literature from Bradford to Whitman.* New York: Dutton, 1976.

Salkey, Andrew. "Inconsolable Songs of Our America: The Poetry of Derek Walcott." *World Literature Today* 56, no. 1 (Winter 1982), pp. 51–53.

Sánchez, Luis Alberto. *Historia comparada de las literaturas americanas.* 4 vols. Buenos Aires: Losada, 1973–1976.

Sanders, Thomas E., and Walter W. Peek, eds. *The Literature of the American Indian.* Beverly Hills: Glencoe, 1973.

Sayers, Raymond. "Contemporary Brazilian Criticism." *Comparative Literature Studies* 1, no. 4 (1964), pp. 287–304.

Shapiro, Karl. "The Critic Outside." *American Scholar* 50 (Spring 1981), pp. 197–210. Decries what is for him the pernicious influence of South American Marxist poets who, via "garish translations," supply North American poets with "large doses of angst, warmed-over surrealism, anti-American hatred, and Latino blood, sweat, and tears."

Shouldice, Larry. "Wide Latitudes: Comparing New World Literature." *CRCL/RCLC,* March 1982, pp. 46–55. An excellent theoretical survey of the problems and possibilities inherent in comparative approaches to New World literature; highly recommended.

Sirois, Antoine. *Montréal dans le roman canadien.* Paris: Didier, 1969. Examines the ways in which Montreal has played a role in both English and French Canadian narrative.

———. "La périodisation dans les littératures du Canada." *CRCL/RCLC* 6, no. 2 (Spring 1979), pp. 119–21.

Smith, A. J. M. *The Book of Canadian Poetry.* Chicago: University of Chicago Press,

1943. Smith argues in this and the following two works that English and French Canadian literature can and should be compared and that in general Canadian literature reflects a tension between the national and the cosmopolitan.

———. *Modern Canadian Verse*. Toronto: University of Toronto Press, 1967.

———. *The Oxford Book of Canadian Poetry*. Toronto: University of Toronto Press, 1960.

Sommer, Doris. "Supplying Demand: Walt Whitman as the Liberal Self." In *Reinventing the Americas*, Chevigny and Laguardia, eds., pp. 68–91. Whitman's reception in Spanish America.

Sontag, Susan. "Afterlives: The Case of Machado de Assis." *New Yorker*, May 7, 1990, pp. 102–8. Calls Machado "the greatest author ever produced in Latin America" and Borges the "second-greatest"; also notes Brazil's isolation, even within Latin America.

Sousa, Ronald W. "Re-evaluation of Luso-American Popular Literature." *New Canadian Review* 2, no. 1 (Winter 1989–90), pp. 47–63.

Staines, David, ed. *The Canadian Imagination*. Cambridge: Harvard University Press, 1977.

Steele, Cynthia. "The Fiction of National Formation: The Indigenista Novels of James Fenimore Cooper and Rosario Castellanos." In *Reinventing the Americas*, Chevigny and Laguardia, eds., pp. 60–67.

Sterne, Richard C. "Hawthorne Transformed: Octavio Paz's 'La Hija de Rappaccini.'" *Comparative Literature Studies* 13, no. 3 (September 1976), pp. 230–39.

Stratford, Philip. *All the Polarities: Comparative Studies in Contemporary Canadian Novels in French and English*. Toronto: E. C. W. Press, 1986.

———. "Canada's Two Literatures: A Search for Emblems." *CRCL/RCLC* 6, no. 2 (Spring 1979), pp. 131–38. An excellent theoretical discussion of the problems and possibilities involved in comparing works of English Canadian literature with those of French Canada.

Struthers, J. R. (Tim). "Alice Munro and the American South." In *The Canadian Novel*, John Moss, ed., vol. 1, pp. 121–33. Toronto: NC Press, 1978.

Sutherland, Ronald. *The New Hero: Essays in Comparative Québec/Canadian Literature*. Toronto: Macmillan, 1977. One of this book's many virtues is its author's explanation of why it is so difficult to categorize Robertson Davies, whose *Fifth Business*, a work richly evocative of Canadian life, is very interestingly compared to Leonard Cohen's *Beautiful Losers*.

———. *Second Image: Comparative Studies in Québec/Canadian Literature*. Don Mills, Ont.: New Press, 1971.

Swann, Brian, ed. *Smoothing the Ground: Essays on Native American Oral Literature*. Berkeley: University of California Press, 1983.

Sylvestre, Guy, Brandon Conron, and Carl F. Klinck, eds. *Canadian Writers/Écrivains canadiens*. Toronto: Ryerson, 1964.

Tatum, Charles, and Harold E. Hinds. "Mexican and American Comic Books in a Comparative Perspective." In *Mexico and the United States: Intercultural Relations in the Humanities*, edited by Juanita Luna Lawhn, Juan Bruce-Novoa, Guillermo Campos, and Ramón Saldívar, pp. 67–83. Texas: San Antonio College Press, 1984.

Torres-Ríoseco, Arturo. "Brazilian Literature." In Torres-Ríoseco, *The Epic of Latin American Literature*, pp. 209–55. Rev. ed. New York: Oxford University Press, 1946.

———. "The Parallel between Brazilian and Spanish American Literature." In Torres-Ríoseco, *New World Literature*, pp. 196–213. Berkeley: University of California Press, 1949. Except for the chapter cited here, this book deals with the development of Spanish American literature.

Tougas, Gérard. *Histoire de la littérature canadienne-française*. Paris: Presses Universitaires de France, 1960. The methodology and orientation of this work are at least partially comparative.

Umphrey, George U. "Spanish American Literature Compared with That of the United States." *Hispania* 26 (February 1943), pp. 21–34.

Valenilla, E. Mayz. *El problema de América*. Caracas: Universidad Central de Venezuela, 1969.

Wade, Mason. *The French-Canadian Outlook*. Toronto: McClelland and Stewart, 1965.

———. *The Search for a Nation*. Toronto: Dent, 1967.

Walker, John. "'Home Thoughts from Abroad': W. H. Hudson's Argentine Fiction." *CRCL/RCLC*, September 1983, pp. 333–76.

Wasserman, Renata R. Mautner. "Re-Inventing the New World: Cooper and Alencar." *Comparative Literature* 36, no. 2 (Spring 1984), pp. 130–45.

Watters, R. E. "A Quest for National Identity: Canadian Literature vis-à-vis the Literature of Great Britain and the United States." *Proceedings of the Third Congress of the ICLA* (1962), W. A. P. Smit, gen. ed., pp. 224–41. Gravenhage: Mouton and Company, 1962.

Williams, Stanley T. *The Spanish Background of American Literature*. New Haven: Yale University Press, 1955.

Willis, Susan. "Caliban as Poet: Reversing the Maps of Domination." In *Reinventing the Americas*, Chevigny and Laguardia, eds., pp. 92–105. Black identity in Caribbean poetry; focuses on Walcott, Césaire, Guillén, and Lamming.

Wilson, Edmund. *O Canada: An American's Notes on Canadian Culture*. New York: Farrar, Strauss and Giroux, 1965.

Wood, Michael. "The Poet as Critic: Wallace Stevens and Octavio Paz." In *Reinventing the Americas*, Chevigny and Laguardia, eds., pp. 325–32.

Zamora, Lois Parkinson. *Writing the Apocalypse*. Cambridge: Cambridge University Press, 1989. Compares the "apocalyptic vision" and "fictions of historical desire" in works by Márquez, Pynchon, Cortázar, Barth, Percy, and Fuentes.

Zolbrod, Paul. *Diné Bahané*. Albuquerque: University of New Mexico Press, 1984.

Zyla, Wolodymyr T., and Wendell M. Aycock, eds. *Ibero-American Letters in a Comparative Perspective*. Lubbock: Texas Tech Press, 1978. Primarily concerned with Spanish America; some references to the United States and Brazil.

Index

✱ ✱ ✱ ✱ ✱ ✱ ✱ ✱ ✱ ✱